MW01282743

Brother-Making in Late Antiquity
and Byzantium

Onassis Series in Hellenic Culture

The Age of Titans: The Rise and Fall of the Great Hellenistic Navies
William M. Murray

Sophocles and the Language of Tragedy
Simon Goldhill

Nectar and Illusion: Nature in Byzantine Art and Literature
Henry Maguire

Adventures with Iphigenia at Tauris: A Cultural History of Euripides' Black Sea Tragedy
Edith Hall

Beauty: The Fortunes of an Ancient Greek Idea
David Konstan

Euripides and the Gods
Mary Lefkowitz

Brother-Making in Late Antiquity and Byzantium: Monks, Laymen, and Christian Ritual
Claudia Rapp

Onassis
Foundation (USA)

Brother-Making in Late Antiquity and Byzantium

Monks, Laymen, and Christian Ritual

Claudia Rapp

OXFORD
UNIVERSITY PRESS

OXFORD
UNIVERSITY PRESS

Oxford University Press is a department of the University of
Oxford. It furthers the University's objective of excellence in research,
scholarship, and education by publishing worldwide.
Oxford is a registered trademark of Oxford University Press
in the UK and certain other countries.

Published in the United States of America by
Oxford University Press
198 Madison Avenue, New York, NY 10016, United States of America

© Oxford University Press 2016

All rights reserved. No part of this publication may be reproduced, stored in
a retrieval system, or transmitted, in any form or by any means, without the prior
permission in writing of Oxford University Press, or as expressly permitted by law,
by license, or under terms agreed with the appropriate reproduction rights organization.
Inquiries concerning reproduction outside the scope of the above should be sent to the
Rights Department, Oxford University Press, at the address above.

You must not circulate this work in any other form
and you must impose this same condition on any acquirer.

Cataloging-in-Publication data is on file at the Library of Congress
ISBN 978–0–19–538933–3

1 3 5 7 9 8 6 4 2
Printed in the United States of America
on acid-free paper

CONTENTS

ACKNOWLEDGMENTS

This book has grown over a long period that included a transatlantic move from Los Angeles to Vienna. It was begun in earnest in 2008–9, when I was fortunate to spend a year as a Visiting Fellow at All Souls College, Oxford, and concluded in fall 2014, when I was a Visiting Fellow at Corpus Christi College. The congenial surroundings and spirit of inquisitiveness that I have come to associate with Oxford for three decades have been an inspiration on both occasions.

In the course of these six years, my work has benefited from the encouragement, advice, and assistance of countless people and numerous institutions. Although I would like to thank them all, I can mention only a few here and in the footnotes. Malcolm Choat deserves special thanks for reading and commenting on chapter 3, as does Daniel Galadza for reading chapter 2. For generous assistance in the study of the manuscripts, I thank Father Justin Sinaites, Archbishop Aristarchos at the Greek Orthodox Patriarchate in Jerusalem, and Stefano Parenti. Special thanks are due to Christine Angelidi, Wendy Bracewell, Philip Booth, Peter Brown, Liz Carmichael, Angelos Chaniotis, Maria Couroucli, Maria Efthymiou, Günter Fuchs, Fiona Griffiths, Gelina Harlaftis, Susan Ashbrook Harvey, Michael Herzfeld, Dirk Hoerder, Mayke de Jong, Nigel Kennell, Derek Krueger, Krystina Kubina, Peter Mackridge, Paul Magdalino, Charis Messis, Arietta Papaconstantinou, George Rousseau, Robert Romanchuk, Christodoulos Papavarnavas, George Rousseau, Vicenzo Ruggieri, SJ, Andreas Schminck, George Sidéris, Robert Taft, SJ, Allan A. Tulchin, Ingrid Weichselbaum, and Robin Darling Young.

Research on parts of this work was carried out during a Fellowship at the Institute for Advanced Studies of the Hebrew University in Jerusalem, and while holding a Visiting Professorship in the Department of Medieval Studies at the Central European University in Budapest—both institutions extending generous hospitality. A research stay at the Max-Planck-Institut für Europäische Rechtsgeschichte in Frankfurt facilitated focused research on the Byzantine legal tradition. The Alexander S. Onassis Public Benefit Foundation sponsored a lecture tour that enabled me to discuss my work in the early stages with audiences at the Seeger Center for Hellenic Studies at Princeton University, as well as at Harvard University and at the Hellenic College and Holy Cross Greek Orthodox School of Theology in Brookline, Massachusetts.

Three institutions have sustained me intellectually and supported my research: UCLA, my academic home for almost two decades, and my new *alma mater*, the University of Vienna. In addition, the Division of Byzantine Research of the Institute for Medieval Research at the Austrian Academy of Science has provided a context of focused enquiry.

Over the years, I have presented aspects of this work in lectures and at conferences, discussed it at dinner tables with friends or in ecclesiastical settings with clergy, monks, and nuns. Often, I was pointed in new directions or provided with additional references. Countless times, I encountered people with roots in the Mediterranean cultures or in the areas of Orthodox Christianity who knew a family member or a friend who was joined in ritual brotherhood in one way or another. Their perspective has enriched my appreciation of the vast spectrum of meaning that brother-making can evoke.

Discharging a debt of gratitude, as a wise person once said, is the only debt that makes one richer. The following pages are a small recompense for the generosity of spirit that I have encountered in the course of this project. If they appear deficient, I hope they will at least present enough material for others to carry the study of this fascinating phenomenon further.

Oxford, on the Feast of Saint Catherine,
November 25, 2014

ABBREVIATIONS

Abbreviations for journals and reference works follow the conventions employed in the *Oxford Dictionary of Byzantium*. The following are most frequently used:

AASS	*Acta Sanctorum*
AB	*Analecta Bollandiana*
AP	*Apophthegmata Patrum*
BZ	*Byzantinische Zeitschrift*
CFHB	*Corpus Fontium Historiae Byzantinae*
Dmitrievskij	A. Dmitrievskij, Opisanie liturgitseskich rukopisej, *vol. 2 (Kiev, 1901; reprint Hildesheim, 1965).*
DOP	*Dumbarton Oaks Papers*
EEBS	*Epeteris Hetaireias Byzantinôn Spoudôn*
JÖB	*Jahrbuch der Österreichischen Byzantinistik*
JThS	*Journal of Theological Studies*
OCA	*Orientalia Christiana Analecta*
OCP	*Orientalia Christiana Periodica*
ODB	*Oxford Dictionary of Byzantium*
PMBZ	*Prosopographie der mittelbyzantinischen Zeit*
RAC	*Reallexikon für Antike und Christentum*
REB	*Revue des Études Byzantines*

SPELLING AND TRANSLITERATION

Consistence in rendering into English personal names and place names that originally appeared in Greek is impossible to achieve without causing offence to eye and ear of any but the most specialized readership. I have used anglicized forms when they are common (Basil, not Basileios; Heraclius, not Herakleios; Athens, not Athena), and transliterated forms otherwise (Nikolaos, Niketas).

For the transliteration of words or sequences of words, I have adopted the intuitive system of "Greeklish,"[1] with the further addition of a circumflex for long vowels (ô for omega, ê for eta). The only exception is *adelphopoiesis*, which is treated as an anglicized word. On this basis, it will be easy to reconstruct the original Greek for those who are familiar with the language, while those who are not will at least be able to read and recognize relevant words and expressions.

---

[1] http://en.wikipedia.org/wiki/Romanization_of_Greek.

MAPS

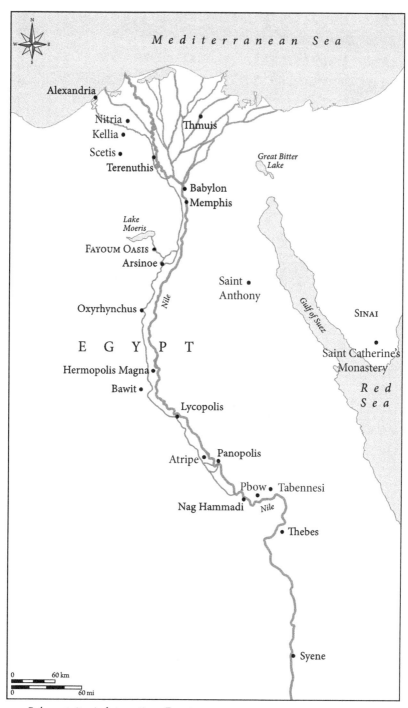

MAP 1 *Relevant sites in late antique Egypt.*

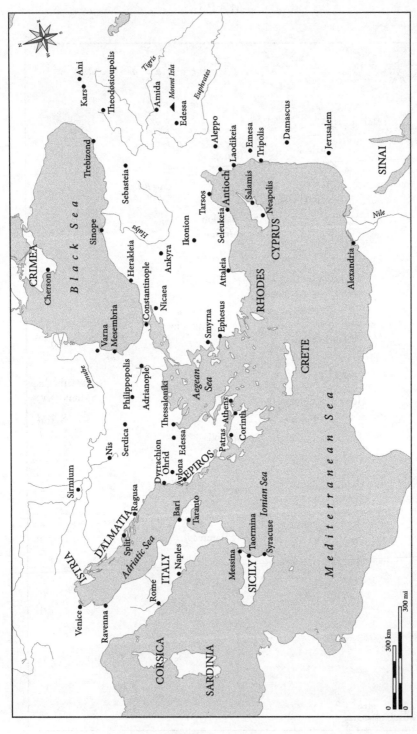

MAP 2 *Relevant sites in Byzantium and the medieval Mediterranean.*

Introduction

The entry point for this study is the prayers for brother-making (*adelphopoi-esis*), a uniquely Byzantine way to create a relation of ritual kinship. They are first attested in a manuscript of the late eighth century and remain a promi-nent feature in the liturgical tradition of medieval Byzantium and beyond. Brother-making of this kind, performed by a priest in a church, was com-monly practiced among Byzantine men, sometimes also between men and women and between women and women, at all levels of society, not just at the court and among the aristocracy. Yet, there was some degree of uncertainty and unease about this relationship. Church leaders and imperial legislators, while aware of its popularity and fully cognizant of their own collusion, made every effort to distance themselves from it.

This raises an interesting set of questions that take us to the inner work-ings of Byzantine society. The purpose and application of *adelphopoiesis* can be studied within three large, and partially overlapping, contexts: within the context of male-male emotional and sexual relations, as a way to formalize a partnership; within the context of ritual kinship strategies, as a way to expand one's family circle; and within the context of Byzantine Christianity, as a way for the church to exercise influence and control. All of these considerations will come to bear, to varying degrees, in the following pages.

Since this material has the potential of becoming a minefield for scholarly disagreement, it may be wise to spell out my own interest in the subject rather than leave it to others to second-guess my motivations. In the twenty years since I first paid attention to the ritual, my own approach to the topic has somewhat evolved. At that time, my abiding interest in the role that living holy men and spiritual leaders, as opposed to dead saints, played in the creation and shap-ing of communities led me to investigate the role of the baptismal sponsor as a spiritual guide and companion of the new Christian-in-the-making during the early centuries, when baptism was sought by adults as a result of personal conversion. I was particularly curious about the responsibility and obligations that went along with baptismal sponsorship, whether in the spiritual realm, in the form of assistance to help a penitent sinner regain the path of virtue, or in the social role of the godfather, after child baptism had become the norm. In the Byzantine tradition, the godfather is known as the "coparent" (*synteknos*) of the biological father, and godparenthood (*synteknia*) was, after marriage, the second important strategy to expand one's kin group in a way that was recognized by the church. Analogous considerations were at work in brother-making, which was a third strategy of ritual kinship, the least onerous of the three with regard to the way it was concluded and the consequences for the next generations. I argued this case in a paper presented in December 1994, at the American Philological Association meeting in Atlanta, entitled "A Different Kind of Parenthood: Baptismal Sponsorship in Late Antiquity." John Boswell's book *Same-Sex Unions in Pre-Modern Europe* (UK title: *The Marriage of Likeness: Same-Sex Unions in Pre-Modern Europe*) had appeared just a few months earlier, and it seemed clear to me that the evidence he had assembled for *adelphopoiesis* in Byzantium offered ample scope for more detailed study. It emerged that Brent Shaw, a Roman historian, who was also present at the conference in Atlanta, and Elizabeth Brown, a historian of medieval France, were at that time also working on ritual brotherhood in their own areas of specialization, and the result of our extensive collaboration was the "Symposium" of three articles, with a long introduction, in the journal *Traditio*, published in 1997.[1]

Since its publication, Boswell's book has become something of a beacon for some, and a lightning rod for others, in the current discussion over the legal institution and church blessings of gay marriage. The number of responses among scholars and by the concerned and interested public has been accordingly extensive. Tracing them would be a task in its own right, a task that others have made theirs.[2]

Among the general flurry of reviews and responses that Boswell's book generated, I was not alone in concluding that the *adelphopoiesis* ritual in Byzantium was not created with the purpose of sanctioning and sanctifying

---

[1] E. A. R. Brown, "Ritual Brotherhood in Ancient and Medieval Europe: A Symposium. Introduction," *Traditio* 52 (1997), 261–83; Brown, "Ritual Brotherhood in Western Medieval Europe," *Traditio* 52 (1997), 357–81; B. Shaw, "Ritual Brotherhood in Roman and Post-Roman Societies," *Traditio* 52 (1997), 327–55; C. Rapp, "Ritual Brotherhood in Byzantium," *Traditio* 52 (1997), 285–326.

[2] Paul Halsall has devoted an entire website, last updated in April 2007, to Boswell's work and the scholarly and popular responses, positive and negative, it continues to elicit: *People with a History: An Online Guide to Lesbian, Gay, Bisexual, and Trans* History. John Boswell Page*. http://www.fordham.edu/halsall/pwh/index-bos.asp. There is now even a Wikipedia article on "*adelphopoiesis*." It focuses largely on critiques of Boswell's book: http://en.wikipedia.org/wiki/Adelphopoiesis.

homosexual relationships, as he seemed to suggest, although I stand firm in my conviction that this evaluation of the historical evidence does in no way undermine the legitimacy of seeking recognition for same-sex partnerships in current societies.

In recent years, my attention has been captured by the ecclesiastical ritual and the need to explain its existence. Why was it created in the first place? What are the possible antecedents for prayers to invoke God's blessing on a relationship of two men? Just as the context of spiritual guidance, including baptism, led to the establishment of the role of the baptismal sponsor, which later developed into the social role of the godfather, was there perhaps a similar pattern for *adelphopoiesis*? This led me back to the social world of early monasticism, where recent studies, augmented by archaeological evidence, have shown that, in addition to living as a hermit or in a large organized community, living arrangements for two or three people were not uncommon. This third option, identified as semi-eremitic or semi-anchoritic monasticism, offers the obvious context for the development of prayers to bless two men as they embark on their spiritual journey with mutual support.

The structure of this book is determined by this line of inquiry. It is divided into six large chapters.

The first chapter gives a brief introduction to social structures in Byzantium, beginning with kinship and the family and the possibilities for the extension of kinship through marriage, godparenthood, or adoption. The focus then moves to male-male relations cast within the framework and language of brotherhood. The second part of the chapter deals with friendship both as a social institution and as an affective relationship, and its interpretation by Christian authors. It concludes with a discussion of homosociability in Byzantium and the history of the study of homosexuality inasmuch as it is relevant to the present study. Throughout this chapter, comparative material from other Christian medieval societies is adduced as necessary in order to highlight the particular features of Byzantine brother-making.

The second chapter, augmented by Appendices 1 to 3 at the end, presents the manuscript evidence for the brother-making ritual beginning with the late eighth century, and elucidates the context of its use based on the history of the manuscripts up to the sixteenth century. The prayers were equally available in Constantinople as the countryside, in parish churches as well as monasteries, and seem to have found particular resonance among orthodox Christians in Southern Italy, perhaps as a way to cement friendly relations with neighbors of other faiths. Further insights about the intent of the ritual—or rather, its lack of similarity with the marriage ritual—are gleaned from a discussion of the liturgical gestures and from an analysis of the prayers.

The third chapter addresses the core issue, the question of the origin of the church ritual for *adelphopoiesis*. It makes a case for early monasticism of the fourth to seventh centuries as the original context for the practice of blessing a bond between two men, making them "brothers." This entails a detailed study of the different aspects of a close relationship between two monastic "brothers": living arrangements, prayer assistance, and the sharing of spiritual capital in the process of penance, as well as emotional perils and sexual temptations. Here, the first of four case studies, on the *Life of Symeon the Fool*, is inserted. It depicts the relationship, told by a hagiographical master narrator of the seventh century, between two casual acquaintances who became monks together and were joined to each other through a prayer ritual. Such brotherhoods of two men continued to be a feature of Orthodox monasticism throughout the Byzantine centuries and beyond, as the conclusion of this chapter shows.

The fourth chapter investigates the practice of *adelphopoiesis* among men of the world. It begins by tracing the expansion of *adelphopoiesis* beyond the immediate social context of monasticism, based on a cluster of hagiographical texts of the seventh century. The use of *adelphopoiesis* by monks to generate connections to the outside world was regarded with great concern by monastic reformers. By the middle Byzantine period, *adelphopoiesis* between laymen was well entrenched as one of several available social networking strategies to expand one's kin group. A second case study presents the relation between the future emperor Basil I and John, the son of the wealthy lady Danelis, in the mid-ninth century, as an example for the employment of the ritual for the purpose of social advancement.

The fifth chapter moves from the description of individual relationships to a study of the prescriptions regarding *adelphopoiesis* by imperial law-givers and ecclesiastical rule-makers. They are unanimous in acknowledging the widespread practice of *adelphopoiesis* through the participation of priests, yet signal their awareness of the dangers it represents, in their view, for the crossing of boundaries between kin groups, social classes, gender, ethnicities, and religions. This is brought to the fore in the third case study, the legal rulings and advice of a bishop-administrator in thirteenth-century Epiros, Demetrios Chomatenos, which shows how men and women of the late Byzantine period interpreted the ritual through their own use.

The sixth chapter presents by way of a postscript further, select evidence for the use of *adelphopoiesis* as a boundary-crossing strategy in post-Byzantine times in the regions of Orthodox Christendom. It is here that the thesis of the book becomes most apparent: Byzantine *adelphopoiesis* was motivated by Christianity and depended on the collaboration of priests, yet did not enjoy official recognition by the church. It can thus serve as an example of a social institution that owed its existence to the people who engaged in it. Institutional control followed behind social practice and was largely confined to first offering and then monitoring the ceremonial.

This book, then, is a very deliberate attempt to treat *adelphopoiesis* within a particular explanatory context. While I make no apologies for that, I have tried to present all the evidence available to me at this point. Others will no doubt draw their own conclusions or add further facets to the picture presented here. My hope is, at the very least, to have contributed to the exploration of Byzantium as a society whose dynamism was to a substantial degree anchored in Christian belief and practice.

{ 1 }

Social Structures

A. Brotherhood Language

Brother-making is a literal translation of the Greek noun *adelphopoiesis*. Other variants are *adelphopoiia, adelphopoiêsia,* and the related adjective *adelphopoiêtos* for a man who has become another man's "brother." This label is attached to the ritual at the center of this book, which created a lasting bond between two men with expectations of social proximity and mutual support, but without any legal consequences for subsequent generations.

The use of brotherhood language implies an ideal of equality,[1] whereas in existing sibling relations, in all societies, there is always a hierarchy between the elder, stronger and the younger, weaker. Real siblings also compete for their parents' love. In foundation myths and popular tales, sibling rivalry is at least as prominent as brotherly support: In the Hebrew Bible, Esau and Jacob are one example of fraternal strife where both brothers survive, while the competition between Cain and Abel results in fratricide, as does the foundation story of Rome involving Romulus and Remus. Positive New Testament models propagated by later Christian authors are the apostles James and John, the sons of Zebedee, and Philip and Bartholomew; both these pairs are also invoked in the ritual prayers for *adelphopoiesis*.

Brother and sister appellations for men and women who are not siblings have a long tradition in the ancient world, in social and religious contexts.

---

[1] This finds its application in Article 1 of the Universal Declaration of Human Rights of the United Nations, adopted December 10, 1948: "All human beings are born free and equal in dignity and rights. They are endowed with reason and conscience and should act towards one another in a spirit of brotherhood." http://www.un.org/en/documents/udhr/.

Their meaning may be stable, analogous to a title or honorific, or fluid, depending on context. In direct address, they were often used in a particular situation as a relational term, to express notional equality or a claim to affective familiarity, regardless of their kinship relation.[2] This included husbands and wives or same-sex lovers.[3] Men and women in early Christian communities employed the language of brother- and sisterhood as a way to emphasize the equality between them. 1 Peter 2:17, for example, reminds the congregation to "love the brotherhood." The erasure of social hierarchies in early Christianity had its root in the twofold belief that all Christian men and women shared a common descent from God the Father, and that they shared brotherhood with Christ through the Incarnation.[4]

The goal of the life of Christian prayer and even more so of the ascetic and monastic life, a mystical experience of complete union with Christ, was sometimes conceived as a form of brotherhood. An experienced spiritual guide in the eleventh century gave this advice to his followers: There are seven different stances that one can assume when praying to God, depending on one's own spiritual state: the lowliest is that of a condemned criminal, then as a debtor, next as a slave, as a paid laborer, as a friend, as a son, and finally, best of all, a position of *adelphopoiêsia* with Christ, when one's own sins are no longer an obstacle to approaching Him freely.[5] Here, the gradual diminution of an individual's distance and inferiority to God is articulated with reference to legal, economic and kinship frameworks, culminating in brotherhood as a relation between equals.

Baptism was the primordial way to join this "family" of Christians and to regard God as one's father, with the resulting claim on all other fellow Christians within the church as brothers and sisters in Christ. The concept of *hyiothesia*, being adopted as a child of God, had great purchase in early Christianity, with the attending horizontal consequences among the fellow faithful.[6] A "brother" is anyone who shares in the Christian faith, as long as he is baptized, whether a lay man or a monk. John Chrysostom observed: "For what is it that creates brotherhood? The bath of rebirth (in baptism), the ability to call upon God as Father."[7] The two most prominent Christian founding

---

[2] E. Dickey, "Literal and Extended Use of Kinship Terms in Documentary Papyri," *Mnemosyne* 67, no. 2 (2004), 131–76.

[3] J. Boswell, *Same-Sex Unions in Pre-Modern Europe* (New York, 1994), 53–107, passim.

[4] As stated, for example, by Athanasius, *Contra Arianos* 2. 62, PG 26, col. 280A.

[5] Nicholas Kataskepenos, *La Vie de saint Cyrille le Philéote, moine Byzantin (†1110)*, ch. 2, ed. and trans. E. Sargologos, Subsidia Hagiographia, 39 (Brussels, 1964), 73. This passage is discussed by P. Halsall, "Early Western Civilization under the Sign of Gender: Europe and the Mediterranean (4000 BCE–1400 CE)," in *The Blackwell Companion to Gender History*, ed. T. A. Meade and M. E. Wiesner-Hanks, 285–306 (Cambridge, 2005), 299.

[6] J. M. Scott, *Adoption as Sons of God: An Exegetical Investigation into the Background of Hyiothesia in the Pauline Corpus* (Tübingen, 1992).

[7] John Chrysostom, *Homilia 25 in Hebraeos*, PG 63, col. 177A.

fathers, Peter and Paul, are thus often depicted in a fraternal relation of equality (which could also have political undertones), sometimes facing each other, as is prominently seen on gold glass representations of the fourth and fifth centuries.

Monasticism is the one distinct social arena within a Christian framework where kinship terms ("father," "mother," "brother," "sister") predominate to the present day.[8] Fraternal language in monasticism implies an essential relation of equality. John of the Ladder, one of the great theorists of monastic spirituality in seventh-century Sinai, includes "co-brotherhood" within the community as one of the key monastic virtues in a spiritual alphabet that he recommends for memorization.[9] Monastic brotherhood often has a vertical component, when a group of disciples gathered around the same spiritual guide and leader whom they regarded as their "father" or *abba*. The same social structures modeled on paternal and fraternal kinship relations were a feature of the philosophical schools of antiquity and Late Antiquity. Another context for the employment of brotherhood language are confraternities, religiously motivated associations of lay people. All of these contexts will be treated in greater detail below.

Being in a relation to one or several others that is assumed to be equal and equitable and hence conceptualized as fraternal is one matter. *Becoming* a brother is another. It is the act of brother-*making* that is of central interest to this study, as reflected in the literal meaning of *adelphopoiesis* (*adelphos* = "brother," *poieô* = "I make"). In the pages that follow, I present the evidence for *adelphopoiesis* in Byzantium and speculate about the origin of the concept, the social practice, and the ritual. The sources sometimes use variants such as *adelphopoiia, adelphopoiêsia*, or the adjective *adelphopoiêtos*. Since I am interested in the ritual and its application in Byzantine society, I assume that the employment of these terms to describe a relation between two men also implies that they had been blessed by the prayers.

This linguistically conservative approach trains the focus on a sound basis of evidence, but also entails the exclusion of potentially relevant material on a broader scale. It means that I have considered only those additional instances where a relation is described as displaying all the signs of a close bond between men that would indicate the ritual of brother-making. Tell-tale characterizations are expressions such as the monastic or theological inflection "spiritual brother" (*pneumatikos adelphos*), or the legal term "brother by arrangement" (*thetos adelphos*), accompanied by an indication that this relation originated between the two men involved[10] and there is mention of a mutual agreement

---

[8] For a recent comprehensive study, see V. Vuolanto, "Family and Asceticism: "Continuity Strategies in the Late Roman World," PhD diss., Tampere, 2008. I am grateful to the author for providing me with a copy of his work.

[9] John Climacus, *Scala Paradisi* (*The Ladder of Divine Ascent*), PG 88, col. 1017, line 14.

[10] This excludes the "brother by arrangement," whom one acquires when one's father adopts a male child.

and a lasting bond. Other forms of affirming a brotherhood bond, such as the exchange of blood, or the swearing of an oath—gestures that are often used together, and sometimes with the further addition of an invocation or a prayer—will be considered only if they are relevant to *adelphopoiesis* in the stricter, ritual sense of the word.

In the pages that follow, I explore the whole range of social constellations that form the context and backdrop for our understanding of *adelphopoiesis*. I begin with kinship relations in Byzantium, then linger on confraternities and sworn brotherhoods, and end with examples of brotherhood compacts from the medieval West.

B. Kinship and the Family

Ritual brotherhood follows the model of biological relations. Notional equality is one defining factor. The other is the creation of a legitimate framework within which ease of access is secured. Byzantium was a society where the boundaries between private and public were clearly delineated, at least for the prosperous classes, where space was accordingly gendered and women had very little mobility outside contexts that were defined by either family or church. It was a society where loyalty was a precious commodity, and survival and prosperity depended on support systems. The extended family or kin group was the basic social unit that offered security. In addition to marriage, several strategies were available to expand the kingroup through the careful selection of suitable men and women: adoption, godparenthood, and brother-making.[11] It is important to understand their similarities of purpose but difference in application and scope.

Marriage

Marriage united a man and a woman in a socially and legally recognized relationship, with the expectation that they would live in the same household and produce legitimate offspring.[12] As a legal instrument, marriage in Byzantium had a long tradition that was defined by the precepts of Roman law. Christian

---

[11] E. Patlagean, "Christianisme et parentés rituelles: Le domaine de Byzance," *Annales ESC* 33 (1978), 625–36; English translation: "Christianization and Ritual Kinship in the Byzantine Area," in *Ritual, Religion and the Sacred: Selections from the Annales, Economies, Sociétés, Civilisations*, ed. R. Foster and O. Ranum, 81–94 (Baltimore, MD, 1982).

[12] A. Laiou, *Marriage, amour et parenté à Byzance aux XIe–XIIIe siècles*, Travaux et mémoires; Monographies, 7 (Paris, 1992); Laiou, *Women, Family and Society in Byzantium*, ed. C. Morrison and R. Dorin (Farnham and Burlington, VT, 2011); H. Hunger, "Christliches und Nichtchristliches im byzantinischen Eherecht," *Österreichisches Archiv für Kirchenrecht* 18 (1967), 305–25; reprinted in Hunger, *Byzantinistische Grundlagenforschung* (London, 1973). For a general treatment of

families may have requested an optional blessing by a priest, but it was only in the ninth century that the ecclesiastical ritual for engagement and marriage was fully developed and that it acquired legal force.

Most women and men in Byzantium were married at one point in their lives, with the possible exception of nuns, monks, and eunuchs. This is true also for the men who engaged in brother-making. Since marriage resulted in the joining of two families, it was the male heads of these families who made it their task to identify a suitable partner for their daughters and sons and to conduct the necessary negotiations. Byzantium was a society where women were expected to bring a dowry into the marriage, while the payment of a bride price by the groom is not attested consistently. If it was offered, it was of a lower value than the dowry. Especially at the highest levels of the aristocracy, including the imperial family, where the rights to large amounts of property were at stake, marriages were a matter of serious diplomacy. Marriage had significant consequences for both families. The exclusive right of primogeniture was not applied in Byzantium, so all the children born to the couple could expect to inherit their parents' property, in varying proportions.[13] Beyond the nuclear family itself, marriage had repercussions for the extended kin group of both husband and wife in terms of determining the future choice of marriage partner. Marriage with a close relative was regarded as incest and strictly prohibited. In the interpretation of Roman law, and its continuation in Byzantium, this meant that marriages were prohibited up to the seventh degree of consanguinity.[14] This affected not only descendants, but also ascendants, so that for example the wife's uncle was not allowed to marry the husband's niece. Such regulations encouraged exogamy on a wide scale, but also had the effect that Byzantine legal experts were frequently consulted in unclear cases.

There was a general expectation that aristocratic families would cast their net of familial ties very widely, and marriage was an obvious way to expand their network. Some rulers became famous for their use of family relations in the service of internal and foreign politics. The founder of the Komnenian dynasty Alexios I Komnenos (1081–1118), for example, himself the offspring of a union between members of two different clans, married into yet a third kingroup. Five of his nine children were daughters, and had between them a total of six marriages to scions of prominent families. His daughter Theodora became the grandmother of the subsequent dynasty of the Angeloi. Although

---

marriage in the middle ages, see J. Goody, *The Development of the Family and Marriage in Europe* (Cambridge, 1983).

[13] A. Laiou, "Family Structure and the Transmission of Property," in *A Social History of Byzantium*, ed. J. Haldon, 51–75 (Chichester, 2009); reprinted in Laiou, *Women, Family and Society in Byzantium*.

[14] Laiou, "Introduction," in *Mariage, amour et parenté à Byzance aux XIe–XIIIe siècles*, 9–20, with a useful diagram on 14.

marriages of members of the imperial family to foreigners were deliberated upon with special care still in the tenth century and accompanied by some anxiety, they became increasingly common in later centuries, especially after the Crusades had brought new neighbors to Byzantium's western and southern borders.

Godparenthood (*synteknia*)

Extension of the kin group could be achieved not only through marriage, but through ritual kinship resulting from baptism. Here, the biological father of a child would select a godparent of the same sex as his daughter or son, who would lend her or his voice to the infant in baptism and take responsibility for the child's Christian upbringing. This relationship is called in Greek "co-parenthood" (the literal sense of *syn* = "together with," *teknon* = "child," i.e., sharing a child in common), the godfather is known as the *synteknos*. The primary relation of importance here is that between the biological father and the godfather of the child. The two men were expected to remain in close contact also at other times and to lend each other mutual loyalty and support. The English designation of "godfather" does not bring out this important facet as well as the German *Gevatter*, the Italian *padrino*, the Spanish *compadre*, or the Modern Greek *koumbaros*. Modern anthropologists thus prefer the term *compadrazgo*. In contrast to marriage, which has a long history, this was a relation that was developed entirely within a Christian framework.[15]

Synteknia, like marriage, results in a relationship of extended kinship. It allows free movement of the two men between their two households and the standing invitation to participate in family feasts—occasions to gain access to the female family members who were otherwise sheltered from the eyes of strangers, with all the dangers to their virtue that this might entail. The godparent's responsibility taken on at baptism usually also extended to the moment of marriage of the godchild, when the *synteknos* took on the role of best man. In the Orthodox tradition, this meant the responsibility of holding the wedding crowns during the marital church ceremony. On the grounds that the spiritual relationship created at baptism is as least as strong as a blood relationship, *synteknia* carried the same incest prohibitions as marriage and affected the choice of marriage partners for the descendants. It did not, however, have any effect on the inheritance of property. While the social benefits and legal consequences of joining two families were the same as for marriage, the economic ones were more limited.

Extensive studies by Evelyne Patlagean and Ruth Macrides have drawn attention to the way in which *synteknia* functioned as a supplemental strategy

---

[15] *Pace* G. Herman, "Le parrainage, l'hospitalité et l'expansion du Christianisme," *Annales ESC* 52, no. 6 (1997), 1305–38.

for the extension of kinship, often used in conjunction with marriage ties between two families.[16] Some emperors carried the potential to create or strengthen ties of loyalty to an extreme, especially when the child awaiting baptism was the firstborn son and designated successor within a dynasty.[17] The first haircut of a child could have a similar initiatory function, and was often performed in conjunction with baptism. It involved an analogous array of participants who were honored with receiving some of the child's hair. The emperor Basil I celebrated the hair-clipping ritual of his second son, Leo (who would later succeed him as Leo VI) with the participation of military men from the capital and from the provinces. Their numbers were so large that the handkerchiefs in which they received the boy's hair stretched "from the chancel barrier of the said chapel (of St. Theodore) as far as the portico of the Chrysotriklinos."[18]

There is one area in which *synteknia* was employed as a hierarchical, paternal relationship and that is in Byzantine interactions with foreign leaders who accepted Christianity and sought baptism.[19] A case in point is the baptism of queen Olga of Kiev in the mid-tenth century, which paved the way for the Christianization of Rus'. It took place in Constantinople and the emperor Constantine VII Porphyrogennetos himself served as her godparent.

Adoption

Another instrument to extend one's immediate kin group was adoption. Filial adoption was usually motivated by the desire to gain an heir. It had a long tradition in Roman law and was used in late Roman and Byzantine society as an inheritance strategy.[20] Adoption as a legal instrument was "christianized" with a church ceremony at the same time as marriage, in the early ninth century.[21] The age of the adopted son was irrelevant, which facilitated the integration of adolescent or adult men into one's family. It is difficult to

---

[16] Patlagean, " Christianisme et parentés rituelles"; R. J. Macrides, "The Byzantine Godfather," *BMGS* 11 (1987), 139–62; reprinted in Macrides, *Kinship and Justice in Byzantium, 11th–15th Centuries* (Aldershot, 2000); and more generally, L. Neville, *Authority in Byzantine Provincial Society, 950–1100* (Cambridge, 2004), 85–98.

[17] G. Dagron, *Emperor and Priest: The Imperial Office in Byzantium* (Cambridge, 2003); first published in French as *Empereur et prêtre: Étude sur le "césaropapisme" byzantin* (Paris, 1996), 45–47.

[18] Constantine Porphyrogennetos, *De ceremoniis* 2. 23, trans. A. Moffatt and M. Tall, *Constantine Porphyrogennetos, The Book of Ceremonies*, 2 vols. (Canberra, 2012), 2: 622.

[19] On this topic, see most recently W. Brandes, "Taufe und soziale / politische Inklusion und Exklusion in Byzanz," *Rechtsgeschichte / Legal History* 21 (2013), 75–88.

[20] R. Macrides, "Kinship by Arrangement: The Case of Adoption," *DOP* 44 (1990), 109–18; reprinted in Macrides, *Kinship and Justice in Byzantium*.

[21] Leo VI the Wise, *Novella* 24, ed. P. Noailles and A. Dain, *Les Novelles de Léon le Sage: Texte et traduction* (Paris, 1944).

gauge how common filial adoption was in Byzantium. It was definitely not entirely arcane, nor was it limited to men who were married. The legislation of Leo VI explicitly allowed childless women and eunuchs to adopt.[22] Adoptions were surprisingly frequent in Byzantine high society and court circles, a case in point being the adoption by the emperor Michael III "the Drunkard" (r. 842–67) of Basil, who shared in his feasts and other leisure pursuits and would succeed him on the throne. They also had their use in foreign politics, as in the case of Bela III, the king of Hungary who was adopted by emperor Manuel I Komnenos (r. 1143–80) as a political move.

Fraternal adoption is a less straightforward issue. The *Codex Justinianus* repeats a rescript of Diocletian that mentions its practice in the border regions, but declares it to be invalid within the empire.[23] It does not seem to have been widespread, and the Church took no interest in it. Byzantine theorists of family relations declared it a conceptual impossibility, because it is not possible to "make" a brother for oneself. The only means to acquire a brother as a result of adoption, they explained, is indirect, if one's father adopts another son. The few narrative sources from Late Antiquity that mention fraternal adoption are at pains to relegate it to the border regions of the empire. It is invoked as an explanatory device for practices such as peace-making under oath, the exchange of blood or of arms, or male-male sex.[24]

C. Other Forms of Brotherhood and the Significance of Oaths

The kin group was a natural point of reference. In classical antiquity, honored and admired teachers were regarded as "fathers," their disciples and followers as their "sons," and thus "brothers" among themselves. Such language signals belonging to a group and at the same time establishes a threshold and boundary that separate this particular group from others. Belonging has its privileges and obligations. It may be an inherited status, but can also be acquired or bestowed. The dividing line can be crossed through a more or less formal act of acceptance or through rituals of initiation. This applies to individual instances of filial and fraternal adoptions as acceptance into a family as much as to the co-optation into larger groups that are conceived as brotherhoods, which it is now time to discuss.

In Late Antiquity, brotherhood terminology was ubiquitous and often vague. Members of Roman associations, such as burial societies or religious clubs, called each other "brother" or referred to the collective membership

---

[22] Leo VI, *Novella* 26 and 27.

[23] *Codex Justinianus* 6.24.7, repeated in the *Basilika* 35.13.17, a compilation of the ninth century (see below, chapter 5).

[24] Shaw, "Ritual Brotherhood in Roman and Post-Roman Societies."

of their association as a "brotherhood."[25] The address "brother" was used to denote a relation of particular closeness, regardless of whether this affection really existed or was merely the product of wishful thinking. The papyrus documentation of pre-Christian and late antique Egypt yields ample evidence for the use of brotherhood language. Husband and wife addressed each other as "brother" and "sister"—a peculiarity of Egypt that may well have its basis in the marriage between siblings or close kin. Holders of the same office would call each other "brother." A person of inferior status could address a superior of whom he was asking a favor as "lord and brother [*kyrios* or *despotês kai adelphos*]."[26] The appellation "brother" could thus also express wishful thinking by staking a claim to equality.

Equality and agreement (*homonoia*), along with friendship (*philia*) and justice (*diakaiotês*) are the intangible values that the earliest brotherhood agreement attested for the Greek world aims to generate. This occurred in Sicily at the end of the fourth or the beginning of the third century BCE and is attested in a famous inscription. Apparently, the city of Nakone had suffered strong divisions, and now a carefully calibrated representational system was devised to bring together members of the opposing factions. These men are referred to as "elected brothers [*adelphoi hairetoi*]." The entire process of brother-making (*adelphothetia*) was sealed with a religious ceremony, in the form of a sacrifice of a white goat, that would be repeated annually.[27]

Colleagues and Brothers

The basic assumption of equality between brothers meant that brotherhood designations were often encountered among people who engaged in the same profession or shared a common goal. Interestingly, the merchant associations and guilds in Byzantium do not seem to have used brotherhood language. The tautological expression "co-brother" (*synadelphos*) was, however, frequently used between high-ranking clergymen, as can be seen, for example, in the letters of John Apokaukos.[28] It is still used in modern Greek to denote a colleague.

---

[25] See esp. P. M. Fraser, *Rhodian Funerary Monuments* (Oxford, 1977), 58–70.

[26] F. Preisigke, *Wörterbuch der griechischen Papyrusurkunden* (Berlin, 1925), s.v. *adelphos*, col. 19–20.

[27] For a discussion of this text, including an English translation, see N. Loraux, *The Divided City: On Memory and Forgetting in Ancient Athens* (New York, 2002; first published in French, 1997), 197–228. Edition by D. Asheri, based on work by G. Nenci, in "Materiali e contributi per lo studio degli otto decreti da Entella," *Scuola Normale Superiore, Annali Classe di Lettere e Filosofia* 12, no. 3 (1982), 771–1103, at 776–7, with further discussion on 1040–45 and 1055–67. See also Decreti di Entella VII (Nenci), IG XIV, III Nenci: http://epigraphy.packhum.org/inscriptions/main.

[28] John Apokaukos used this term with preference for Bonditzes and Ximaras, see *Letters* 57, 74, 76, 81, 100. Also Theophylaktos of Ohrid, *Letter* 61.65, ed. P. Gautier, CFHB 16, no. 2 (Thessaloniki,

Something like corporate solidarity has also been postulated for the eunuchs who formed a distinct social group at the imperial court. On occasion, this translated into joint enterprises: two eunuchs purchased a property outside Rome together, and two other eunuchs made arrangements to share the same tomb, whether out of economic considerations or because of personal attachment remains unclear.[29] These are interesting cases of the pursuit of shared interest similar to the known instances of *adelphopoiesis*, even though they do not employ brotherhood language.

The environment par excellence where corporate solidarity and a strong *esprit de corps* were articulated within an exclusively male context was the military. The challenges of warfare, far removed from one's family and kin group, at a time when one's life was constantly on the brink and survival depended on the assistance of others, provided a natural seedbed for homosocial and homophilic relations. It is a well-known phenomenon at all times in history that long after their discharge, veterans experience greater closeness with their mates from the trenches than with their families.[30] A prominent example from ancient Greece are the Theban soldiers, discussed at length by Boswell and Davidson.[31] Within this group, an older and a younger fighter formed pairs who remained close both on the battle lines and in the camp. Fraternal language, however, is absent from the description of these relationships.

In the Byzantine army, brotherhood rhetoric is surprisingly rare. An exception is the *Handbook on Military Strategy* by the general-turned-emperor Nikephoros II Phokas (ca. 912–69), which placed great emphasis on the small

---

1986). Note also the frequent instances of *synadelphos* in the *Prosopographisches Lexikon der Palaiologenzeit.*

[29] M. McCormick, "Emperor and Court," in *Cambridge Ancient History*, vol. 14: *Late Antiquity: Empire and Successors, AD 425–600*, ed. A. Cameron, B. Ward-Perkins, and M. Whitby (Cambridge, 2008), 152.

[30] Dick Bowen, a British veteran who had participated in the D-Day landings in 1944 that paved the way for the Allied victory over Hitler's Germany despite devastating casualties, has visted the gravestones on Gold Beach in Normandy every year since then. Pointing to the endless row of grave markers, he explained to a reporter: "These are all my mates. These and these and these." John Lichfield, "All the Dead are my Mates," *Independent on Sunday*, June 7, 2009, 6. Oberstleutnant Philipp von Boeselager (1917–2008) describes in his memoirs the steps that led to his participation in the plot of July 20, 1944, to kill Hitler. In this environment, where loyalty and secrecy were a matter of life and death, his most intimate relation was with his brother Georg, who rose to the rank of colonel of the cavalry. Georg had concluded a pact with three other friends to ensure their burials on German soil, whatever the effort. Philip eventually discharged this obligation on behalf of his brother. After the death of Karl von Wendt in Rzhev in Romania in 1942, he carried his body, in a specially outfitted map box, for eighteen months in order to fulfill his promise. P. von Boeselager, with F. and J. Fehrenbach, *Valkyrie: The Plot to Kill Hitler* (London, 2009), 168–70; originally published in French as *Nous voulions tuer Hitler: Le dernier survivant du complot du 20 juillet 1944* (Paris, 2008).

[31] J. N. Davidson, *The Greeks and Greek Love: A Bold New Exploration of the Ancient World* (New York, 2007); published in the United Kingdom as *The Greeks and Greek Love: A Radical Reappraisal of Homosexuality in Ancient Greece* (London, 2007).

unit of the *bandon*, where men who spent all their waking hours together were bound by ties of "kinship and friendship."[32] Nikephoros put his own advice into practice during the Arab siege of Chandax in Crete, when he addressed his soldiers as "brothers and co-fighters."[33]

That the *adelphopoiesis* ritual could be adapted for such a purpose within a military environment, at least in post-Byzantine times, is suggested by the version of the prayers in a single manuscript of the sixteenth century (Appendix 1, no. 59). It assumes that three men are involved in creating the brotherhood bond and, instead of invoking Biblical figures as exemplars, it mentions a triad of military saints, Demetrios, George, and Theodore.[34] In Byzantine art, these three are usually depicted in Roman military costume, either on horseback or on foot, individually or in varying constellations, in groups of two, three, or four, sometimes more. Demetrios is often shown together with George, while George frequently appears together with Theodore, who was believed to be his biological brother. The cult of military saints accompanied the imperial revival of the tenth century when Byzantium registered increasing success on the battlefield. A systematic evaluation of the evidence would be a great *desideratum* of art historical scholarship. Suffice it to mention here two iconographic types of particular interest. The first shows two military saints either facing each other or facing the viewer and above them a bust of Christ who extends his arms in blessing over both of them in a gesture usually known from depictions of married couples.[35] Equally striking are those post-Byzantine icons that show two military saints, George on the viewer's left and Demetrios on the right, each on his horse with his arms around the other's

---

[32] E. McGeer, *Sowing the Dragon's Teeth: Byzantine Warfare in the Tenth Century* (Washington, DC, 1995), 38–39.

[33] Theophanes Continuatus, ed. I. Bekker (Bonn, 1838), 478. I thank Ioannis Stouraitis for this reference.

[34] A possible parallel occurs in the Coptic tradition, where a group of three military men of different regional origins, from Anatolia, Arabia, and Persia, is venerated as martyrs of the Diocletianic Persecution. In the narrative, they variously address one another as "brother", "friend," and "buddy, comrade" (*socius*): *Martyrium S. Theodori, Orientalis nuncupati, fortis I. Christi martyris, et sociorum eius martyrum, quos dominus ad eumdem martyrii agonem invitavit, scilicet S. Leontii Arabis, ac beati Panygiridis e Persarum gente*, in I. Balestri and H. Hyvernat, *Acta Martyrum*, CSCO Scriptores Coptici 3, no. III/1 (Paris, 1908), 30–46.

[35] George and Theodore on a Steatite plaque now in Berlin, Staatliche Museen, cf. I. Kalavrezou-Maxeiner, *Byzantine Icons in Steatite* (Vienna, 1985), pl. 49 (no. 100). George and Demetrios on a sardonyx cameo in the Cabinet des Médailles, Paris, cf. E. Babelon, *Catalogue Camées* (1897), pl. XL (342), as mentioned in the *Princeton Index of Christian Art*. Byzantine emperors in the ninth and tenth centuries, when the empire was engaging in military confrontation along its eastern and northern frontiers, placed greater emphasis on military saints. See M. White, *Military Saints in Byzantium and Rus, 900–1200* (Cambridge, 2013), 64–93, esp. 85 for martyr saints in military costume being depicted in groups of two or three, and P. L. Grotowski, *Arms and Armour of the Warrior Saints. Tradition and Innovation in Byzantine Iconography (843–1261)* (Leiden and Boston, 2010), 104–23, on the imperial encouragement of the veneration of warrior saints.

shoulders. Demetrios leans toward George, their cheeks touching, their halos converging, and their glance no longer frontally directed at the viewer.[36]

Religious Confraternities

Byzantium does not yield particularly rich evidence for confraternities, but they are attested at various moments. Their formation was usually religiously motivated. They were part of the web of relations in a Christianized society in which the Church provided the framework and eventually attempted to control all forms of organization, even if they were spontaneously formed at the initiative of individuals.[37] The earliest instances were the *philoponoi* in fourth-century Egypt, but soon such charitable lay associations were also known in Constantinople, under the name of *spoudaioi*.[38] A confraternity of men in ninth-century Constantinople acted as a kind of burial society. It was a form of grass-roots organization of the economically and socially disadvantaged who, by pooling their scant resources, were able to provide for each other what, individually, they would not have been able to afford, a decent Christian burial. No paupers' burial in a mass grave for them. The men in this "brotherhood" could be certain that there would be a coffin and a proper funerary cortège to accompany them to their last resting place in a designated and marked grave. The membership obligations did not extend beyond the act of burial. There is no mention of prayers offered on behalf of dead members, comparable to the manner that the *memoria* of the deceased was

---

[36] In 1771, Ioannes the son of Athanasios, son of a family of painters and himself a prolific creator of icons and murals, painted an icon of the Dormition of the Virgin for the church of the Koimesis of Archimadreio in Ioannina which includes in the center of the lower panel a depiction of Saints George and Demetrios, in close embrace, but each on his own horse. On the painter, see E. Drakopoulou, *Hellênes zôgraphoi meta tên halôsê (1450–1850)*, vol. 3 (Athens, 2010), 333–37. The same iconography is also present, with slight variations, in an icon in the Church of Hagios Nikolaos in the village of Makrino in the Zagori region. I am grateful to Christos Stavrakos for sharing this information with me.

[37] H. Leclerq, "Confréries," *Dictionnaire d'archéologie et de liturgie chrétienne*, vol. 3, pt. 2 (Paris, 1914), cols. 2553–60, offers evidence, including two inscriptions from sixth-century Pisidia, for early Byzantine lay associations whose members were known as *spoudaioi* or *philoponoi*. The most recent overall treatment, with further references, is J. Baun, *Tales from Another Byzantium: Celestial Journey and Local Community in the Medieval Greek Apocrypha* (Cambridge, 2007), 371–85.

[38] S. Pétridès, "Spoudaei et Philopones," *Échos d'Orient* 7 (1904), 341–48; H.-G. Beck, *Kirche und theologische Literatur im byzantinischen Reich* (Munich, 1959), 138–39; E. Wipszycka, "Les confréries dans la vie religieuse de l'Égypte chrétienne," *Proceedings of the Twelfth International Congress of Papyrology, Ann Arbor, 13–17 August 1968*, ed. D. H. Samuel, 511–25 (Toronto, 1970); reprinted in Wipszycka, *Études sur le christianisme dans l'Égypte de l'antiquité tardive*, Studia Ephemeridis Augustinianum 52 (Rome, 1996); P. Horden, "The Confraternities of Byzantium," in *Voluntary Religion*, ed. W. J. Shiels and D. Wood, 25–45, Studies in Church History 23 (Oxford, 1986); E. J. Watts, *Riot in Alexandria: Tradition and Group Dynamics in Late Antique Pagan and Christian Communities* (Berkeley, 2010).

maintained by confraternities in the Latin West and written down in German medieval manuscripts known as "Verbrüderungsbücher."[39]

This was not the only kind of confraternity in Constantinople. Equally motivated by Christian charity, but this time directed to others beyond the group, several laymen formed a confraternity at the public baths that were maintained by various churches, to assist the sick and those in need.[40] A similar kind of confraternity is implied in the priestly prayers of unknown date that are preserved in a manuscript copied in Constantinople in 1027 (Paris, Bibliothèque Nationale, Coislin 213; Appendix 1, no. 8). The "brothers" in this group regularly experienced ritual purification in spirit and body, as they stood, naked, in the bath associated with the Blachernae complex dedicated to the Mother of God. The cohesion among this brotherhood was enforced by their joint prayers for those in their group who had died, and for those who were absent, the latter being mentioned by name. The men were expected to embrace each other at two moments in the proceedings. The manuscript even preserves the ritual for the acceptance of new members, the "Prayer to make a brother with regard to the holy bath." It invokes God's blessing for the new member's future service to the weak and the sick.[41] These prayers document a charitable organization of dedicated laymen who formed close bonds of spiritual responsibility for one another, even beyond death. The mention of their own need of purification and the repeated embrace leaves ample room for speculation about the homosocial aspect of their gatherings. In addition to the care of the sick and the dead, confraternities in Constantinople and elsewhere dedicated themselves to the cultivation of particular acts of worship. In the capital, a religious confraternity took care of an icon of the Mother of God (Theotokos) in the Chalkoprateia church. This "service of the brothers" is mentioned in a sermon that was composed in the late tenth or early eleventh century.[42] A similar practice was observed and described in Constantinople in the eleventh and fifteenth centuries. There are no Byzantine sources for this, only the reports by Western visitors. They

---

[39] G. Dagron, "'Ainsi rien n'échappera á la réglementation': État, église, corporations, confréries: À propos des inhumations à Constantinople (IVe–Xe siècle)," in *Hommes et richesses dans l'Empire byzantin*, ed. V. Kravari, J. Lefort, and C. Morrison, 155–82 (Paris, 1991). The statutes of a professional association of Christian men who provided burial and other forms of assistance to each other and celebrated banquets together survives in Syriac, probably from the pre-Islamic period: S. Brock, "Regulations for an Association of Artisans from the Late Sasanian or Early Arab Period," in *Transformations of Late Antiquity: Essays for Peter Brown*, ed. P. Rousseau and M. Papoutsakis, 51–62 (Farnham and Burlington, VT, 2009). For the West, see J. Autenrieth, D. Geuenich, and K. Schmid, *Das Verbrüderungsbuch der Abtei Reichenau*, MGH, Libri memoriales et necrologia, n.s. 1 (Hanover, 1979).

[40] P. Magdalino, "Church, Bath and Diakonia in Medieval Constantinople," in *Church and People in Byzantium*, ed. R. Morris, 165–88 (Birmingham, 1990).

[41] Text in Dmitrievskij, *Euchologia*, 1042–52, *Euchê eis to poiêsai adelphon eis to hagion lousma*, 1051.

[42] E. Dobschütz, "Maria Romaia: Zwei unbekannte Texte," *BZ* 12 (1903), 173–214, at 201–02.

commented on the intriguing and colorful sight of men and women forming a weekly procession to accompany with psalmody an icon of the Virgin Hodegetria ("who shows the way", i.e., by pointing with her hand to the Christ child in her lap) from one church to another where it was to remain until its solemn relocation the following week.[43]

Groups of pious men and sometimes women dedicated to religious service are also attested outside Constantinople. In eleventh-century Thebes, at that time a prosperous city thanks to the silk industry that made this region an attractive target for foreign raids, a number of women and men, some of them clerics, were joined in the confraternity of Saint Mary of Naupaktos for the common purpose of worship, prayer assistance in times of illness and need, and collective responsibility for burial and commemoration. Their original membership list of 1048 is preserved in a manuscript copy of 1089 and contains the names of clergy, laymen, and women. They called themselves an *adelphotês* ("brotherhood") and declared their intention to provide for one another in illnesses and funerals, to lend each other prayer assistance, and to avoid strife.[44] In Epiros, a manuscript copied in 1225 in the region of Ioannina contains a list of names that follows the request for commemoration. Thirty-nine people are mentioned, a quarter of them are religious (priests, monks, a nun), the rest women and men in equal proportion, and several of the names are of Slavic origin. Günter Prinzing made a convincing argument for identifying this group as a religious confraternity, although the manuscript entry lacks any designation of this group, and hence also any kinship language.[45]

The people in these lists were far removed from the splendor of the imperial palace or the fine dwellings of the aristocracy. They are the kind of women and men of middling status who feature as nameless bystanders or as part of anonymous crowds in the narratives of Byzantine historians. They appear more frequently, often equally anonymously, in hagiographical accounts, where they are identified by their respective pathology—the man with a hernia, the woman with a breast tumor—as they sought healing from a holy man or at a famous sanctuary. These religious confraternities attest to people's resourcefulness in forming associations based on ability and need. They are the same kind of people for whom the prayers in the *euchologia* (prayer books) were written and performed. And it is not too far-fetched to assume that in addition to getting married and acting as godfathers, the men in these communities also exercised the option of forging ties of *adelphopoiesis* to their mutual advantage.

---

[43] K. N. Ciggaar, "Une description de Constantinople traduite par un pèlerin anglais," *REB* 34 (1976), 211–67; Ciggaar, "Une description de Constantinople dans le Tarragonensis 55," *REB* 53 (1995), 117–40; Pero Tafur, *Travels and Adventures, 1435–1439*, trans. M. Letts (New York and London, 1926), 141–42.

[44] J. Nesbitt and J. Wiita, "A Confraternity of the Comnenian Era," *BZ* 68 (1975), 360–84.

[45] G. Prinzing, "Spuren einer religiösen Bruderschaft in Epiros um 1225? Zur Deutung der Memorialtexte im Codex Cromwell 11," *BZ* 10, no. 2 (2008), 751–72.

Several of our prayer-book manuscripts (*euchologia*) from the orthodox communities in South Italy, which date from the eleventh and twelfth centuries, also include on fly-leaves (and thus clearly as a later addition) lists of names, usually in twos or threes, accompanied by the request for prayers for their souls: (Appendix 1, manuscripts nos. 9 and 13). It is possible that these were independent prayer associations of lay people. It is equally conceivable that these manuscripts were kept in a monastery and that people from the surrounding region had their names inscribed in the hope of benefiting in the afterlife from the prayers of the monks. In this instance, these annotations would fit the pattern known from medieval Germany as Verbrüderungsbücher.[46] These are lists of names of laymen, rarely lay women, who joined the monastery in an economic sense, through generous donations during their lifetime or even by naming it as heir to their property, and profited in a spiritual sense, by benefiting from the prayers of the monks for their soul. This is a neat system of exchange of spiritual for monetary capital. In thirteenth-century Calabria, a region where many of the manuscripts containing the *adelphopoiesis* prayers originated, it was common practice for laymen in anticipation of their death to designate a monastic community as their legitimate heir while at the same time joining the monks as a "brother."[47] This practice is not well studied for Byzantium, but it is attested, at least once, for Mount Athos in the year 1013, in a donation made by Maria, the widow of John of Thessaloniki, and her husband, Constantine Lagoudes. Maria considers herself to be brought up "practically from my mother's womb" by the monastery (a striking detail in itself) and wants to retain this association. As they donate extensive properties in Hierissos, wife and husband both expect "from this day forward" to be "united in the spirit" with the monks, "becoming one soul" with them, "and being (monastic) brothers of the Laura ourselves." The document then confirms that they are inscribed in the *diptycha* of the monastery for commemoration in prayer.[48]

The purpose of all these fraternally conceived communities was the communal exercise of and mutual support in a particular religious practice, whether joint prayers and icon veneration, burial assistance, or posthumous commemoration. They evolved within the framework of the institutional Church, but without any regulation by it, either because they were considered negligible, due to the small number of people involved, or because their

---

[46] Autenrieth, Geuenich, and Schmid, *Verbrüderungsbuch der Abtei Reichenau*. Other examples exist for Salzburg and St. Gall.

[47] P. De Leo, "L'adoptio in fratrem in alcuni monasteri dell'Italia meridionale (sec. XII–XIII)," *Atti del 7° Congresso internazionale di studi sull'alto Medioevo: Norcia, Subiaco, Cassino, Montecassino, 29 settembre–5 ottobre, 1980* (Spoleto, 1982), 657–65; see also A. Bébén, "Frères et membres du corps du Christ: Les fraternités dans les *typika*," *Cahiers de civilisation médiévale* 44 (2001), 105-19, at 116-17.

[48] *Actes de Lavra* no. 17, Archives de l'Athos 1, ed. G. Rouilland and P. Collomp (Paris, 1937), 47–50.

purpose was not considered to be of sufficient interest to warrant the establishment of control mechanisms.

Notarized Brother-Making as a Household Strategy outside Byzantium

Brother-making had many advantages, depending on the circumstances of the two people involved. As an extension of kinship, it conferred rights and privileges and facilitated interaction on the model of the family. This had further ramifications, for families were not only groups of people, but also lived in households and thus formed economic entities that were based on ownership of and access to property (land), goods (animals), and services (laborers and servants). In the late middle ages, in Latin documents from Spain, the South of France, and the Adriatic, brother-making appears as a legal instrument that is officially notarized. There is no record of the confirmation of this arrangement in a religious ritual or by the Church, although it may have happened nonetheless.

The motivating factor for such *affrèrements* in the Mediterranean in the late medieval and early modern period, from Spain and Southern France to Italy, where they are called *affratellamento*, was the extension of kinship with an aim to profit from legal regulations that facilitate economic exchange between family members. These relations had a utilitarian character and were based on contractual agreements. They gave family status to an arrangement that was entered into voluntarily by heads of households that may or may not have been related. Such arrangements fit into a wide spectrum of household types, from small nuclear families to multigenerational households to several nuclear families of the same kingroup living in the same household. *Affrèrement* became available in the late middle ages (the earliest cases date from the eleventh century), gained prominence in the fourteenth century, and is attested until the early eighteenth centuries, as several regional studies have shown.[49] There is a fundamental difficulty in studying this phenomenon: *affrèrements* are known exclusively from legal documents, and find no reflection in contemporary historical narratives. This is in notable contrast to Byzantine *adelphopoiesis*, where, in addition to the rich manuscript tradition of the ecclesiastical ritual itself, we have narrative descriptions and legal prescriptions, but no legal documentation of the practice.

The contracts of *affrèrement* from Southern France studied by Allan Tulchin involve two or more individuals who declare their intent to combine their possessions, hold them in joint ownership, and pass them on equitably

---

[49] The most recent study is A. A.Tulchin, "Same-Sex Couples Creating Households in Old Regime France: The Uses of the *Affrèrement*," *Journal of Modern History* 79 (2007), 613–47, at 618–27, with further references.

to their heirs. This is couched in language that emphasizes their desire to live together as brothers, sharing "one bread and wine."[50] Sometimes, a man and woman entered a contract of *affrèrement* prior to marriage, which was advantageous if the woman was poor, as it eliminated the need for a dowry. In other cases, two men who were young and unmarried entered into such arrangements. In such instances, the expressions of affection in the contracts may be more than just commonplace phrases, and perhaps point to an emotional attachment between the two men. This assumption gains further support from the evidence of late medieval and early modern burials in the same tomb of two unrelated men, which has been documented for France as well as England. Tulchin thus concludes that these contracts could be used "to formalize same-sex loving relationships."[51] Of course, whether or not such relationships included a sexual component cannot be known. That is a modern question on which the medieval sources remain silent.

Sicilian Local Customs

Local historians report two occasions in the eleventh and twelfth centuries, respectively, of what they identify as a particular Sicilian custom of sworn brotherhood between two men of the highest echelon of society. The first episode relates to a brotherhood agreement concluded between a Muslim and a Christian, in the year 1072. At the time of the Norman conquest, the Arabs of the town of Castrogiovanni were deliberating how best to defend themselves "whether by deceit or by arms." One of the most powerful among them, Ibrahim (Brachiem), entered into a pact of adoptive brotherhood with Serlo, the nephew of Count Roger I, "by ear [*per aurum*], as was their custom." The rest of the story is dramatic: Ibrahim sent gifts to Serlo, addressing him as his "adopted brother," along with a message alerting him to a planned incursion by a small band of Arabs set on plundering the land. What he did not say was that the number of invading Arabs amounted to 700 knights and 200 foot soldiers. Serlo promptly fell into an ambush when he pursued the seven Arabs that had marched ahead to bait him and he was killed.[52] The ingredients of this relationship run the whole gamut of what an *adelphopoiesis* relation might entail: a mutual agreement of brotherhood, gift giving, the exchange of privileged information, the assumption of loyalty and support,

---

[50] Ibid., 622.

[51] Ibid., 639.

[52] Geoffrey Malaterra 2. 46, ed. E. Pontieri, *De rebus gestis Rogerii Calabriae et Siciliae comitis et Roberti Guiscardi Ducis fratris eius*, Raccolta dei Storici italiani, vol. 1 (Bologna, 1927), 54, lines 5–6; trans. K. B. Wolf, *The Deeds of Count Roger of Calabria and Sicily and of his Younger Brother Guiscard by Robert Malaterra* (Ann Arbor, 2005), 126. A footnote to the Latin text comments that pulling each other's ear was a Muslim custom. Wolf's translation "verbally" should be dismissed. I am grateful to Alex Metcalfe for drawing these references to my attention.

but also the betrayal of trust that later Byzantine authors such as Kekaumenos would warn about. The mention of established custom is intriguing: does this refer to a Sicilian custom of brother-making, or perhaps more specifically to the affirmation of their mutual promise through ear-pulling, a custom well attested since the early middle ages, especially in Bavaria?[53]

The second incident relates to a brotherhood that was contracted between a court official and a high-ranking cleric, in the mid-1150s, when Maio of Bari, the power-hungry and unpopular chief minister of King William I (r. 1154–66), concluded a compact with Hugh, the archbishop of Palermo. He subsequently introduced Hugh to the court and depended on his support to influence the king. The historian Falcandus reports that

> these two, in accordance with the Sicilians' custom, formed an alliance of brotherhood [*fraterne fedus societatis*], and bound themselves with a mutual oath that each would support the other in every way, and that they would be of one mind and purpose both in good and in bad circumstances; anyone who harmed them would become the enemy of both.[54]

In both these cases, the brotherhood agreement facilitated the creation of a strategic alliance of a Sicilian nobleman with men of comparable social status, but who moved in different social spheres, the one a Muslim, the other a clergyman. Fascinating as they are in their own right, these cases suggest why *adelphopoiesis* was so popular in Southern Italy and Sicily that almost one-third of the manuscripts containing the ritual can be associated with this region. In an area where Greek-speaking Orthodox Christians lived together with Catholic and Muslim neighbors, brotherhood arrangements—in whatever way they were concluded—provided a convenient tool to seek accommodation and to pursue relationships to mutual advantage.

A Brotherhood Contract and its Dissolution in Late Fifteenth-Century Ragusa

A series of legal documents for the conclusion of brotherhood on the Italian model of *affratellamento* by contract survives in the archives of the city of Ragusa (Dubrovnik), a wealthy trading port on the Adriatic that was in close contact with the Italian peninsula.

---

[53] On the custom of ear-pulling in a legal context, see W. Brown, *Unjust Seizure: Conflict, Interest, and Authority in Early Medieval Society* (Ithaca, NY, 2001), passim.

[54] Falcandus, trans. G. A. Loud and T. Wiedemann, *The History of the Tyrants of Sicily by "Hugo Falcandus,"* 1154–69 (Manchester and New York, 1998), 62 (slightly modified). Latin text at http://www.thelatinlibrary.com/falcandus.html.

On January 24 and again on January 29, 1487, two men from Breno (Zhupa Dubrovachka, a small agricultural area south of Ragusa), Andreas and Vuk (Vuchich or Vochic in the manuscript), made an oral agreement which was notarized. Vuk was already married to Andreas's sister Cuiete, and they had a daughter, Marussa. Now they agreed to treat each other as brothers, "as if they had been born from the same parents." This is explained as "to stay and to reside together, sharing the same bread and the same wine, as is the custom of good brothers." They further agreed to share their immobile possessions of inherited and rented land and houses, and their moveable possessions, such as animals, an agreement that also extends to their heirs and legal successors.[55]

Five years later, their compact was dissolved. Kinship language was no longer employed. Andreas and Vuk agreed in a further notarized document of February 29, 1492, to divide all their property, including a house and animals. On July 15, 1492, Andreas and Vuk declared in a deposition that they had received the promised amount from their settlement and separation.[56]

Whether they benefited from the church ritual of *adelphopoiesis*, we cannot know. But the fact remains that theirs was an already existing close relation prior to the legal agreement. Perhaps the marriage of Andreas's sister to Vuk was a way to cement a personal friendship between the two. Or this marriage led to a greater degree of closeness and interaction between two men who had initially been distant. With their notarized agreement, they sought to make this relation even closer by sharing the same home and the same resources. Whose house they lived in is not specified, however, neither do we know about the marital status of Andreas, but since care is taken in the document to mention heirs and successors, he too must have been married or expected to get married. These were people of moderate wealth, who are recorded as both renters and owners of land, cattle, and a house.

This is the only instance of which I am aware of an official record of the severance of a brotherhood agreement, and is thus an indirect confirmation of its binding nature as a contract. In this sequence of three legal documents, there is no mention of any involvement of the Church, no prayers, no oath, no exchange of significant objects or substances (such as blood), only a valid declaration that was later archived. Although concluded between two men who were already related by marriage, this was brotherhood strictly for the purpose of economic benefit and could thus easily be dissolved.

In the regions under Byzantine cultural influence, such as Romania at the end of the middle ages, legal brotherhood arrangements for the sake of

---

[55] Dubrovnik, State Archives, Diversa notariae, vol. 67, fol. 66. I am greatly indebted to Barisa Krekić for making his transcription of these documents available and for discussing this case with me.

[56] Ibid., vol. 71, fol. 126v. The documentation is incomplete, but the figure of seventeen *hyperpyra* is mentioned.

exercising joint ownership were equally common. They could involve small items like fruit trees, or larger goods, like land and mills, and they were contracted among distant relatives, or even among heads of monasteries.[57] In the core lands of Byzantium itself, a small handful of legal documents attest to the practice of generating written, binding agreements regarding ownership of property and labor when a (future) son-in-law or daughter-in-law entered the household of his or her in-laws either as minors after their engagement, or at marriage—a practice that can be traced to the eighth century and seems to be most prevalent in the eleventh and twelfth centuries.[58] The joining of a household is described with a formula similar to the *unum panem, unum vinum* of the Latin documents of *affrèrement*, as sharing "the same roof, the same food [*homostegos, homodiaitos*]." But these are cross-generational, hierarchical relations where brotherhood language has no place. They serve as a reminder that strategies for social and economic benefit were as varied as the people and situations who dictated their use.

Sworn Brotherhoods

An entirely different case was the so-called brotherhoods. The Greek word is either *ph(r)atria*, etymologically related either to the Latin *frater* ("brother"), or to *hetairia*, derived from the Greek *hetairos* ("companion," "associate"). These are never mentioned in a positive light and are often shrouded in secrecy. This is reflected in a further designation of such groups as "sworn associations," *synômosiai*.

These were mostly secular associations, usually involving young men eager to improve their social status by gaining access to power through whatever means, including violence.[59] The confirmation of relationships through an oath was not unknown in medieval Byzantium, but these were always regarded with suspicion. In the Byzantine lexica of the sixth, ninth, and tenth centuries, the word *synômosia* (literally, "swearing an oath together") is defined neutrally enough as "friendship accompanied by oaths", that is, sworn friendship.[60] These could also be conspiracies and thus the thirteenth-century Lexicon of Pseudo-Zonaras explains "*synômosia*: plotting against others, and

---

[57] P. H. Stahl, "La consanguinité fictive: Quelques exemples balkaniques," *Quaderni fiorentini per la storia del pensiero giuridico moderno* 14 (1985), 122–47, at 138–40, quoting N. Iorga, *Anciens documents de droit roumain* (Paris and Bucharest, 1930).

[58] D. Simon, "Byzantinische Hausgemeinschaftsverträge," in *Beiträge zur europäischen Rechtsgeschichte und zum geltenden Zivilrecht: Festgabe für Johannes Sontis*, ed. F. Baur, K. Larenz, and F. Wieacker, 91–128 (Munich, 1977).

[59] In a slanderous way, the label of *phratria* could also be attached to the adherents of a different Christian doctrine, as done by Nikephoros, *Refutatio et eversio*, passim.

[60] Hesychius, *Lexikon* 2747: *synômosia: hê meth' horkôn philia*, repeated by Photius, *Lexikon* 556, and *Suda* 1612. All citations from the Thesaurus Linguae Graecae online. For conspiracies (*synômosiai*), see the detailed study by J.-C. Cheynet, "Foi et conjuration à Byzance," in *Oralité et lien*

making a bond with each other through oaths, not to cease from the pointless plot until it is accomplished."[61]

It is in this unsettling sense that sworn friendships between several people are also equated with boys' clubs (*phatria, phratria*) and mentioned in connection with insurrection (*stasis*) in a sixth-century handbook of military strategy,[62] and associating with plots against the emperor, punishable by death, in the *Ekloga*, the great codification of law of the eighth century.[63] As potentially destabilizing action-groups that could easily unsettle the established order and even cost an emperor his throne, they were always regarded with great suspicion.[64] The Council of Chalcedon reinforced secular law by prohibiting such groups also within the church.[65] This was not without reason: a cursory glance at the statistics shows that of the ninety-four emperors (and the rare empresses) who ruled between 330 and 1453, thirty-six lost their throne in an insurrection. Instability of rulership was part of the Byzantine political system.[66] No surprise, then, that rule-makers and legislators, both imperial and ecclesiastical, concerned themselves with these associations, issuing strict and wholesale prohibitions.

Ecclesiastical brother-making, by contrast, initially remained distinct from such groups, restricted as it was to two men. It was only in the early fourteenth century that *adelphopoiesis* was equated with the kind of brotherhood that involved several men. Even later, in a manuscript dated 1522 (Appendix 1, no. 59), we encounter the only instance of ritual prayers for *adelphopoiesis* that involve three men. The earlier practice of a bond between two men persisted—whether between monks, between monks and laymen, or just between laymen—but the expansive application of *adelphopoiesis* in post-Byzantine times is worthy of note, and will be discussed further in chapter 6. It confirms the potential flexibility of the relation and is testimony to the resourcefulness of the people who employed it.

---

social au Moyen Âge (Occident, Byzance, Islam): Parole donnée, foi jurée, serment, ed. M.-F. Auzépy and G. Saint-Guillain, 265–79, Centre de recherche d'histoire et de civilisation de Byzance, Monographies 29 (Paris, 2008).

[61] Pseudo-Zonaras, *Lexikon* 1687.

[62] Maurikios, *Strategikon* 1.6.4.

[63] *Ecloga* 17. 3, cf. *Ecloga aucta* 17.4.

[64] H.-G. Beck, "Byzantinisches Gefolgschaftswesen," *Bayerische Akademie der Wissenschaften, Philos.-hist. Kl., Sitzungsberichte* 1965, no. 5 (Munich, 1965).

[65] *Acts of the Council of Chalcedon*, Canon 18, *Acta Conciliorum Oecumenicorum*, ed. E. Schwartz, vol. 2: *Concilium Chalcedonense* (Berlin and Leipzig, 1936); repeated at the Quinisext Council in 692 (Mansi 11, col. 960A).

[66] R.-J. Lilie, "Der Kaiser in der Statistik: Subversive Gedanken zur angeblichen Allmacht der byzantinischen Kaiser," in *Hypermachos. Studien zur Byzantinistik, Armenologie und Georgistik: Festschrift für Werner Seibt zum 65. Geburtstag*, ed. C. Stavrakos, A.-K. Wassiliou, and M. K. Krikorian, 211–33 (Wiesbaden, 2008).

Oath-Taking and *Adelphopoiesis*

As their designation as "oath communities" (*synômosiai*) indicates, the dangerous kinds of confraternities were confirmed by the swearing of an oath. This requires further investigation, since the ecclesiastical *adelphopoiesis* ritual also involves a gesture that is reminiscent of taking an oath on a Gospel book. Generally speaking, oaths affirmed either the sincerity of an intention, or the truth of a statement. They found application in law courts and proved a useful tool in social relations and economic interactions. By the sixth century, at the latest, oaths on the Gospel were a common part of judicial proceedings. Although church fathers, invoking the second commandment, were quick to condemn the practice of swearing oaths, the church soon developed from opponent of oaths to its guarantor, in the felicitous phrase of Olivier Delouis.[67]

Oaths could be taken in a church or chapel, with the right hand on a sacred object, Gospel book, icon, relics, or a cross, invoking God as a witness—the same gestures that are present in the *adelphopoiesis* ritual. By the early ninth century, the emperor Leo VI reaffirmed: "The judge should give an oath at the beginning of the proceedings, and the officer at the moment of his promotion." The imperial legislator then goes on to explain that this is only an apparent contradiction between imperial and religious law, since both are interested in assuring that only truth be spoken.[68]

Oaths were a regular feature of the late Roman and early Byzantine state, a practice attested since the mid-fifth century that also has parallels in the early medieval West.[69] New officers were required to swear an oath of loyalty to the emperor and the empire in an oral ceremony, a written copy of which was deposited in the imperial archives. This represents, as Mikhael Nichanian observes, the continuation of a Roman practice within a ritual context, for the purpose of reinforcing vertical power structures. In the eighth century, this oath was extended to include the promise of support for the emperor's heir and successor—a precaution to ensure dynastic succession in a system where rulership was far from stable.[70] Byzantine authors of the eleventh century and later frequently report on oaths of loyalty by court officials and aristocrats at moments of transition in the imperial office, in the later period even for the appointment of a junior emperor (*kaisar*) and designated successor. By the fourteenth century, at the very latest, when one of the great intellectuals of his

---

[67] O. Delouis, "Église et serment à Byzance: Norme et pratique," in *Oralité et lien social*, ed. Auzépy and Saint-Guillain, 212–46, reference at 232.

[68] Leo VI, *Novella* 97, ed. Noailles and Dain, 317–19.

[69] N. Svoronos, "Le serment de fidelité à l'empereur byzantin et sa signification constitutionnelle," *REB* 9 (1951), 106–42; reprinted in Svoronos, *Études sur l'organisation intérieure, la societé et l'économie de l'Empire byzantin* (London, 1973). W. Fritze, "Die fränkische Schwurfreundschaft der Merovingerzeit," *Zeitschrift der Savigny-Stiftung für Rechtsgeschichte, Germanistische Abteilung* 71 (1954), 74–125.

[70] M. Nichanian, "Iconoclasme et prestation de serment à Byzance: du contrôle social à la nouvelle alliance," in *Oralité et lien social*, ed. Auzépy and Saint-Guillain, 81–101, quotation at 83.

time, Manuel Moschopoulos, composed a little treatise on "political oaths," all subjects of the emperor were expected to swear an oath of loyalty. This was not only a safeguard that protected imperial power against insurrections, but was also interpreted as an expression of the collective political will of the citizenry.[71]

Oaths also regulated the relations between the emperor and the Patriarch of Constantinople. On several occasions in the fifth century, the emperor was required to give assurances of the orthodoxy of his beliefs, in line with the teaching of the church. The tables turned during the period of iconoclasm, which brought the innovation of an oath of loyalty to the emperor that was required of a new patriarch.

With their frequent application in different contexts, oaths were a serious and grave matter, a promise made in the presence of God that could not be broken. A number of monastic treatises of the eleventh and twelfth centuries addressed to cenobites and solitary monks offered strong admonitions to avoid taking oaths, even in matters as trivial as buying and selling merchandise at the market.[72] Sometimes, however, the breaking of an oath served a greater good. In an edifying story from seventh-century Palestine, a man asked an *abba* (spiritual father) for assistance in the reconciliation with his "brother." The latter listened to admonishments, but declared himself unable to be reconciled "because I swore on the cross." The *abba* persuaded him that it is not only acceptable, but can be necessary to change one's mind, to break oaths that lead to perdition, and to repent.[73] Many Byzantine prayer books contain prayers of release and pardon for people who had broken their oath. These sometimes appear directly before or after the *adelphopoiesis* prayers, perhaps pointing to an interpretation of brother-making along those lines, as a sworn contract.

The central gesture of the *adelphopoiesis* ritual, the imposition of the hands of both men on the Gospel codex, is the same as that for the swearing of an oath. The avoidance of enmity and strife and the promise of mutual support and loyalty are central to the prayers for *adelphopoiesis*. Some prayers go even further in suggesting that they are signaling a new beginning in a relation between two men, following a period of confrontation. This is especially true for the prayers in the Old Church Slavonic version of the *Euchologium Sinaiticum*, and for those prayers that mention mutual forgiveness.[74] George Sidéris has emphasized the importance of such oaths of peace-making in middle and late Byzantine social history, and suggested that brother-making emanated from the practice of oath

---

[71] P. Guran, "Une théorie politique du serment au XIVe siècle: Manuel Moschopoulos," in *Oralité et lien social*, ed. Auzépy and Saint-Guillain, 161–85. See also R. Rochette, "Empereurs et serment sous les Paléologues," in *Oralité et lien social*, 157–67.

[72] Cf. D. Krausmüller, "Moral Rectitude vs. Ascetic Prowess: The Anonymous Treatise On Asceticism (Edition, Translation and Dating)," *BZ* 100 (2007), 101–24.

[73] John Moschus, *Pratum spirituale (The Spiritual Meadow)*, 216, trans. Wortley, 192–93.

[74] Prayers D and F (Appendix 3).

taking.[75] The crucial difference from *adelphopoiesis*, however, is that in none of the manuscript versions of the ritual do the two men speak in their own voice. The only voice that is heard is that of the priest who speaks the prescribed prayers over them. The entire intent and meaning of the relationship that is concluded in the eyes of God and presumably also witnessed by bystanders must be deduced from the text of the prayers alone. Moreover, the earliest attestations of the noun *adelphopoiesis* or the adjective *adelphopoiêtos* occur in Byzantine hagiography of the seventh century, with at least one of the partners being a cleric, a monk, or a holy man. It would be difficult to explain these relationships as the result of reconciliation following a conflict. Further, *adelphopoiesis* relations are characterized by the same set of expectations of loyalty and concrete support as fraternal kinship relations and this is confirmed in many narratives of the middle and late Byzantine periods. Reconciliation through an oath, by contrast, is weaker. It marks the end of a period of confrontation, but entails very little in the way of promise for the future, except neutrality.

Blood Brotherhood

Blood brotherhood is defined as a relation between two or more men (rarely women) that is confirmed through the drinking of each other's blood, often a small drop dissolved in a cup of red wine. It usually accompanies the swearing of an oath or affirmations of peace at the conclusion of a confrontation. Ethnographers and folklorists have found ample evidence for blood brotherhood in all societies, especially those where masculinity is affirmed through real or ritualized violence and the wielding of weapons. Greek and Latin authors of antiquity and the middle ages display a certain unease about blood brotherhood, associating it with a foreign Other, whose engagement with this practice can serve as a further way of labeling him as "barbarian," as Klaus Oschema has persuasively shown.[76]

Thus blood brotherhood was reported as being practiced by the Scythians in ancient times, and by the Cumans who concluded an anti-Byzantine alliance with the Crusaders in this way,[77] or indeed by the formidable Mamluk ruler Saladin, who was said to have been the blood brother of Count Raymond III of Tripoli, of Isaak Dukas Komnenos, the ruler of Cyprus, and of the Byzantine emperor Isaak II Angelos.[78]

---

[75] G. Sideris, "L'*adelphopoièsis* aux VIIe–Xe siècles à Byzance: Une forme de fraternité jurée," in *Oralité et lien social*, ed. Auzépy and Saint-Guillain, 281–92.

[76] K. Oschema, "Blood-Brothers: A Ritual of Friendship and the Construction of the Imagined Barbarian in the Middle Ages," *Journal of Medieval History* 32, no. 3 (2006), 275–301. See also B. Shaw, "Ritual Brotherhood in Roman and Post-Roman Societies," *Traditio* 52 (1997), 327–55.

[77] Joinville, *Histoire de St. Louis* 97.

[78] J. Burgtorf, "'Blood-Brothers' in the Thirteenth-Century Latin East: The Mamluk Sultan Baybars and the Templar Matthew Sauvage," in *From Holy War to Peaceful Cohabitation: Diversity of Crusading and the Military Orders*, ed. Z. Hunyadi and J. Laszlovszky (Budapest, forthcoming).

The extent of the practice of blood brotherhood and whether it followed established patterns or customs is difficult to know, thus making it impossible to establish whether it had a stable ritual enactment or social application. As many reports of ritual brotherhood in different historical periods and geographical regions show, there was in the eyes of the observers and commentators a great deal of slippage between blood brotherhood, sworn brotherhood and the *adelphopoiesis* ritual, which led them to surmise that the last is a sanitized version of the others in Christian guise. Several such instances in post-Byzantine times will be presented in chapter 6. This cannot be excluded, of course, but is hard to prove in the absence of any mention of the exchange of blood when Byzantines make other Byzantines their brothers through *adelphopoiesis*.

Brotherhood Compacts in the Latin West

While Byzantium has preserved ample evidence for an ecclesiastical ritual to conclude brotherhood between two men, the sources for the medieval West, especially Germany and England, report relations of brotherhood entered through a legal agreement or compact (*foedum*). This usually took the form of a solemn oath, was sometimes affirmed by the exchange of blood, and on occasion the actual act of agreement was followed by the celebration of the Eucharist. In some instances, a written declaration was made in a sealed document. The two men took responsibility for each other on the battlefield, including the obligation to pay ransom in case one of them was captured, inherited each other's quarrels and feuds, and were prepared to take care of each other's kin, should the necessity arise. Compacts of this kind are reported at the highest level of society, involving the aristocracy, knights, and kings, beginning in the eleventh century.[79] This was already noted in the seventeenth century by the great French scholar Du Cange, who not only provided ample evidence for medieval brotherhood agreements between two men for the purpose of fighting and maintaining their honor, but also drew attention to the fact that these were often sealed in conjunction with a celebration of the Eucharist.[80] Modern scholars have found it convenient to label them "brotherhood in arms" or "adoptive brotherhood." Their discussions focus on weighing the utilitarian, emotional, or sexual motivations that led to the conclusion of such compacts. These close relations between two men

---

[79] M. Keen, "Brotherhood in Arms," *History* 47 (1962), 1–17; P. Chaplais, *Piers Gaveston: Edward II's Adoptive Brother* (Oxford, 1994), 14–20.

[80] C. Du Fresne, Sieur Du Cange, *Glossarium mediae et infimae latinitatis*, Dissertation 21: *Sur l'Histoire de Saint Louis: Des adoptions d'honneur en frère, et, par occasion, des frères d'armes*, ed. L. Favre (Paris, 1887), 10: 67–71. http://sul-derivatives.stanford.edu/derivative?CSNID=00003340& mediaType=application/pdf or http://ducange.enc.sorbonne.fr.

were celebrated in literary works in medieval Latin, a feature that is strikingly absent from Byzantium, where the bulk of our evidence is ritual, legal or historiographical.

Two cases in particular stand out, both of them in the early fourteenth century, the time when brother-making in Byzantium had become so widespread as a boundary-crossing strategy that church and empire became vociferous in their attempts to monitor and control it. In England, the future King Edward II in his late teens concluded a compact of brotherhood with a young knight from Gascony, Piers Gaveston. He gave him an equal share of power and favored him with gifts and public displays of affection, such as sharing with him his table and his bed. Accused twice of disloyalty by other nobles, Piers Gaveston was murdered in 1312. Their relation was based on personal acquaintance and personal sympathy, although the intensity of their attachment is left to the imagination of its interpreters. Contemporary sources invoke the comparison to the Old Testament models of David and Jonathan to describe their relationship—a reference that is absent in Byzantine texts on *adelphopoiesis*—and are critical of Piers's favored position.[81]

Also from medieval England come the remarkable tombstones that speak to the wish of two men to be united in death and that have been the subject of intensive study, most recently by Alan Bray. These range in date from the eleventh to the fifteenth centuries, although the tradition continues: Henry Cardinal Newman was buried in 1890 at his own wish in the same tomb at Oratory House in Rednal near Birmingham as was his lifelong spiritual companion Ambrose St. John. The most remarkable medieval tombstone is that of Sir John Clanvowe and Sir William Neville, their two helmets being depicted as facing each other as if in a kiss and their coats of arms impaled, as was common for married couples. They were buried in Galata, the Latin-inhabited suburb Constantinople in 1391. John Clanvowe's close companion was said to have been so desolate over his death that he refused to eat and passed away two days later. They had known each other and acted as a pair since their late teenage years, long before they reached the shores of Byzantium.[82]

In Germany, by contrast, the brotherhood that Friedrich the Beautiful concluded in 1325 with Ludwig the Bavarian was preceded by bitter fighting between the former, a Habsburger, and the latter, a Wittelsbacher, for the royal throne. The understanding they reached was the result of ecclesiastical intervention. It was brokered by their respective father confessors and sealed by the celebration of communion, a sacrament whose celebration included

---

[81] The most recent treatment is Chaplais, *Piers Gaveston*. See also E.A.R. Brown, "Ritual Brotherhood in Western Medieval Europe."

[82] See most recently J. M. Bowers, "Three Readings of *The Knight's Tale*: Sir John Clanvowe, Geoffrey Chaucer, and James I of Scotland," *Journal of Medieval and Early Modern Studies* 34 (2004), 279–307.

the ritual exchange of a kiss of peace. Their accord was made public through displays of familiarity such as sharing table and bed, and affirmed through their mutual address as "brother." Henceforth, justice was dispensed in their regions in both names. It has been suggested that this arrangement of dual kingship ("Doppelkönigtum") may have been inspired by historical precedent further south and east: the distant memory of Roman adoptive emperors, the Tetrarchy installed by Diocletian in the late third century, and the Byzantine system of appointing a junior emperor with extensive (although not equal) powers to groom him for succession, and indeed Byzantine brother making.[83]

D. Friendship and Christianity

One Soul in Two Bodies

What if the relation that the *adelphopoiesis* ritual cements had its origins in lay society? This would lead us to an investigation of its antecedents in friendship—*philia* in Greek, *amicitia* in Latin—in the ancient and late antique world. There is a vast amount of scholarship on friendship in the ancient and medieval world, its social dimensions, the emotional and affective bonds that support it, and its literary expression. Especially within the genre of epistolography friendship is affirmed and articulated, reflected upon by the correspondents. There is an extensive vocabulary of friendship. A frequent topos is the affirmation that the two friends share "one soul in two bodies," a topos that was sometimes also used in the context of *adelphopoiesis* in Byzantium. Ancient friendship is further marked by the exchange of gifts, and the letter exchanged between friends is often welcomed as a precious gift of words and sentiments in itself. There is also the expectation of concrete assistance through the extension of favors, especially by social networking, much as the old saying defines the aim of friendship: to help each other's friends and to harm each other's enemies.

Lifelong friendships were often forged during the formative years that young men spent during their education preparing for a later career. This would be the first time they had left their family and home town and they were thrown together as strangers in a new location. Such friendships extended into their later lives, when each pursued his own professional advancement. It could lead to the establishment of networks and was often expressed and evoked in letters or in fond reminiscences.[84] The camaraderie generated by

---

[83] M.-L. Heckmann, "Das Doppelkönigtum Friedrichs des Schönen und Ludwigs des Bayern (1325–1327): Vertrag, Vollzug und Deutung im 14. Jahrhundert," *Mitteilungen des Österreichischen Instituts für Geschichtsforschung* 109 (2001), 53–81, at 62–64, with further literature.

[84] E. J. Watts, *City and School in Late Antique Athens and Alexandria* (Berkeley, CA, 2006), 8–11; Watts, "Student Travel to Intellectual Centers: What Was the Attraction?" in *Travel, Communication and Geography in Late Antiquity*, ed. L. Ellis and F. Kidner, 13–23 (Aldershot, 2004); D. Konstan,

this shared experience often found expression in brotherhood language. The emperor Julian the Apostate, for instance, still considered Priscus as his "dearest and most-beloved brother," long after they had both studied philosophy together and Priscus had attracted disciples of his own.[85]

Even when young men remained in their ancestral home, the sharing of their educational experience had a transformative effect and often resulted in close bonds, as ancient authors readily acknowledged. Thus the Roman rhetorician Quintilian comments on the advantage of boys being taught along with others, rather than alone: "I say nothing of friendships which endure unbroken to old age, having acquired the binding force of a sacred duty; for initiation in the same studies has all the sanctity of initiation in the same mysteries of religion. And where shall he acquire that instinct which we call common feeling, if he secludes himself from that intercourse which is natural not merely to mankind but even to dumb animals?"[86] Philo of Alexandria in the early first century CE commented that the communities of the Therapeutae and Essenes, who are often considered as social and religious parallels to the early movement of followers of Jesus of Nazareth, honored their spiritual superiors like fathers and mothers, "in a closer affinity than that of blood, since to the right-minded there is no closer tie than noble living."[87] Ancient and late antique history knows many examples of small communities that formed around the central figure of a teacher, dedicated to the pursuit of particular kinds of knowledge and understanding, often accompanied by the adoption of a distinctive lifestyle or diet. Such groups were understood to be modeled on the family, with the leader as the "father" and the followers as his "sons" and as "brothers" to one another. The obligations this entailed, including the passing on of the intangible heritage of the fathers' teachings, were considered analogous to those within a family.[88] Acceptance into such a group signaled a solemn commitment, and was often sealed with an oath. A fine example is the so-called Hippocratic Oath, as reported by Galen in the second century CE:

> I swear by Apollo the physician and by Asclepius, by Health and Panacea, and by all the gods as well as goddesses, making them witnesses: to bring the following oath and written covenant to fulfillment, in accordance with my power and judgment; to regard him who has taught me this knowledge and skill as equal to my parents, and to share,

---

"How to Praise a Friend," in *Greek Biography and Panegyric*, ed. T. Hägg and P. Rousseau, 160–79 (Berkeley, CA, 2000).

[85] Julian Apostata, *Ep.* 1, *Ep.* 5.

[86] Quintilian, *Institutio Oratoria* 1. 2. 20.

[87] Philo of Alexandria, *De vita contemplativa* 72.

[88] S. C. Barton, "The Relativisation of Family Ties in the Jewish and Graeco-Roman Traditions," in *Constructing Early Christian Families: Family as Social Reality and Metaphor*, ed. H. Moxnes, 81–100 (London and New York, 1997).

in partnership, my livelihood with him and to give him a share when he is in need of necessities, and to judge the offspring coming from him as equal to my male siblings, and to teach them this knowledge and skill, should they desire to learn it, without fee and written covenant, and to give a share both of rules and of lectures, and of all the rest of learning, to my sons and to the sons of him who has taught me and to the pupils who have both made a written contract and sworn by a medical convention but by no other.[89]

The confirmation of the student's acceptance of his filial role in an oath resonates with the forms of serious commitment in the context of monastic brotherhood and lay brother-making. The Hippocratic Oath, accompanied as it was by a written covenant, took on a legally binding character. It was much more than a notional, emotional, or even intellectual commitment. It included the obligation of the disciple to share his livelihood with his teacher and to lend support if the latter was in need. The acceptance of the student into the teacher's family also extended to his obligations across the generations, as he was expected to share with the biological sons of the teacher his "inheritance" of everything he had learned from their common "father."

Two treatises about friends and friendship by Plutarch, the Greek philosopher and statesman of the first century CE, may be taken as an expression of the prevailing sentiments and accepted code of conduct in the Roman Empire. *On Having Many Friends* (*De amicorum multitudine; Peri polyphilias*) values the quality of a few genuine friendships over the quantity of many friendly relations. Friendship, Plutarch explains, is based on familiarity which is easily generated in contexts of conviviality and feasting, especially if drinking is involved. The articulation of friendship consists of mutual assistance in professional and economic matters and also entails participation at family feasts, such as weddings and funerals. By this definition, a friend belongs to the outer circle of the family, and indeed Plutarch sees the friend as similar to a brother. In fact, the bond can be even closer. Plutarch uses words such as "binding together" (*syndeô*) and "intertwining" (*symplekô*) and speaks of the "bond of friendship" (*katazeugos philias*, based on the root *zygos*, yoke). These words are echoed in the prayers for brother-making that we will encounter later. To put his definition of friendship in a nutshell, Plutarch used the common expression of one soul in two bodies, but also coined the strangely modern-sounding pun that friendship means to call one's companion one's counterpart or "Other" (*prosagoreuein hetairon hôs eteron*).[90]

---

[89] Trans. H. von Staden, "'In a Pure and Holy Way': Personal and Professional Conduct in the Hippocratic Oath," *Journal for the History of Medicine and Allied Sciences* 51 (1996), 406–08 (slightly adjusted).

[90] Plutarch, *De amicorum multitudine*, relevant passages at 93E, 94A, 95C, 96D, and 96E–F.

Biological brotherhood as the imperfect model of true friendship is the topic of Plutarch's short treatise *On Brotherly Love* (*De fraterno amore; Peri Philadelphias*), dedicated to Nigrinus and Quietus. Brotherhood, he explains here, is the preparation and training ground for friendship, but is often fraught with tension because of hierarchies in age, innate competitiveness between brothers, or competition over the paternal inheritance.[91] It has been noted that in his discussion of brotherhood, Plutarch, just like Paul of Tarsus a generation before him, is consistent in avoiding the language, metaphors, and lexicon of friendship.[92] Real brotherhood is not necessarily like friendship, in other words, but real friendship is like ideal brotherhood.

Concepts of ancient friendship, especially as articulated in letter writing, remained strong in Christian Late Antiquity.[93] Many Christian authors stressed the importance of having a "friend," a mirror for one's soul in the pursuit of spiritual perfection. The ideal friend is someone at more or less the same level of advancement, so that a dynamic of mutual instruction and assistance could prevail and secure the growth of each partner individually.[94] Especially in the centuries when the acceptance of Christianity was still a conscious choice made by adults, the shared faith in the new religion added a further dimension to a friendship between two men and provided additional nourishment for their personal interaction and letter exchange. The same epistolographic topoi continue to be used, but Christianity offered an opportunity to expand the repertoire to familial language. David Konstan in his extensive study of friendship in the classical world noted that "the preferred metaphors for Christian solidarity were derived from kinship, for example brothers or father and son, rather than from the domain of *amicitia* or *philia*."[95] The Christian notion of *caritas*, directed at more than one person, eventually crowded out the ancient concept of *amicitia*.

John Cassian, who was responsible for the translation of the Egyptian monastic ideal into the Latin linguistic and cultural idiom, included in his *Conferences* a separate chapter "On Friendship" that reports a conversation of Abba Joseph with Cassian and his monastic companion Germanus.[96] Abba Joseph set up the indissoluble affection within a family as the model for a pure and lasting friendship and then explained the challenges that endanger

[91] H. D. Betz, ed., *Plutarch's Ethical Writings and Early Christian Literature* (Leiden, 1978).

[92] R. Aasgaard, "Brotherhood in Plutarch and Paul: Its Role and Character," in *Constructing Early Christian Families*, ed. Moxnes, 166–82.

[93] D. Konstan, *Friendship in the Classical World* (Cambridge and New York, 1997).

[94] C. White, *Christian Friendship in the Fourth Century* (Cambridge, 1992). On the importance of the teacher-friend in philosophical instruction, see I. Hadot, "The Spiritual Guide," in *Classical Mediterranean Spirituality: Egyptian, Greek, Roman*, ed. A. H. Armstrong, 436–59 (London, 1986), 446–48. See also the important book by L. Carmichael, *Friendship: Interpreting Christian Love* (London and New York, 2004).

[95] Konstan, *Friendship in the Classical World*, 156–57.

[96] John Cassian, *Conferences*, ch. 16.

monastic friendships, in particular negative emotions such as anger or indifference, or imperfections in the monastic virtues of detachment from possessions or the self. Although it is not very pronounced in Cassian, the Christian concept of friendship as it was developed by the Latin church fathers in Late Antiquity expanded the definition of the relationship between two friends by introducing God as *tertium quid*. Thus Augustine in his *Confessions* reflects on a childhood friendship: "Yet ours was not the friendship which should be between true friends, either when we were boys or at this later time. For though they cling together, no friends are true friends unless you, my God, bind them fast to one another through that love which is sown in our hearts by the Holy Ghost, who is given to us."[97] In Augustine's understanding, that was to be hugely influential in the Latin middle ages, divine love is what animates and sustains a true friendship between Christians.[98]

This became the subject of much reflection among Latin authors in the high middle ages. The notion of *amicitia* was developed as a way to conceptualize God's relation to the world through the coming of Christ and its consequences for the interaction of man with fellow man. This was especially true for what was believed to be the most evolved form of a Christian community, the large monastery. Within Western monasticism, *amicitia* played such an important role that many authors were at pains to define and circumscribe it. In Irish Christianity, the soul-friend acted as a spiritual guide and companion on the individual's pilgrimage towards perfection in the faith, in much the same role as the spiritual father in the Greek tradition. Monastic friendship became a central feature of Cistercian spirituality in the twelfth century in the writings of Aelred of Rievaulx in England, despite a constant undercurrent of fear, from earliest times, of so-called special friendships that might lead to separation from the community and undermine its cohesion.[99] Formalized friendships within a fixed social framework continued to play a very important role in Western medieval society. As Gert Althoff has shown, there was a ritualized aspect to friendships among the higher echelons of society. Friendships were entered through a sworn compact, confirmed by feasts, expressed in gestures of affection, including sleeping in the same bed, or sitting on the same horse—all intended to ensure public recognition of a special relationship.[100] Further studies have tried to elucidate the relation between Christian friendship and courtly love.[101]

---

[97] Augustine, *Confessions* IV 4.

[98] For an extensive treatment of this topic, see Carmichael, *Friendship*.

[99] B. P. McGuire, *Friendship and Community: The Monastic Experience, 350–1250* (Kalamazoo, MI, 1988; repr. Ithaca, NY, 2010).

[100] G. Althoff, *Verwandte, Freunde und Getreue. Zum politischen Stellenwert der Gruppenbindungen im Mittelalter* (Darmstadt, 1990). Althoff, "Friendship and Political Order," in *Friendship in Medieval Europe*, ed. J. Haseldine, 91–105 (Stroud, 1999).

[101] See especially C. S. Jaeger, *Ennobling Love: In Search of a Lost Sensibility* (Philadelphia, PA, 1999).

Medieval friendship was no private matter, but a social affair and a political statement. In the Latin middle ages, *amicitia* was therefore invoked and enacted not only in relations between kings and the nobility, but also in the interaction with foreign rulers.[102] In the early modern societies of Europe, characterized by large social realignments, especially in the numerical expansion and rise to greater prominence of the aristocracy, the loyalty and support that could be expected from a friend provided an essential safeguard against twists of fate and misfortune.

Published posthumously in 2003 after the author's death from AIDS, and thus under inauspicious circumstances similar to Boswell's *Same-Sex Unions*, Alan Bray's *The Friend* put male-male and female-female friendship firmly on the map of social history. Based on the solid evidence of joint tombstones of two men from late medieval times such as that of Clanvowe and Neville mentioned above, complemented by a loving letter exchange between two nineteenth-century women, one of them married, who maintained a sexual relationship with each other, and augmented by various historical narratives, Bray draws a convincing picture of emotional attachment and lifelong commitment, with or without a sexual component, between two men or two women. He shows that in late medieval and early modern England, such relations were possible, accepted, and recognized, and he explores their articulation in the rhetoric not of kinship, but of friendship.

But to what degree can this be applied to the Greek East? Compared to the Latin West, there is a notable absence of theoretical treatises on friendship by Byzantine authors. Of course, feelings of attachment and affection in the sense of our modern understanding of friendship existed between individual men.[103] And "friends" (*philoi*) and "friendship" (*philia*) were also recognized as a social category, but the general concept did not receive the same attention among Byzantine authors as it did among their Western counterparts. It seems that in Byzantium, the prevailing model to express and interpret social relationships was that of the family.[104]

Gregory of Nazianzus's depiction of his relation with Basil of Caesarea (d. 379) in his funerary oration on his deceased friend, is rightly famous in this regard. They had met as adolescents during their student years in Athens, long before the former became bishop of Caesarea and the latter was appointed to the see of Constantinople. They soon became inseparable, sharing the same roof, the same meals, the same desire for the pursuit of a life of

---

[102] Althoff, *Verwandte, Freunde und Getreue*.

[103] M. Mullett, "Byzantium: A Friendly Society?" *Past & Present* 118 (1988), 3–24; Mullett, "Friendship in Byzantium: Genre, Topos and Network," in *Friendship in Medieval Europe*, ed. Haseldine, 166–84.

[104] As argued, for example, by A. P. Kazhdan and G. Constable, *People and Power in Byzantium: An Introduction to Modern Byzantine Studies* (Washington, DC, 1982, repr. 1991), 32.

philosophy in the Christian vein—similar to the pairs of friends who jointly sought initiation into the monastic life whom we will encounter later. Even within their group of like-minded friends, they were recognized as a pair. Gregory's reminiscences about their time together are painted in the warm glow of friendship experienced as *eros*, perhaps best translated here as "fervent attraction," without the slightest hint of a physical component. Mention is made of being a yoke-pair (*homozygos*) and "one soul in two bodies" with all the pain and anguish that ensued when they parted to go their separate ways. These are key expressions that will resurface again and again in the descriptions of brother-making, first among monks and later also among lay people in Byzantine times. This kind of *eros* finds its expression in *philia*, a friendship between equals. The balance shifted once Basil accepted a position of authority as bishop of Caesarea in Cappadocia. Now the language that Gregory employed for its description changes as implied hierarchies make themselves felt, as Jostein Bortnes has shown. Gregory's affection for Basil was now articulated from the vantage point of a disciple's *eros* for his teacher, or of a monk for his spiritual guide, but it was *eros*, nonetheless, experienced as a strong attraction.[105] Whether the relation was between equals or between men of different status, there remained an intimate connection between *eros*, friendship, and the ardent desire and physical quest for self-improvement through the pursuit of Christian asceticism.

After the great letter collections of the Greek church fathers of the fourth and fifth centuries, there is a lull in this kind of writing until the middle Byzantine period. In the early ninth century, it is the letters of Theodore the Studite, the monastic reformer, that resume this tradition. Especially during the times when he was exiled for his opposition to imperial marriage strategies and icon policy, he relied on an extensive network of close associates and supporters, many of them women. In Theodore's letters, however, friendship was not the predominant mode of interaction, but rather a supplemental articulation of relationships that were defined in other ways. Peter Hatlie observes: "Most people declared as friends [by Theodore Studites] were also blood relatives, spiritual kin, his own monks, relatives of his monks and so forth. . . . The general impression is that friendship in itself lacked sufficient moral force to hold people together in times of need. For Theodore and others, it normally constituted a mere calling card and gateway to a more meaningful kind of relationship."[106] For all the rhetorical fireworks in the classical tradition that epistolary partners liked to exchange as though their letters

---

[105] J. Børtnes, "Eros Transformed: Same-Sex Love and Divine Desire. Reflections on the Erotic Vocabulary in St. Gregory of Nazianzus's Speech on St. Basil the Great," in *Greek Biography and Panegyric*, ed. Hägg and Rousseau, 180–93.

[106] P. Hatlie, "Friendship and the Byzantine Iconoclast Age," in *Friendship and Friendship Networks in the Middle Ages*, ed. J. Haseldine, 137–52 (London, 1990), 143.

were small, gift-wrapped packages, friendships by themselves were often not strong enough to endure tests and crises. The frequent lament of writers of the iconoclast period of the eighth and ninth centuries about the unreliability of friendship shows that, in and of itself, it was a weak relationship unable to withstand larger social or political pressures.

Epistolography experienced a revival in the late eleventh and twelfth centuries under the Komnenian dynasty, which pursued a distinctive policy of strengthening its position through an expansion of its social networks on the model of the family. The elite that was connected through ties of friendship and kinship exchanged letters on an increasing scale.[107] These men shared an appreciation of classical Greek authors which they had acquired in long years of education, sometimes under the same teachers, and chose to articulate their sentiments for one another in the ancient idioms of friendship, but now with an admixture of kinship language. The intellectual revival under the Palaiologan dynasty, when Byzantium's political power was waning, saw a similar proliferation of epistolographic activity. To the intellectuals of the thirteenth and fourteenth centuries, friendship was an assertion of a shared foundation in classical learning, best experienced in a small circle of like-minded men of the same status. This could involve not only listening or reading, but could extend to critiquing each other's work, and even making additions to it.[108]

In a seminal article of 1988, Margaret Mullett draws attention to friendship (*philia*) as a social force in Byzantium. She adopts a useful anthropological distinction between three kinds of friendship: emotional friendship, instrumental friendship, and unequal ("lop-sided") friendship in the form of patronage.[109] Friendship was articulated in ways that were similar to the treatment of family members, with the single but weighty exception that friends could be chosen, but family members could not. The exception to this general rule, one might add, is *adelphopoiesis*, which could turn a friend into a "brother" and thus add a further dimension of meaning and additional possibilities for interaction to an existing friendship. Friends enjoyed the same privileges and obligations as members of the family. "Made brothers" did, too. Conviviality, sharing of food and drink, visits to each other's houses, the exchange of gifts and letters, and the addition of further kinship relations through marriage or godparenthood all played their role. There is a

---

[107] Mullett, "Byzantium," 19, speaks of a "sudden rash [*sic*] of discussion of friendship"; and Mullett, "Friendship in Byzantium."

[108] C. Dendrinos, "Co-operation and Friendship among Byzantine Scholars in the Circle of Emperor Manuel II Palaeologus (1391–1425) as Reflected in their Autograph Manuscripts," paper given at the conference "Unlocking the Potential of Texts: Perspectives on Medieval Greek," Centre for Research in the Arts, Social Sciences, and Humanities, University of Cambridge, July 18–19, 2006. http://www.mml.cam.ac.uk/greek/grammarofmedievalgreek/unlocking/pdf/Dendrinos.pdf.

[109] Mullett, "Byzantium," 16.

heightened need for friendship when social structures are fluid and individuals have to fend for themselves in building their own support networks. As Mullett suggests, this may explain the popularity of brother-making, especially in the late Byzantine period, if the generalizing statements in the legal documentation discussed in chapter 5 are a reliable guide.

E. Homosociability in Byzantium

The History of Scholarship

Did they or did they not? The question of whether the men we will encounter on the following pages had sexual relations remains the proverbial elephant in the room, and it seems best to address the issue right away so that it does not encumber our study any further. It is, implicitly, also a question of whether John Boswell's approach to the interpretation of *adelphopoiesis* as resembling a "gay marriage rite" is the only possible path. Much of the answer depends on the definition and interpretation of male-male relations, whether spiritual, emotional, or physical. This merits a short detour into the history of sexuality and its study, inasmuch as they are relevant to the work at hand.

The study of sexuality was pushed into the mainstream of historical inquiry in the late 1970s and early 1980s by Michel Foucault in his three-volume work *The History of Sexuality*,[110] precisely because of his guiding question: in what way do power structures shape and define how people conceptualize, act out, and experience sexual conduct—their own and that of others?[111] Power, in Foucault's approach, is inherently negative, because it is restrictive. Power is based on mechanisms of inclusion and exclusion, on the clear demarcation of "us" and "them" in a discourse where homosexuality is inevitably marginalized or pushed into oblivion as the ultimate alterity. As David Halperin shows in *Saint Foucault*, Foucault's academic writing as well as his political activism in Paris and in Berkeley were driven by the desire to explore the possibility of new relationships, whether stable affective bonds or fleeting encounters for the simple sake of physical pleasure, that would be created outside established power structures.[112] In Foucault's view, the power structure par excellence that is responsible for labeling all sexual acts as evil is the Christian church. The instrument it uses to control not just the conduct, but also the minds of the faithful is the system of confession and penance. These are the ultimate

---

[110] M. Foucault, *The History of Sexuality*, vol. 1: *An Introduction*, vol. 2: *The Use of Pleasure*, vol. 3: *The Care of the Self* (New York, 1978–84).

[111] It should be noted, however, that Foucault's emphasis in this work is on the adult male subject, whether as a consequence of the sources available to him or as a result of his own position as an openly homosexual man.

[112] D. M. Halperin, *Saint Foucault: Towards a Gay Hagiography* (New York and Oxford, 1995).

target of criticism in Foucault's work, although the last volume of his trilogy *The Care of the Self*, which was published posthumously in 1984, covered only the pagan authors of the Roman Empire.

John Boswell's grand view of medieval history and the role of marginal groups within it was shaped by a multiplicity of vantage points. A professor of medieval history at Yale, he shared with Foucault an interest in the historical conditions which are conducive to the formation of behaviors and ideas. These two scholars also have in common the sad fate of not living long enough to see their most influential books in printed form. Boswell died in 1994, a few months before the publication of his *Same-Sex Unions in Pre-Modern Europe* (published in Britain under the title *The Marriage of Likeness*). Foucault died exactly a decade earlier, before the French publication of the second and third volumes of his *History of Sexuality*. But in contrast to Foucault, Boswell was deeply at home in the middle ages and throughout his entire oeuvre was in no rush to lay blame on the Catholic church—perhaps not unrelated to his conversion to Catholicism from Episcopalianism in his teenage years.

Where Foucault was interested in institutions (the Catholic Church, the French state) as power structures and their effect on the construction of male sexuality, Boswell asked a different set of questions that concern the thought world and literary expression of medieval men. Where Foucault worked from the top down, Boswell moved from the inside out. The *opus magnum* that established his reputation as a historian of homosexuality, *Christianity, Social Tolerance and Homosexuality*, was published in 1980.[113] The phrasing of the title is significant. Rather than taking an accusatory stance in defense of an oppressed minority against the overpowering paternalistic institution of the Catholic Church, Boswell in this book concentrated on Christian doctrine and Biblical hermeneutics in order to show that there is nothing inherent in Christian belief and teaching that condemns people whose erotic desire is directed towards the same sex. Prohibitions, insofar as they are expressed, concern the specific sexual act of anal penetration, whether its object is a man or a woman. It was only in the course of the thirteenth century, Boswell showed, that the Christian church singled out, and thereby for the first time recognized "homosexuals," alongside Jews and heretics, as a distinct group whose members warranted proscription and persecution simply by virtue of being identified as such by others, whether or not they engaged in acts labeled as criminal. This was possible, Boswell argued, because in the preceding centuries, expressions of attraction, spiritual love and eroticism had undergone significant changes. The twelfth century saw the flourishing of courtly love. In poetry and romances, men would give voice, in urgent and expressive

---

[113] J. Boswell, *Christianity, Social Tolerance and Homosexuality: Gay People in Western Europe from the Beginning of the Christian Era to the Fourteenth Century* (Chicago, 1980).

words, to their attraction to women. This love was not for consummation, as the object of desire was always married. Monasteries, however, constituted an entirely different context, a form of a male-only society where affective bonds were infused with spiritual meaning and could be expressed in sexual acts.

In this book, Boswell also made the helpful distinction between "homosexual" and "gay," explaining his use of "homosexual" as referring to same-sex eroticism and related behavior, while "gay" was taken to refer to "persons who are conscious of erotic inclination toward their own gender as a distinguishing characteristic."[114] This definition is significant in the context of the ongoing debate between the "essentialist" and the "constructivist" interpretations of homosexuality, which mirrors the "nature-versus-nurture" debate. Do all societies at all times have a portion of men who are sexually attracted to other men? Or is male-male sex the result of specific societal contexts and thus subject to historical and cultural change? Boswell's careful choice of terminology, as well as the appearance of both "homosexuality" and "gay people" in the title of his book, seems to indicate that he occupied a middle ground between those two positions. This is a safe position to assume, for siding with the "essentialists" would make one a poor historian, while as a self-identified gay man, Boswell must have been acutely aware of the limitations of the "constructivist" position. In the heat of this debate, he issued a call for moderation from his unique perspective as a medieval historian when he compared the extreme positions of essentialists and constructivists to those of realists and nominalists in the problem of universals.[115] David Halperin has in recent years revived this discussion by reminding his readers that "homosexuality" as a category is a creation of the nineteenth century. The polar opposition between hetero- and homosexuality, Halperin shows, is a modern construct which it would be misguided to project onto earlier societies.[116]

In 1982, Boswell was invited to present the Fifth Michael Harding Memorial Address, named for the founder of the Gay Christian Movement, and on this occasion further elaborated on the idea of monasticism as the seedbed for new expressions of male-male affection.[117] This gave him the opportunity to speak for the first time in public about his new research on brotherly unions. The lecture is a remarkable document, as it shows Boswell cautiously juggling his identities as a gay man and as a church-going Catholic. He began by noting that "there is no inherent opposition between Christianity and homosexual behavior", but then explained

---

[114] Ibid., 44.

[115] J. Boswell, "Revolutions, Universals and Sexual Categories." *Salmagundi* 58–59 (1982–83), 89–113.

[116] D. M. Halperin, *One Hundred Years of Homosexuality* (New York and London, 1990), 40–41.

[117] J. Boswell, *Rediscovering Gay History: Archetypes of Gay Love in Christian History* (London, 1982).

that in the course of the fourth to sixth centuries, "procreative justification became the way most Christians limited and legitimized sexuality,"
in heterosexual relations that were strikingly devoid of any expectation
of love or mutual attraction. The core of his argument was the discussion of three archetypes of gay love in monastic communities. The first
kind was conceptualized in analogy to family love, as evidenced in the
liberal use of kinship designation of "father," "brother," and "sister." The
second kind was associated with *paideia* in the sense of education and progress in knowledge, wisdom, and spirituality, a love that developed between
teachers and their students. The third kind was "romantic love," which may
or may not have been consummated physically, and that may also have
assisted in the spiritual growth of the two monastics involved.[118] Boswell
then unveiled what he considered "one particularly attractive archetype
of romantic love that might exist between gay people", namely Byzantine
brother-making, citing long passages of the ritual from an unidentified
source that includes the wearing of wedding crowns.[119] Boswell had the
initial hunch to seek the origins of *adelphopoiesis* within the context of
male monastic communities, but without further developing this idea in
the final presentation of his research twelve years later in *Same-Sex Unions
in Pre-Modern Europe*.[120] A vast area of possibilities for further study thus
remained wide open, a gap which the present study hopes to address.

The most recent milestone in scholarship on male-male relationships in
antiquity and beyond is the publication of James Davidson's *The Greeks and
Greek Love*, which focuses on ancient Greece.[121] His work is significant in its
methodology, which represents a conscious break from the "sodomania," as
he calls it, of previous scholars especially in the wake of Kenneth Dover's
seminal 1989 book *Greek Homosexuality*.[122] The main obsession is no longer
the sexual act in itself, nor are the superior or inferior position of the partners
engaged in anal intercourse interpreted as signaling social hierarchies and
fixed codes of conduct, as Dover had argued on the basis of literary sources,
vase painting, and Roman legislation.[123] Instead, Davidson allows for a much
wider range of expressions of male-male affection, attraction, and interaction
in Greek antiquity, with considerable regional variations that are best documented for Crete, Thebes, Athens and the Macedonian court. He also argues

---

[118] Ibid., 15–17.

[119] Ibid., 18–21.

[120] Boswell, *Same-Sex Unions*. For responses by various scholars to Boswell's work within the
framework of male and female same-sex attraction in antiquity and the middle ages, see M. Kuefler,
ed., *The Boswell Thesis: Essays on Christianity, Social Tolerance, and Homosexuality* (Chicago and
London, 2006).

[121] Davidson, *Greeks and Greek Love*.

[122] K. Dover, *Greek Homosexuality* (Cambridge, MA, 1978; repr. with a new postscript 1989).

[123] *Codex Theodosianus* 9.7.6.

that the age difference between the two partners was not significant enough to permit the use of the modern term "pederasty," with all its criminal implications. The practices of courtship rituals between the older *erastês* (lover) and his *erômenos* (beloved) were subject to accepted norms and closely observed by the participants and the authors who report on them: philosophers, rhetors, poets, and lawmakers. Especially in Athens, Davidson argues—an heir to the Foucaultian approach more than he cares to admit—these practices are inscribed in the larger context of societal structures where they acted as a stabilizing factor that balanced divergent tendencies: "It was a bridge between the culture's structurally given gaps, between age classes, between men who were not related, between endogamous 'in-marrying' families with their weddings of cousins to cousins and uncles to nieces, between the human and the divine."[124] Yet, the magnitude of the societal impact of "Greek love" remains unclear, since, as Davidson himself points out, perhaps no more than 10 percent of the adult male population may have been engaged in the pursuit of such relationships, at least in Crete or in Sparta, at a certain time in their lives.[125]

An undercurrent throughout Davidson's substantial and richly documented book is the assumption that the prototypical relationship is that of two men in a lasting, stable, publicly recognized relationship. Such a relationship had its origin in the gymnasium where the athletic male physique was on display and masculine strength was measured in competition. Military training looms not far behind, and Davidson explains in great detail the relevance of male "yoke-pairs" or *syzygies* on the battlefield, whether in the pairing of the mythological figures of Achilles and Patroclus in the Trojan War, made famous by Homer, or the Sacred Band of Thebes, as described centuries later by Pausanias. He calls them "wedded couples" because their relation is confirmed by an oath or a pledge, thus anchored in an invocation of a divinity, whether Apollo or Eros.[126]

The application of selective criteria for the definition of marriage by Davidson as well as Boswell has elements of a magician's hat-trick, pulling out a rabbit instead of a scarf. Both scholars, in their own way, insinuate that Byzantine *adelphopoiesis* corresponds to their definition of the essential element of marriage and therefore ought to be generally regarded as an equivalent of the entire phenomenon. Davidson's and Boswell's works are important contributions that lay out with great nuance the social and emotional aspects of male-male relations and their perception and representation in Greek antiquity and the Latin middle ages. But they leave the Byzantinist in search of a better grip on *adelphopoiesis* dissatisfied.

---

[124] Davidson, *Greeks and Greek Love*, 499.
[125] Ibid., 334.
[126] Ibid., 473.

Male-Male Relations in Byzantium

There is a general willingness in recent scholarship to consider the wider parameters of homoeroticism and homosociability, so that "Did they or did they
not?" becomes an increasingly irrelevant question to ask of any individuals. That
some of "the Byzantines" as an aggregate society enjoyed male-male sexual relations can be taken for granted, just as it is taken for granted that most Byzantine
men lived in stable household arrangements with women, either in concubinage
or in marriage, depending on social class. One did not exclude the other.

Byzantine sources that speak about male-male sexual desire can be grouped
into three categories: the most explicit are condemnations and prohibitions,
usually by the church, more rarely in imperial law. Blanket condemnations of
homosexual acts (more precisely, sexual acts between men, or anal penetration regardless of the gender or age of the receiving partner) by the church or
in imperial law point only to the existence of the proverbial iceberg, without
revealing its actual shape or size. Second come narrative sources that refer to
male-male sexual encounters, but such mentions are extremely rare. Third are
texts that speak about masculine longing and desire for a male counterpart,
but do so in very opaque language. This leaves a lot of room for interpretation.
The sources do not usually reveal the concrete circumstances of such connections and their place in society. What does it mean if two men or two women
sleep in the same bed?[127] If the Patriarch of Constantinople shares his bedroom with a "cell-mate," whose designation eventually becomes a title and the
office of *synkellos*?[128] If the author of a theological treatise, Symeon the New
Theologian, speaks in mystic language of his longing for physical union with,
and indeed penetration by, Christ? It is difficult enough to gauge the extent
of male-male sexual activities and their social context, whether in a structured environment (the home, the army, the monastery) or casually (in bath-
houses, with prostitutes). It is even more taxing to gain an understanding of
the value and interpretation attributed to such relationships by the actors and
other contemporaries. As Dion Smythe observes: "The evidence for same-sex
desire in Byzantium is sparse, and its interpretation relies on the recognition
of possibilities rather than identifying certainties."[129]

---

[127] *Miracula Theclae* 46, ed. G. Dagron, *Vie et miracles de saint Thècle*, Subsidia hagiographica 62
(Brussels, 1978), 408; *Life of Basil the Younger*, ed. and trans. Talbot et al.: the pious woman Theodora
declares in the "Vision of Theodora" that she never shared a bed with a woman and thus was never
tempted to have lesbian sex.

[128] Synkellos of the Patriarch of Alexandria: John Moschus, *Pratum spirituale* 127, 148. Ignatius
the Deacon, *Life of Patriarch Tarasius*, ed. Efthymiadis, 16n58 on the history of the *synkellos*.

[129] D. Smythe, "In Denial: Same-Sex Desire in Byzantium," in *Desire and Denial in Byzantium:
Papers from the Thirty-First Spring Symposium of Byzantine Studies, University of Sussex,
Brighton, March 1997*, ed. L. James, 139–48 (Aldershot, 1999), 139; K. Pitsakis, "Hê thesê tôn homo-
phylophilôn stê Byzantinê koinônia," in *Hoi perithôriakoi sto Byzantio*, ed. C. Maltezou, 171–269
(Athens, 1993).

For all these reasons, the study of homosexuality, homoeroticism, and homosociability in Byzantium is relatively recent. And it is still rare that an entire conference and subsequent volume are devoted to the theme of "Desire and Denial in Byzantium."[130] The work of legal scholars such as Speros Troianos and Konstantinos Pitsakis and of literary scholars such as Cristian Gaspar, Stratis Papaioannou, and others is beginning to make inroads into this rich and rewarding, if complex, field of inquiry.[131] Derek Krueger has drawn attention to the narrative construction of male-male pairings in the early monastic literature and suggested that there is conscious elision surrounding these relations. The two men involved, the people around them, the narrators of these stories and the reading audience of these tales were all caught up in mindsets of their own and the discourses of their times, resulting in an ample interpretive space of ambiguity. "One monk's *agape* might be another monk's *eros*."[132] Charis Messis has argued that *adelphopoiesis* should be interpreted within the general framework of homosociability, as an attempt by ecclesiastical authorities to assert control over one of the very few relations in the Byzantine social structure that, like friendship, could exist between equals.[133]

My approach is pragmatic when it comes to human relations, and positivist when dealing with the sources. It can be taken for granted that men engaged in sexual encounters with other men, in Byzantium as in any other society, and that there was an emotional, affective component to many such relations. But this did not depend on the presence and practice of the brother-making ritual. My interpretation of the narrative depictions of the practice of *adelphopoiesis* will leave room for such interpretations and draw attention to particularly suggestive language in individual cases, but without making any further claims. I readily admit that this does not address Foucault's question of the place of sexual relationships within the power structures and hierarchies of Byzantine society. Boswell had taken up this challenge by suggesting that Byzantium should be seen as a medieval society that offered exceptionally rich

---

[130] *Desire and Denial in Byzantium*, ed. James.

[131] Some relevant titles are S. Troianos, "Kirchliche und weltliche Rechtsquellen zur Homosexualität in Byzanz," *JÖB* 39 (1989), 29–48; Pitsakis, "He thesê tôn homophylophilôn stê Byzantinê koinônia"; A. A. Demosthenous, *Friendship and Homosexuality in Byzantine 11th and 13th Centuries* (Thessaloniki, 2004) (in Greek); S. Papaioannou, "On the Stage of *Eros*: Two Rhetorical Exercises by Nikephoros Basilakes," in *Theatron: Rhetorische Kultur in Spätantike und Mittelalter*, ed. M. Grünbart, 357–76 (Berlin and New York, 2007); M. Masterson, "Impossible Translation: Antony and Paul the Simple in the *Historia Monachorum*," in *Boswell Thesis*, ed. Kuefler; J. Børtnes, "Eros Transformed."

[132] D. Krueger, "Between Monks: Tales of Monastic Companionship in Early Byzantium," *Journal of the History of Sexuality* 20, no. 1 (2011), 28–61, at 37–38.

[133] C. Messis, "Des amitiés à l'institution d'un lien social: l'"adelphopoiia' à Byzance," in *Corrispondenza d'amorosi sensi: L'omoerotismo nella letteratura medievale*, ed. P. Odorico, N. Pasero, and M. P. Bachmann, 31–64 (Alessandria, 2008).

documentation for a positive attitude of the Christian church toward homo-sexuality through the creation of a male commitment ritual. My analysis of the prayers will, I hope, show that the ecclesiastical ritual of brother-making was not formulated with a view to include a sexual dimension. It is difficult to see any further than that when the bedroom lights are out.

There is, however, plenty of light in other areas which permit a meaningful analysis of the ritual and its significance over the long trajectory of Byzantine history. The first attestation of prayers for *adelphopoiesis* in the Barberinus graecus 336 of the late eighth century and the discussion of the prayers in chapter 2 that follows serve as a pivot from which we can proceed in two directions. Chapter 3 will go back in time in search of the origins of *adel-phopoiesis*. I will suggest that the precedent for brother-making blessed by prayers can be found in the collective experiment of creating an alternative society that is represented by the early monastic movement. The remainder of the book will advance forward in time and move from the monastic world to that of lay society, where brother-making takes on social significance as one of several kinship strategies to secure loyalty and support in a society where strong institutions were absent and prosperity and well-being depended on one's own networks, whether inherited or created.

The Ritual of *Adelphopoiesis*

Imagine the following scene: Two men enter a church together. They step in front of the table on which the Gospel is laid out, and place their hands on it, one on top of the other. The priest speaks prayers over them, asking that God may grant them his peace, love, and oneness of mind. Then they embrace and from now on are regarded as "brothers." What has been performed here is the ritual of *adelphopoiesis*, literally the "making of brothers."

The importance of the relationship generated by this ritual for Byzantine society is beyond question. The stories that involve emperors, patriarchs, and aristocrats and are recorded by historians and hagiographers of the middle and late Byzantine periods, discussed in chapter 4, testify to that. In this regard, Byzantium is no different from the medieval West, where kinship strategies were combined with the politics of friendship and patronage to weave the fabric of society. But Byzantium offers a more intricate pattern, because of the liturgical evidence that survives. Prayers for "brother-making" are preserved in sixty-six manuscripts that span the eighth to the sixteenth centuries.

Any study of Byzantine brother-making must begin by taking this evidence into account and attempting to make sense of it. This is not an easy task, for two reasons: first, there is the debt that scholarship owes to John Boswell, who was the first to recognize the importance of the ecclesiastical tradition of brother-making and undertook a detailed study of its manuscript attestation. This debt must be acknowledged prior to any disagreement with his conclusions that the Byzantine ritual of *adelphopoiesis* between two men was structurally, and hence also functionally, comparable to marriage. The second difficulty in studying the liturgical evidence lies in the fact that we are faced with a living tradition that evolved over centuries of time and in different locations. What is more, this is a tradition that was invested with different shades of meaning by its practitioners according to their own circumstances. Not all of this is recoverable with any degree of completeness or consistency—our evidence is simply not sufficiently comprehensive across time and space. But a careful and attentive study of the liturgical evidence in the manuscripts can help to isolate the features associated with brother-making by those who engaged in its practice. In three steps, we will narrow the focus and move from the material object of the manuscript to the text of the ritual and its placement within a manuscript and then on to the individual spoken prayers. The manuscripts tell the story of the chronological distribution, regional location, and social communities in which brother-making was practiced. The position of the ritual within a manuscript, the prayers that precede and follow it, may indicate the importance and significance it was accorded, while the prescriptions for ritual gestures point to parallels with other ecclesiastical rituals. Finally, the prayers themselves, their language, imagery, and content, reveal the intent of the relationship of *adelphopoiesis*.

A. Ritual Practice: A Present-Day Blessing among Pilgrims to Jerusalem

Before launching into the dry and dusty world of medieval prayer-books, an initial word of caution about the relation of ritual to written text is in order. Ritual depends on performance. Every enactment, no matter how frequently and diligently repeated, will involve variances great and small, and thus communicate different nuances of meaning and significance to practitioners and observers. The practice of ritual does not depend on a written tradition, although it may eventually be written down. Inversely, the presence or absence of written instructions is no indicator of the presence or absence of ritual practice, nor does it indicate the importance accorded to it by active or passive participants. There will always be a gap between written ritual and lived experience. The blessing of personal relationships can be as simple as a prayer, whether these relationships have their origin in friendship, a shared pilgrimage experience, or a joint commitment to the monastic life. And a prayer can be as simple as an encounter with a valued person, say a spiritual advisor, a priest, or a monk, where a conversation about matters of the faith and a heartfelt expression of a wish for well-being introduces God into the conversation and glides effortlessly into a prayerful invocation of divine assistance or the actual performance of a blessing. Prayers, especially when recited in a location charged with religious significance and in a formal context, can acquire a ritualized aspect and may have implications even without the active cognizance of the participants at that moment, so that their collusion in accepting that meaning may only follow the event.

This is what happened in the sister-making that two American women experienced in the Church of the Holy Sepulcher in Jerusalem in 1985. They were both scholars of Syriac Christianity traveling to the churches and monasteries in Syria and Israel: Robin Darling Young, now a professor of spirituality at Catholic University of America in Washington, DC, and Susan Ashbrook Harvey, now Willard Prescott and Annie McClelland Smith Professor of History and Religion at Brown University. At the time, it seemed to be a lovely moment on a scholarly pilgrimage, but almost a decade later, when John Boswell's *Same-Sex Unions in Pre-Modern Europe* was published in 1994, Robin Darling Young decided to include her recollections in her review of Boswell's book:

> The ceremony took place during a journey to some of the Syrian Christian communities of Turkey and the Middle East, and the other member of this same-sex union was my colleague Professor Susan Ashbrook Harvey of Brown University. During the course of our travels we paid a visit to St. Mark's Monastery in Jerusalem, the residence of the Syrian Orthodox archbishop. There our host, Archbishop Dionysius Behnam Jajaweh, remarked that since we had survived the rigors of Syria and Eastern Turkey in amicable good humor, we two women must be good friends indeed. Would we like to be joined as sisters the next morning after the bishop's Sunday liturgy in the Church of the Holy Sepulchre? Intrigued, we agreed, and on a Sunday in late June of 1985, we followed the bishop and a monk through the Old City to a side chapel in the Holy Sepulchre where, according to the Syrian Orthodox, lies the actual tomb of Jesus. After the liturgy, the bishop had us join our right hands together and he wrapped them in a portion of his garment. He pronounced a series of prayers over us, told us that we were united as sisters, and admonished us not to quarrel. Ours was a sisterhood stronger than blood, confirmed in the outpouring of the Holy Spirit, he said, and since it was a spiritual union, it would last beyond the grave.[1]

Both scholars have been willing to revisit this event, and I am deeply grateful for their inquiries into the circumstances and precedent for these prayers. Thanks to their efforts, it was possible to trace the Syrian Orthodox Patriarch of Jerusalem who performed this liturgy, the late Archbishop Mar Dionysius Behnam Jajaweh. He sent these reminiscences from his place of retirement at

---

[1] R. Darling Young, "Gay Marriage: Reimagining Church History," *First Things: The Journal of Religion, Culture and Public Life*, November 1994, http://www.firstthings.com/article/1994/11/gay-marriage-reimagining-church-history. Susan Harvey, however, in a conversation on April 7, 2009, did not remember a joining of hands. Neither Susan Harvey nor Robin Darling Young recall the placing of hands on a Gospel book during this ritual occasion. Both of these gestures are common in the Byzantine ritual of brother-making.

the Monastery of the Virgin at Tell Wardiat, near Hasake in north-eastern Syria.[2]

> I came to know about this when I was a monk and a secretary for the monastery of St. Mark [in Jerusalem] in 1953. The custom is found among the Syrian Orthodox faithful, and especially among those of Tur Abdin who come to visit the holy land. It is not found within other (i.e., non-Syrian Orthodox) Christian traditions. Those who come on pilgrimage to the holy land do because of strong faith; they want to take part in this tradition of becoming brothers and sisters with each other to serve as a remembrance, as a blessing, as a way of getting to know each [other] and as a means to take a significant step in one's personal life history. They do it because of their love for and faith in the blessing that they get during this pilgrimage to the holy land and to the holy sepulcher. Many western tourists who used to come to the holy land and heard about this kind of tradition used to ask us to practice it with me as a spiritual man and as someone who lives in the holy land. And I used to respond positively to their requests. And since this kind of custom is a natural one, based on a personal volition, a personal faith, and is not a church rite, there are no specific prayers that should be said for it. Only supplications and prayers are done at the holy sepulcher whether two or ten together hold hands above this holy site. They pray together saying (for example): "O Lord Jesus, make your grave the basis of spiritual brotherhood and faith-filled love among us so that we may live in you not only during our pilgrimage to your thresholds and the stages of your salvation only, but that we may carry the blessing of your grave with us to our homes and countries and we may act in accordance with the memories and impressions of this visit and that we may correspond to each other as brothers and sisters in your holy name." This kind of prayer is repeated during their visits to Golgotha, "Hajar al-mughtasil" ("the washing stone"), the prison of Jesus Christ, and the cave of the cross. And then afterwards they go out and they hug each other and kiss each other spiritually and in faith and love, and then greet each other as brothers or sisters when they write to each other. I had the chance to practice this tradition with many people from east and west, with men and women, and we keep this in our hearts even though I now have less communication or meetings with them.

---

[2] The mediation of this email exchange in April 2009, and the translation of the Archbishop's response from Arabic into English, was very generously undertaken by Metropolitan Eustathius Matta Roham. I would like to extend my sincere gratitude to all the scholars who have contributed to this exchange.

These prayers were intimately tied to the pilgrimage experience, and are introduced as being unique to the Syrian Orthodox in Jerusalem. From a ritual point of view, the practice, as remembered by the archbishop, involved prayers pronounced by the liturgist, but uttered in the voice of the participants. The prayers were integrated into a pilgrimage movement itself, as they were repeated at five locations within the Holy Sepulcher building complex, beginning with the Syrian chapel of the Holy Sepulcher, and then continuing to Golgatha, the Stone of Unction, the Prison, and the Cave of the Cross, perhaps not necessarily in that sequence. The archbishop emphasizes in his letter that the impetus for the recital of such prayers came from the pilgrims who requested them. In the case of the academic travelers, however, it was the archbishop who suggested this special gesture to the two scholars who had been unaware of this custom. In addition to the description of the archbishop, Robin Darling Young and Susan Harvey remember the presence of a monk and of a deacon, the latter holding either a lit candle or a thurible with incense.[3]

The archbishop remarks that this "is not a church rite, there are no specific prayers that should be said for it." It is easy to imagine that the prayer he offers as a suggestion of what *might* have been said was adapted and altered when it was pronounced for other people, as the occasion required. It is a tradition that was perpetuated through practice, not in writing. Indeed, neither the *Prayers [sic] Book for Various Occasions for the Use of the Clergy*, published in 1993 by the late Archbishop Mar Athanasius Yeshue Samuel, nor the two medieval manuscripts containing the *Pontificale of Michael the Great* (Vat. syr. 51 and Vat. syr. 57) contain such a prayer.[4] Lived traditions of this kind are always unstable in their survival, as they depend on the people who maintain them. During a visit to the Syrian Orthodox Monastery of St. Mark in Jerusalem in June 2010, Father Shemun Can received me most kindly and in conversation was emphatic that no such practices exist today.

The groups of pilgrims who received this blessing from the archbishop may or may not have been acquainted with one another prior to their journey. Gender was irrelevant, as was the number of participants, or indeed their Christian denomination. In the case of the two women scholars, however, the archbishop recognized that they were friends and remarked that their bond was stronger than that of biological sisters. According to his explanation, the prayers had the dual purpose of strengthening the ties between the fellow pilgrims and of encouraging them as they carried the transformative effect of the pilgrimage experience back to their homes. Pilgrimage is

---

[3] I am grateful to Susan Ashbrook Harvey for sharing her reminiscences with me during a conversation in Providence, RI, April 7, 2009.

[4] Again, I depend on information generously offered by Susan Ashbrook Harvey.

essentially a displaced monastic experience with an expiration date, and—like monasticism—is bound to transform human relations. Spiritual kinship as "brothers" and "sisters" seems to be the most appropriate way to conceptualize such relations, applying to lay men and women the same designation as that for monks and nuns.

The prayer practice of the Syrian Orthodox in Jerusalem is strikingly similar to the experience of Symeon the Fool and his "brother" John that is reported in a hagiographical account of the seventh century, the *Life of Symeon the Fool* by Leontius of Neapolis, which will be discussed in detail in chapter 3. Symeon and John met while on pilgrimage to Jerusalem and then, struck by the strong desire to continue this manner of life, they made the spontaneous decision to become monks together. Their future life as hermits and spiritual "brothers" in adjacent abodes in the desert was blessed through the prayers of the abbot of a monastery in the Jordan valley. The purpose of the prayers for the Syrian Orthodox pilgrims to Jerusalem, as much as for the monastic initiates Symeon and John, was to strengthen them in their resolve, as they transitioned from a shared traveling experience of dislocation in time and space to a regular and stable life imbued with new spiritual meaning, and to offer them the assurance of a lasting commitment of mutual support on the continuation of their spiritual journey through life.

B. The Manuscript Evidence in Byzantine
Prayer Books (*Euchologia*)

Hagiographical stories and other narratives discussed in chapter 4 indicate that such prayers were common and describe how they served to affirm relationships of loyalty and mutual support. The back story to such narratives is the existence of the ritual and its ample attestation through all periods of Byzantine history. It is thus essential to begin with an investigation of Byzantine prayer books.

Euchologia (sing. *euchologion*) are made for the use of the clergy. Some manuscripts have only the text of the prayers, while others specify whether they are pronounced by a priest or by a deacon, at what moment they make the sign of the cross, and what liturgical objects—such as candles, censers, or liturgical fans (*rhipisteria*)—they might be using. In addition to the celebration of the Eucharist and other sacramental liturgies, *euchologia* include prayers that are said not at the altar, behind the iconostasis, but in the congregational space of the church or in other locations. For this reason, the codices tend to be small in size (about the size of a paperback), so that the priest can hold the *euchologion* in his left hand as he performs the prayers. Usually, an *euchologion* contains the eucharistic liturgies of St. John Chrysostom and/or St. Basil, rituals of marriage and baptism, rituals for death and burial, ordination to various ranks in the clergy, and often also monastic initiation rites for men and women. These may appear in varying combinations and sequence. In addition, they may include so-called small prayers related to everyday concerns—anything from the first day of school to the grape harvest. These prayers and the mundane matters they address render *euchologia* a very rich source for the lived reality of the women, men, and children of Byzantium.[5]

The content of the prayers in any given manuscript offers some indication of the kind of community in which they were used. Prayers for taking farm animals to pasture or for setting sail to go fishing allow insight into the geographical location of the community and its economic basis. A few manuscripts contain prayers that relate to the imperial court, such as those for the departure of imperial war ships, and thus are easily located in the capital of Constantinople. Further variation among the manuscripts depends on the presence of so-called rubrics, that is, instructions for the liturgical gestures. Palaeographical study can identify the script style of a manuscript as typical for a particular region, whether Southern Italy, Constantinople, or elsewhere. *Euchologia* are thus "in essence, a message of old, local and cultural situations and customs," as Vicenzo Ruggieri observed.[6]

Euchologia are neither pretty to look at nor valuable. They were utilitarian objects and subject to heavy use. The only decoration of *euchologia*, if any, consists of decorative bars and elaborate initials underlaid with red, blue, green, or yellow color, which also have the practical purpose of helping the liturgist find his place on the page. Many are made of reused parchment that was cheaper and more readily available than freshly prepared skins of goat, sheep, and calf that were used for manuscripts intended as luxury objects. A large number of the *euchologia* in the collection of the Holy Monastery of St. Catherine in the Sinai, for example, contain such palimpsest (rewritten) folia.[7]

The study of *euchologia* is still in its infancy, not least because their number is so large. The earliest Byzantine *euchologion* that survives in manuscript form dates from the late eighth century and, luckily, preserves the prayers for ritual brotherhood. Throughout the centuries, each priest, each church, each monastery had at least one, and usually several prayer books in their possession. These may have been of recent production or of an earlier date. At the time of the Council of Florence (1438–39), Constantine XI Palaeologus assumed that there were about 2000 *euchologia* in circulation.[8] Scholars have

[5] A new research project, "Daily Life and Religion: Byzantine Prayer Books as Sources for Social History," at the Division of Byzantine Research, Institute for Medieval Studies, Austrian Academy of Sciences, intends to explore this rich material.

[6] V. Ruggieri, "The Cryptensis Euchology Gamma beta XI," *OCP* 52 (1986), 325–60.

[7] See the forthcoming dissertation by Giulia Rossetto, University of Vienna, "The Sinai *Euchologia* Written on Re-Used Parchment. Communities of Production and Use."

[8] V. Laurent, ed., *Les "mémoires" du Grand Ecclésiarque de l'Église de Constantinople Sylvestre Syropoulos sur le Concile de Florence (1438–1439)* (Rome, 1971), 476.

estimated that, if a systematic study of these manuscripts were to be undertaken today, about 400 *euchologia* in manuscript form ought to be considered,[9] but the actual number that survives is surely much larger than that.

If the prayer books are any indication, brother-making was an important part of the religious life of Byzantium. John Boswell identified sixty-two Greek manuscripts, ranging in date from the eighth to the seventeenth centuries, that contain the prayers for *adelphopoiesis*. Chrêstos Panagou in a recent study added four further manuscripts unknown to Boswell.[10] In 1901, the Russian scholar Dmitrievskij consulted 162 *euchologia* for his catalog, ranging in date from the eighth to the nineteenth centuries. More than one-fifth of Dmitrievskij's sample include prayers for brother-making. The survival of this ritual in the manuscripts is thus no accident of transmission, but rather confirms the importance of brother-making to Byzantine society.

The frequent occurrence of the ritual in the *euchologia* also indicates that this was a part of social life that was understood by all involved within the interpretive framework of Christianity, and that it was the representatives of the church, the priests, who exercised control over its practice through the performance of the relevant prayers.

Appendix 1 lists the sixty-six Greek and two non-Greek manuscripts up to the sixteenth century that include *adelphopoiesis* that I have considered, forty-three of them in the original.[11] My list ends with the greater availability of printing, a century before Boswell's cut-off point. It indicates the current location of the manuscript, its date, and (wherever possible) its regional origin, the relevant folio numbers, the title of the entry, and the first words (*incipit*) of the prayers, references to the most recent studies, and in the last two columns, the rituals or prayers that immediately precede and follow it. Further manuscripts that contain the ritual will no doubt be identified in the future.[12]

Boswell's list of manuscripts has proved enormously helpful, although he does not make clear on what basis he assembled it, nor does he indicate which manuscripts he consulted in the original. In his preface, he makes oblique reference to Mount Athos and to the Vatican, but without specifying whether he had first-hand access to these materials.

---

[9] S. Parenti, *L'eucologio slavo del Sinai nella storia dell'eucologio bizantino*, Filologia Slava 2 (Rome, 1997), 11–12.

[10] C. Panagou, *Hê adelphopoiêsê: Akolouthia tou evchologiou . . .* (Athens, 2010). His study is based on a total of thirty-nine manuscripts. The new manuscripts that Panagou added are: Grottaferrata Gamma beta 10 and Athens, National Library, nos. 2064, 2724, 2795. He omits, however, sixteen manuscripts listed by Boswell.

[11] I have not been able to identify the prayers for brother-making in two of the manuscripts on Boswell's list, and have added five further manuscripts to that list, four based on the work of Panagou (nos. 5, 31, 48, 61), one identified by Constantinides and Browning (no. 60).

[12] I will strive to maintain an updated version of Appendix 1 (List of Manuscripts) online, both on academia.edu, as well as on my institutional website at the University of Vienna.

It would require a lengthy study in its own right to do full justice to the liturgical tradition of *adelphopoiesis*. Such a study would have to expand on the interpretive work of Panagou[13] and would require not only a detailed textual comparison of the different versions of *adelphopoiesis*, but also close attention to the larger framework of the development of the Byzantine liturgical tradition and its manuscript transmission—a study that may well exceed an individual scholar's lifetime.

The variations between manuscripts begin already with nuances in the title. While most use the common word *adelphopoiesis*, some employ the variant nouns *adelphopoiia* (Appendix 1, nos. 14, 48, 60), *adelphopoiêsia* (nos. 4, 12, 25), or the circumlocutions "to make *adelphopoiesis*" (no. 58), or "to make brothers" (no. 22).

Chronological Distribution of the Manuscripts

A closer look at the distribution over time of *adelphopoiesis* in the prayer book manuscripts confirms its enduring appeal throughout the middle and late Byzantine periods. No prayer books survive in manuscript form prior to the eighth century. The prayers for *adelphopoiesis* appear in the earliest extant prayer book, the Barberini *euchologion*, written in majuscule letters in the late eighth century and now in the Vatican Library (Barberinus graecus [Barb. gr.] 336).[14] Manuscripts of such an early date, prior to the adoption of minuscule writing (*metacharaktêrismos*), are very rare in general. One further manuscript dates from the ninth century. From then on, the chronological distribution of *euchologia* containing prayers for *adelphopoiesis* mirrors that of the Byzantine manuscript tradition in general. Five manuscripts can be assigned to the tenth century, which was a time of cultural revival and increased manuscript production during the heyday of the Macedonian Renaissance. It was also the time when aristocratic families were gaining new prominence in the social life of Byzantium. This social trend continued in the eleventh century, from which six manuscripts survive. But these are still outliers. The bulk of Byzantine manuscripts—whether they preserve Christian homilies and early Byzantine historians or Platonic dialogues and ancient Greek tragedies—that are today accessible in libraries across Europe and elsewhere date from the twelfth to the fourteenth centuries. No fewer than sixteen *euchologia* can be dated to the twelfth century. The thirteenth

---

[13] Panagou, *Hê adelphopoiêsê*.

[14] S. Parenti and E. Velkovska, *L'eucologio Barberini gr. 336* (Rome, 1995; rev. ed., 2000). For a critical review of the first edition, and especially its editorial techniques, see A. Jacob, "Une édition de l'Euchologe Barberini," *Archivio storico per la Calabria e la Lucania* 64 (1997), 5–31. For a critique of the second edition, see Jacob, "Une seconde édition 'revue' de l'Euchologe Barberini," *Archivio storico per la Calabria e la Lucana* 66 (1999), 175–81.

century, in the aftermath of the Fourth Crusade and the establishment of the Latin Kingdom in Constantinople (1204–61) was a time of political upheaval. Yet, manuscript production did not come to a complete standstill, especially outside Constantinople. Fifteen of our *euchologia* survive from this period, most of them associated with large monastic centers at Patmos, on the Sinai, at Mount Athos, or in South Italy. The same pattern of provenance applies to the five manuscripts of the fourteenth century, and the additional eight manuscripts of the fifteenth century. The Fall of Constantinople to the Ottomans in 1453 may have spelled the end of the Byzantine Empire, but its religious traditions continued. The survival of Christianity in the areas that either had been part of the Byzantine Empire, such as Greece and some of the islands in the Eastern Mediterranean, or had been missionarized by Byzantium, such as Russia and Serbia,[15] constitutes an important element in "Byzance après Byzance," in the apt phrase of the Rumanian scholar Nicolae Iorga. With the progression of time, the survival rate for manuscripts increases. Ten manuscripts can thus be attributed to the sixteenth century. The manuscript transmission does not stop after that, but since the prayers for *adelphopoiesis* were first made available in print on a large scale in the seventeenth century, this provides a convenient end point for the present investigation.

Adelphopoiesis in Print

The first attestation in print occurs in an *euchologion* published in Venice in 1545 of which only two copies are known to exist.[16] It was in the context of counterreformation scholarship in the early seventeenth century that the wide circulation in print of Byzantine liturgical texts was assured, thanks to the work of the Dominican scholar Jacob Goar. He based himself largely on manuscripts that he studied in the Vatican library and in the Monastery of Grottaferrata near Rome that had been founded by the Greek-speaking monk Nilus of Rossano in Calabria in 1004, prior to the ecclesiastical separation of Rome and Constantinople. Goar's *Euchologion* was intended as a book for study, not for liturgical use, and is still unsurpassed as a reference work. Its first edition was printed in 1638 in Venice, which had a large population of

---

[15] For the history of the ritual in Serbian prayer books, where it is attested since the fourteenth century and seems to follow the Greek ritual closely, see L. Kretzenbacher, "Serbisch-orthodoxe 'Wahlverbrüderung' zwischen Gläubigenwunsch und Kirchenverbot von heute," *Südost-Forschungen* 38 (1979), 163–83.

[16] I have consulted the volume in Oxford, Bodleian Library, Byw. M 7.13. The publication details are on the last page, indicating that the volume was printed in Venice, in the house of Nikolaos Sophianos and his associates Markos Samariaris and Nikolaos Eparchos, on December 12, 1545. A second copy is in Munich, cf. E. Legrand, *Bibliographie hellénique ou description raisonnée des ouvrages publiés en grec par des Grecs*, vol. 1 (Paris, 1885; repr. Brussels, 1963), 272 (this was the only copy known to Legrand).

Greek merchants and was home to several Greek printing presses. For the
updated edition eleven years later, Goar incorporated variant readings from
several manuscripts in Italy and Paris.[17] The revised 1730 version is widely
available in a 1960 reprint (and on Google Books).[18] There is thus no need to
suggest, as Boswell has done, that a study of these prayers requires privileged
access or arcane knowledge.[19]

Goar approached the ritual with apparent unease, but he was too conscien-
tious a scholar to suppress it entirely. Instead, he manipulated the interpretation of *adelphopoiesis* with the subtle means available to an editor. He based
himself, although not with great accuracy, on a twelfth-century manuscript
in the Vatican Library (Barb. gr. 329).[20] In his printed volume, he entitled it
"Liturgy for spiritual brotherhood" (*akolouthia eis adelphopoiian pneumatikên*), an expression that is never used in the liturgical manuscripts. It is
tucked away near the end of the volume, immediately following a prayer for
the reconciliation of enemies—thus suggesting an interpretive context for
adelphopoiesis that in the manuscript tradition is not very frequent. And he
prefaces the prayers with the following cautionary note: "It ought to be known
that, although this ritual has been prohibited by ecclesiastical and imperial
law, we have nevertheless printed it exactly as we have found it in many other
codices."[21] The same sequence as in Goar is observed in the 1873 edition of the
Euchologion, the standard reference of the Greek Orthodox liturgy.[22]

The accessibility of the prayers for *adelphopoiesis* in print was expanded
greatly by the work of the Russian scholar Alexei Dmitrievskij. On the basis
of a large number of manuscripts throughout the Orthodox world, including
those at St. Catherine's monastery in the Sinai and in the monastic libraries
on Mount Athos, he published a detailed catalog of *euchologia*. Thirty-seven
out of his total sample of 162 manuscripts, or about 23 percent, contain prayers
for *adelphopoiesis*.[23]

---

[17] A. Strittmatter, "The 'Barberinum S. Marci' of Jacques Goar," *Ephemerides liturgicae* 47 (1933),
329–67. The manuscripts used by Goar are listed on 330ff., note 4. There is an online version of the
Paris 1647 edition: http://books.google.fr/books?id=YrpFAAAAcAAJ&dq=euchologion+goar&pg=
PP1&redir_esc=y#v=onepage&q=euchologion%20goar&f=false.

[18] http://books.google.fr/books?id=zKQ-AAAAcAAJ&dq=goar+euchologion&pg=PP7&re
dir_esc=y#v=onepage&q=goar%20euchologion&f=false.

[19] Boswell, *Same-Sex Unions*, ix–xi.

[20] A. Jacob, "Les euchologes du fonds Barberini grec de la Bibliothèque Vaticane," *Didaskalia* 4
(1974), 131–222, at 154.

[21] J. Goar, *Euchologion, sive rituale Graecorum* (Venice, 1730; repr. Graz, 1960), 706–09.

[22] *Euchologion* (Rome, 1873), 482–84. Miguel Arranz in his reconstruction of the liturgy as practiced in Constantinople in the eleventh century chose the label "adoptive brotherhood" for *adelphopoiesis*: M. Arranz, *L'eucologio costantinopolitano agli inizi del secolo XI. Hagiasmatarion &
Archieratikon (Rituale & Pontificale) con l'aggiunta del Leiturgikon (Messale)* (Rome, 1996), 355.

[23] By comparison, his index lists 102 manuscript attestations for prayers associated with baptism
and 173 for prayers associated with marriage, a long ritual which consists of several prayers that are
listed individually—hence their large number.

English translations of some versions of the Byzantine ritual were first made available by John Boswell, on the basis of eight manuscripts.[24] While he took care to present a broad selection of manuscript versions, ranging in date from the tenth to the sixteenth centuries, his translations must be used with caution as they often exaggerate certain nuances of meaning for the sake of bolstering his interpretation. Translations of two versions of the ritual, but without exact specification of their original source, were made accessible by Paul Halsall on the Internet Medieval Sourcebook.[25] Appendix 3 offers my own translations of the prayers for brother-making.

Regional Provenance of the Manuscripts

The *euchologia* manuscripts not only attest to the continued relevance of *adelphopoiesis* in Byzantium across time, but also imply its use in the different regions within the Orthodox world. Some indicate the place where they were copied. Some contain references to the region where they were used in the form of later annotations in the margins or ownership entries. And others allow speculation regarding the region of their use on the basis of the liturgical traditions which their prayers reflect.

The current location of a manuscript is an unreliable indicator of its past relevance and use. The great libraries in the Vatican (thirteen of our manuscripts), Athens (six manuscripts), Paris (five manuscripts), and St. Petersburg (two manuscripts) amassed their holdings since the Renaissance largely on the base of treasure-hunting, purchase, or appropriation at the initiative of royalty and scholars. Utilitarian and undecorated, devoid of any interest for the study of classical antiquity, prayer books were not among the most sought-after objects of these collectors. If they reached these libraries at all, it was mostly because they were bundled together with other items, as part of a larger purchase or a gift, or as a final resting place after the closure of a church archive or a monastery. Still, these high-status depositories can on occasion harbor individual codices that are of great importance for the study of the liturgy, as is the case with the oldest liturgical manuscript in Greek, the Barberinus graecus 336, which is now preserved in the Vatican Library.

As might be expected, the largest number of prayer books are still to be found in monasteries. The libraries of St. Catherine's monastery in the Sinai (fourteen of our Greek manuscripts, one Church Slavonic manuscript;

---

[24] Boswell, *Same-Sex Unions*, 291–341, using Grottaferrata ms. Gamma Beta VII; Grottaferrata ms. Gamma Beta II; Paris, Bibliothèque Nationale, ms. Coislin 213; Paris, Bibliothèque Nationale, ms. gr. 330; Vatican, ms. gr.1811; Sinai, ms. gr. 966; Athos, Panteleimon, ms. 780; Istanbul, Holy Sepulcher, ms. 615.

[25] http://www.fordham.edu/halsall/source/2rites.html.

FIGURE 2.1 *Manuscripts at the Holy Monastery of St. Catherine that contain the prayers for brother-making.*
Source: Holy Monastery of St. Catherine

Figure 2.1), the Athos monasteries (twelve manuscripts), the Badia Greca in Grottaferrata (seven manuscripts), and the Monastery of St. John the Theologian in Patmos (three manuscripts) are old foundations that have been continually inhabited since the middle ages. Saint Catherine's monastery was founded in the sixth century and the Monastery of St. John the Theologian in Patmos in the late eleventh century, just to indicate the oldest and the youngest among them. Here, we may expect a higher incidence of *euchologia* that were actually in use or treasured for their value as gifts or as preserving older liturgical traditions. But here, too, generalizations about the current location of a manuscript as indicating its place of origin can be perilous. One of the manuscripts at St. Catherine's monastery, for example (Sinai, ms. gr. 966; Appendix 3, no. 41), points to its original production and use in Southern Italy, over 2000 km away.

By far the largest number of manuscripts that can be assigned to a certain region, at least eighteen, point to the Greek-speaking communities of Southern Italy that practiced the Orthodox rite. Apulia, Calabria, and parts of Sicily were under the political authority of the Byzantine emperor and under the ecclesiastical authority of the Patriarch of Constantinople until 1071, when the administrative and military stronghold of Bari was taken over by the

Normans. Greek language and culture had deep roots there. The region became home to Greek settlers already in the eighth and seventh centuries BCE, and was known since Roman times as Magna Graecia. After the end of imperial rule in Rome in the late fifth century CE, it retained an important function as Constantinople's bridgehead in the West. Even after 1071, the Greek-speaking communities continued to follow Orthodox practices, and several monasteries and churches in Italy, first and foremost Grottaferrata near Rome and St. Salvatore in Messina, acted as spiritual, liturgical, and administrative centers. This function included the preservation of the written heritage in Greek, and led to the development of a distinct and recognizable script.

At least fourteen of our manuscripts can be identified as having been copied in Southern Italy on paleographical grounds (nos. 7, 13, 16?, 17, 21, 22, 23, 25, 26, 27, 36, 37, 38, 41, 44). Other manuscripts carry marginal annotations in Latin or in Latin written with Greek letters, which point to their use in bilingual communities (nos. 13, 25),[26] while other manuscripts (nos. 1, 9) seem to reflect the liturgical usage common in this region.

The preponderance of manuscripts associated with Southern Italy raises some interesting questions. Is this merely a result of the extensive survival of Greek liturgical manuscripts from this region? Or is it a significant indication of the popularity of *adelphopoiesis* among these communities? In order to argue for this latter possibility, it would be necessary to establish what percentage of all the surviving *euchologia* of Italo-Greek origin included the prayers for *adelphopoiesis*, and then to compare this to other regions of the Byzantine realm—an undertaking that goes beyond the aims of this book. It would also be helpful to know more about the relations between Catholic and Orthodox Christianity at all levels, not just in terms of baptism and liturgical allegiance, but also in terms of recourse to different sets of legal and religious customs available to the men and women who lived in this area of confluence and simultaneous presence of different traditions.[27]

In archival sources of the western Mediterranean, evidence is beginning to come to light about legal contracts of *affratellamento* (French: *affrèrement*) between two men that created joint ownership of property and shared household agreements, along with attestations of brotherhood arrangements of laymen with monasteries. Such contracts, as we have seen in chapter 1, are known from Spain, the South of France, and Italy, beginning in the twelfth century. Is it possible that the popularity of *adelphopoiesis* in the Southern Italian manuscripts stems from the fact that in this region people used the Greek

---

[26] A further bilingual manuscript is the Sinaiticus, ms. gr. 977 (no. 57), which contains liturgical texts in two columns, in Greek and Arabic. Would it go too far to see here an indication of the use and usefulness of *adelphopoiesis* as a means to cross linguistic and ethnic boundaries?

[27] L. Safran, *The Medieval Salento: Art and Identity in Southern Italy* (Philadelphia, PA, 2014), was not yet available to me.

prayer ritual, perhaps in conjunction with legal *affratellamento*, according to the practices of their day?

C. The Ritual of *Adelphopoiesis* as Evidence for its Social Context

The *euchologia* usually consist of well over 100 and often close to 200 folia. The core is the eucharistic liturgy either of St. John Chrysostom and/or of St. Basil, as well as the liturgies for betrothal and wedding, baptism, and burial. In addition, an *euchologion* may contain any number of small prayers that address specific concerns or situations. These appear in different quantities and sequence, and with a considerable degree of variation from manuscript to manuscript. In this manner, the specific assembly of texts within an *euchologion* reflects the spiritual concerns and liturgical needs of the community for which it was made, although here, too, the possibility cannot be excluded that an *euchologion* was simply copied in its entirety from its original, without adaptation.

A few inferences can be drawn on the basis of this information: the *adelphopoiesis* ritual is present in manuscripts used in monastic communities (nos. 3, 4, 23, 65), as well as in those used by lay congregations (nos. 7, 8, 10, 58, 59, 60, 61). It enjoyed wide regional distribution and was known among communities that followed the liturgical tradition of Syria and Palestine (nos. 10, 35, 57), as well as those of Constantinople (nos. 2, 8, 30, 33). As has already been noted, it is especially well attested in the manuscripts of Southern Italian provenance, where the liturgy was exposed to the influence of both the Constantinopolitan and the Syro-Palestinian traditions.

The Position of *Adelphopoiesis* in the Manuscripts

In the sequence of texts within the *euchologia*, the section on *adelphopoiesis* has no fixed place. In three manuscripts (nos. 37, 39, 60), in fact, brother-making was not included in the original arrangement and sequence of texts, but added later, almost as an afterthought. This may well indicate a grass-roots interest in the ritual that exceeded the expectation of the priests and scribes responsible for the manuscript's original content.

A faint pattern is discernible that suggests an implied association of brother-making with Christian initiation. This requires some explanation. The basic assumption is that the sequence of prayers within an *euchologion* follows a meaningful pattern that consists of clusters of prayers on a certain theme (illness and death, for example, or childbearing, birth, and churching, i.e., a woman's first visit to church after she had given birth). The immediate context of the preceding or following prayer, as noted in the final two columns of the table of manuscripts in Appendix 1, may thus bring to the fore the associations evoked by brother-making at the time when a manuscript was copied.

Counting the prayers before and after brother-making, four great thematic clusters emerge: numerically the smallest (eight occurrences) are prayers regarding the swearing or breaking of an oath, or prayers of reconciliation between enemies. The next largest group (fifteen occurrences) consists of the liturgies of engagement and wedding, including the removal of wedding crowns, or prayers for a second marriage. The third-largest group is of prayers of Christian initiation (thirty-seven occurrences), which includes not just baptism, but also the tonsuring of a monk or the veiling of a nun, the first haircut of a child, or a young man's offering of his first growth of beard. The third option, and by far the most numerous (sixty-four occurrences), is that of random and unrelated prayers, such as those for harvesting or for the departure of battle ships. If any meaning is to be attributed to our findings, then, it is that the most pronounced association of *adelphopoiesis* by proximity is established with prayers for Christian initiation. There is thus no overwhelming reason to follow either Boswell, who associates *adelphopoiesis* exclusively with marriage, or Panagou, who sees a relation by proximity to filial adoption.[28]

Liturgical Variations in the *Adelphopoiesis* Ritual

The *euchologia* under consideration here are prayer books that provide the script, as it were, for priests in the performance of their role as liturgists. The validity of a ritual, once it is established by a long tradition of practice, rests on the exact repetition of the right words at the correct moment. The basic components of the *adelphopoiesis* ritual are the prayers whose number, sequence, and exact meaning will be discussed in detail below. In addition, many manuscripts also include instructions for the priest and sometimes a deacon, the so-called rubrics. From the point of view of the liturgist, they are of lesser importance than the text of the prayers. The written form of the prayers ensures that the correct wording is used every time that they are recited. Gestures, by contrast, can be learned and memorized, and they were often written down a long time after they first came into use. Hence the distinction in the title to this section in the manuscripts between "prayer" (*euchê*), "order (of service)" (*taxis*), and "liturgy" (*akolouthia*). By far the greatest number of manuscripts, a total of forty, indicate that they are offering the text of one or several prayers, although four of these (nos. 4, 14, 24, 29b) also include rubrics for the liturgist. A further twenty-four contain instructions for ritual gestures

---

[28] Boswell, *Same-Sex Unions*, 187; Panagou, *Hê adelphopoiêsê*, 97–109, cf. 145.

and movements, eighteen of them labeled as *akolouthia*, three as *taxis*, and another three as *taxis kai akolouthia*.[29]

The study of ritual, whatever its context, poses inherent problems, especially when these rituals were practiced and codified in the past and are accessible to us only in writing. A comparison of large numbers of manuscripts allows historians of the liturgy to reconstruct prayers and rituals in their original form. Robert Taft, a prominent scholar of the Byzantine liturgy, has argued for the possibility of isolating elements in the liturgy and tracing their evolution back to their origins. In such an enterprise, the emphasis is on the function of the liturgy in its historical context as it evolved over time, rather than the desire to establish its original version. Such an approach has been successfully applied to the study of the eucharistic liturgy.[30] The general assumption is that the simple prayers by themselves represent the earliest stage. Rubrics that add further instructions for liturgical gestures and additional invocations represent later additions.

But does a written version of the ritual prescribe actual practice as it was just taking shape, or does it reflect the result of a long evolution? Does the Barberini *Euchologion* of the late eighth century present a newly formulated ritual practice, or does it merely offer the earliest surviving attestation in manuscript form of a prayer that had developed over an unspecified period of time? If the latter, can we identify the original building blocks that were combined to form the ritual in the first place, which may provide further clues to its origin? The long historical trajectory of this relationship as it continues to appear in the manuscripts throughout the duration of the Byzantine Empire also raises the possibility that the ritual may have been adapted to suit particular circumstances at any given time. Does the fact that all but one versions mention only two men exclude the possibility that three or more men could have been joined in *adelphopoiesis*? And could the ritual have been adapted for relations between men and women, as the narrative evidence suggests? There are no satisfying answers to these questions at the present moment.

The evolution of the sacramental liturgy was not a uniform process, but occurred simultaneously in different regions whose traditions, over time, intersected and overlapped. As Robert Taft notes: "The Byzantine liturgical system ... is actually a hybrid of Constantinopolitan and Palestinian rites, gradually synthesized during the ninth to the fourteenth centuries in the monasteries of the Orthodox world, beginning in the period of the struggle

---

[29] The total numbers in this discussion of the liturgy do not always add up, because there are some gaps in the information available to me.

[30] R. F. Taft, *Beyond East and West: Problems in Liturgical Understanding* (Washington, DC, 1984), ch. 10, 151–64: "The Structural Analysis of Liturgical Units: An Essay in Methodology"; ch. 11, 167–92: "How Liturgies Grow: The Evolution of the Byzantine Divine Liturgy." See also S. Parenti, "Towards a Regional History of the Byzantine Euchology of the Sacraments,' *Ecclesia Orans* 27 (1910), 109–21.

with Iconoclasm."[31] These two traditions merged and mingled in their use by the orthodox communities in Southern Italy—the region that has preserved the richest manuscript attestation for brother-making. It is important to bear in mind, then, that the liturgical tradition represented in any given manuscript may stem from a very different region than the current location of the codex would indicate.

To underline the centrality of *adelphopoiesis* to the ritual and social life of Orthodox Christianity, it cannot be emphasized enough that it is contained in the earliest surviving prayer book manuscript, the Barberini *Euchologion* (*Euchologium Barberinum*) in the Vatican Library (no. 1). It dates from the second half of the eighth century, coinciding with the first phase of iconoclasm. On palaeographical grounds, the manuscript can be assigned to Calabria, in Southern Italy. As the earliest liturgical manuscript to survive, it is of great value for our understanding of religious practices in Byzantium.

The liturgical prayers it contains may well have been developed and used at an earlier date. For instance, it features prayers attributed to Patriarch Germanos, who was deposed in 730. There is some disagreement over the origin of the prayers and rituals in this manuscript, whether Syro-Palestinian or Constantinopolitan, but there can be no question of their adaptation to Southern Italian use.[32] Stefano Parenti, who most recently edited the manuscript, together with Elena Velkovska, argues that it seems to represent the religious traditions not primarily of Constantinople, but of Palestine and Syria.[33] This is the same region as the earliest attestations of prayers to bless the bond between two monks that we will encounter below in the *Life of Symeon the Stylite* and the *Life of Symeon the Fool*. And it takes us closer to the middle of the seventh century, when hagiographical texts first mention the term *adelphopoiêtos*.

A different approach was taken by Miguel Arranz. He included the *Euchologium Barberinum* in a group indicative of the ritual practices in the Byzantine capital of Constantinople, whose most important witness for the ritual in the orbit of the imperial court is Paris, Bibliothèque nationale, Coislin 213. This manuscript (no. 8) can be located precisely in space and time: it was copied in 1027 for Strategios, who was priest at the patriarchal church and

---

[31] R. F. Taft, *The Byzantine Rite: A Short History* (Collegeville, MN, 1992), 16.

[32] The only prayer contained in the *Barberini Euchologium* is Prayer A (*Ho poiêsas ton anthrôpon*), which is also attested in Grottaferrata Gamma beta VII (no. 3), a manuscript of the first half of the tenth century, which in this part reflects the concerns of hard-working agricultural communities in Southern Italy. G. Passarelli, *L'eucologio cryptense Gamma beta VII (sec. X)*, Analekta Blatadon 36 (Thessaloniki, 1982), 61.

[33] Parenti, Velkovska, *L'eucologio Barberini gr. 336*. I am grateful to Stefano Parenti for facilitating my visit to the library at the Badia Greca di Grottaferrata and for generously sharing his expertise in Byzantine liturgical manuscripts with me. André Jacob further notes that the Syro-Palestinian influence on the liturgical tradition of Southern Italy and Sicily continues well into the twelfth century and perhaps later: A. Jacob, "La prière pour les troupeaux de l'Euchologe Barberini: Quelques remarques sur le texte et son histoire," *OCP* 77 (2011), 1–16, at 14.

several chapels in Constantinople. The collection of prayers it contains reflects the usage that Constantinople had in common with Palestine and the Sinai, on the one hand, and Southern Italy, on the other.[34] Arranz reconstructed the original form of the Byzantine *euchologion* as it was developed at the patriarchal church of Hagia Sophia in Constantinople in the eighth and ninth centuries, based on seven manuscripts (Barberinus graecus 336, our no. 1; St. Petersburg 226 [Euchologium Uspenskij],[35] our no. 7; Sevastianov 474 [Moscow];[36] Sinai 959, our no. 10; Grottaferrata Gamma beta I,[37] our no. 33; Coislin 213, our no. 8; and Athens 662,[38] our no. 30). With the exception of the Mosquensis, all the manuscripts in this imperial group contain prayers for *adelphopoiesis*. The "imperial" manuscript group established by Arranz proves that ritual brotherhood was part of the standard repertoire of prayers at the very center of the Byzantine empire at least from the eleventh century, but probably somewhat earlier—the same time as the historical sources suggest its increasing popularity among laymen.[39]

Two further observations about the liturgical manuscripts can be made: first, a small cluster of three manuscripts of the sixteenth century all share the same misreading of Prayer A: Sinai, gr. 977 (no. 57); Jerusalem, *Metochion tou panagiou taphou* (no. 59); and Athens, National Library (no. 61). They all contain a prayer that begins uniquely *Ho poiêsas ton ouranon kai tên gên kat'eikona sou kai homoiôsin* ("Who made Heaven and earth in your image and likeness"). This is probably a variant of Prayer A, *Ho poiêsas ton anthrôpon kat'eikona sou kai homoiôsin* ("Who created man in your image and likeness"). The scribe must have misread the *nomen sacrum* for *anthrôpon* (*anon*) as the *nomen sacrum* for *ouranon* (*ounon*) and then augmented it with the familiar formula *kai tên gên*. This is where the similarities

---

[34] Arranz, *L'eucologio costantinopolitano*. Its content is paralleled by the manuscripts Athens 662 and Grottaferrata Gamma beta I, both of the thirteenth century. P. L. Kalaitzidis, "To hyp' arithm. 662 cheirografo-euchologio tês Ethnikês Bibliothêkês tês Hellados," PhD diss., Pontificio Istituto Orientale, Rome, 2004.

[35] A. Jacob, "L'euchologe de Porphyre Uspenski, Cod. Leningr. gr. 226 (Xe siècle)," *Le Muséon* 78 (1965), 173–214; P. Koumarianos, *Il codice 226 della Biblioteca di San Pietroburgo: L'eucologio bizantino di Porfyrio Uspensky* (London, ON, 1996), 101. Koumarianos edits only the eucharistic liturgies from this codex, but gives a complete table of contents, which includes as nos. 219–20 on fols. 114r–115r (mentioned on p. 101) the prayers for brother-making.

[36] This manuscript does not contain prayers for *adelphopoiesis*. See S. J. Koster, "Das Euchologion Sevastianov 474 (X. Jhdt.) der Staatsbibliothek in Moskau," PhD diss., Pontificio Istituto Orientale, Rome, 1996.

[37] G. Stassi, "L'euchlogio Gamma beta 1 'Bessarione' di Grottaferrata," PhD diss., Pontificio Istituto Orientale, Rome, 1982, 127.

[38] Kalaitzidis, "To hyp' arithm. 662 cheirografo-euchologio tês Ethnikês Bibliothêkês tês Hellados."

[39] Arranz, *L'eucologio costantinopolitano*, 42. Arranz's effort, 355–56, to trace the development of the liturgical prayers even further stands in need of revision based on the findings presented here.

end, however. There is no agreement between the three manuscripts in the sequence of prayers before and after *adelphopoiesis.*

A second observation regards a few individual manuscripts that show the greatest liturgical creativity and may well form a cluster. Grottaferrata Gamma beta VII (no. 3), copied in the first half of the tenth century for monastic use, begins with the common Prayer A, but then contains one prayer (Prayer C) that is only shared with another manuscript of southern Italian origin, Sinai, ms. gr. 966 of the thirteenth century (no. 41), and a further prayer that is otherwise unattested (Prayer D). A similar case is represented by Escurial, X.IV.13 (no. 17), copied in the twelfth century in Salento. The *akolouthia* begins with the second most frequent Prayer A, and then adds Prayer K, that it has in common only with Sinai, ms. gr. 966 of the thirteenth century (no. 41), and Prayer L, which has no parallel elsewhere. These three manuscripts not only reflect the same regional usage, spread over three centuries, but also demonstrate that individual prayers continued to be developed.

In summary, the study of the manuscript tradition of the *adelphopoiesis* ritual yields three important insights with regard to its geographical dissemination and its demographic application:

1. It was known (and presumably practiced) in Syria, Palestine, Cyprus, Constantinople, and among the Greek-speaking communities of Southern Italy.
2. It was known (and presumably practiced) in court circles as much as in agricultural communities.
3. It was known (and presumably practiced) in monastic as well as lay communities.

Commemoration of Two or More People in the Manuscripts

Some of the liturgical manuscripts show traces of use in the form of annotations, either in the margins or on the fly-leaves at the end of the manuscript. Men and women inscribed their names, with further additions regarding their status or declarations of their intentions. Such annotations may be frustrating for the historian in search of "hard" evidence, as they usually fail to give any indication of a date, but they are direct and tangible affirmations of a long tradition of use and appreciation of *euchologia* as associated with the church and its rituals. Only a few observations can be noted here, as these annotations would repay further, independent study.

Particularly intriguing is Grottaferrata Gamma beta II of the eleventh century (no. 9), which contains the ritual for *adelphopoiesis* on fols. 86v to 87v. The manuscript contains at its end a fly-leaf, written at a later date, with a so-called *diptychon*, that is, a list of names of the deceased that ensures their remembrance in prayer.[40] The writing is in a small hand and difficult to read. The list begins with the names of men and women, identified as husband and wife, and their sons. Further down the page, God is invoked several times on behalf of two men who are mentioned together, without further explanation of their relationship. They are neither identified as monks, nor are they labeled as father and son, or uncle and nephew. A typical entry is simply: "Remember, o Lord, your servant [singular!] Theodore and Philip and forgive them [!]. Remember, o Lord, your servant [singular!] Basil and Matthew and forgive them [!]." It is especially the request for joint forgiveness, as indicated by the plural "them," that seems to suggest the kind of committed brotherhood bond that is under consideration here, although we are unable to speculate further whether the two men were monastic or lay brothers.

Diptycha for the commemoration of the dead also appear in the *euchologium* Vaticanus graecus 1811 (no. 13), copied in 1147 by the scribe Petros in Southern Italy. On a loose sequence of four folia (83v, 84v, 96v, 99v), commemoration is made of living and dead people, men and women. Some of them were priests, others officials in Apulia and Sicily; even the Norman king Roger of Sicily is mentioned. Here, too, individuals are commemorated in pairs: men and women, men and men, women and women, for example, Constantine and Eirene, Peter and Apollinarius, Kale and Zoe. The paired commemoration is striking and may perhaps be explained through the application of *adelphopoiesis* between members of the same religious association. A similar case is known in thirteenth-century Epiros, where the fly-leaves of a manuscript list the names of thirty-nine people—priests, monks, a nun, as well as women and men of the laity—who perhaps belonged to a religious confraternity.[41]

The Slavonic Ritual of Brother-Making

Just as *adelphopoiesis* is attested in the oldest surviving Byzantine *euchologion*, it also appears in the oldest prayer book in Old Church Slavonic, the shared ancestor language of Bulgarian and Russian. The *Euchologium Sinaiticum* (Sinai glag. 37, included in Appendix 1 after no. 10) was copied at the end of the eleventh century.[42]

The Slavs must have adopted the prayers for brother-making,[43] along with other Christian rituals, in the process of Christianization which began in the

---

[40] Grottaferrata Gamma beta II, fol. 150r (fol. 151r).

[41] Prinzing, "Spuren einer religiösen Bruderschaft in Epiros um 1225?".

[42] J. Frček, *Euchologium Sinaiticum: Texte slave avec sources grecques et traduction française*, PO 24/5 (Paris, 1933). For the dating, see 625. See also the detailed study by R. Nachtigal, *Euchologium Sinaiticum* (Ljubljana, 1941–42), 20. I am grateful to Georgi Parpulov for his generous help with this section of my work.

[43] Frček, *Euchologium Sinaiticum*, 658 and 661. Frček wants this ritual to be understood as fraternal adoption, as his French translation makes clear.

ninth century—indirect confirmation of the importance of brother-making in the middle Byzantine period that was then exported along with other Christian practices. *Pobratimstvo*, as they call it, would become very important among the Slavs, where this tradition was maintained into very recent times, enjoying great popularity especially among the Serbian people.[44]

The manuscript does not survive in full, and in its present state does not contain separate treatments of the full eucharistic liturgy, nor liturgies for marriage or baptism. It begins with prayers for the benediction of water. Next come four prayers for the cutting of hair or beard, followed by the ritual of brother-making. The next section of prayers is concerned with agricultural matters: sowing, harvesting, the planting of vines.

The brotherhood ritual begins with an introductory invocation by the deacon, followed by what is labeled "First prayer for *adelphopoiesis*" (equivalent to Greek Prayer A). Then follows a reading from the Gospel of John about Jesus washing the feet of his disciples (John 13:1–17)—the ultimate example of brotherly love. Next comes a prayer in front of the table (*trapeza*) (equivalent to Greek Prayer B). The priest kisses both brothers, then they kiss each other. The third prayer is said silently by the priest. This prayer (*o tês agapês phytourgos*) addresses God as the teacher of peace who has granted us to receive each other in love as his adopted sons. It does not feature in any of the Greek *adelphopoiesis* rituals, but is known in the Greek tradition in the context of peace-making or reconciliation.[45] The subsequent prayers, including the Lord's Prayer, are again said aloud. Then follows the partaking of the presanctified gifts, that is, the eucharistic bread and wine that had been consecrated on a prior occasion.[46] At the conclusion of the ritual, the priest takes the "older brother" by the hand, who then takes the hand of his "younger brother," and they all go to share a meal—a rare reference to the common feast that follows the ecclesiastical ritual and that underlines its public character.

Two features stand out in this early attestation of the practice of *adelphopoiesis* within the sphere of influence of Byzantine Christianity: the explicit instruction to partake of the eucharistic elements, a feature that appears in the Greek tradition only twice, in the twelfth century (no. 25) and in the sixteenth century (no. 59), but seems to have been common in the Slavic tradition, as it also appears in the fourteenth-century middle Bulgarian Zaykovski

---

[44] See chapter 6 below. Kretzenbacher, "Serbisch-orthodoxe 'Wahlverbrüderung,'" gives details about the liturgical tradition in Serbia, beginning with the fourteenth century. He notes that in the ritual that he observed between a man and a woman in 1966 and between two men in 1977, the priest handed the partners a cup of red wine, from which they sipped in turn, three times.

[45] The text is similar (not identical) to the Greek prayer for reconciliation in Goar, *Euchologion*, 706.

[46] Frček, *Euchologium Sinaiticum*, 658–61. On the eucharistic component of this ritual, see also M. Arranz, "La Liturgie des Présanctifiés de l'ancien Euchologe byzantin," *OCP* 47 (1981), 332–88, at 382–85.

Trebnik,[47] and the inclusion of a prayer for the reconciliation of enemies, which is absent from the Greek manuscripts.

This suggests that by the time the Slavonic ritual tradition was established the conciliatory potential of the prayers for brother-making must have been a guiding concern for the clergy, translators, and scribes who produced this version. A different interpretation is offered by Thomas Pott, whose detailed analysis of the liturgy concludes that the blessing of an existing relationship between two men by the church transforms it into a spiritual relation of brotherhood within the context of the spiritual siblinghood of all baptized Christians that is signified by the church.[48]

The Latin Tradition

One manuscript of the fourteenth century contains a Latin version of brother-making. It comes from Zadar in Croatia and thus belongs to the Adriatic region where, as in Southern Italy, Latin and Greek, Catholic and Orthodox lived side by side, interacted in daily life, and conducted business and commerce. In such an environment, the creation of kinship ties through Christian rituals, from standing witness at baptisms and weddings to marriage, acquired particular relevance. The frequent admonition of Byzantine authors to avoid such relations is eloquent testimony to this widespread practice.

The Latin ritual is preserved in a manuscript of the late fourteenth century in the Church of St. John in Trogir, Croatia (inserted in Appendix 1 after no. 44), published by the Dominican scholar Antonin Zaninović in 1971.[49] According to Alan Bray, the scholar who worked on this text most recently, it "seems to have been compiled by Catholic Franciscan friars when they arrived around 1370 in the area."[50] Similar to the Slavonic version, this ritual includes the celebration of the Eucharist. This fact is central to Bray's argument that in Latin Christianity, brotherhood compacts that served to establish a relation of voluntary kinship characterized by mutual support were essentially sworn promises whose eternal validity was guaranteed through the invocation of the eucharistic presence of Christ. Bray does not explain how his emphasis on

---

[47] B. Holosnjaj, "Zajkovski Trebnik N. 960 der Nationalbibliothek 'Hl. Kirill und Methodij' in Sofia (Bulgarien)," PhD. diss., Pontificio Istituto Orientale, Rome, 1995, 46, 61–65, where it is labeled as "fraternal adoption."

[48] T. Pott, "La 'Prière pour faire des frères' de l'Euchologe slave du Sinaï (Xe siècle): Essai d'approche théologique," *Studia Monastica* 38, no. 2 (1996), 269–89.

[49] O. A. Zaninović, "Dva Latinska spomenika o sklapanju pobratimstva u Dalmaciji," *Zbornik za narodni zivot i obicaje Juznih Slavena* 45 (1971), 713–24. Not accessible to me.

[50] A. Bray, *The Friend* (Chicago and London, 2003), 126. Text and English translation of the ritual, 130–33. For Bray's understanding of the communal aspect of the liturgical celebration, see also his "Friendship, the Family and Liturgy: A Rite for Blessing Friendship in Traditional Christianity," *Theology and Sexuality* 13 (2000), 15–33.

the importance of the Eucharist as essential for the conceptualization of the ritual tallies with his insistence that the actual swearing of the oath took place in a public ceremony outside the church doors, on the porch. Nor does he address the question of why the ceremony that he takes to be representative for the Latin rite as practiced throughout Latin Christianity—his main focus is on early modern England—is preserved in only this one manuscript, from an area where Catholic and Orthodox Christians lived side by side. Chapter 6 will present some scenarios from the Balkan regions in the late middle ages, where ties of voluntary brotherhood were a popular strategy to reach out across social, ethnic, and religious boundaries.

It is difficult to generalize on the basis of this evidence about the church involvement in the formation of fraternal bonds in the West. Brotherhood relations concluded by oath or even by drinking or mixing blood, by contrast, are known to have been practiced, as has been noted.[51] One further description of ecclesiastical participation in brother-making in the Latin West adds to the puzzlement, rather than helping to solve it. This is the tendentious report by Gerard of Wales, whose purpose it is to depict a custom in Ireland as threateningly alien.

> Among the many other deceits of their perverse ways, this one is particularly instructive. Under the appearance of piety and peace, they come together in some holy place with the man with whom they were eager to be united. First they join in *compaternitatis foedera* [literally "covenants of co-parenthood," translated by Bray as "spiritual brotherhood"]. Then they carry each other three times around the church. Then, going into the church, before the altar, and in the presence of relics of the saints, many oaths are made. Finally, with a celebration of the mass and the prayers of the priests they are joined indissolubly as if by a betrothal [*tanquam desponsatione*]. But at the end, as a greater confirmation of their friendship and to conclude the proceedings, each drinks the other's blood: this they retain from the custom of the pagans, who use blood in the sealing of oaths. How often, at this very moment of a betrothal, blood is shed by these violent and deceitful men so deceitfully and perversely that one or the other remains drained of blood! How often in that very improper hour does a bloody divorce follow, precede or even in an unheard-of-way interrupt the betrothal![52]

Alan Bray focuses on the ecclesiastical component of this description, the celebration of the mass and the subsequent prayers by the priest, and observes: "The heady mix in Giraldus' description invokes the spiritual

---

[51] Oschema, "Blood-Brothers."
[52] Translated by Bray, "Friendship, the Family and Liturgy," 18 (modified), who also gives the Latin text.

kinship of *compaternitas*, the binding force of betrothal and the liturgical form of sworn brotherhood—a form whose culmination in this account is the Eucharist."[53] Bray argues that in the Latin West, brother-making was indeed a church affair, but was integrated into the celebration of the Eucharist. This would also explain the absence of any trace of a separate ritual: "The indirect effect (of its incorporation within the existing strictures of the Eucharist) has been to make the friendship of the Latin west far less visible to the historian than its Byzantine counterpart in that both were part of a phenomenon that once comprehended Byzantine and Latin Christianity alike."[54]

This connection to the Eucharist is an attractive proposition with obvious potential for present-day pastoral and liturgical purposes, but does not strike me as an entirely convincing explanation for the absence of any Latin ritual prescriptions. After all, a few versions of the Byzantine ritual assume that it is performed in conjunction with a full eucharistic liturgy, while others mention only the partaking of the presanctified gifts, and the majority do not mention any liturgical context at all, leaving it open whether the prayers for *adelphopoiesis* were integrated into a regular service, followed it, or were performed on a separate occasion.

Liturgical Gestures and Their Significance

It has already been noted that about half of the *euchologia* under consideration here include instructions for the priest, beyond the simple prayers. At its root, the ritual consisted of two prayers unaccompanied by further instructions, and this is how it appears in the three earliest manuscripts. Liturgical instructions are noted only sporadically beginning with the late tenth century (no. 4), but become more frequent beginning with the twelfth century and are almost ubiquitous from the fifteenth century onwards.

Boswell argued for the similarity of structure, and hence of function, of *adelphopoiesis* with marriage, based on a number of ritual gestures.[55] For this reason alone, it is necessary to revisit the evidence by placing it in a broader context of Byzantine ritual practice. It will emerge that an even stronger argument can be made for similarities with rituals of Christian initiation, especially at baptism.[56]

---

[53] Ibid., 19.

[54] Ibid., 31.

[55] Boswell, *Same-Sex Unions*, 206. In this part of Boswell's work the lack of a final revision, due to his failing health, is most painfully obvious.

[56] The evidence adduced here reflects my current state of knowledge based on the manuscript information available to me. For general background, see K. Ritzer, *Formen, Riten und religiöses Brauchtum der Eheschliessung in den christlichen Kirchen des ersten Jahrtausends*, Liturgiewissenschaftliche Quellen und Forschungen 38 (Münster, 1962); K. Stevenson, *Nuptial Blessing: A Study of Christian Marriage Rites* (New York, 1983).

Boswell adduces six ritual gestures, which will be treated here in the order in which they appear in the *adelphopoiesis* celebration:

1. The imposition of both hands on the Gospel book.[57] This gesture is well established from the fourth century as accompanying the solemn swearing of an oath. This is the reason for its inclusion in the *adelphopoiesis* ritual as much as in the wedding liturgy.[58] But it is by no means exclusive to marital or brotherhood relationships, nor is it constitutive of them. The imposition of both men's hands, usually one upon the other, on the Gospel book as the priest speaks the first prayer over them simply offers visible confirmation of the seriousness of their intention.[59]

2. The binding of the joined hands with a stole, which is an important gesture in the marriage ritual, reaching back to the *dextrarum iunctio* (joining of right hands) in the Roman wedding ceremony.[60] Boswell insists that the binding of the right hands is "a part of both heterosexual weddings and same-sex unions,"[61] supporting this assertion with reference to four of the rituals in his appendix of translations.[62] The first and second of these (Grottaferrata Gamma beta VII, no. 3; Grottaferrata Gamma beta II, no. 9) are *adelphopoiesis* rituals which do not mention the binding of hands at all, the third is a sixteenth-century marriage (!) ritual from England. Only the fourth manuscript (Constantinople, Patriarchate 615 [757], now in Athens, no. 59), which dates from the post-Byzantine period, mentions the binding of the hands of the brothers by the priest.[63] Boswell does not seem to have noticed that Jerusalem, Metochion tou Taphou 182 (8), of the fifteenth century (no. 53) specifies that the two men should join their right hands. This is very meager documentation of a relatively late date, and certainly does not suffice to imagine, as Boswell does, "the sight of a couple standing hand-in-hand at the altar."[64]

---

[57] Boswell, *Same-Sex Unions*, 206. At least eleven of our manuscripts mention this (nos. 9, 13, 17, 22, 23, 27, 35, 41, 43, 48, 53?, 59, 61?, 66?).

[58] This was common from the fourth century: John Chrysostom, *Hom.* 15. 5 ad populum Antiochenum, PG 49, col. 160; Palladius, *Historia Lausiaca* 38, 6–7 (Palladio, *La storia Lausiaca*, ed. and comm. G. J. M. Bartelink, trans. M. Barchiesi [Rome, 1974], 196). See also E. Seidl, *Der Eid im römisch-ägyptischen Provinzialrecht*, vol. 2 (Munich, 1935), 48–52; P. Koukoules, *Byzantinôn bios kai politismos* (Athens, 1949), 3: 352–54.

[59] Yet, they do not exchange promises, a feature that further distinguishes this ritual from the nuptial liturgy.

[60] Boswell, *Same-Sex Unions*, 206.

[61] Ibid., 209.

[62] Ibid., 208.

[63] Dmitrievskij, 43.

[64] Boswell, *Same-Sex Unions*, 206. It is conceivable that Boswell was led to his assertions about the "binding" of the two men by the liturgical books of the Russian Orthodox Church, which indeed prescribe that both be "bound with a belt" while holding each other's hands in front of the tetrapodion. See, for example, the sixteenth-century manuscript discussed in K. Nikol'skii, *O sluzhbakh*

3. The priest's use of a hand-held cross, which is also part of the wedding ritual.[65] Only one text for the ritual for *adelphopoiesis*, in the twelfth-century manuscript Sinai, ms. gr. 973 (no. 14), has the priest holding a ceremonial cross over the hands of both men in order to bless and confirm their oath.[66] However, the post-Byzantine tradition in Greece and in Russia mentions the use of a hand-held cross by the priest. It is possible that the modern Greek expression *stavradelphos* (literally "cross-brother") is connected to this practice in later centuries.

4. The occasional use of swords.[67] Boswell later admits that the use of swords is "never prescribed in the text" of the *adelphopoiesis* ritual,[68] but cites examples from two marriage rites.

5. The imposition of crowns on the couple, held by the best man, as they stand in front of the altar, an integral part of the Orthodox marriage ritual.[69] While admitting that "same-sex union rites only rarely mention crowning,"[70] Boswell adduces two pieces of evidence for the crowning of the two brothers: The first is the manuscript Grottaferrata Gamma beta II (no. 9), where—following the ritual for brotherhood—the manuscript mentions the prayer for the removal of crowns, which is introduced under the new heading of "Canon of the church for the wedding."[71] The manuscript continues with additional texts relating to marriage. In other words, this passage deals with the removal of crowns in a marital context, although Boswell prefers to interpret this prayer as belonging to the *adelphopoiesis* ritual that precedes it. The second piece of evidence is the prohibition reported by the fourteenth-century jurist Constantine Harmenopoulos that it is not possible for monks "to receive children from holy baptism, and to hold wedding crowns, and to make *adelphopoiia*."[72] Boswell here confuses "holding the crowns" at a wedding, that is, being the best man, with being the recipient of this coronation in a nuptial ceremony.

6. The triple circling of bride and groom around the *tetrapodion* (the table on which the accoutrements of the ceremony are placed), led by the priest, and followed by the best man who holds the crowns over their heads. It is important to note that the triple circling of the couple is not attested as part of the marriage ceremony before the fourteenth century;[73] it has since become

---

russkoi tserkvi byvshikh v prezhnikh pechatnykh bogolushevnykh knigakh (St. Petersburg, 1885), 373 and 376.

[65] Boswell, *Same-Sex Unions*, 206.

[66] Dmitrievskij, 122.

[67] Boswell, *Same-Sex Unions*, 206.

[68] Ibid., 211.

[69] Ibid., 206.

[70] Ibid., 209.

[71] See Boswell's edition, 347, and his translation, 297–98.

[72] Constantine Harmenopoulos, *Epitome canonum*, PG 150, col. 124 C–D.

[73] D. Gelsi, "Punti sull'ufficio bizantino per la 'incoronazione' degli sposi," in *La celebrazione cristiana del matrimonio: Simboli e testi. Atti del II Congresso internazionale di Liturgia, Roma,*

common practice in the Orthodox Church, and is known as the "Dance of Isaiah."[74] Until the fourteenth century, triple circling was reserved for the baptismal ritual (the priest leading the godfather who carried the child)[75] and the consecration of deacons, priests, and bishops.[76] This ritual gesture is usually interpreted as a manifestation of initiation to a new status.[77] In the wedding ritual, it is also seen as an expression of joy as the newlywed couple joins with the whole church in "dancing with the Holy Martyrs," who are invoked in the accompanying chant, while the priest holds them both by the hand and leads them in a triple procession around the *tetrapodion*, the best man following behind, holding the wedding crowns over their heads.[78]

In the *adelphopoiesis* ritual, the circular walk is not part of the core liturgical celebration as it was written down in the middle and late Byzantine periods. It is, however, attested in an early fourteenth-century Serbian manuscript,[79] in the Russian Orthodox ritual of the fourteenth and fifteenth centuries,[80] and in the post-Byzantine Greek manuscript Athos Kutlumousiou 341 (sixteenth to seventeenth centuries, no. 64).[81] These attestations may be regarded as further evolutions of the Byzantine tradition, but not as indicative of the original intent of the ritual. However, it is worth noting that the circular walk makes its first appearance in the fourteenth century in both the brotherhood ritual and the nuptial ceremony. This would suggest that the inclusion of this gesture in both rituals has to be traced back to the baptismal liturgy as a common source.

27–31 maggio 1985, ed. G. Farnedi (Rome, 1986), 301. I follow the authority of Gelsi on the question of the earliest attestation of the triple circling. Boswell, *Same-Sex Unions*, 210, insists that the triple circling is found already in the wedding ritual of the thirteenth-century manuscript Patmos 104, but as it is cited by Dmitrievskij, 156, the wedding ritual in the Patmos manuscript does not specify triple circling. It merely mentions the singing of the troparion "Holy Martyrs" (which later became the standard accompaniment for triple circling) and the fact that the removal of the wedding crowns is performed by the priest in the house of the newlyweds. Ritzer, *Formen, Riten und religiöses Brauchtum*, 146, note 558 (not 145), whom Boswell cites in support of his assertion about the triple circling, merely comments on the existence of the troparion in the Patmos manuscript.

[74] The triple circling forms part of the marriage ritual given by Goar, *Euchologion*, 319.

[75] Ibid., 291. Boswell, *Same-Sex Unions*, 210n65, demonstrates his awareness of the baptismal connection.

[76] Goar, *Euchologion*, 208 (deacon), 242 (priest).

[77] Gelsi, "Punti sull'ufficio bizantino per la 'incoronazione' degli sposi," 302.

[78] Symeon of Thessaloniki, *De sacris ordinationibus*, PG 155, col. 373B.

[79] Boswell, *Same-Sex Unions*, 322.

[80] See, for example in U. Bamborschke et al., *Die Erzählung über Petr Ordynskij: Ein Beitrag zur Erforschung altrussischer Texte* (Berlin, 1979), 98–99. I am much indebted to Gail Lenhoff for her help with the Russian material.

[81] Boswell, *Same-Sex Unions*, 210n67, asserts that this is the case, presumably on the basis of his reading of the manuscript. I have not been able to verify this since Dmitrievskij, 953, gives only the title, but not the text of this ritual.

In short: the ritual of *adelphopoiesis* itself does not show any significant resemblance to that of marriage during the Byzantine period. In fact, it is distinguished from the marital ritual by the absence of the exchange of rings (technically part of the engagement ceremony which precedes the Byzantine marriage rite) and the absence of the crowning of the couple.[82] When specifications are given for the *adelphopoiesis* ritual, this refers most frequently, thirteen times to be precise, to the conclusion of the ceremony, when the newly confirmed brothers either embrace or bow to one another (nos. 9, 13, 23, 24, 27, 29b, 35, 41, 50, 53, 59, 63, 66). Next in prominence, with at least eleven occurrences, is the gesture of placing their hands on the Gospel to affirm their commitment (nos. 9, 13, 17, 22, 23, 27, 35, 41, 43, 48, 53?, 59, 61?, 66?). In nine manuscripts, the brothers also kiss or bow down to the Gospel at the conclusion of the ritual (nos. 9, 13, 23, 24, 27, 29b, 35, 41, 53, 61, 66). Some slight variations may be significant for our understanding of the relationship dynamics between ritual brothers: one manuscript (no. 43) specifies that the "older" brother places his hand on top of that of the "younger," thus implying a hierarchical relation in which the former literally has the upper hand. And one post-Byzantine manuscript (no. 59) mentions that the prayers are said not for two, but for three brothers and supports this by the invocation of heavenly assistance of three military saints: George, Demetrios, and Theodore.

For the participants and bystanders, the most important elements that constitute this ritual were simple: the moment of commitment, when the men's desire for a brotherhood relation is solemnly confirmed by the priest's prayers while they both demonstrate the sincerity of their intentions by placing their right hand on a Gospel book, and the concluding moment, when they enact their new relationship in an embrace, a kiss, or a bow (the Greek verbs *aspazesthai* or *proskynein* can cover all these meanings).

D. The Prayers: History and Purpose

At the beginning of this chapter, we saw how a prayer could be formulated to address a specific spiritual situation and how it became the core of a ritual practice at the holy site of Christ's Sepulcher in Jerusalem. All that was required was the presence of a priest and deacon holding a censer, and the two pilgrims whose friendship was about to be affirmed as a spiritual sisterhood.

We then extracted as much information as possible regarding the use of the ritual from the manuscripts, based on their history as objects. The next step is to investigate the prayers that they contain. For the prayers are the

---

[82] Boswell elsewhere concedes the absence of the exchange of rings: *Same-Sex Unions*, 215. He also admits that "same-sex union rites only rarely mention crowning," 209.

essential building blocks of the rite. As anyone who acts as a liturgist will readily acknowledge, the most important aspect of performing a Christian ceremony consists of speaking the prayers just as they are transmitted and written down. The liturgical gestures (when and in what direction to make the sign of the cross, for example) may be repeated from memory, but the prayers must always be read.

In the following, in an attempt to trace the distribution of the prayers over time and space, the sixteen different prayers for *adelphopoiesis* will be correlated with the provenance of the manuscripts. In a second step, the text of the prayers themselves will be analyzed in order to better understand their declared purpose. It will emerge that these prayers could have been used for a variety of purposes, from blessing monastic pairs and establishing bonds of spiritual brotherhood for more than two people to creating peaceful sibling relations between two or more laymen, perhaps even to end conflicts.

The Chronological and Geographical Distribution of the Prayers

Even before the transmission in parchment codices begins in the late eighth century, there is the intriguing possibility of an early attestation of prayers for spiritual brotherhood. The Deir Balizeh Papyrus of the late sixth or early seventh century preserves, in addition to an early version of the eucharistic liturgy and other liturgical texts, ten fragmentary lines of a prayer that mentions God as the giver of love (*agapê*) and brotherly love (*philadelphia*), who has granted the bond of peace (*en tô syndesmô tês eirênês*), and then uses for a concluding invocation the same words of Psalm 113:5–6 that are used in Prayer I, *Ho en hypsistois katoikôn*.[83] Since the papyrus was found at the site of a large late antique monastic *koinobion*, it is possible that this represents the trace of an early prayer of brother-making from the same period when, as has been noted before, monastic and hagiographic literature mention blessings for two monks.

The manuscripts of the Byzantine *euchologia* show great variation in the selection and sequence of the prayers for *adelphopoiesis*. While the provenance of manuscripts as evidence for the practice of *adelphopoiesis* has been studied above, here the individual prayers serve as a starting point. A total of sixteen prayers appear in different combinations and sequence in the fifty-seven manuscripts whose content is known to me. This is illustrated in the Table of Prayers in Appendix 2. The nature of these texts and their

---

[83] C. H. Roberts and B. Capelle, *An Early Euchologium: The Dêr-Balizeh Papyrus Enlarged and Re-Edited*, Bibliothèque du Muséon 23 (Louvain, 1949), 18–19, 39–41, who assume a date in the fifth or sixth century. See most recently J. van Haelst, "Une nouvelle reconstitution du papyrus liturgique de Dêr-Balizeh," *Ephemerides Theologicae Lovanienses* 45 (1969), 444–55.

manuscript transmission resist the application of the methods of classical philology to create a neat stemma with the aim of reconstructing the original version. The best that can be achieved are some disjointed observations.[84]

In the manuscript distribution over time, some prayers predominate. Prayer A, *Ho poiêsas ton anthrôpon*, first attested in the late eighth century, and Prayer B, *Ho panta pros sôtêrian*, first attested in the ninth century, constitute the basic core of the *adelphopoiesis* rite. All manuscripts, with one exception (no. 14), contain either Prayer A or Prayer B, sometimes together, or in combination with further prayers. The oldest attested prayer (Prayer A) is found in about one-third fewer manuscripts (in thirty to be exact) than the second-oldest prayer, which appears in forty-one manuscripts (Prayer B) (Figures 2.2–2.4).

This core was augmented, but not consistently. In the tenth century, three new prayers made their first appearance in conjunction with either Prayer A or Prayer B, but they are much rarer by far. Prayer C, *Ho endoxazomenos en boulê hagiôn*, is present in only two manuscripts that are three centuries apart (nos. 3, 41). Prayer D, *Anthêron hêmin kai polypothêton hê tês agapês euôdia*, is attested only once (no. 3). Prayer E, *Ho panta pros to sympheron*, occurs in a manuscript identified as pointing to Constantinopolitan use (no. 7) and in an eleventh-century manuscript of unidentified origin (no. 14). Of the relevant tenth-century manuscripts, Grottaferrata Gamma beta VII, made for monastic use (no. 3), proves to be the most innovative as it contains two of the new prayers.

In the eleventh century, one new prayer, Prayer F, *Ho ton choron tôn hagiôn sou apostolôn*, is attested for the first time, in Paris, Bibliothèque Nationale, ms. Coislin 213, dated 1027 and produced for the court circles in Constantinople (no. 8). It also appears in the additional two manuscripts of the "imperial *euchologion*" identified by Miguel Arranz (nos. 30, 33) and one codex presented as a gift to Hagia Sophia (no. 59). This would indicate a prevalence of use among laymen in an urban environment and, more specifically, the capital. In addition, Prayer F appears in a manuscript possibly associated with Palestine (no. 35) and a further manuscript (no. 47) that reflects the concerns of a lay community.

The twelfth century offers the greatest degree of variation, with the appearance of six new prayers, Prayers G to L. All of them are preserved in manuscripts with a Southern Italian connection. Prayer G, *Ho einteilamenos hêmin agapan allêlous*, is limited in chronological attestation to the twelfth century and in geographical attestation to Southern Italy, with a total of four occurrences (nos. 13, 21, 22, 25). Prayer H, *Hê tachinê akoê, ta tachina splagchna*,

---

[84] One small cluster of manuscripts shares the same variant text of Prayer A. They all date from the early sixteenth century: Sinai, ms. gr. 977 (no. 57), Jerusalem, Metochion to Taphou, ms. 789 (no. 59), and Athens, National Library, ms. 2064 (no. 61).

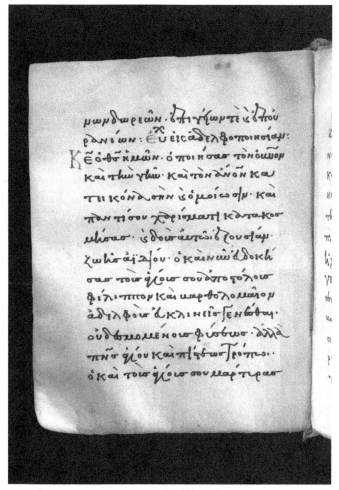

FIGURE 2.2 *Codex Sinaiticus graecus 1036 (twelfth to thirteenth centuries), folio 56 verso: beginning of Prayer A.*
Source: *Holy Monastery of St. Catherine*

occurs only once (no. 14). Prayer I, *Ho en hypsistois katoikôn*, is first encountered in twelfth-century Southern Italy (no. 22) and with a total of six attestations seems to have enjoyed popularity almost exclusively in this region until the fourteenth century (nos. 25, 26, 41, 44; only no. 42 is of unknown provenance). Prayer J, *Ho en tê kata sarkou sou oikonomia*, also makes its first appearance in the twelfth century (no. 24) and from then on sporadically, but consistently for a total of six occurrences until the sixteenth century (nos. 29a, 46, 50, 53, 66). Prayer K, *Ho dia tês aphatou sou oikonomias kataxiôsas adelphous kalesai tous hagious sou apostolous*, appears twice, first in the twelfth century (no. 17) and then in the thirteenth century (no. 41). Prayer L,

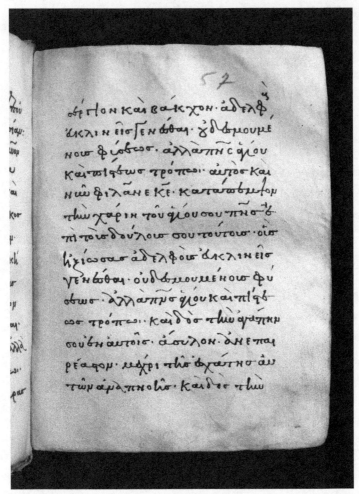

FIGURE 2.3 *Codex Sinaiticus graecus 1036 (twelfth to thirteenth centuries), folio 57 recto: continuation of Prayer A.*

Source: *Holy Monastery of St. Catherine*

Ho eipôn tois hagiois sou mathêtais kai apostolois eirênen tên emên didômi hymin, the last in our list of the twelfth-century Southern Italian prayers, occurs only once (no. 17).

One new prayer appears in each of the thirteenth, fourteenth, fifteenth, and sixteenth centuries: Prayer M, *Ho kataxiôsas dia tês sês epiphanias*, appears for a total of three times, twice in the thirteenth century (no. 32), including once in a manuscript associated with Calabria (no. 36), and once in the sixteenth century (no. 66). Prayer N, *Ho enischysas tois hagiois sou mathêtais kai apostolois*, occurs only once, in the fourteenth century (no. 48). Prayer O, *Ho synathroisas tous hagious sou*, is of a rather late date, as it occurs in a fifteenth-century Athos

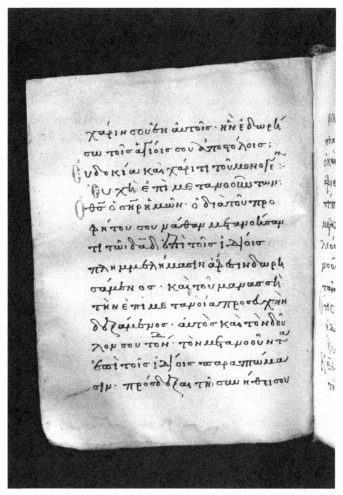

FIGURE 2.4 *Codex Sinaiticus graecus 1036 (twelfth to thirteenth centuries), folio 57 verso: end of Prayer A.*
Source: Holy Monastery of St. Catherine

manuscript (no. 50) and a second one of the same period that is closely related in content (no. 53). Prayer P, *Ho dia stomatos Dauid*, appears twice, both times in sixteenth-century Athos manuscripts that preserve the same sequence of prayers (nos. 63, 65), and may thus indicate a formulation largely for monastic use.

In sum, the chronological pattern indicates a fully developed basic structure, consisting of Prayer A and/or Prayer B, that remains stable until the tenth century. Then diversification sets in, with the use of other prayers in conjunction with either or both of the two "core" prayers. Three new prayers made their first appearance in the tenth century, and in the eleventh century, further prayers were developed in Constantinople. Diversification occurs on an even larger scale in the twelfth to fourteenth centuries in Southern Italy. In the fifteenth century, Mount Athos emerges as a further region where the ritual receives additions. All these conclusions, it must be emphasized, are valid only on the assumption that the survival of manuscripts has not skewed the evidence in favor of one or the other century, region, or prayer, and has yielded a sample that can be regarded as sufficiently representative for our purposes. They are also predicated on the assumption that the date of the manuscript attestation of a prayer is an accurate indication of the earliest period of its use.

These findings tally well with observations made on the basis of other types of evidence throughout this study. They affirm that the blessing of brotherhood bonds that originated in the monastic environment continued to be valued among monks (including the monastic communities on Mount Athos), that the ecclesiastical affirmation of brotherhood compacts gained popularity in the court circles of Constantinople in the middle Byzantine period, and that laymen of the late Byzantine period appreciated the possibility of the expansion of their family through this bond of ritual kinship, especially among the rural communities of Southern Italy, where the social and cultural influence of the Orthodox Church outlasted the grip of the imperial government in Constantinople.

The Prayers and Their Meaning

Apart from their geographical and chronological distribution in the manuscripts, the text of the prayers themselves (translated in Appendix 3) can offer some indications of their purpose and intent. All these prayers follow the usual pattern of division into three parts. They begin with an invocation that addresses God, with reference to a particular divine attribute that is relevant to the plea that follows. The longest part is the prayer request itself. Here, the names of the brothers-to-be may be mentioned, and the nature of their expected relationship is sketched with a few significant words. In some instances, this is illustrated by positive or negative models from the Hebrew Bible or the New Testament. Finally, there follows a doxology, praising God for qualities that are relevant to the purpose of the prayer. Most frequent, attested in forty-one manuscripts, is Prayer B:

> Lord our God, who has granted everything for our salvation, and who has ordered us to love [agapan] one another and to forgive each other's trespasses. Even now, benevolent Lord, that these your servants who love one another with spiritual love [pneumatikê agapê] have come to your holy church to be blessed by you:
>
> Grant them faith without shame [pistin akataischynton], love without suspicion [agapên anhypokriton], and just as you granted your peace to your holy disciples, grant also to them everything that they ask for their salvation and grant them eternal life.

For you are a merciful and benevolent God, and to you we raise up our praise, the Father, the Son and the Holy Spirit.

Second in frequency with thirty attestations is Prayer A, represented in the earliest liturgical manuscript, the *Euchologium Barberinum* of the late eighth century:

> Lord God, ruler of all, who has created man in your image and likeness and has given him eternal life, who has deemed it right that your holy and most famous apostles Peter, the head, and Andrew, and James and John the sons of Zebedee, and Philip and Bartholomew, become each other's brothers, not bound together by nature, but by faith and through the Holy Spirit, and who has deemed your holy martyrs Sergius and Bacchus, Cosmas and Damian, Cyrus and John worthy to become brothers:
>
> Bless also your servants NN and NN, who are not bound by nature, but by faith. Grant them to love one another, and that their brotherhood remain without hatred [*amisêton*] and free from offense [*askandaliston*] all the days of their lives through the power of your Holy Spirit, the intercession of the All-Holy [Mother of God], our immaculate Lady the holy Theotokos and ever-virgin Mary, and of holy John the forerunner and baptizer, the holy and truly renowned apostles and all your holy martyrs.
>
> For you are the unity and security and lord of peace, Christ our God, and to you we raise up glory and thanks.

These prayers are simultaneously expressions of a wish and declarations of intent of the two men involved. The relationship is anchored in the realm of God's divine love ("who has granted everything for our salvation," and "who has created man in your image and likeness"), which is its *raison d'être* and which it reflects. This intersects with the other interpretive axis, the concept of kinship, with the emphasis on a bond between men that is not "by nature," but spiritual.[85] The prayers draw with a few deft strokes the vague outline of the desired new quality of the relationship between the two: mutual love and the absence of strife—the very ideal of a relation between brothers. But beyond these contours, we miss the coloring. It is particularly frustrating that we are unable to speculate about the impetus that brought the men to the church. Was it genuine personal affection or the end of a quarrel? The culmination of a long-standing friendship or a measure of expediency to seal an agreement between recent acquaintances? A shared experience of pilgrimage or monasticism or the need to gain an ally in more mundane matters?

---

[85] The same language is used by Byzantine churchmen and jurisprudents to define the role of the *synteknos* (godfather) when they explain the marriage prohibitions that result from this connection between two families.

In Byzantine Christianity, the ultimate and all-pervasive frame of reference was Holy Scripture. The mere mention of a well-known biblical figure, such as the apostle Peter, could invoke, like a cipher in short-hand, the entire story of his life. The same is true, by extension, for famous saints, such as Demetrios or George. The saintly exemplars that are mentioned in some of the prayers may thus provide further keys to their interpretation. Prayer A is the only prayer that sets up an extensive list of saintly prototypes, other prayers refer to them on a more selective scale. The exemplars in Prayer A are divided into two groups, apostles and martyrs. The apostles Peter and Andrew were biological brothers, as were James and John, the sons of Zebedee (the only exemplars mentioned in Prayer J). Philip and Bartholomew were also believed to be brothers, and engaged in missionary journeys along with their sister Mariamne. Peter and Paul, although not biological brothers, were often depicted and invoked together in Western Christendom, and thus it is not surprising that they appear in Prayer I and Prayer M, both of which are recorded for the first time in manuscripts made for lay use in Southern Italy. Conspicuously absent from this list of positive examples are David and Jonathan, the prototypical affective male-male relationship of the Hebrew Bible.[86] The reference to these biblical exemplars of brotherhood—including the negative example in Prayer E of Cain who killed his brother Abel—makes it abundantly clear that the prayers were intended to replicate "through the spirit" a relationship between brothers of the same father and nothing else. There is an interesting aspect of cross-gendered imagery in Prayers E and J, which refer to the five wise virgins of Matthew 25:1–13, whose reward for guarding the light in their lamps is the invitation to the heavenly bridegroom's wedding feast.

The martyrs who are invoked in Prayer A all found their death in the Great Persecution of Diocletian—which incidentally provides a *terminus post quem* of 311 for the composition of the prayer in its current form, while the plea to the Theotokos would place it after the Council of Chalcedon in 451, when the status of the Holy Virgin as the Mother of God was affirmed. In the Byzantine tradition, the martyrs invoked in Prayer A usually appear in pairs, whether celebrated in hagiographical texts or depicted on icons and frescoes. Sergius and Bacchus were military men, and Cosmas and Damian were physicians who offered their services free of charge. The latter were twins—the closest nonhierarchical biological relation imaginable.

The great exceptions in this list are Cyrus and John. Like the other two pairs, they suffered martyrdom together under Diocletian, but unlike the other examples, they came from different families and background. Cyrus hailed from Alexandria and practiced as a physician who refused payment,

---

[86] Their example is invoked, however, in the fourteenth-century medieval Bulgarian version of the ritual, cf. Holosnjaj, "Zajkovski Trebnik," 46, 61–65.

hence the Greek epithet *anargyros*, which he has in common with Cosmas and Damian. John, who had completed a career in the army, attached himself to Cyrus as his disciple. Their cult is first attested on the occasion of the translation of their relics to Canopus in 414 by Patriarch Cyril of Alexandria. It was popularized in writing by Sophronius, Patriarch of Jerusalem from 634 to 639, one of the authors of the seventh century (as will be seen in chapter 4) to articulate close spiritual and affective bonds in his hagiographical and theological works.

Prayer B contains very evocative Greek expressions that require comment: "faith without dissembling" (*pistis akataischyntos*), "love without suspicion" (*agapê anhypokritos*), and "free from offense" (*askandalistos*). Similar phrases appear in Prayers A, E, G, and O. It is easy to read into them, as Boswell has done, an implicit acknowledgment of the "love that dare not speak its name," in the famous words associated with Oscar Wilde. But Christian liturgical language is far more expansive and inclusive than that.

"Faith without dissembling" (or "faith without shame") is a regular expression in the Greek liturgy, not specific to brother-making. It is usually part of a prayer for Christian faith that is openly professed, not shamefully hidden, and articulates a wish for strength to put one's faith into practice so that one does not bring shame on oneself.[87]

"Love without suspicion" (*anhypokritos*) is a love devoid of hypocrisy or pretense, a "genuine love" that cannot be mistaken by its recipient in the honesty of its intention.[88] The King James version translates the expression from Romans 12:9: "Let love be without dissimulation."[89] It is the kind of love that the first disciples of Christ had toward one another and the love that abbots were expected to cultivate toward their flock of monks.[90] In this very sense, a prayer in the Divine Liturgy of St. Basil asks for God's love as the source for genuine and pure love of one's neighbor.[91] It is primarily a love that is articulated within a community of the faithful,[92] but that can also single out an individual within that context.[93]

In the evocation of a relationship "devoid of scandal," it is not clear who might be offended or scandalized (the Greek word *skandalon* can mean either offense or scandal), whether an outside observer of the relationship or one of

---

[87] I am grateful to Jannis Grossmann and Martin Petzolt for their helpful comments on this issue.

[88] Thus also Pseudo-Zonaras, *Lexikon*, s.v. "alpha', 177, line 17.

[89] See also 2 Corinthians 6:6 "love unfeigned."

[90] Basil of Caesarea, *Homilia dicta tempore famis et siccitatis* (*Sermon at a Time of Famine and Drought*), PG 31, col. 325, line 18; Basil of Caesarea, *Regulae morales*, PG 31, 812, line 52; *Rule of Christodoulos for the Monastery of Patmos*, ch. 28, line 23; *Typikon for the Monastery of the Holy Virgin Eleeousa*, 80, line 11.

[91] Basil of Caesarea, *Liturgia*, PG 31, col. 1633, line 20.

[92] *AP Alphabetical Collection*, 440, line 35. *Sancti Pachomii vita tertia*, 282, line 8.

[93] Thus, for example, the relation of Sabas, the leader of Palestinian monasticism, and his successor Theodore: Cyril of Scythopolis, *Life of Sabas*, ed. Schwartz, 166, lines 6–8.

the men involved. The former sense would be required in order to make the case for a strong male-male affective bond that transgresses socially acceptable boundaries. The latter, however, is at least equally valid and definitely more appropriate, not only within the context of the wording of the prayer that focuses only on the participants, but also given the historical trajectory of the *adelphopoiesis* relation. The avoidance of causing offense to a close associate through one's conduct is clearly intended in a word of advice to be mindful of the fear of God that is reported to have been issued by Ephrem the Syrian: "Beloved, when you bring someone to your cell, take care that he departs again without having taken offense."[94] In the strict ascetic environment that Ephrem had in mind, the spiritual equilibrium of an individual monk and that of an observer or visitor could easily be disturbed by witnessing infringements of comportment, in speech or eating habits. Whether the prayers affirm a spiritual bond or are the private equivalent of a nonaggression pact, their declared intent is that henceforth each partner has the obligation to conduct himself with regard to the other so as to give no reason for shame, suspicion, or offense.

Prayers A and B, as has been noted, are by far the most popular and common. They often appear together in conjunction, although they suggest different shadings of meaning. With its reference to saintly couples, Prayer A (as well as Prayers I, J, and M) would be most suitable for the affirmation of spiritual relationship between two men, while Prayer B's emphasis on salvation and its mention of peace (also Prayers D, E, G, J, K, N, O) could have been applicable to relations that were potentially fraught with tension. This aspect is particularly pronounced when the need for forgiveness of sins and transgressions is mentioned (Prayers B, E, G, K). It is easy to imagine such prayers put to good use among laymen in the reconciliation of enemies. Several prayers expressly state that two men were involved (Prayers A, D, I, K, M, N), while others (Prayers C, E, F, G, H, J, O, P) mention collective bodies of holy figures ("the council of the saints," "the choir" of disciples, the heavenly gathering of apostles) and suggest that these words might have been recited in rituals involving more than two men. Here, we might imagine small groups of men within a monastic context, such as those discussed in chapter 3. The ritual was not conducted in privacy, but assumed the presence of a community. Prayer E, first attested in a manuscript for use in lay communities, makes explicit reference to the presence of witnesses during the ritual, while Prayers B, F, G, and N emphasize that the participants have gathered in a church for the purpose of attaining the priest's blessing.

As we have seen, the actual wording of the *adelphopoiesis* prayers leaves ample room for interpretation and adaptation to different purposes. They

---

[94] Ephrem the Syrian, *Ad imitationem proverbiorum*, ed. Phrantzolas, vol. 1, 251.

could be used to bless a close spiritual friendship of two monks, or to help two laymen to end a quarrel—or perhaps as an encouragement of two laymen who were on the same spiritual journey or pilgrimage, or indeed to make peace between two monastic brethren. The possibilities are manifold and only confirm the value of the ritual which was founded precisely in its adaptability.

We have squeezed the evidence of the liturgy dry, and yet there are several questions that remain unanswered: who else was present during the ritual, the wives and children of the newly confirmed spiritual brothers, or only male friends or relatives? Was it possible for more than two people to receive the prayers at the same time, as some manuscripts seem to indicate? Was this an exclusive relationship, or was one man able to conclude *adelphopoiesis* with more than one man in the course of his life? What happened when a man and a woman wanted to receive the prayers? This last scenario is known from hagiographies, historical narratives, and official prohibitions, but not provided for in the liturgical texts. This observation sounds a final cautionary message: we must be careful not to overinterpret the evidence of the *euchologia* as prescriptive or even descriptive. They offer glimpses of possibilities of the lived experience; nothing more and nothing less.

{ 3 }

The Origins

SMALL-GROUP MONASTICISM IN LATE ANTIQUITY

A. Monastic Beginnings

This chapter investigates the possible antecedents of *adelphopoiesis* and argues for its origin within the monastic milieu of Late Antiquity. The focus will be on the East, where the documentation in Greek, Coptic, and Syriac written texts is most ample and documentary sources and archaeology complete the picture. Taken together, this evidence is sufficient to make this argument, if not watertight, then at least convincing.[1]

The liturgical tradition discussed in the previous chapter offers two entry points for further investigation. The first is the relative proximity and possible similarities of the *adelphopoiesis* prayers to the rituals of Christian initiation. The prayers that transformed two men into brothers were probably understood by some of their Byzantine practitioners to belong in the same context as the initiatory rites of baptism and hair clipping. This opens up the question of the social application of *adelphopoiesis* in the centuries when it had become a popular social-networking strategy among the laymen of Byzantium. Baptism, the Christian initiation ritual par excellence that involves godparenthood, offers many points of connection and comparison to brother-making.

At baptism, the sponsor takes spiritual responsibility for the neophyte and thus becomes his spiritual "father." This places him alongside the biological father, to whom he now stands in a relation of spiritual kinship that also

---

[1] Boswell, *Same-Sex Unions*, 218, acknowledged the difficulty of determining whether the ritual "represents the Christianization of an ancient same-sex rite—and if so, which one—or a Christian innovation."

has consequences for their offspring in the form of marriage prohibitions. The Orthodox baptismal ritual included the cutting of small amounts of hair from the baptizand's head. Baptism was only one form of Christian initiation and commitment by an individual woman or man. Other such moments of offering oneself up to God were marked by the ritual of hair clipping, whether offering the first growth of beard, or the cutting of hair at monastic initiation for both women and men. In all these instances, a sponsor (abbot, spiritual father, baptismal sponsor, godfather) takes on the role of spiritual guide, who assists in the crossing of the threshold to a more committed Christian life. Such assistance, as shall be seen below, could also be offered between equals, in a nonhierarchical relationship.

The second entry point for further investigation lies in the origin of the *adelphopoiesis* prayers in the Syro-Palestininan liturgical tradition of which the *Barberini Euchologium* is the first manifestation. Although the manuscript itself dates from the late eighth century, it probably reflects common usage that reaches back to the seventh century, if not earlier, that is, to the time when that area was still under Byzantine rule prior to the Arab conquests. There is also the intriguing evidence of a prayer on a papyrus of this time that invokes the same key concepts and phrases as the *adelphopoiesis* ritual. During this period, Christian communities from Egypt to Syria had developed a distinctive tradition of asceticism that was articulated in a variety of living arrangements, from lay associations to large organized monasteries, and with a remarkable preponderance of men pursuing the monastic life in pairs, as shall be shown below. It is perhaps more than coincidence that the first literary treatments of *adelphopoiesis* which employ that term occur among hagiographic and monastic authors whose network spans the entire religious and cultural region of Egypt, Palestine, Syria, and Cyprus. All of these indications combined suggest an origin of the prayers for *adelphopoiesis* in the ascetic tradition of Egypt.

Understanding Early Monasticism

The common narrative of monastic origins begins with Anthony of Egypt (d. 356).[2] The son of wealthy, Greek-speaking Christian parents in Lower Egypt, he left his village and his sister at a young age, disposed of his inheritance, and lived in a sequence of isolated settings in search of ever greater seclusion from the world. His fame spread already during his lifetime thanks to a steady stream of visitors from near and far, including messengers from the emperor in Constantinople and philosophers from India. Anthony was

---

[2] For an introduction to the history of monasticism and its literature, see W. Harmless, *Desert Christians: An Introduction to the Literature of Early Monasticism* (Oxford and New York, 2004).

immortalized in the description of his life and times by Athanasius, Patriarch of Alexandria and staunch defender of Nicene orthodoxy. It enjoyed wide circulation in Greek, was soon translated into Latin, and provided the blueprint for all later hagiographies. Although he lived as a hermit, in the eyes of later authors, Anthony became the heroic founding father of monasticism in general, especially after Benedictine monasticism—enclosed communities of dozens of monks, leading a structured daily life, according to a written rule, under the direction of a highly regulated hierarchy of officers led by an abbot—became common in the middle ages in western Europe.[3]

In modern scholarship, Pachomius is generally recognized as the founder of communal monasticism. The son of Coptic-speaking parents in Upper Egypt, he encountered Christianity when he was a conscript in the Roman army, and soon after his release sought baptism. After instruction in the ascetic tradition from nearby hermits, he was first joined by his younger brother John and soon gathered a large community of followers who lived together according to tightly organized rules in a walled enclosure. Not long after his death, the Pachomius's foundation at Pbow had 1300 men, and had spawned a sister monastery for women, as well as several other foundations.[4] In Greek and Latin Christianity, Pachomius lacks the posthumous fame as a founding figure that Anthony enjoyed, although his *Rule* was translated into Latin by Jerome, and his *Vita* circulated in Coptic and in Greek.

Since Pachomius lived several decades after Antony, it is often assumed that cenobitic (communal) monasticism is a later offshoot of eremiticism (the solitary, anchoritic life) in the evolution of monastic lifestyles. Cenobitic monasticism is marked by the presence of dozens, often hundreds of monks who live in a walled enclosure and follow the same daily rhythms of worship and working, eating and sleeping. Cenobitic settlements could be enormous. At Oxyrhynchus, according to a perhaps excessively optimistic estimate, there were 10,000 monks and 20,000 nuns.[5] Self-sufficiency in economic and social terms was of prime importance. The Monastery of Isidore in the Thebaid, for example, was an elaborate affair. According to the *Historia Monachorum*, it was "fortified with high brick walls and housed a thousand monks. Within the walls were wells and gardens and all that was necessary to supply the

---

[3] J. Leclerq, "Saint Antoine dans la tradition monastique médiévale," in *Antonius Magnus Eremita*, ed. B. Steidle, 229–47, Studia Anselmiana 38 (Rome, 1956).

[4] *Historia Lausiaca* 32.8, ed. Bartelink, 156, line 69. For background, see Harmless, *Desert Christians*, 115–63.

[5] *Historia Monachorum* 5.6, ed. E. Schulz-Flügel, *Tyrannius Rufinus, Historia monachorum sive De vita sanctorum patrum*, Patristische Texte und Studien, 34 (Berlin and New York, 1990), 283, trans. N. Russell, *The Lives of the Desert Fathers: The Historia Monachorum in Aegypto* (London and Kalamazoo, MI, 1981), 67. For ease of reference, I follow the old pagination, which is indicated in brackets in Schulz-Flügel's edition.

needs of the monks, for none of them ever went out ... Among the brethren there were only two elders who went out and fetched supplies for them."[6]

The extensive posthumous fame of Anthony thanks to his prominent hagiographer points to a systemic problem in the study of early monasticism: our understanding of this phenomenon tends to be telescoped through the lens of later developments. In search of the origins of medieval monasticism as it was practiced in the Latin West, we too often follow the reading list of medieval monks and nuns who derived their knowledge of Egyptian monasticism from the *Golden Legend*, John Cassian, and Jerome. This is legitimate if we wish to appreciate medieval monasticism in the way it understood itself and created its own history. But if, as scholars of our own time with our own curiosities, we strive to bypass this identity-shaping tradition, we must go back to the Greek and Latin sources of Late Antiquity that were composed by the visitors, temporary disciples, and admirers of some of the most famous monks in Egypt. An even more coherent picture of Christian asceticism in Egypt will emerge when we turn to the Coptic texts and the archaeological record, combined with documentation from papyri and inscriptions. One of the results of such study close to the ground, as it were, is the abandonment of the simple dichotomy of anchoritic versus cenobitic organizational forms, pitching Anthony against Pachomius as the protagonists of these supposedly opposing lifestyles. In fact, the distinction between eremiticism and cenobiticism is of greater concern to modern readers than it was to late antique Greek authors. These latter apply the term *monastêrion* to any monastic dwelling of monks, whether inhabited by one or by hundreds. The modern translator of the Greek version of the *History of the Monks in Egypt* into English thus finds himself compelled to render the same word as "hermitage" or "monastery," depending on context, giving the false impression of two different setups—a cautionary lesson to bear in mind when reading texts in translation.[7]

In the past decade, archaeologists, Coptologists, and those who read their work have subjected such dichotomies and master narratives to scrutiny and revision.[8] First of all, it is important to acknowledge the simultaneous existence of a large variety of monastic models, depending on the size of the group and its distance from society, a distance that is determined largely by the economic activity that provided the support and livelihood for these

---

[6] *Historia Monachorum* 17.1–3, ed. Schulz-Flügel, 348, trans. Russell, 101.

[7] Russell, *Lives of the Desert Fathers*, 124n14.

[8] D. Brakke, "Research and Publications in Egyptian Monasticism, 2000–2004," in *Huitième congrès international d'études coptes (Paris 2004): Bilans et perspectives, 2000–2004*, ed. A. Boud'hors and D. Vaillancourt, 111–26 (Paris, 2006); E. Wipszycka, "Recherches sur le monachisme égyptien, 1997–2000," in *Coptic Studies on the Threshold of a New Millennium: Proceedings of the Seventh International Congress of Coptic Studies, Leiden, 27 August–2 September 2000*, ed. M. Immerzeel and J. van der Vliet, 831–55 (Leuven, 2004), 838.

monks. The fluidity between monastic lifestyles is played out in the lives of individual ascetics.

The respective merits of living by oneself and living in a community were hotly debated among monks. They find hagiographical expression in the story of Paisios and Isaias, two sons of a merchant who decided after their father's death to pursue the monastic life. They divided up their inheritance, but then followed different paths: one gave up his property and became a hermit, the other used his wealth to found a monastery. After their death, their followers began to squabble about the greater merits of one or the other of the two. The issue was settled only when *Abba* Pambo had a vision of both of them in paradise together—a compromise that offered the audience the certainty that both were valid choices.[9]

For instance, Sarapion in Arsinoe was "the father of many hermitages and the superior of an enormous community numbering about ten thousand monks."[10] The story of *Abba* Apollo near Hermopolis in the Thebaid, recorded in the *History of the Monks in Egypt*, reveals how one great ascetic could experience a sequence of different living arrangements and inspire others along the way. Apollo was the spiritual director of 500 hermitages in the desert, but at the end of his life, he founded a large communal monastery with an additional 500 men. He had begun his ascetic career by living in a cave. Later he lived in the desert, where he attracted disciples who settled in cells near him and followed a regular weekly schedule of communal meals.[11] Following this, there seems to have been a further interlude of cave dwelling and it was during this time that Apollo attracted five disciples who lived there with him.[12] During his desert years, he had lived together with "his own elder brother" who predeceased him. Apollo later saw his brother in a dream, "seated on a throne beside the apostles—he had left him his virtues as an inheritance—and he was interceding with God for him, entreating him to take him quickly from this life and give him rest with him in Heaven."[13] Here we encounter two motifs that are common to this type of narration: the disciple (in this case, Apollo) who inherits the status and achievements of his teacher (here designated as his "elder brother"), and the expectation that two men who had spent many years of their life together as monastic brothers (in this case, also as biological brothers) would be united in the afterlife as well.

Over the course of his lifetime, Apollo experienced the whole spectrum of social formations, in caves and in the desert, by himself, or together with his

---

[9] *Historia Lausiaca* 14, 1–6, ed. Bartelink, 58, line 1, to 62, line 50.

[10] *Historia Monachorum* 18. 1, ed. Schulz-Flügel, 349, trans. Russell, 102.

[11] Ibid. 8.2–9, ed. Schulz-Flügel, 286–89, trans. Russell, 70–71. Cf. 8.18, ed. Schulz-Flügel, 292, trans. Russell, 73.

[12] Ibid. 8.38, ed. Schulz-Flügel, 298, trans. Russell, 76.

[13] Ibid. 8.17, ed. Schulz-Flügel, 291–92, trans. Russell, 72.

brother, with a group of five followers, then as the "father" of a large number of disciples who lived independently in the desert in cells, and finally as the founder of an enclosed monastery with large membership, probably that of Bawit, whose communal life would have been more regulated.

Since its inception in the fourth century, eremitic monasticism quickly gained in popularity. This is particularly well documented for the settlements of Nitria, Kellia, and Scetis that lie to the west of the Nile Delta. The monastic settlements in Nitria originally consisted of scattered hermitages. By the time the author of the *History of the Monks in Egypt* paid his visit, about 394/5, they were populated by Egyptians and by people from elsewhere. This work describes the travels and visits to the monks in Egypt, and offers snippets of their wisdom and observations of their way of life, as they were recorded by a visitor from "foreign lands," probably Palestine. Sometimes, the narrator traveled in a group of seven,[14] sometimes he seems to have been on his own. By the time this journey took place, desert asceticism motivated by Christianity had entered its third generation and a variety of lifestyles were available for its pursuit, not just in the western Nile Delta but also further south, in the Fayum Oasis, and even as far upstream as Lycopolis (Asyut).[15] The monks in Nitria, we are told in the *History of the Monks in Egypt*, lived in rather close proximity, just outside of eyesight from one another, but at a distance that allowed them to convene every week.[16] Palladius, who visited this region in the 390s and wrote down his observations around 420 in the *Historia Lausiaca*, offers further details. According to his generous estimate, Nitria was home to 5,000 monks. Such rapid growth had consequences for the usual custom of resettling a hermitage that had become available after the death of its inhabitant. The dwelling of Nathanael, for instance, had once been remote, but within a few decades was no longer claimed by any potential new resident because of overcrowding of the desert space. The *abba*'s fellow ascetics and contemporaries showed his abandoned cell to Palladius, who comments that it is no longer inhabited: "For he [Nathanael] had built it at a time when the anchorites were still few."[17]

In addition to living the cenobitic life in a large, structured community or to pursuing the eremitic life in solitude, there existed a further model of monasticism. This was for individuals who lived independently in small groups of two, three, or more. Palladius observed that the monks in Nitria "have different ascetic practices [*politeias*], each one according to his ability and desire. Thus it is possible to live by oneself, in twos, or in a group of

---

[14] Ibid. 1.13, ed. Schulz-Flügel, 253, trans. Russell, 54.

[15] Russell, *Lives of the Desert Fathers*, 20–22.

[16] *Historia Monachorum* 20, 7, ed. Schulz-Flügel, 358, trans. Russell, 106.

[17] *Historia Lausiaca* 16. 1, ed. Bartelink, 64, lines 7–8. Translation mine.

many."[18] Some of these groups lived in close proximity to villages and cities and encountered the disdain of contemporaries for their social and economic ties to the outside world.

John Cassian was the first to criticize them in his recollections about his pilgrimage to the Egyptian monks:

> There are three kinds of monks in Egypt, of which two are admirable, the third is a poor sort of thing and by all means to be avoided. The first is that of the *coenobites*, who live together in a congregation and are governed by the direction of a single Elder: of this kind there is the largest number of monks dwelling throughout the whole of Egypt. The second is that of the *anchorites*, who were first trained in the coenobium and then being made perfect in practical life chose the recesses of the desert.... The third is the reprehensible one of the *Sarabaites*.[19]

Cassian's explanation of their characteristics reveals his disdain for ascetics who lack the rigor of hermits as well as the organized structure of cenobites and live in close interaction with the "world," maintaining economic autonomy while donating their profits to charity:

> in no sort of way [do they] practise discipline, or are [they] subject to the will of the Elders, or, taught by their traditions, [do they] learn to govern their wills or take up and properly learn any rule of sound discretion; but ... either continue in their homes devoted to the same occupation as before, though dignified by this title [of monk], or building cells for themselves and calling them monasteries remain in them perfectly free and their own masters, never submitting to the precepts of the Gospel, which forbid them to be busied with anxiety for the day's food, or troubles about domestic matters.... [They are] puffed up by the fact that they are bestowing something on the poor.[20]

Cassian's condemnation of this "third kind" of monks was reiterated not much later by Jerome, who called them Remoboth,[21] and taken up in the sixth century in the preamble to the *Rule of Benedict*. The wide popularity of Benedict's *Rule* as the foundational charter of Western monasticism ensured

---

[18] Ibid. 7.2, ed. Bartelink, 38, lines 9–12. Translation mine.

[19] Cassian, *Conferences* 18.4, trans. NPNF, 519.

[20] Ibid. 18.7.2, trans. NPNF, 524.

[21] Jerome, *Ep.* 22.34. On the difficulties in establishing the precise meaning of these terms, which are clearly intended to be derogatory, and further bibliography, see J. Horn, "Tria sunt in Aegypto genera monachorum: Die ägyptischen Bezeichnungen für die 'dritte Art' des Mönchtums bei Hieronymus und Johannes Cassianus," in *Quaerentes scientiam: Festgabe für Wolfhart Westendorf zu seinem 70. Geburtstag*, ed. H. Behlmer, 63–82 (Göttingen, 1994); M. Choat, "Philological and Historical Approaches to the Search for the 'Third Type' of Egyptian Monk," in *Coptic studies on the Threshold of a New Millennium*, ed. M. Immerzeel and J. van der Vliet, vol. 2, 857–65 (Leuven, 2004).

that this variety of monastic arrangements receded into the obscurity of opprobrium. Modern scholarship, largely in the wake of the pioneering studies of James Goehring, is beginning to recognize this gathering of a "third kind of monk" as a distinct category of monastic lifestyle by labeling it as "semi-anchoritic" or "semi-eremitic."[22]

Despite the harsh words by Latin authors, it was not uncommon in the earliest phase of Western monasticism to encounter monks who lived in small groups of two or three. Such was the case with several generations of the Jura Fathers: John and Armentarius, who were following in the footsteps of Romanus, Lupicinus, and Eugendius. Although Armentarius is said to have had his own cell within the monastery, he and John are both addressed together as "devout brothers" with "twin affections."[23]

Semi-anchoritic monasticism has by now evolved into a distinct investigative category of its own, occupying the vast middle ground between eremitic and cenobitic monasticism. Because it is so extensive, it is also a category with blurry boundaries. Upon closer scrutiny, the sources reveal that the living arrangements of monks are best imagined as a sliding scale, with the potential for fluctuation even within the lifetime of an individual. While it is easy to recognize as a solitary someone who lived on his own in a cave as a hermit, does this designation still apply to an old monk who lived in his own enclosure, assisted by a younger disciple? And what if he had two disciples? Or if he lived with another hermit and they both had the same disciple? Or if the second senior partner was accompanied by his own disciple, resulting in a group of four? These are precisely the kinds of monastic living arrangements at the focus of the following pages, as they can provide the key to understanding the shape of committed spiritual relationships between two men or in very small groups, relationships for which the prayers were developed that would later inspire Byzantine brother-making.

Archaeological Evidence for Semi-anchoritic Monasticism

The medieval master narrative of monastic origins postulated the chronological primacy of communal over eremitic monasticism, and thus perpetuated the assumption of a binary opposition between monastic lifestyles that

---

[22] His articles are collected in J. Goehring, *Ascetics, Society and the Desert: Studies in Early Egyptian Monasticism* (Harrisburg, PA, 1999). See also M. Giorda, *Il regno di Dio in terra: Le fondazioni monastiche egiziane tra V e VII secolo* (Rome, 2011). For some of the following, see C. Rapp, "Early Monasticism in Egypt: Between Hermits and Cenobites," in *Female "vita religiosa" between Late Antiquity and the High Middle Ages: Structures, Developments and Spatial Contexts*, ed. G. Melville and A. Müller, 21–42 (Zürich, 2011). On monks living as pairs, see also E. Wipszycka, *Moines et communautés en Égypte (IVème au VIIIème siècle)* (Warsaw, 2009), 389.

[23] F. Martine, ed., *Vie des pères du Jura*, SCh 142 (Paris, 1968), chs. 1–3, pp. 238–40; trans. T. Vivian et al., *The Life of the Jura Fathers*, Cistercian Studies Series, 178 (Kalamazoo, MI, 1999), 97–98.

corresponded to the spiritual path advocated by church leaders. The eremitic life, which posed its own spiritual challenges to the hermit and resisted external control by abbots and bishops, was regarded by medieval authors as the rare and perilous pinnacle of monastic living, accessible to only a few, and only after many years of training in a communal setting. Modern scholarship, along the same lines, has followed Athanasius's story in the *Life of Antony* and postulated a progression in the history of monasticism that mirrors the life path of Antony himself, from being a solitary to attracting a group of disciples and imitators. Since first Stephan Schiwietz and later Derwas Chitty established a coherent chronological sequence for the monastic movement and drew attention to the regional differences in Egypt and Palestine, archaeological excavations have further enriched the picture and thus also rendered it more complex. Peter Grossmann's work offers a first effort at a systematization of this vast body of material.[24]

Archaeological findings offer a better understanding of the living arrangements of monks living in small groups of two or more. Especially relevant is the site of Kellia in the western Nile Delta that has been excavated by French and Swiss scholars since the 1960s. Spread out over a territory of about 27 square kilometers, 1600 monastic dwellings have been identified, ranging in date from the fourth to the ninth centuries (Figure 3.1). Many of the hermit's cells from the late fifth, sixth, and seventh centuries that have been excavated in Kellia provide living space not just for the anchorite himself, but also for a disciple who would have assisted him in the tasks of daily living, including the preparation of meals and the reception of visitors.[25] One hermitage features, in addition to the dwelling for one *abba*, symmetrical accommodation for two disciples.[26] Other monastic dwellings were originally constructed for one *abba* plus disciple and then enlarged to accommodate a second elder and his assistant.[27] In kinship terms, these men may be identified as "father" and "son" or as "brothers," depending on the particular situation. The literary depictions of the complexities of these relationships will concern us below.

A model study, with the use of space syntax analysis, undertaken by Nicola Aravecchia has shown the progression of living space over time,

---

[24] S. Schiwietz, *Das morgenländische Mönchtum*, 3 vols. (Mainz and Vienna, 1904–38); D. J. Chitty, *The Desert a City: An Introduction to the Study of Egyptian and Palestinian Monasticism under the Christian Empire* (London, 1966; repr. 1977); P. Grossmann, *Christliche Architektur in Ägypten*, Handbook of Oriental Studies, vol. 26 (Leiden, Boston, Cologne, 2002), 245–315.

[25] M. Krause, "Das Mönchtum in Ägypten," in *Ägypten in spätantik-christlicher Zeit. Einführung in die koptische Kultur*, ed. M. Krause, 149–74 (Wiesbaden, 1988), 154. Grossmann, *Christliche Architektur*, 259. I am grateful to Peter Grossmann for his generosity in sharing the results of his recent research with me.

[26] Kellia, Kom 490 of Qusur al-Ruba'iyyat: R.-G. Coquin, "Évolution de l'habitat et évolution de la vie érémitique aux Kellia," in *Le site monastique copte des Kellia. Sources historiques et explorations archéologiques. Actes du Colloque de Genève, 13 au 15 août* (Geneva, 1986), 266, with note 14.

[27] Kellia QI z 31, Kellia QI z 52, Kellia QR 24.

FIGURE 3.1 *Kellia, monastic dwellings ("hermitages")*
Source: P. Miquel et al., eds., Déserts chrétiens d'Égypte *(Nice, 1993), figure 106.*

based on the arrangement and accessibility of rooms within each monastic enclosure. In the earliest phase that is also reflected in the popular works of monastic literature of the fourth and fifth centuries, there was a strict hierarchical division of space between the hermit and his one disciple, who acted as his assistant and a gatekeeper for his visitors. While the elder's cell and oratory were tucked away in a corner of the complex that was difficult to reach, the disciple's cell abutted the courtyard, kitchen, and storage facilities for which he was responsible. As time progressed, the spatial arrangements within each enclosure became more equitable, with the result that by the eighth century, an enclosure could house as many as six monks, each with his private rooms, but with shared access to the oratory and a large hall for taking communal meals.[28]

It was not only in the eremitic setting that two monks (or on occasion three, two brothers and a disciple) could live together. The cenobitic life also offered opportunities for two men to live in close quarters. The White Monastery was a huge operation founded by Aba Pgol, uncle of the famous Aba Shenoute in the fourth century. It may have counted as many as 2200 monks,

---

[28] N. Aravecchia, "Hermitages and Spatial Analysis: Use of Space at Kellia," in *Shaping Community: The Art and Archaeology of Monasticism*, ed. S. McNally, 29–40 (Oxford, 2001).

and each cell within the monastery was shared by two monks.[29] This may not have been a unique case. According to the *Rule of Pachomius*, the dormitories in the Pachomian monasteries were built to house ten monks, but if we are to believe Palladius's *Historia Lausiaca*, the original "Rule of the Angel" that provided Pachomius with instructions on how to shape his community specified that within the monastic enclosure, the monks should live in cells in groups of three.[30]

At the Monastery of the Archangel Gabriel at Naqlun, in the Fayum Oasis, there are several hermitages that are purpose-built for two monks who share the space on equitable terms. This extensive site has been excavated since 1986 by a Polish team. There are early rock-cut hermitages, a large cenobitic complex and a cemetery, parts of it incorporated into the current rebuilding of the monastery by Coptic monks. The monastic site experienced its first heyday in the sixth century, although its origins reach back to the fifth century. Various parts of it continued to be inhabited until the fourteenth century. Of particular interest are the eighty-nine hermitages, largely founded in the sixth century, most of which were intended for habitation by two monks. The spatial arrangement within these hermitages suggests that the hermits who lived there were of equal status, as "brothers." They consist of two adjoining suites of two or three rooms each, with a shared kitchen and courtyard in the center. There are no facilities for storage of foodstuffs or for baking, which suggests that the hermits depended on regular deliveries of bread, water, and wine. In other words, they may well have represented the "third kind" of monastic lifestyle that was so abhorrent to John Cassian and Jerome. In the eighth century or later, the economic system at Naqlun seems to have changed to greater independence from helpers and middle men, as storage bins set into the floor of the hermitages began to be used. These dwellings continued to be inhabited until the beginning of the twelfth century.[31] The site of Naqlun confirms what the Greek and Coptic authors of Late Antiquity indicate: that living as a hermit and being recognized as such by one's admirers, visitors, and followers did not necessary mean living in total isolation, but could entail some form of companionship and communal living arrangements.

---

[29] Krause, "Mönchtum in Ägypten," 159.

[30] *Historia Lausiaca* 32.2, ed. Bartelink, 152, lines 17–18. E. Wipszycka, "Les formes institutionelles et les formes d'activité économique du monachisme égyptien," in *Les formes institutionelles et les formes d'activité économique du monachisme égyptien*, ed. A. Camplani and G. Filoramo, 109–54 (Leuven, 2007), has come to the conclusion, based on the floor plans of a variety of monasteries, that there were no large dormitories. These sleeping arrangements are believed to reflect the living arrangements.

[31] W. Godlewski, "Excavating the Ancient Monastery at Naqlun," in *Christianity and Monasticism in the Fayoum Oasis*, ed. G. Gabra, 155–71 (Cairo and New York, 2005). The small cemetery nearby contains about 250 burials of the sixth and seventh centuries. Most of the burials there were of laypeople, not monks.

An analogous establishment at Deir el-Bachit in western Thebes has been excavated since 2004 by a German team. So far, extensive facilities for the storage and preparation of grain and of other provisions have been brought to light, as well as spaces for two looms and a number of terracotta vessels, testifying to a prosperous settlement. The seating arrangements at meal times were unusual, consisting of a total of six large circles with benches along the circumference and a table in the middle. Since up to twelve people could be seated at one of these *Sitzringe*, the monastic community must have counted seventy-two monks at most. Two of them, it seems, lived in individual but adjacent cells, each outfitted with a bed built of mud. Did they consider themselves joined in a spiritual brotherhood bond? The necropolis is yet awaiting full excavation, but already gives evidence of rows of multiple individual tombs of the same size. One tomb was larger, visible from a distance because of a coat of white paint, and more easily accessed by a pathway paved with burnt bricks. It may have been the final resting place of the founding *abba*.[32]

Similar arrangements suggesting a mixture of large and small social groups within the same community existed elsewhere. Near Esna (Greek Latopolis) in Egypt, French excavators brought to light fifteen hermitages from the late sixth and early seventh centuries. Each of them was designed for one or two ascetics, often with not one but two oratories, and sometimes with additional space for a disciple. This monastic settlement soon fell into disuse and oblivion.[33]

Recent archaeological findings, confirmed by an attentive reading of the sources, thus render obsolete the great master narrative of monastic origins that takes its lead from the chronological primacy of Antony to Pachomius and presents the dyad of eremitical and cenobitical monasticism in neat progression. Instead, we are faced with the simultaneous availability of several options for monastic living, not only in larger communities and as individuals, but also in smaller groups including the smallest pairing, that of two monks.

Written Sources

Written works that relate to the experience of monasticism, either of hermits or of people living in organized monasteries, whether men or women, are plentiful. Within this milieu, some individuals enjoyed a reputation as holy men because their prayers had special efficacy and thus became

---

[32] For an overview, accompanied by instructive photographs, see http://www.aegyptologie. uni-muenchen.de/forschung/projekte/deir_el_bachit/deb1/index.html.

[33] S. Sauneron and R.-G. Coquin, *Les ermitages chrétiennes du désert d'Esna*, vol. 4: *Essai d'histoire* (Cairo, 1972); for the larger context, see also E. Wipszycka, "Apports d'archéologie à l'histoire du monachisme égyptien," in *The Spirituality of Ancient Monasticism: Acts of the International Colloquium, Cracow-Tyniec, 16–19 November 1994*, ed. M. Starowieyski, 63–78 (Cracow, 1995), 65.

renowned for their ability to work miracles. Their biographies, written up as works of hagiography, contribute further to our knowledge of monasticism.

While these texts are populated with men, women, and children from every walk of life, and while they are filled with lively details about daily living that are not otherwise accessible, they are also notoriously difficult to interpret. Hagiographers wanted to edify, not inform, and historical accuracy was not their aim. Moreover, in order to prove that the individuals they describe followed a recognizable pattern of praiseworthy conduct, hagiographers had recourse to recycling well-known stories that had become commonplace. This means that the same story may be told of individuals who lived at different times and in different places. It is difficult for the modern interpreter to judge whether these individuals were simply following established codes of conduct, in which case these stories reflect actual repeated experiences, or whether their hagiographers chose to represent them in this way, in order to prove that their protagonists fitted the established mold. But even if it does not reflect actual historical fact, such representation must be taken seriously as it attests to the enduring value of expectations of certain kinds of conduct. Even dubious cases are worth mentioning by an author only if they are plausible; in other words, if there is a consensus of author and audience that events *may* have happened in the way that they are described.

Duplication of stories may also occur between different language traditions. The experiences of early monasticism were originally recorded in Greek and Coptic, and later translated into Armenian, Georgian, Syriac, and Arabic. Translations from Greek into Coptic are particularly frequent. These translations often take liberties, small or large, and embellish or improve upon their original text, so that it is not always easy to tell if a story preserved in another language is entirely new or whether it represents a reworking of a story that was already in circulation—a problem not dissimilar to the transmission of the *Sayings of the Desert Fathers* that Guy has studied in the different language traditions.[34]

In the following discussion, we will encounter many stories that seem to repeat the same experience. It would be futile to attempt to quantify this information or produce an exact count of the number of monks at any given time who lived in pairs. Still, the repeated telling of these stories at different points in time affirms that authors and audiences of successive generations assumed that such pairs of "brothers" were neither unusual nor unimaginable, but rather a common form of monastic living.

---

[34] J.-C. Guy, *Recherches sur la tradition grecque des Apopthegmata Patrum*, Subsidia hagiographica 36 (Brussels, 1962).

Kinship Terminology in the Monastic Environment

The aim of every monk is to leave the world behind, and that includes his family. He substitutes his biological ties and perhaps those of marriage with a new society of men who share the same purpose in search of spiritual advancement. Yet, as Andrew Crislip has noted, "the new monastic family operated on two levels, on the level of language and self-understanding and on the level of social supports: it provided both a mental framework for the monastic's socialization and incorporation into the new community and all the necessities of life for its members."[35] In this context, relationships were conceptualized in kinship terms: "father," "son," and "brother." These terms were crucial in establishing one's place in the alternative world of monasticism, where they denote one's ancestry and membership in a particular kinship group that was achieved not through bonds of blood and marriage, but through a shared purpose and the acquisition of knowledge and skills. The shared purpose is the quest for spiritual perfection, the knowledge and skills can range from biblical interpretation to the order of psalmody, and from the art of weaving palm leaves to survival training in the desert.

In contrast to worldly families where relationships are predetermined and remain fixed, the relation between two people in the monastic milieu could take on different shadings and different designations, depending on circumstance. Apa Moyses, a famous hermit in Egypt, was in the habit of gently rebuking anyone who called him "father" by explaining: "God is the father of us all, but we are all brothers. However, many among you have attained the dignity of being called a 'father.'"[36] A spiritual father would thus usually call his disciple his "son," but on those occasions when he was humbled by the latter or learned something valuable from him, he may have chosen to refer to him as "brother" or even as *abba* ("father"). A monk would usually call his fellow monk "brother" but in a particular situation may have addressed him as *abba* as a sign of respect. In a contrasting development, kinship terminology became formalized and ritualized to such an extent that "brother" became the generic term for "monk," while "father" in the generic sense referred to someone in a superior position, either an "abbot" or a priest. The language of kinship became so normative and pervasive in the monastic context that it was biological brotherhood that called for additional qualifiers. The sources for early monasticism therefore often identify biological brothers as "sons of the same father" or as "genuine brothers" (*adelphoi gnêsioi*).

---

[35] A. Crislip, *From Monastery to Hospital: Christian Monasticism and the Transformation of Health Care in Late Antiquity* (Ann Arbor, MI, 2005), 58. See 55–67 for the monastery as a substitute for the social unit of the family household. Vuolanto, "Family and Asceticism."

[36] W. Till, *Koptische Heiligen- und Martyrerlegenden*, OCA 108 (Rome, 1936), 2: 79.

The ubiquitous application of kinship language in monastic literature poses a particular challenge for the present study, in that it is not always clear whether a text mentioning someone's "brother" intends simply another monk, or the specific closer relation as a fellow monk in a committed relationship. The written sources offer only a keyhole though which we can glimpse relations depicted at that particular moment as fraternal. Their origin, however, may be widely different: they may be an elder and his disciple, or two monks of equal age and status. And in either case, the setting may be the solitude of the desert or a community of other monks of whatever size.

The phrasing of a story about how one man's charity can bring another to compunction that is told in the *Systematic Collection of the Sayings of the Desert Fathers* is indicative of the problems in this regard: *gerôn tis ekathezeto meta adelphou koinobion.* "An old man [*gerôn*] established a *koinobion* with a brother [*meta adelphou*]."[37] Assuming that "brother" without further qualification refers to a fellow monastic, this sentence permits us to imagine several scenarios of varying intimacy and duration: a monastic partner who lived with the elder in a committed relationship that is conceptualized as a bond between two siblings, a disciple who lived with the elder in a permanent arrangement, or even a visitor who was also a monk and shared the elder's ascetic life for a limited period of time.

Or consider the story of how Pachomius was initiated into the monastic life. He sought out Apa Palamon, an experienced elder, who accepted him, and clothed him in a monk's cloak—a ritual act of transformation into a new state of being. Then they prayed together "with joy" and "lived together as one man."[38] This emphasis on oneness of purpose rings a distant echo of the classical language of friendship. Based on this description alone, theirs would appear to be the relation of a monastic pair on equal footing, if it were not for the vesting ceremony that makes clear that this is a relation between elder and disciple.

Once we are open to the possibility of paired monasticism—and the sheer quantity of instances of two monks who are clearly living in such a way is compelling—then this opens up the way to a careful and attentive reading of the monastic literature so that whenever a "brother" is mentioned, we must be guided by the context whether to interpret this as a generic term referring to monastic brethren in the common pursuit of virtue or in the specific sense

---

[37] *AP Systematic*: 13.15 = Nau 281; see also *AP* Regnault, 143–44, Nau 619: an *abba* goes with his brother into the desert, where they share in common a routine and fasting habits. The new translation of the Alphabetic Collection of the *Apophthegmata Patrum* by John Wortley appeared too late to be considered here: J. Wortley, *Give me a Word: The Alphabetical Sayings of the Desert Fathers* (New York, 2014).

[38] *Life of Pachomius (Bohairic)*, ch. 10, trans. A. Veilleux, *Pachomian Koinonia*, vol. 1, Cistercian Studies Series, 45 (Kalamazoo, MI, 1980), 32.

of a close relation modeled on biological fraternity and indicating a stable, committed, and recognized relationship.

Fathers, Sons, and Discipleship in the Monastic Context

In ancient thought about social relations, the primary relationship is that between a father and his son. In monastic terms, this meant a relation between an elder or *abba* and his disciple. Their relationship was hierarchical, based on age or experience. Biologically the relationship was very close, in that the son stood to inherit his father's property and would pass on that inheritance to his own offspring. In monastic terms, the inheritance would first of all be the acquisition of immaterial goods—absorbing the *abba*'s teaching, observing and imitating his way of life—but it might involve the more tangible aspect of inheriting his worldly belongings, especially his garment or his monastic cell. The disciple also acted as a servant, assisting his "father" in his physical needs, such as monitoring visitors and preparing meals and being of general help as the elder approached the end of his life. The *abba* in his turn was responsible for his "son's" spiritual progress, not only in this world, but also beyond. John Cassian, whose adaptation of Eastern monasticism was soon to dominate in the medieval West, considered this arrangement as normative, even within a larger community.[39]

The acceptance by a "father" of a "son" was accompanied by acts and gestures that acquired ritual character. It is important to dwell on these rituals of initiation in detail because the prayers that accompany the cutting of hair and putting on of a new garment would in later centuries be fixed and preserved in prayer books (*euchologia*), where they often appear in close proximity to the prayers for *adelphopoiesis*. Entry into the monastic state was as important a crossing of a threshold as was initiation through baptism. Indeed, monastic initiation is often considered to be a "second baptism." As has been noted above, there are significant similarities between baptism in all its ramifications and *adelphopoiesis*. A large number of the men whom we will encounter in the following entered into a one-on-one monastic brotherhood as disciples of the same *abba*, and thus would have undergone these initiation rites together, perhaps augmented by further prayers to bless their relationship.

We can glean some details about the significant acts and gestures of a father's acceptance of a disciple from the Coptic *Life of Samuel of Kalamoun*, the founder of a monastery east of Fayum, who died shortly before the year 700. The *Life* was composed in the second half of the eighth century by Isaac, a priest and monk in the monastery. Samuel began his monastic career in the desert of Scetis as a disciple of the hermit Agathos, who was

---

[39] Cassian, *Institutes* II 12, 3.

instructed by an angel about the great future of his new charge. As soon as the angel left, a knock was heard on the door and Agathos opened it with the words: "Welcome, Samuel, my son! God has sent you to me so that you may serve me in my old age." He prayed over the tunic, the hood, and the holy cloak, saying: "May the God of my holy fathers, saints Macarius and Anthony, be with you, Samuel my son, and be your protector in all your sufferings." He taught him humility in thought and conduct, and instructed him to say at all times: "Forgive me, I beg you, and teach me." Samuel then prostrated himself before Agathos, kissed his hands and feet, and asked: "Remember me, my lord and father (Agathos). May God forgive me my sins and give me the means to fulfill His will." And indeed, Agathos died after three years and an illness of three months, "during which Samuel served him in the fear of God and in spiritual love." After Agathos's death, their bond lost nothing of its intensity as "his spirit upon Samuel, his son and disciple, increased twofold, like Elijah and Elisha, and he was his heir forever."[40]

This is a relationship that oscillates with different facets. Agathos was expecting a disciple who could also act as his servant and support him in his waning years, but addressed him immediately as a "son," a designation that conveys social hierarchy as well as familial affection. The ritual acceptance of Samuel into the *abba*'s household that also launched the young man on his ascetic quest consisted of dressing him in monastic garb and pronouncing a prayer that invoked an even longer line of monastic ancestors who had lived two centuries earlier, Macarius and Anthony, whom Agathos regarded as his distant forefathers on the desert path to perfection. Samuel was thus integrated into a new family lineage. He responded by showing his complete obedience and devotion, first in the act of prostration at Agathos's feet and the kissing of his hands, then in the continuous practice of humility and persistent request for instruction. The father-son relationship was fulfilled when Samuel assisted Agathos in his final days. It is rare to find "spiritual love" explicitly mentioned between monastic fathers and their disciples-sons, but the sentiment is not uncommon between monastic "brothers." After Agathos's death, Samuel's transition from disciple to son was complete. He inherited the full weight of the spirit of his master, not just temporarily, but in perpetuity, which is reinforced by the hagiographer's comparison to Elisha receiving the mantle from Elijah. As a fatherless son, Samuel was now himself able to become a father to other novice monks. The story continues by explaining that Samuel retained all the ascetic practices that Agathos had taught him and thus became to his own "brothers" like a "father, master, and guide to virtue."[41]

---

[40] My translation, based on the Italian translation of the Coptic text in T. Orlandi, *Vite di monaci copti* (Rome, 1984), 229–30, passim.

[41] My translation, based on the Italian translation of the Coptic text in Orlandi, *Vite di monaci copti*, 230–31.

As this example shows, the first step in confirming one's acceptance of a disciple was to dress him in a new outfit. It was a visible transformation in outward appearance, and signaled membership in a new social group. Thus the person who was the agent of that transformation—in this instance, the spiritual father—also carried a grave responsibility: for the worthiness of the new monk and for his continued progress. Receiving the cloak meant acceptance into the "family" of one's spiritual father. It was an act that was not to be taken lightly. When *abba* Amoi, who resided near Natron, took on John as his disciple, he first spent some time in instructing him. Then he shaved John's head and put new monastic garments on the ground. Next, they both spent three days and nights fasting and in prayer on those garments. Then an angel signed the garments three times with the cross and Amoi put the garments on John.[42]

The next step in monastic initiation was the assignment of living quarters. Concrete arrangements depended on location, resources, and the particular choice of ascetic lifestyle. An aspiring solitary could set up a cell of his own. At Nitria, newcomers were welcomed and new cells easily erected from mud bricks, in a communal effort of the established hermits. "If there were many [aspiring hermits] who came to him wishing to be saved, he [Ammonius] called together the whole community, and giving bricks to one, and water to another, completed the new cells in a single day."[43] A disciple could take up residence in the same dwelling as his "father."[44] After the death of the older "father," the inheritance of his younger disciple-son not only included his virtues, but also ownership of his cell, so that the cycle could continue, with a younger disciple now being recruited as an assistant to the new master of the cell.[45]

Pachomius, for instance, became the spiritual apprentice of Palamon, and they lived together in perfect unison. At a certain moment, Pachomius was instructed in a divine vision to move to Tabennisi where he would foster a monastic community, and Palamon agreed to join him in this relocation. They built a small dwelling for themselves and, at Palamon's suggestion, made a contract (*diathêkê*) never to part from each other.[46] Recognizing the

---

[42] *Life of John Kolobos*, ed. E. Amélineau, *Histoire des monastères de la Basse-Égypte: Vies des Saints Paul, Antoine, Macaire, Maxime et Domèce, Jean le Nain etc., Texte copte et traduction française*, Annales du Musée Guimet 25 (Paris, 1894), 397.

[43] *Historia Monachorum* 20.10, ed. Schulz-Flügel, 361, trans. Russell, 106.

[44] *AP Alphabetical*: Daniel 5: "When shall we, too, settle down, in a cell, Father?"

[45] *Historia Monachorum* 9.5–6, ed. Schulz-Flügel, 309, trans. Russell, 80: "He told us that in that place where he himself had his seat there had lived a holy man called Amoun, whose disciple he had been." *Historia Monachorum* 8.17, ed. Schulz-Flügel, 291, trans. Russell, 72: During his desert years, Apollo had lived together with "his own elder brother," who predeceased him. Apollo later saw him in a dream, "seated on a throne beside the apostles—he had left him his virtues as an inheritance—and he was interceding with God for him, entreating him to take him quickly from this life and give him rest with him in Heaven."

[46] Pachomii, *Vita Prima* 12, ed. Halkin, 8; see also P. Rousseau, *Pachomius: The Making of a Community in Fourth-Century Egypt* (Berkeley, CA, 1985), 65–66.

possibility of Pachomius's departure, the elder may have wished to secure his assistant's presence in his old age. As soon as it became known that Palamon's death had created a vacancy, Pachomius was joined in this residence by his biological brother John.[47]

A monastic cell was a precious commodity in and of itself. It was also a place of seclusion and, indeed, secrecy, as the following story illustrates. It is told by Paul of the Evergetinos monastery, who in the tenth century compiled a long treatise of monastic wisdom largely from known sources. This narration, which has no parallel elsewhere, is said to originate "From the Gerontikon." A young man wished to become the disciple of a hermit. He went to the desert and when he noticed a cell that looked like a tower (i.e., it probably had more than one floor), he resolved to become the servant of its owner "until death." But the owner told him to go away and seek his spiritual reward rather in a monastery (*en monastêriô*), because he was living with a woman. The newcomer remained firm in his purpose, regarding it as immaterial whether she was "a woman or a sister." After a while, the elder and the woman, prompted by bad conscience, decided to leave their dwelling and live elsewhere. They gathered their personal belongings and departed, but the newcomer ran after them, only to be rebuked with the words: "You have the cell now, go sit in it and take care of yourself." Then he explained: "I did not come because of the cell, but in order to serve you both." This brought them to compunction. The woman joined a monastery, the old man returned to his cell, "and thus they were all saved, thanks to the perseverance of the brother."[48] The morale of the tale is the role reversal that occurs when a novice assists an elder in mending his ways. The story is built on the premise that the junior inhabitant of a cell acted as a servant to his elder, thereby claiming his stake to inherit this property. Indirectly, it also reveals that cells could have two inhabitants, not always of the same sex.

A further step in the process of monastic initiation from "father" to "son" was an introduction to the routines of daily living. Partial exposure may have already been provided during a trial period prior to the final acceptance of the disciple by his teacher or preceding the acceptance of a postulant into a monastery. Such instruction could vary in length from several days to several months, depending on the terrain. It was vital for those who took up residence in remote desert locations, basically akin to our modern "survival training." The novice hermit had to be shown the location of sources of water, firewood, and edible plants; he had to be familiarized with the daily changes of light, darkness, sun, and shade; he had to become accustomed to

[47] *Life of Pachomius* (Bohairic) 19, trans. Veilleux, 41.

[48] Paul Evergetinos, *Evergetinos, êtoi Synagogê tôn theophthoggôn rhêmatôn kai didaskaliôn tôn theophorôn kai hagiôn paterôn*, ed. Victor Matthaios, vol. 1 (Athens, 1957), ch. 27.3, 243–44. French trans. L. Regnault, *Les sentences des pères du désert*, 169–70.

seasonal climate patterns; and he had to learn to identify dangerous animals or to anticipate the attacks of brigands. He had to train himself to endure these harsh conditions while reducing his intake of food and water, and interrupting his sleep for regular prayer. Further vital information for survival in the desert was a mental map of helpful resources—whether the locations of other hermits nearby or the vicinity of major roads that would bring travelers, visitors, and possibly middlemen for the sale of the hermit's handicrafts, usually ropes or baskets made from woven palm leaves. All of these wayfarers were also a source of provisions offered as gifts or as payment, as the case may have been.

The Coptic *Life of Onnophrius* describes this process. It was written by Paphnutius, who prominently inserts himself into the latter part of the narrative. He is likely to have been one of the ascetics of that name who were held in high esteem in Scetis at the end of the fourth century.[49] According to the *Life*, Onuphrios began his monastic life in a community near Hermopolis Magna in the Thebaid but, struck by the desire for the desert life as a hermit, he marched for six or seven miles into the mountainous desert until he found a hermit in a cave who welcomed him as "my fellow worker in the Lord." Onuphrios continues his reminiscences: "I went in and I stayed with him for a few days. I learned from him about God and he taught me how to do the works of the desert." Next, his teacher took him deeper into the desert until, after four days of walking, they reached a small hut which was to become Onuphrios's abode. The teacher remained with him for a full month of instruction in the ways of the desert "until I knew how to do the good work which it was right for me to do." He was then left in complete solitude until the teacher died and Onuphrios buried him.[50] The story repeats itself on the narrative plane that reaches into the present, when the narrator of the *Life*, Paphnutius, was accepted by Onuphrios as his disciple, addressing him as "brother." They walked for two or three miles until they reached a hut, where the *abba* declared: "Do not be afraid, my brother in God, for the Lord has sent you to care for my body and bury it." Next follows the death scene. The young man expressed his fervent desire to accompany his teacher in death, that is, to die with him at the same time, but was told that this was not God's plan. Paphnutius then tried to negotiate at least privileged access to Onuphrios in the afterlife: "Bless me, my father, that I may stand before God and as I have been worthy to see you on earth so may I be worthy to see you in the other world before the Lord Jesus Christ." In return, he did not receive a promise, but a blessing for a blameless life in the hope of future acquittal before the

---

[49] Paphnutius, *The Life of Onnophrius*, trans. T. Vivian, *Histories of the Monks of Upper Egypt and the Life of Onnophrius by Paphnutius*, Cistercian Studies Series 140 (Kalamazoo, MI, 1993), 42–50.

[50] Ibid., 152–55.

tribunal of God. Onuphrios died and Paphnutius buried him in a cleft in the rocks.[51]

The dominance of the teacher-disciple relationship in early monasticism makes it impossible to quantify these social relations between two ascetics. Was it really as ubiquitous as the monastic writings would have us believe? What are the limits of the application of the kinship model? In nature, one has only one father, but for a monk, it was not uncommon to seek out a sequence of teachers, each of whom he would regard as a "father." Many of the narratives of Egyptian monasticism are based on this premise: the author of the *History of the Monks in Egypt* as well as Palladius and Cassian were all visitors and temporary disciples of many of the *abba*s that feature in their descriptions. "Father" could thus be used as a generic designation for an older, experienced monk who was in a position to share some of his spiritual capital, teachings, or prayers with others. But the designation of "father" and "son" could also be used in a much stricter sense for a committed and enduring relationship between one disciple and his *abba*. In this instance, the *abba* took full responsibility for the spiritual progress of his disciple for the duration of their association, not only through his teaching and example, but also through his prayers. This bond was expected to extend even into the afterlife. As shall be seen below, there are numerous stories that describe a spiritual father's care for his deceased disciple. He sometimes asked for a vision to ascertain his disciple's place in the afterlife, or applied his fervent prayers to intercede on behalf of his deceased disciple in order to improve his posthumous fate. The disciple, in turn, was entitled to his share of the father's spiritual or tangible capital, not just in the form of intercessory prayer but also the right to his cell and personal belongings, such as clothing or books. Just as the father-son relationship is the basic building block of social hierarchies, the teacher-disciple relationship provides the primordial pattern for the interaction between two men in the context of the ascetic movement and monastic practice.

B. Small Monastic Groups and Paired Monks in Documents

Kinship designations were not limited to the kind of hierarchical relations that are largely encountered in an eremitic setting. Within monastic communities, individual monks were called "brother" or "father" and addressed each other on those terms. Besides such general applications, there seems to have existed a particular kind of brotherhood relationship between two men, forged for the purpose of mutual help in the common quest for spiritual

---

[51] Ibid., 157–60.

perfection, often under the guidance of a spiritual father. It is the argument of this book that this kind of relationship constitutes the monastic origin of *adelphopoiesis*.

This next step in our investigation takes us to the semi-anchoritic environment outlined above as the middle ground between eremitic and cenobitic monasticism. The archaeological evidence has already been discussed. But the most persuasive attestation for small-scale monasticism and monastic pairings comes from papyrus documents, either in the form of letters or in the form of contracts and agreements. In addition, there are limestone ostraka and graffiti. Unlike narrations that are colored by the experience and intent of the author, such documentary evidence presents us with an immediate and unadulterated view of a specific situation, even as it often employs formulaic language.

One set of papyrus letters originates from a community of monks and laymen and laywomen centered on the figure of Nepheros. He was regarded by his correspondents as a holy man who dispensed moral guidance, spiritual advice, prayers, and the occasional miracle. Around him was a community of disciples, who were variously addressed or referred to as "fathers" or "brothers." Particularly relevant for this study is the presence of monks who are addressed in pairs: a papyrus letter addressed to Nepheros conveys the greetings of Serapion to a long list of people.[52] Many of them are mentioned along with their "brother," for example: "I embrace Apoutis with his brother Syros . . . I embrace Keimai and his brother Paris."

Further epistolographical documentation comes from sixth-century Palestine, in the letters that circulated in the joint names of Barsanuphius and John. The particular type of asceticism and withdrawal from the world that Barsanuphius had chosen to pursue near Gaza as the path to perfection included his refusal to interact face to face with disciples and visitors. This did not amount to a complete and total rejection of human relationships, however. Barsanuphius was most intimate with his "brother" John, although he maintained "brotherly" relations with several other individuals such as Euthymios and Andrew.[53] The close relation between Barsanuphius and John is reflected in the joint transmission of the letters of advice, 850 in total, which they both dictated in response to queries and requests by insiders and outsiders of their community.

---

[52] B. Kramer, *Das Archiv des Nepheros und verwandte Texte*, Aegyptiaca Treverensia, 4 (Mainz, 1987), no. 12, 74–75. For background to some of the following discussion, see C. Rapp, "'For Next to God, You are My Salvation': Reflections on the Rise of the Holy Man in Late Antiquity," in *The Cult of Saints in Late Antiquity and the Early Middle Ages: Essays on the Contribution of Peter Brown*, ed. J. Howard-Johnston and P. A. Hayward, 63–81 (Oxford, 1999).

[53] See also J. Hevelone-Harper, *Disciples of the Desert: Monks, Laity and Spiritual Authority in Sixth-Century Gaza* (Baltimore, MD, 2005).

The first fifty letters in this collection are addressed by Barsanuphius to John and give eloquent testimony to their intimate and personal relationship. Barsanuphius is older in years and more advanced in his spiritual quest. Assuming the role of a guide, teacher, and instructor, he writes to John letters of support, encouragement and instruction. The beginning of their association is marked by a significant gesture. The first letter accompanies Barsanuphius's *koukoullion* (hood) which he sent to John as a protection against evil and temptations, "a gift of God you are receiving from my hands"—the bestowal of new garments, as we have seen, being a key moment in the acceptance of a disciple.[54] It was a very personal gift, a token of their association and a tangible reminder of Barsanuphius's care for him,[55] which John was enjoined to keep until his death, without passing it on to anyone else. This hierarchical aspect of their relationship is alluded to when John addressed Barsanuphius as "father."[56] But inasmuch as John had embarked on the same spiritual quest as Barsanuphius, he was also his "brother." The intensity of their union is striking. Not only did they pray for each other,[57] their relation was marked by "love,"[58] and "mutual desire";[59] they had "one heart,"[60] and "one spirit";[61] they were of one soul.[62] Their association extended even beyond death: their lives were joined forever and they expected to live together as "brothers" even in the life to come.[63]

This kind of fraternal relationship was not limited to John. Barsanuphius also addressed other hermits, most notably Paul[64] and Euthymius,[65] as "brothers," again emphasizing their unity of thought and spirit. Aware of his sinful state, he begged each of them for prayers on his behalf[66] while he, in his own turn, offered up his supplications for them.[67] The closeness of Barsanuphius's fraternal relation with Euthymius was cemented when he sent the latter his hood as a token, as he had done with John, and further strengthened by the fact that they expected to be buried together in the same tomb.[68] The whole

---

[54] Barsanuphius and John, *Letters*, ed. F. Neyt and P. de Angelis-Noah, *Correspondance*, 5 vols., SCh 426, 427, 450, 451, 468 (Paris, 1997–2002), *Ep.* 1, cf. *Ep.* 47, for the sending of another "little present."

[55] Ibid., *Ep.* 44.

[56] Ibid., *Ep.* 22, 23.

[57] Ibid., *Ep.* 16, 27.

[58] Ibid., *Ep.* 36.

[59] Ibid., *Ep.* 22.

[60] Ibid., *Ep.* 22, 27, and 28.

[61] Ibid., *Ep.* 13.

[62] Ibid., *Ep.* 16.

[63] Ibid., *Ep.* 6 and 7.

[64] Ibid., *Ep.* 57, 58.

[65] Ibid., *Ep.* 59, 64, 68, 71.

[66] Ibid., *Ep.* 63, 67.

[67] Ibid., *Ep.* 62, 63.

[68] Ibid., *Ep.* 60, 69.

collection of letters is permeated by the idea that a fraternal relationship based on mutual prayer and the bearing of each other's burdens provides a safeguard against the dangers on the path to perfection and a remedy against the punishment that ensues if one individual has stumbled on his way. Euthymius, for one, expressed the hope that, on the Day of Judgment, Barsanuphius's abundant good deeds would also be counted in his own favor.[69] Here we encounter the notion of shared spiritual capital, mutual prayer assistance, and the anticipation of being joined in death—a shared tomb and a continued association in the afterlife. As shall be seen, these are recurring features typical of monastic paired relationships.

Beyond letters that survive through manuscript transmission, there is some relevant material in the documentary papyri. These documents of mundane transactions allow us concrete glimpses of the lived reality of the men and women in late antique Egypt. They affirm what literary sources tend to overlook, the possibility for monastic women to live in pairs. The first instance is that of a spiritual mother, or *amma*, who lived with her spiritual daughter in an elder-disciple relationship. A certain Nonna is mentioned "together with her ever-virgin daughter."[70] A second example is two sisters who shared ownership of a property: In a papyrus from the city of Oxyrhynchus, dated June to July 400, Aurelia Theodora and Aurelia Tauris, both of them daughters of Silvanus, agreed to rent to Aurelius Joses, son of Judas, a Jew, a ground-floor room that is described as a dining hall, along with a cellar in the basement. What distinguishes these two biological sisters is that they are identified in this legal document as *monachai apotaktikai*, female ascetics who have renounced the world, although they may still have lived in their original village context.[71]

The evidence for men is by far more numerous. A papyrus from the monastic settlement at Labla in the district of Arsinoe in the year 511 deals with the property rights of two monks and reveals an interesting back story of the dangers of shifting allegiances. Aioulios, the legal owner of the monastic cell which he inhabits with his "brother" Eulogios made a written promise "that after my death my cell will belong to Eulogios. . . . If I leave Eulogios during my lifetime, my cell will belong to Eulogios, or if I bring any layman or monk to be senior to (?) Eulogios into my cell without permission of Eulogios, my cell will belong to Eulogios." Having received such assurances of the permanence of Aioulios's commitment to honor the status of Eulogios as his only equal companion and sole heir, the latter in turn declares in the same document that "it is not lawful for me to cast you away from me while you

---

[69] Ibid., *Ep.* 60.

[70] P. Mich. Inv. 431 = SB 16 12620, ed. princeps H. C. Youtie, "Short Texts on Papyrus," *Zeitschrift für Papyrologie und Epigraphik* 37 (1980), 211–19, at 216–17.

[71] *P. Oxy.* 44.3203.

live, until you die."[72] Their relationship was understood to have a contractual
nature that lasted for their entire lifetime. This written contractual commitment resolves a conflict caused by the recent introduction of a third person.
But at the time when Aioulios and Eulogios began living under the same roof,
there must have been the expectation of shared ownership of the monastic
property and an exclusive relationship between the two owners.

Monastc pairs could also live as part of a large community, as a papyrus
from Jeme near Thebes attests.[73] It contains the formal application issued by
John "and Shenoute my brother" to become members of a monastic community and the promise to obey its rules.

> I, John and Shenoute my brother write unto my father Apa Zacharias and
> our father Apa Jacob and Apa Theodore and all the brethren according
> to their names, [saying,] since I myself have desired in my heart's desire,
> together with my brother, not by constraint, but by my own decision,
> and am come and have requested from our father Apa Zacharias and
> Apa Jacob, that their pity might reach me and my brother, that we might
> be worthy to take part in prayer with them; but they desired to require
> a declaration at our hands, namely, that we will walk in the ordinance,
> after the manner of all the brethren that walk in obedience, [and] that
> we will go nowhere without asking [leave], nor will [do] aught whereat
> your heart should be pained beyond all the brethren.[74]

This setup was later unsettled by the introduction of a third person. On
the back of the papyrus, John sought forgiveness from the monastic elders
because he had "brought a man in to my dwelling without asking [leave]
of the elders according to the canon." In this instance, John's offense was
disobedience of the rules of the *koinobion*. There is no mention of personal
hurt or the need to make amends toward his "brother" Shenoute. The duration and purpose of the presence of this additional man remains obscure,
and the relation of John and Shenoute is equally opaque. Even if they were
biological brothers, this does not exclude a living arrangement of paired
monasticism.

The Monastery of Phoibammon near Thebes, on the west bank of the Nile,
across from Luxor, provides further documentary evidence for such pairings

---

[72] B. C. McGing, "Melitian Monks at Labla," *Tyche* 5 (1970), 67–94, at 89; see also Wipszycka,
Moines et communautés, 85.

[73] It is not clear whether the community in question should be identified with the Monastery of
Phoibammon discussed below. I wish to thank Jennifer Cromwell for bringing this papyrus to my
attention.

[74] British Museum Or. 9536, ed. W. E. Crum, *Varia Coptica* (Aberdeen, 1939), no. 6, pp. 9–10.
See also W. C. Till, *Die koptischen Rechtsurkunden aus Theben*, Österreichische Akademie der
Wissenschaften, Philosophisch-historische Klasse, Sitzungsberichte 244/3, no. 77 (Vienna, 1964),
234–35.

within a *koinobion*.[75] A limestone ostrakon probably dating from the first two decades of the seventh century mentions two monks, Peter and Solomon. They applied to enter the Monastery of Phoibammon, but at the same time expressed their wish to remain together. They declared their willingness to observe all the rules and to be held accountable in case of infringements, including the anticipation of punishment.[76] A little later, in the years 634–35, the testament of the head of the same community offers further evidence for paired living within a monastic community. It is a rather long document, missing the occasional word or sentence. It has not yet been published in the Coptic original and is known only from a German study by Walter Curt Till.[77] Peter, the current abbot of the monastery, passed on the legal rights to the property and its organization to his successor Jacob. He explicitly declared that this included the right to accept monks, and to "take another monk to you," that is, to enter into a paired relationship. In the further context of this long document, Peter mentioned David and Jacob, who must have been a pair. Jacob must have run foul of his superiors, for he was criticized for his "senselessness" and his "haughtiness," which led him to leave the monastery three times, only to seek and be granted readmission.[78] A dramatic moment had occurred recently when Jacob and David had both agreed to depart from the monastery together. Soon thereafter, Abbot Peter fell gravely ill and David then returned to ask for readmission to the community. This required a written declaration in the presence of three other monks: that David would leave Jacob and that he would further abstain from exchanging objects with Jacob or from leaving objects in Jacob's cell. David also prayed in the presence of many laymen and monks that he would act accordingly. Clearly, the relationship between David and Jacob enjoyed formal recognition and was considered to have some kind of legal force, probably the same kind of property rights that Eulogios expected after the death of his elder brother Aioulios in the papyrus mentioned above. On the other hand, the document implies that Jacob lived in his own cell, and it is not clear whether he shared it with David. Because the relationship between Jacob and Daniel was publicly known and legally valid, its dissolution was complex. As a first step, it required a written affirmation, witnessed by three people, of renunciation by the elder David of

---

[75] M. Krause, "Die Beziehungen zwischen den beiden Phoibammon-Klöstern auf dem thebanischen Westufer," *BSAC* 27 (1985), 31–44; Krause, "Zwei Phoibammon-Klöster in Theben-West," *Mitteilungen des Deutschen Archäologischen Instituts, Abteilung Kairo* 37 (1981), 261–66.

[76] British Museum 8, in A. Biedenkopf-Ziehner, *Koptische Ostraka*, vol. 1: *Ostraka aus dem Britischen Museum in London* (Wiesbaden, 2000), 120–25.

[77] Till, *Koptische Rechtsurkunden aus Theben*, 144–48. See also M. Krause, "Die Testamente der Äbte des Phoibammon-Klosters in Theben," *Mitteilungen des Deutschen Archäologischen Instituts Abteilung Kairo*, 25 (1969), 57–67.

[78] This makes it doubtful that he is the same Jacob who is mentioned later in the document as Peter's designated successor.

the younger Jacob. In a second step, it also entailed a promise before God, in the form of a prayer by David. This, too, was witnessed by a large group of people—insiders and outsiders of the monastery. David's prayer had a double function, similar to an oath: to invoke God's assistance and to declare before his community his newly forged purpose of desisting from his attentions to Jacob. This was an important ritual moment. The fact that a prayer accompanied the dissolution of a paired monastic relationship would suggest that prayers and declarations of some kind had also been performed when it was formed.

Some 300 km north of the Monastery of Phoibammon, between Assiut and Ashmunein, lies the Monastery of Bawit which yields further documentary information about monks who lived in close association of two or three. The monastery, a large complex for monks and nuns that included several churches, was founded in the late fourth century by Apa Apollo, probably to be identified with Apollo of Hermopolis mentioned above. It continued in use into the Muslim period, with its last traces dating to the tenth century. On the walls of these buildings, women and men left graffiti of their names. Especially striking are those instances where one man is mentioned with "his" brother. If that man was a monk, there is a strong likelihood that this was not a biological, but a monastic brother with whom he stood in a privileged relationship. Thus there are inscriptions by "Apa Petros, the father of the cell. My brother Phib, the musician," or "Amon, the man of Phenaoulaas. Jeremias, his brother," and an invocation, "remember Anub, the most humble, and Apa Paphnutius, his brother, that God may watch over them in peace."[79]

Of relatively late date is a series of four contracts that span the years 833 to 849. They indicate that joint ownership of monastic properties between men known as "brothers"—whether monastic or biological, or both—remained common throughout Egyptian Christianity even under Arab rule. These contracts deal with the sale and ownership of a monastic property that was originally owned jointly by two sons of Samuel the camelherd, namely Joseph, who was a priest and archimandrite, and his brother Markos. The external parameters of the property as well as its interior arrangement are clearly delineated in the contracts. Within the property lay a cell that was originally known to belong to Brother John and Brother Houmise, but which then passed into the ownership of only one brother. At a later stage, the entire property was the joint possession of three monks who are identified as "apotactics."[80]

---

[79] J. Maspero and E. Drioton, *Fouilles exécutées à Baouît*, Mémoires de l'Institut français d'archéologie orientale du Caire, vol. 59 (Cairo, 1931–43), inscriptions no. 80, 119, graffito no. 389.

[80] L. MacCoull, "The Bawit Contracts: Texts and Translations (Plates 36–54)," *BASP* 31 (1994), 141–58; M. Krause, "Die koptischen Kaufurkunden von Klosterzellen des Apollo-Klosters von Bawit aus abbasidischer Zeit," in *Monastic Estates in Late Antique and Early Christian Egypt: Ostraca, Papyri, and Essays in Memory of Sarah Clackson (P. Clackson)*, ed. A. Boud'hors et al., 159–69, American Studies in Papyrology 46 (Cincinnati, OH, 2009).

The fluidity of ownership and living arrangements is tangible in these contracts: the same property was owned, and presumably inhabited, by one, two, or three men, all of them monastics, all of them identified as "brothers."

Archaeology and documentary evidence trace the outlines on the ground, as it were, of close monastic relationships. In order to get a view from within the walls, we have to look through the window of monastic literature in search of information about the origin, development, and articulation of paired monastic relationships.

C. Small Groups of Monks in the Monastic Literature

Archaeology has shown, and papyrus documentation and epistolography have confirmed, that monks lived in small groups. Often this meant living as a pair and being recognized as such by others. When such a relationship was confirmed by a ritual act such as an oath or consecrated by prayer, this brings us close to the origins of the prayers for *adelphopoiesis*. When in the course of their relationship the men involved took mutual responsibility for each other, remained loyal, and offered each other support, then this is only a short step removed from the application of this relationship among lay society that will concern us in the next chapter.

The monastic literature of Late Antiquity provides significant evidence of monastic men living in pairs or in smaller groups of three and four.[81] This requires attentive reading. The *Sayings of the Desert Fathers*, edifying snippets of the teachings of the most famous *abba*s and *amma*s of the fourth and fifth centuries, depict the context of such teaching only with the broadest brushstrokes. Although paired monks appear frequently in the *Sayings*, they often leave us guessing about the concrete circumstances of the life that the two monks led together.[82] When we are told that two brothers visited an *abba* together,[83] should we assume that this was a temporary arrangement of convenience for the sake of travel or that these two also lived together as monks when they were not traveling? When two brothers are said to have lived together or to reside in close proximity,[84] does this mean that they had encountered one another as disciples of the same *abba* who is no longer alive? Or are we looking at two men who already knew one another in the world and made a joint decision to become monks together?

---

[81] For largely Western evidence, see E. Ferrarini, "'Gemelli cultores': Coppie agiografiche nella letteratura latina del VI secolo," *Reti Medievali Rivista* 11, no. 1 (2010), 1–17.

[82] Theodore and Lucius are mentioned as living together, as are Saius and Moue, and Matoes and his unnamed "brother," *AP Alphabetical*: Theodore of Enaton 2; *AP Alphabetical*: Saius 1; *AP Alphabetical*: Matoes 9.

[83] *AP Alphabetical*: Pambo 2; *AP* Nau 288.

[84] *AP* Nau 6.

In contrast to the snapshot character of the *Sayings*, extended hagiographical narratives in the form of saints' *Lives* offer information regarding the development of relations over an extended period of time. Their detailed description of the origin, character, shape, and evolution of paired monastic brotherhood can help to distinguish a pattern. With an eye sharpened for the telltale details, it becomes possible to identify the same kind of pattern in the more terse depictions of early monastic writing. The following observations are based on a reading of late antique monastic literature from Egypt, Palestine, and Syria, regardless of literary form, whether *Sayings*, collections of edifying anecdotes such as the *History of the Monks in Egpyt*, or *Lives*.

It is useful to begin with those stories of the association of two men, or paired monks, as I call them, where the context in which their relation originated can be known. There are three possible scenarios: (1) a tie of biological brotherhood, (2) a preexisting friendship formed prior to the adoption of a monastic life, and (3) an association that originated within the monastic context. The sources do not always permit a clear distinction between the last two. I shall treat these in turn.

Biological Brotherhood

In some instances, birth brothers become spiritual brothers by jointly leaving the world and attaching themselves to the same monastic "father." Thus Ainesios and Eustathios became disciples of Elpidios;[85] two brothers became disciples of Macarius;[86] two unnamed brothers were the disciples of an equally unnamed *abba* in Nitria;[87] and another two brothers were disciples of the same elder within a larger community;[88] and many more examples can be found. Similar pairings also appear in the Latin West: Honoratus of Arles began his monastic life together with his biological brother Venantius. As co-disciples of Caprasius, they ascended to "one shared summit of virtue."[89]

When two brothers according to the flesh also became brothers in a monastic context, this allows for the construction of narrative scenarios that play on this paradox. Real sibling relations imply a hierarchy based on age and can be marked by rivalry and competition, while monastic brotherhood was expected to be an idealized harmonious relation between equals. Especially revealing in this context are affirmations that spiritual brotherhood resulted in a role reversal among siblings. A famous case is that of Pachomius, who was joined by his younger brother John. After the latter observed how Pachomius chased

---

[85] *Historia Lausiaca* 48.3, ed. Bartelink, 238, lines 21–22.

[86] *AP Alphabetical*: Macarius 33.

[87] *AP* Regnault, 90–91, AP Nau 521.

[88] *AP* Regnault, 242–43, Butler, Paradise 2.388.

[89] Hilarius of Arles, *Vie de Saint Honorat* 10.1, ed. M.-D. Valentin, SC 235 (Paris, 1977), 94.

away a crocodile at close quarters by invoking God's help, he declared: "The Lord knows, my brother, that every day I used to say that I am your elder by the flesh, that was why every day I would call you my brother. From this day forward I will call you my father because of your firm faith in the Lord."[90] The timing of John's arrival, immediately after the death of Palamon, when "he heard that Pachomius was in a place alone,"[91] suggests that his original motivation had been the search for a place to live. But he soon shared not only Pachomius's exacting ascetic regime, but also his limited items of monastic clothing.

Such stories of spiritual role reversals are not uncommon. The story is told of two hermits who were biological brothers, the younger of whom is considered to be the "elder" because he was the first to take the monastic habit.[92]

In other instances, biological seniority prevailed, but was worthy of comment: In the early seventh century, two brothers from Cyprus lived together in the same cell in the Judaean desert, affiliated with the Laura of Kalamon. Heracleides, the older and more experienced of the two, had been joined there by his younger brother George, who recognized his brother's position of seniority although it was he himself who had the greater spiritual gifts.[93]

There is some ambivalence about the relative precedence of biological versus spiritual brotherhood. Thus the story is told of a hermit who went to a *koinobion* where his brother was the abbot. He sought to live in a cell in his brother's establishment, but received the moral lesson that he belonged in the desert and that family relations, which it clearly had been his intention to exploit, bring no advantage.[94] At the opposite extreme are two biological brothers who lived in separate cells and refused to visit one another precisely because they were blood relations.[95] The point of this story is that ties of biological brotherhood are so strong that intensified efforts are required to supplant them with spiritual fraternity.

The constant zeal (*zêlos*) in outdoing oneself and outpacing others in spiritual and ascetic progress is a commonplace in monastic literature. But when it occurred between monks who were also biological brothers, it took on the distinctive flavor of sibling rivalry. Thus two biological brothers who had joined the same monastery continued to be in competition, not for worldly goods, but in the attainment of virtue.[96] Even more revealing is the story of two biological brothers who lived together in Scetis. When one fell ill, the other asked

---

[90] *Life of Pachomius (Bohairic)* 20, trans. Veilleux, 43.

[91] Ibid. 19, trans. Veilleux, 41.

[92] *AP Systematic:* 10.175 = Nau 246.

[93] C. Houze, ed., "Sancti Georgii Chozebitae confessoris et monachi vita auctore Antonio eius discipulo," *AB* 7 (1888), 95–144, chs. 3–9, pp. 100–05.

[94] *AP Systematic:* 7.62.

[95] *AP* Nau 21.

[96] *AP* Nau 294.

the priest to pray for his brother. When the priest arrived, accompanied by several monks, they began to argue among themselves about theology and the question of *dynamis* (power). In the meantime, the sick brother was about to die, when the other brother announced that he would show "who has the power [*dynamis*]." He asked for a mat, bowed down, and then died himself, predeceasing his brother, who followed shortly afterwards. Both were then buried together.[97] More than a practical joke to shame the participants who were distracted by their heated discussion about the power of God, this story also shows that the healthy sibling claimed for himself to have greater power than his brother in his ability to hasten his death at will. Between biological monk-brothers, there was also the ever-present danger of bickering and complaining about annoying habits, and some stories highlight how discord is kept at bay.[98]

Blood ties of brotherhood could not be entirely obliterated by entry into the monastic life. These men continued to be recognized as biological brothers—that is the precise point about the stories that are told about them. But their hierarchy based on age could be redefined by seniority based on monastic experience. However, more often than not, their relationship was marked by all those traits that are common among siblings: competition and complaint, offset by the expectation of mutual support and the knowledge that their relationship is permanent and interminable.

Yet, as an ideal, biological brotherhood offers a constant point of reference for monastic pairings. Surprisingly, though, there are very few stories about twins, who would be the perfect embodiment of an idealized fraternal relationship. One romanticized story of biological brothers who became monks is particularly noteworthy as it is the foundation legend of a Coptic monastery that still functions in Egypt, Deir al-Baramus, or the "Monastery of the Romans," located in the Wadi Natrun in the western Nile Delta. Its distinctive architectural feature is two tall towers that are said to have been the dwelling of the Roman Brothers. The tale of the Roman Brothers is told in several, ever more elaborate versions, both in Greek and in Coptic. Its transmission history itself speaks for its great popularity. The story first appears in the middle of the fourth century, and was further developed over the subsequent century and a half. The earliest versions in the Greek and Coptic *Apophthegmata* mention two very young men, foreigners, with barely the first growth of beard, who sought to be apprenticed to *abba* Makarios in Scetis. Because of their youth and their wealthy background, Makarios was doubtful of their ability to endure the rigors of the desert life. But when he visited them three years later, they received him with all solemnity in a proper cell, where

---

[97] *AP* Nau 4.
[98] *AP* Regnault, 91–92, Nau 523; *AP Systematic*: 15.112 = Nau 77.

they observed a well-organized schedule of work, meals, and prayers. During their nightly psalmody, Makarios saw that they were surrounded by a divine light—a sign of their supreme attainment of monastic virtue. Soon thereafter, they died within three days of each other.[99]

By the fifth century, the story of the two brothers was integrated into the Coptic *Life of Makarios*. They were now said to hail "from parts of the Roman Empire," their burial place "beside the cave [where they had lived]" was identified, and they were claimed as eponymous founders: "the whole area came to be called that of the Romans and is called that to this day."[100] A century later, they had received names (Maximus and Domitius), and a distinguished family lineage (their purported father was the emperor Valentinian I), and they were the subjects of their own hagiographical account, the Coptic *Life of Maximus and Domitius*. Needless to say, Valentinian did not have sons by that name, and this is only one of many errors of fact in the story.[101] Historical accuracy is less important in this text than the message, which romanticizes Egyptian monasticism as a place of escape and a safe haven for those seeking an alternative lifestyle, away from the restrictions and temptations of the imperial court. The storyline is driven by the motifs of deliberate alienation and distance on the part of the brothers and the desperate search for them by their father, mother, and sister. This entire tale of biological brothers who become monastic brothers is based on the paradox of family ties which must be severed in a monastic context, but can regained in a new way.

Paired Sisters

The late antique and medieval sources were composed within a societal and political context that left little space for women, especially if they were acting on their own, removed from male associations and society. True, we hear about biological sisters who followed their brothers' vocation and were set up by them in monastic communities of women, such as the sisters of Anthony and of Pachomius, or later in the West, the sister of Caesarius of Arles. Several patristic authors praise the women of their acquaintance from whose generosity they had benefited, such as Jerome and Paula, Rufinus and Melania, John Chrysostom and Olympias. But apart from the documentary evidence presented above, very little is known about women who lived by themselves as hermits and even less about women who lived in pairs.

---

[99] Makarios 32, 273D–277B; *Apophthegmata of Makarios the Egyptian*, ed. Amélineau, *Histoire*, 207–11; trans. T. Vivian, *Saint Macarius the Spiritbearer: Coptic Texts Relating to Saint Macarius the Great*, Popular Patristics Series (Crestwood, NY, 2004), 56–59.

[100] Vivian, *Saint Macarius*, Introduction, 42. These are Vivian's quotations.

[101] The motif of imperial lineage was probably caused by confusion with the two pupils of Apa Arsenius, who were identified as sons of the emperor Valentinian I.

A notable exception comes from Theodoret of Cyrrhus, a bishop with monastic leanings in fifth-century northern Syria, who not only speaks frequently and with great fondness of his mother, but also includes in his *Historia Religiosa* a chapter on two women ascetics who lived together, Maryana and Cyra. The author introduces them on the principle of "equal opportunity" and with explicit reference to the paradox of the supposedly weaker sex performing great ascetic feats as a way of inciting the men in the audience to greater zeal. The description leaves open how Maryana and Cyra came to know each other, but suggests that they were perhaps biological sisters. They were of noble upbringing and sufficiently wealthy and independent to purchase a small piece of property outside their home town of Beroea, where they settled their female servants in a separate building. Then they walled themselves up in a small enclosure without a roof, communicating with the outside world and receiving what little food they required through a window in the wall. Theodoret, who knew them personally and had the privilege of being allowed to see them, reports that they not only engaged in extended fasts, even while traveling to Jerusalem and to the shrine of St. Thekla in Seleucia, but that when they were in their enclosure they also wore iron chains around the neck, waist, hands, and feet—bearing heavy chains was a distinctive feature of monasticism outside Egypt. He does not comment further on their relationship other than to exclaim "so much has divine love for the Bridegroom driven them mad."[102]

Preexisting Friendship and the Formative Effect of Schooling

Many monks lived in pairs as a result of their own choice. Like biological brothers who became monks together, these relationships originated in the world and then carried over into the monastic realm. Unlike biological ties, however, these relations were the result of a personal decision and entered by mutual consent while the two were still in the world, brought together by close ties of friendship. At a certain moment, they took a joint decision to embrace the ascetic life. At that point, they had a choice of lifestyles: they could enter a large monastic community together, where their relationship was, however, in danger of being discouraged or at the very least diluted within a larger social group. They could become co-disciples of the same *abba*, where the principle of obedience required them to accept living arrangements that may not have been to their liking. Or they could simply decide to take up residence together, independently of others, whether as hermits in separate, but adjacent cells, or under the same roof in the same hermitage. Paired monastic

---

[102] Theodoret of Cyrrhus, *Historia Religiosa* 29, ed. P. Canivet and A. Leroy-Molinghen, *Théodoret de Cyr, Histoire des moines de Syrie: Histoire Philothée* (Paris, 1979), trans. R. M. Price, *History of the Monks of Syria*, Cistercian Studies 88 (Kalamazoo, MI, 1985), 183–85.

relationships that have their origin in preexisting friendship always have an affective and emotional dimension to them that may be absent in those cases where chance (or providence) has brought together individual disciples of the same *abba* who partner up, for whatever reason, in the course of their discipleship.

The pursuit of monasticism or of the ascetic life is often compared to the learning experience in a school room—a learning process that does not merely consist in absorbing verbal lessons, but also involves a concrete physical aspect in the mastery of ascetic practices. This is more than an effective metaphor or simile. Experienced monastics acted as fathers to groups of younger monks, and provided teaching on a regular basis. Excavations of monastic settlements confirm that some larger establishments not only had space for the accommodation of disciples and visitors, but U-shaped rooms suitable for teaching that were equipped with benches arranged around a seat for the instructor in a central location, sometimes on a raised platform. This arrangement was clearly borrowed from the classrooms of late Roman institutions of learning, such as those of the fourth to seventh centuries recently excavated at Komm-el Dikka near Alexandria.[103]

The bonding experience would have been even stronger when not only minds, but also souls were at stake. A Christian example is Gregory of Nazianzus's *Panegyric* on his friend Basil, the later bishop of Caesarea: "As time went on, we pledged our affection for one another ... we were everything to each other, housemates, table companions, intimates who looked towards one goal—making our affection for one another grow warmer and more secure."[104] Many pairs of friends are known to have undertaken their initiation into Christianity together, whether seeking baptism or turning to monasticism. Minucius Felix used the intimate language of friendship for Octavian; they both converted to Christianity together.[105] Augustine reports in his *Confessions* that Ponticianus and his friend, both of them engaged to be married, converted together after reading the *Life of Anthony.*[106] John Cassian, the propagator of Egyptian monasticism for a Latin audience, undertook his journey to Egypt with Germanus. He explains that they were inseparable from the moment they both decided to enroll in the "spiritual army," and from then on lived together, in cenobitic monasteries or in the desert. They were so inseparable that others commented on their union (*sodalitas*) and shared monastic purpose, remarking that they were one mind and one soul in two bodies.[107]

---

[103] P. Grossmann, "Bemerkungen zu den Discipuli-Räumen in den Hermitagen von Kellia" (unpublished, 2008), with gratitude to the author for sharing his work.

[104] Gregory of Nazianzus, *Oratio 43: In Praise of Basil the Great* 19.

[105] Minucius Felix, *Octavius*, ch. 1.

[106] Augustine, *Confessions* 8.6.

[107] John Cassian, *Conferences* 1.1.

When Cassian and Germanus visited *abba* Joseph, one of the grand old men of the desert, he wanted to know if they were brothers. Their response was that they were not brothers "in the flesh, but in the spirit [*spiritali . . . fraternitate deuincti*]," and that since the beginning of their monastic quest they had been joined by a strong bond (*indiuidua semper coniunctione sociatos*).[108] This conversation is recorded at the beginning of book 16 of Cassian's *Conferences*, in which *abba* Joseph speaks at great length about spiritual friendship, its immense value for the practice of virtue, and the many perils that can endanger it. When he was finished, Cassian says, the old man had "incited in us an even more ardent desire to preserve the perpetual love of our union [*sodalitatis perpetuam caritatem*]."[109] Integrated into Cassian's *Conferences*, the report of this conversation served the dual function of giving external validation to Cassian's relation with Germanus and of providing inspiration and guidance to others about the proper conduct in such monastic friendships.

Cassian and Germanus are not the only men to become spiritual brothers and to go in search of instruction by older, more experienced desert fathers.[110] Palladius of Helenopolis was probably joined to Aphthonios in a bond of spiritual friendship that was couched in the terms of brotherhood. Palladius composed his *Historia Lausiaca* around 420, after he had become bishop of Helenopolis in Bithynia. The work records the travels he undertook in Egypt in the 390s together with several companions, visiting monks and hermits, profiting from their wisdom, absorbing their edifying tales, and sharing their daily rhythm of life, even if only for brief periods of time. At the end of his work, Palladius speaks with great personal warmth and admiration about "the brother who has been with me since youth until this present day," praising his ascetic virtues and remarkable ability to withstand the sexual temptation of women.[111] Earlier in his work, Palladius speaks in similar terms of fondness and admiration of "the good Aphthonios" who "became my true friend."[112] In the seventh century, we may think of a similar pair, John Moschus and Sophronius the Sophist, whose travelogue is known as the *Spiritual Meadow*. They shared an interest in the monastic life and deepened their association

---

[108] Ibid. 16.1.

[109] Ibid. 16.28.

[110] Dionysius Exiguus, who also hails from "Scythia," addressed two monastic pairs in his letters, John and Leontius, and Felicianus and Pastor, the latter surrounded by a monastic community: *Acta Conciliorum Oecumenicorum* 1.5, 294; cf. *Acta Conciliorum Oecumenicorum* 4.2, 196.

[111] Palladius, *Historia Lausiaca* 71.1–4, ed. Bartelink, 288, lines 1–290, at line 35. Translation mine. Bartelink comments, 402, that this person is surely not Palladius's biological brother Brisson, mentioned in his *Dialogue on the Life of John Chrysostom*, and suggests that Palladius is using this literary device to refer to himself. Flusin, too, regards this reference to Palladius's "brother" as a literary device to mask an autobiographical remark: B. Flusin, "Démons et Sarrasins: L'auteur et le propos des Diègèmata stèrikta d'Anastase le Sinaite," *Travaux et mémoires* 11 (Paris, 1991), 381–409, at 398.

[112] Palladius, *Historia Lausiaca* 32.8, ed. Bartelink, 156, lines 69–71.

while traveling to the monks in Egypt. Their writings evince a pronounced interest in spiritual male-male bonds which will concern us again below.

Pilgrimage

Education and travel, the experience of the classroom and of pilgrimage, were the times when young men of means were thrown together for long stretches of time under challenging circumstances.[113] These were the occasions when they left their home towns and their families and forged associations with others of the same age, in which a combination of utilitarian purpose and genuine sentiment often led to a lasting personal attachment. Pilgrimage took the classroom experience to the road and had an even deeper emotional effect, hence the desire to honor this experience with a special blessing, as the Syrian Orthodox Archbishop did in 1985, as we have seen, when he blessed the spiritual sisterhood of two women scholars.

The Syriac *Life of Severus* is an explicitly apologetic treatise by Zacharias of Mytilene intended to clear the good bishop of Antioch from any suspicions on the basis of the extensive pagan education he had enjoyed in Alexandria, in grammar and rhetoric, and in Berytus (Beirut), in jurisprudence. It is an interesting documentation of the dynamics of a communal learning experience, shared belief, and divergent levels of religious commitment—some of which result in close male-male associations, others not. The author himself was a close associate of Severus. They had met in the classrooms in Alexandria, "listening to the same teachers and sharing the same life."[114] When Severus, who was a year further ahead in his studies, decided to continue his education as a legal expert at the elite institution of Berytus, he asked Zacharias to follow him the next year. Zacharias, however, was further advanced in his commitment to Christianity, and therefore was reminded that it was his responsibility to encourage Severus to seek baptism. On the one free day of the week that their legal studies allowed, he led them in their joint study of the writings of the church fathers. As Zacharias was more spiritually advanced, Severus chose him to sponsor his baptism, although ecclesiastical politics prevented this from happening. Severus later entrusted to him the safeguarding of his possessions before he went on pilgrimage to Jerusalem. This close association based on a long acquaintance and a shared formative experience could have led to a declaration of mutual support in religious purpose. But this was not to happen, because Zacharias, by his own admission ("I . . . had lost my wings"), found himself unable to pursue the rigorous asceticism that Severus

---

[113] Watts, "Student Travel to Intellectual Centers ," 13–23.

[114] *The Life of Severus by Zachariah of Mytilene*, trans. L. Ambjörn, Texts from Christian Late Antiquity, vol. 9 (Piscataway, NJ, 2008), ch. 10, p. 6.

eventually adopted as his lifestyle.[115] So it was in the company of another man, Anastasius from Edessa, "who shared his willingness and was roused to a similar zeal," that Zacharias eventually went into the desert.[116]

A subplot of the *Life of Severus* revolves around the eradication of pagan thought and cults, and mentions another pair, Athanasius and his companion Stephen. They had turned away from their studies at the same time under the spiritual guidance of a certain Salomon: "As through a sign from God, they both received the yoke of true philosophy from the Great Salomon," abbot of the monastic community at Enaton.[117] "Yoke" is the word used for joining a pair of oxen, often applied metaphorically to couples joined in marriage, but also used for monastic pairs. Indeed in the following chapter, the two are referred to as "the holy couple."[118] There is the suggestion that they were united in death as well, when Athanasius is said to have "joined" the divine Stephen.[119]

Hints of a preexisting relationship are also present in some *Sayings of the Desert Fathers*. There is the story of two monks who were wondering what level of perfection they had reached until, led by divine providence, they were shamed by the humility, chastity, and poverty of a simple shepherd. Clearly, these two monks had embarked on their monastic life together and any progress they made in the spiritual life was a joint experience.[120] A similar story is told of Chronios, who left his village, went into the desert, dug himself a well, and built a cell. After a few years, a group of twenty monks had gathered around him. "With him lived [synôkêse] a certain Jacob, who came from the same area, who was called *chôlos*."[121] The same geographical origin of Jacob and Chronios would suggest that their association pre-dated their monastic life. More explicit is the story of *abba* Or, who built a cell together with Theodore, and the report of the two brothers who had met and decided to live together.[122] The evolution from friendship to joint monastic commitment is also attested in the story of the two friends who made an agreement to become monks and live a virtuous life. Even as one of them was later called to become the leader of a *koinobion*, while the other remained an anchorite, their relation retained its strength and continued to be recognized as such by others.[123] How

---

[115] Ibid., ch. 89, p. 92.

[116] Ibid., ch. 96, p. 100.

[117] Ibid., ch. 14, pp. 10–11.

[118] Ibid., ch. 15, p. 12.

[119] Ibid., ch. 44, p. 42.

[120] *AP Alphabetical*: Eucharistos 1, PG 65, 168D–169C. Another instance: Isaac and Abraham live together: Isaac 3, PG 65, 224D–225A.

[121] Palladius, *Historia Lausiaca* 41, 1–2, ed. Bartelink, 226, lines 1–15.

[122] *AP Alphabetical*: Or 1; *AP Alphabetical*: Niketas 1.

[123] *AP* Nau 461.

else would the narrator of this tale know about it and deem it worthy of passing on to posterity?

So far, we have presented stories of the formation of attachments between two men that led to a joint living arrangement in the monastic context. It is easy to imagine these stories as precursors of those that will concern us next, of two disciples serving the same spiritual father.

Co-disciples of the Same *Abba*

It was not uncommon for an elder to have not one, but two disciples. Nor was it rare for a monastic family to be headed not by one, but by two men, who shared this responsibility.

The *Life of Anthony* tells us that he had two younger disciples to assist him, presumably living together at some distance from his cell. Also, Macarius the Egyptian is reported to have had two disciples in his desert abode in Scetis, one who acted as his assistant in handling the stream of miracle-seeking visitors, and another who lived as an ascetic in a nearby hermitage of his own.[124] Near the border to the Sasanian Empire lived Milesius, who also had two disciples.[125] And then there is Daniel of Scetis, whose *Life* describes him as having one disciple, and then adds "together with this disciple lived a brother by the name of Sergios." The association of these two quickly came to an end with the death of Sergios, after which Daniel granted the remaining disciple *parrhêsia* "because he loved him very much." Daniel and his disciple are then depicted as traveling together to visit another holy man, Mark the Fool, in Alexandria. *Parrhesia* means freedom of access and liberty of speech, and by allowing his disciple this privilege, Daniel essentially elevated him from an original father-son or teacher-disciple relationship to one of equality. Prompted by a sentiment of affection, he invited his erstwhile disciple and "son" to become his "brother."[126]

The relation between co-disciples and their spiritual father was not always harmonious. In such cases, the two might decide to depart and establish themselves independently, in effect becoming a monastic pair. Such was the case with Eulalius and Petronius. They ran away from the monastery together, to the great distress of their spiritual father.[127]

Poimen was a very well-known leader of a monastic community that generated its own tradition of teaching, as is evident from the 187 Sayings attributed

---

[124] Palladius, *Historia Lausiaca* 17.3, ed. Bartelink, 70, lines 16–19.

[125] *AP Alphabetical*: Milesius 2.

[126] L. Clugnet, *Revue de l'Orient chrétien* 1900, 60, lines 1–7.

[127] Theodore the Stoudite, *Parva catechesis* 133, ed. Auvray (Paris, 1891), 164, cited in I. Hausherr, *Spiritual Direction in the Early Christian East* (Kalamazoo, MI, 1990): first published in French as *La direction spirituelle en Orient autrefoi*, OCA 144 (Rome, 1955), 62–63.

to him in the *Alphabetical Collection* of the *Sayings of the Desert Fathers*. In this collection, Anub appears as an older biological brother of Poimen, who readily submits to the greater monastic wisdom of his sibling, in a spiritual role reversal.[128] Poimen was no stranger to the waxing and waning of social arrangements within monastic groupings. On one occasion, he was visited by two "brothers" who complained that they lived with someone, presumably an *abba*, but without deriving any spiritual profit from this setup—a potential first step to striking out on their own.[129] And, indeed, this is a situation that Poimen himself may have experienced. An interesting story recounts how Paisios, a (biological?) brother of Poimen, found a bag of coins and said to his brother Anub: "You know that the language of Poimen is very harsh. Let's go and found our own monastery and live there untroubled." Anub first agreed and they departed together. But he then lost the coins on purpose while they were crossing a river, and thus the two returned to their brother.[130] This story suggests that certain funds were required to establish an independent monastic abode, even if only for two people.

A revealing story of two runaway co-disciples is also reported from early sixth-century Syria. Severus, bishop of Antioch, responded to a legal query by John Scholastikos of Bostra as to whether disciplinary action against two monks who had left their monastery fell under the authority of the bishop or the abbot. The two had been admitted to the monastery, presumably together, and had been ordained to the deaconate. "Afterwards, they cleaved to one another and departed from the monastery." The abbot must have been aware of their whereabouts, since "he sent the anathema through a man to them that they should not be together at all and not speak with one another and drink wine"—advice which they flouted the same day. There is no description of the emotional or affective content of their relationship, nor of their spiritual aspirations, only the insinuation that friendly conversation accompanied by alcohol consumption would create ample opportunity for improprieties, probably of a sexual nature.[131]

In some rare cases, a disciple felt compelled to seek approval from an older *abba* for his choice of a monastic partner. This was the hypothetical question posited by a "brother" to an *abba*: "If I go to an *abba* and tell him that I want to live with such-and-such a person, and he knows that this won't be to my benefit, how should he answer without talking badly about the other

---

[128] *AP Alphabetical*: Poimen 108, PG 65, col. 348 D.

[129] *AP Regnault*, 261, Armenian 2.112 (33) A.

[130] *AP Regnault*, Nau 448; see also P. Rousseau, "Blood-Relationships among Early Eastern Saints," *JThS* 23 (1972), 135–44, at 142–43; W. Harmless, "Remembering Poemen Remembering," *Church History: Studies in Christianity and Culture* 69 (2000), 483–518.

[131] A. Vööbus, *The Synodicon in the West Syrian Tradition*, CSCO 367–68, Scriptores syri 161–62 (Louvain, 1975–76), vol. 1, 197–98 (text), vol. 2, 185 (translation). Translation and discussion of this passage in Krueger, "Between Monks," 45–6.

elder?"[132] Ostensibly, this is a *Saying* about the avoidance of false rumors or gossiping, but it offers us a glimpse of the mechanisms that might lead to the establishment of a paired monastic relationship within a large spiritual family. The way the question is phrased creates a hypothetical scenario in which the intended monastic partner is known to the *abba* whose advice is sought.

The different facets of the relationship between two co-disciples of the same *abba* that these examples have revealed invites further scrutiny. If they joined their *abba* at different moments in time, this might create occasion for tensions. If, on the other hand, they had known one another for a long time prior to making the decision to enter the monastic life together, then one would expect their friendship to be redefined in spiritual terms. After sharing the experience of being schooled and tutored in the traditional curriculum of the world, they then may have sought to continue and intensify that experience in a monastic setting under a spiritual father as their new teacher. In the latter case, the initial acceptance by the father of the pair of his new disciples would include not only the usual steps of hair clipping and clothing in a new garment, but also some kind of prayer to seal and sanctify the lateral connection between the two. It is my assumption that the origin of the *adelphopoiesis* ritual lies in the prayers performed by a spiritual father on just such an occasion. Evidence to support this will be offered below.

Living Arrangements

The living arrangements of these paired or coupled monks could vary. Some seem to have lived in the same abode, others had separate dwellings or gardens.[133] But even if paired monks resided under different roofs, they often found occasion to spend time together, either in conversation and prayer at night or during Saturday and Sunday. This was the routine of *abba* Semyas and *abba* Aron, who lived together in the desert, each in his own cell, but visited each other at night for pious conversation.[134] *Abba* Paisios and *abba* Isaiah in Scetis also lived in their own cells, but on Saturdays and Sundays, after going to church, Isaiah stayed in the same cell as Paisios.[135] The *Life of Paisios* tells the story of a further utilitarian attachment that the holy man had formed: his hagiographer John establishes his credentials as an author and eyewitness by explaining that he shared a cell with Paisios at the beginning of the saint's ascetic quest, when they had both been the disciples of *abba* Pambo. "[F]or we were of the same mind and we practiced the same life and diet according to the canon which we received from our spiritual father

---

[132] *AP* Regnault, 76, Nau 476.
[133] *AP* Nau: 343; *AP* Nau 413; *AP* Regnault, 142, Nau 618.
[134] *AP* Regnault, 301, Ethiopic Coll. 13. 52.
[135] *AP* Regnault, 307–08, Ethiopic Coll. 13. 79.

[Pambo], strengthening each other in the faith and striving together for the salvation of our souls."[136] But soon Paisios's extraordinary zeal for asceticism in solitude became so obvious that their relationship reached a crossroads. John thus suggested to his companion that they submit the matter to God in prayer: "Let us entreat God, therefore, to reveal His will to us, and we shall do according to His divine wishes. Either that we should stay here and struggle together in one place, or that we should be separate from one another." After a night spent in prayer, the divine answer was clear: Paisios retreated further into a desert cave while John stayed behind. This separation is reported without the slightest hint of an emotional involvement.[137] The same *Life* also recounts that Paisios near the end of his life sought an association of mutual monastic support with the hermit Paul, a relationship that is described by the same John in much warmer tones: they are called "friends" and known to be "inseparable." Indeed, one died shortly after the other and they found their permanent resting place in the same shrine in a monastery in Pisidia of which John, the author of this story, was also a member.

Ritual Beginnings

Now that the widespread practice of small-group and paired monasticism has been documented, and the different paths that led two men to live the monastic life together have been explored, the next question to ask is whether their relation was confirmed by a ritual, analogous to the acceptance of a disciple by his spiritual father. This could be an act or gesture, such as an oath, a promise, or a prayer. In the sources, a solemn promise or affirmation of commitment is often mentioned in passing, not as a particular point of emphasis. It surfaces with regular frequency in stories of paired monks whose relationship is put under strain, and where a reminder of their mutual commitment is needed. We will encounter many such examples also in the discussion of vicarious penance further below, after one partner in a monastic pair yields to sexual temptation.

A casual remark in the *Spiritual Meadow* informs us that in the monastic community of Theodosios in Palestine, "two brothers were there who had sworn an oath to each other that they would never be separated from each other, either in life or in death."[138] In seventh-century Sinai, John Climacus reports a case of paired monks who mutually agreed to a period of separation because their close association had given rise to rumors of impropriety: "I have

---

[136] John the Little, *Life of Paisios*, included in Nikodemos Hagioreites, *New Eklogion*, and now part of *The Great Synaxaristes of the Orthodox Church*, trans. L. Papadopoulos and G. Lizardos (Jordanville, NY, 1998), 10.

[137] Ibid., 10–11.

[138] John Moschus, *Pratum Spirituale* 97, trans. Wortley, 78–79.

known young men who were bound to each other [*proskeimenous*] in accord with God, but who, to avoid harm to the conscience of others, agreed to avoid each other's company for a time."[139]

A story in the *Sayings of the Desert Fathers* relates how four men "made an agreement" and shook hands on it (the Greek text says that they literally "gave each other their right hands"), "so that, after living in this life with one soul and one mind, they would be united again in Heaven."[140] Three of them were monks, while the fourth acted as their servant. After the death and burial of two of the monks, the servant benefited in a moment of spiritual and physical danger from the prayerful intercession of the elder. After the death of the remaining two, a clairvoyant monk had a vision of all four of them together in the same place. With its cast of characters, this narrative is indicative of the small-group living arrangements of semi-anchoritic monasticism, where the hierarchies between monastic life and servitude are sometimes made explicit and sometimes deliberately elided.

Contractual relationships of mutual support, prompted by a strong calling to the practice of Christian virtue, have their origin in the monastic setting, but could also be practiced by particularly pious lay people. A good illustration is the tale of Eulogios reported in the *Historia Lausiaca*. He was a pious city-dweller, a highly educated man from a privileged background, who "neither wanted to enter into a community, nor seek perfection as a solitary."[141] He finally settled for the unconventional arrangement of becoming the caretaker of a severely disabled man. Their relationship, fraught as it eventually became, was defined by a firm and indissoluble commitment to a lifelong association that ended with their deaths, a few days apart. When Eulogios first set eyes on the disabled man (who remains nameless throughout the story), he "makes a contract [*tithetai diathêkên*]" with God, offering his lifelong service to the man in anticipation of his own eternal salvation. For fifteen years, their secluded life together was amiable and peaceful, until the disabled man began to rebel (*apostasiazein*) against Eulogios, demanding to eat meat and to enjoy the company of others in the marketplace. He drove Eulogios to such despair that the latter came close to abandoning him. It was only the fear of divine retribution that held Eulogios back from breaking his compact with God. "I have given my right hand to God that I would be his caretaker, and that I shall

---

[139] John Climacus, *Scala Paradisi*, PG 88, col. 1065; trans. C. Liubheid and N. Russell, *John Climacus, The Ladder of Divine Ascent* (New York, 1982), 250.

[140] The only published version of this tale (*BHG* 1445g) is a French translation: L. Regnault, *Les sentences des pères du désert. Nouveau recueil: Apophthegmes inédits ou peu connus*, 2nd ed. (Solesmes, 1970), 131. I also consulted the Greek original, a manuscript of the tenth or eleventh century, Paris, Bibliothèque nationale, Coislin 126, fols. 329v–330r, where the relevant sentence reads: *dexias edôken allêlois hina homopsychôs kai homophronôs zêsantes en tô aiôni toutô homou palin en ouranois heurethôsin.*

[141] *Historia Lausiaca* 21.3, ed. Bartelink, 106, lines 21–23. Translation mine.

be saved through him, and he shall be saved through me."[142] In his distress, Eulogios took his unhappy companion to seek the advice of Anthony. The *abba* addressed strong words of admonishment to both of them, demanding that they return together to their monastic abode and await there the completion of their days, which should be imminent. And indeed, Eulogios died forty days later, followed three days later by his disabled companion.[143]

This is an interesting variant of a relation between two men that is based on a compact. Especially noteworthy is the fact that the two had no prior contact. The driving motivator for this relation is not a preexisting personal acquaintance, but Eulogios's desire as a layman to dedicate himself to the practice of charity. All the elements that are characteristic of paired monks are present here: a lifelong commitment that begins with prayers to God, the anticipation of a spiritual reward for both parties, and a joint death which, as we shall see, is part of the phenomenology of these paired relationships. What further makes this relationship unusual is that, as a compact between unequal partners, it is initiated by the able-bodied Eulogios, not by the handicapped man. The true message of this story, then, must be that in terms of outward physical ability, Eulogios may indeed be at an advantage, but in terms of spiritual perfection, he is the one with a need for another on whom to practice his charity. His spiritual interest lies in mastering the challenge of social role reversal when he, as a rich man, becomes the "caretaker," as he calls himself, of a nonfamily member and social outcast. It is remarkable that the narrator of this tale conceptualizes Eulogios's initial commitment in terms of a firm "contract" with God that involved "giving the right hand [to God]." This goes to prove how legal terminology was pervasive in use and flexible in application. "Giving of the right hand" is the equivalent of today's "shaking on it" to seal an agreement, often one that is informal and oral. The joining of right hands was also part of the legal contract of marriage in the Roman tradition.

Also remarkable about this story is that it is located on the outer periphery of the monastic life. Eulogios's desire to lead a pious life and to dedicate himself to good works does not lead him to the gate of a monastery, or to the dwelling of a spiritual father, but out into the streets of his city. His was not an isolated case. There are similar stories of laymen who seem to have paired off in their pursuit of a pious life, even if this was not accompanied by withdrawal from the world. Such relationships are reported, although rarely, among laymen both in Egypt and in Syria. Some pious travelers to Egypt, for example, observed that: "Two elders living in the world received us as their guests in the church on their property," which was located on an estate six miles from Rossos.[144]

---

[142] *dexias edōka*, line 89, cf. line 50.

[143] *Historia Lausiaca* 21.2–14, ed. Bartelink, 106, line 15, to 114, line 116. Translations mine.

[144] *Pratum Spirituale* 87, trans. Wortley, 70.

For Syria, John of Ephesus's account of biographical anecdotes of holy men, his *Lives of the Eastern Saints*, includes a segment on Theodore, who held high office at the court of Justinian, but nonetheless pursued a life of poverty and asceticism "with another brother of his whose name was John, so that they were both chamberlains of the king, while living in fasting and constant prayers, and sorrow and tears and works of charity." While he lived in the capital, Theodore's generosity to the poor and needy was so extensive that even the author of this story himself had benefited from it. Near the end of his life, Theodore retreated to the estate where his model and teacher Mishael, a skeptic of Justinian's neo-Chalcedonian imperial politics, had lived. Upon his death, he was buried in the same tomb as Mishael, while his brother John continued to live on for a number of years.[145]

The Institutionalization of Paired Monasticism

Although it is first attested in Egypt, small-group and paired monasticism also existed in Palestine and Syria from the fifth century onwards. The sources for these regions often follow the life of a monastic establishment over several generations. They show that monastic pairs were a regular feature that surfaced again and again in the history of a monastic institution.

Palestinian monasticism became prominent in the Judaean Desert and is best known to us through the sequence of biographies composed by Cyril of Scythopolis in the mid-sixth century. The founding figure who assembled a loose confederation of hermits and cenobitic monks was Sabas. He had been trained by Euthymios, and then lived variously as a hermit or in association with a series of existing monastic communities, until he himself began to attract disciples of his own.[146] One of his disciples was an Armenian by the name of Jeremias, who arrived with two disciples of his own, Peter and Paul. These two were held in such esteem that Sabas allocated them the cave where he himself had lived in an earlier phase of his life.[147]

Later, Sabas also founded a *koinobion* whose leadership was held jointly by more than one person—the famous Monastery of Mar Saba that is still active today, although difficult of access, as it is located on the West Bank and does not permit female visitors. Sabas's first appointment went to Paul, an older experienced anchorite, together with the latter's disciple Theodore, who was in charge of the administration. After Paul's death, Theodore took his

[145] John of Ephesus, *Lives of the Eastern Saints*, ed. E. W. Brooks, PO 17, 18, 19 (Paris, 1923–26), ch. 57, p. 200 (546)–206 (552).

[146] For background see, J. Patrich, *Sabas, Leader of Palestinian Monasticism: A Comparative Study in Eastern Monasticism, Fourth to Seventh Centuries* (Washington, DC, 1995).

[147] Cyril of Scythopolis, *Life of Sabas*, ch. 20, ed. E. Schwartz, *Kyrillos von Skythopolis*, TU 49, no. 2 (Leipzig, 1939), 105, trans. R. M. Price, *Cyril of Scythopolis, Lives of the Monks of Palestine*, Cistercian Studies 114 (Kalamazoo, 1991), 114.

position and selected two of his kin as administrators, his brother Sergius and his uncle Paul.[148] In this manner, the setup of the founding fathers of this institution represents an interesting combination of spiritual and biological kin.

Sabas himself cultivated a close association with Theodosius, who would later become his successor. This Theodosius belonged to the third generation of monks in this area, having received his training from two men, Marinus and Luke, who themselves had been disciples of the great Euthymius. If Sabas's community was the spiritual athletes' arena, Theodosius's establishment was the training ground where young novices received their first formation. Although Sabas and Theodosius did not share living arrangements, their relationship is described in the terms of ancient friendship, reinterpreted within a Christian framework: "For they were one in soul and one in mind, breathing each other more than the air, so that the people of Jerusalem called their godly concord and unity a new apostolic pairing of Peter and John."[149] The word employed here is the already familiar expression of a yoke-pair (zygê), which is regularly used for marital couples. Their responsibilities were distinct, but complementary: Theodosius was in charge of the cenobitic establishments, while Sabas was responsible for the anchorites and those who lived in cells.[150]

An entire chapter in the *Life of Sabas* is devoted to praising their harmonious and mutually supportive association. Sabas "maintained the most unfeigned and sincere love [agapên anhypokriton kai gnêsiotatên] toward the above-mentioned *abba* Theodosius, while he in his turn maintained the same sincerity towards our father Sabas."[151] These are the same words that are used in the ritual prayers for *adelphopoiesis*: unfeigned or "without suspicion"— further proof that the ritual was inspired by monastic relationships. Their close association did not go unnoticed by the monks around them, including those who later shared their memories of Sabas with the hagiographer Cyril of Scythopolis: "They could be seen visiting each other and conversing together frankly with spiritual affection."[152] Although we are not informed about a formalization of the association between Sabas and Theodosius, in the eyes of their contemporaries they formed a pair and their relation found expression in frequent visits and conversations distinguished by frankness of speech (parrhêsia). These features will later become recognizable in the application of *adelphopoiesis* between laymen, the most famous instance being the emperor Basil I, who granted freedom of access and *parrhêsia* to his "spiritual brother" John, the son of Danelis.

---

[148] Ibid., ch. 27, ed. Schwartz, 112, trans. Price, 121.

[149] Ibid., ch. 29, ed. Schwartz, 114, trans. Price, 123. The pairing of the apostles Peter and John is unusual. The prayers for *adelphopoiesis* have Peter joined either with Andrew, or with Paul.

[150] Ibid., ch. 56, ed. Schwartz, 151, trans. Price, 161.

[151] Ibid., ch. 65, ed. Schwartz, 166, trans. Price, 175.

[152] Ibid., ch. 65, ed. Schwartz, 166, trans. Price, 176.

More evidence for monastic pairings in several generations comes from late antique Syria—the region where, according to Jerome, the detestable "third kind of monks" that represented the semi-eremitic life were most frequent. The *Life of Symeon the Stylite* (d. 459) shows how common it was for two monks to be in a close lifelong relationship that was described in terms of the language of close friendship. Long before taking up residence on top of a pillar near Antioch, Symeon the Stylite began his monastic career in a community that had originally been founded by Ammianus and Eusebius, and which spawned a second establishment headed by Eusebonas and Abibion, who had been disciples together in the first monastery. Their relation is characterized as "one soul in two bodies."[153] With Symeon spending most of his life alone atop a pillar, monastic brotherhood bonds jumped one generation and resurfaced in the next: the Syriac *Life of Symeon the Stylite* describes how Symeon, when he felt his death approaching, called the two disciples whom he designated as leaders of the community. "He grasped those two by their hands and gave charge to them about each other, that they love one another. He also set them over their companions."[154] The prayers that were pronounced in such a context, informally at first, but perhaps at a certain point repeated often enough to become customary, must be the origin of the prayer for *adelphopoiesis* as it is preserved in the Byzantine *euchologia*.

The story leaves open whether these two disciples of the famous stylite had been closely associated prior to this moment or whether it was Symeon's dying wish that turned them into a pair. But it offers an important indication of an *abba*'s prayer to bless and consecrate an association of two monks. The presence of three monastic pairs in four generations of a monastic family shows that the pattern that we first encountered in fourth- and fifth-century Egypt was common in other regions of Byzantium as well and continued to be important in subsequent centuries. Bridging the two locations, Palestine and Syria, is the remarkable story of Symeon the Fool and his companion John, which will receive more detailed treatment in chapter 4.

D. Temptations and Challenges

The crucial difference between biological brotherhood and spiritual brotherhood lies in their emotional economy. While siblings are expected to be

---

[153] Theodoret of Cyrhus, *Historia Religiosa* 26.4.

[154] They are then appointed superiors over the community of monks that had gathered around Symeon. Although the dying man's blessing could conceivably be interpreted as being rather pragmatic, in preempting any divisions within the community, the insistence on "love" and related terms is significant. Similar vocabulary is employed in the *adelphopoiesis* ritual. For the entire history of Symeon and his early cult, see D. Boero, "Symeon and the Making of a Stylite," PhD diss., University of Southern California, 2015.

mutually supportive of one another, in reality they may often be in competition or disagreement. Spiritual brotherhood is a different matter, especially when two men come to the joint decision to live together as monks, whatever the origin of their association may have been.

Living in close proximity, mastering together the challenges of nature, sharing in worship—these situations would be conducive to the development of affective bonds, if they had not existed prior to the relation or indeed prompted it. Such attachment would be intensified when the two lived under the same roof and shared a daily rhythm of worship, working, eating, and sleeping. Our texts do not dwell on this aspect of monastic living at close quarters, unless something is amiss. It is only then that we hear of the dangers that such proximity could present, either to the body or—more importantly—to the soul. If we read these scattered episodes against the grain, we can detect the intensity of emotional involvement and personal attachment that some of these brothers must have experienced. And we can appreciate the firm commitment that existed between the two partners that had sometimes been affirmed by a promise or an oath. These moments of crisis, when the unity and tranquility of a monastic pair were threatened, throw into high relief the stuff that these relations are made of.

In one simple story, two monks were observed in a bloody physical altercation. When asked to intervene, *abba* Poimen simply responded: "They are brothers—they will make peace again."[155] This is, of course, the expectation that prompts the identification of close paired relations with biological brotherhood in the first place. But the reality of monastic living posed its own challenges and created tensions. The chapter "On Friendship" in John Cassian's *Conferences* is in fact largely devoted to this issue, as *abba* Joseph of Thmuis shares his advice and experience with Cassian and his monastic companion, Germanus. The relationships he describes are exactly like those we have encountered in the material from Egypt, including the binding nature of their commitment. In this passage, Cassian frequently puts the word "contract" (*foedus*) into *abba* Joseph's mouth.

> But we have known many set on this purpose, who though they had been joined together in companionship [*sodalitatem deuincti*] out of their burning love for Christ, yet could not maintain it continually and unbrokenly, because although they relied on a good beginning for their friendship, yet they did not with one and the same zeal maintain the purpose on which they had entered, and so there was between them a sort of love only for a while, for it was not maintained by the goodness of both alike, but by the patience of the one party, and so although it is

---

[155] *AP Alphabetical*: Poimen 173, PG 65, 361B–C.

held to by the one with unwearied heroism, yet it is sure to be broken by the pettiness of the other.[156]

The greatest dangers, *Abba* Joseph explained, are a lack of detachment from possessions or from the self, which finds an outlet in willfulness, anger, haughtiness, and competition.

At the conclusion of the conversation, *abba* Joseph repeated his warning against relationships that begin with ardent oaths of friendship, either out of worldly love or out of need and necessity, but that soon result in an imbalance and hierarchies that create resentment.[157] The wise *abba* seems to have been well aware that monastic pairings might have their origin in a multitude of overlapping motivations, personal love or the expectation of material gain not least among them.

First, there is the expectation of one partner that the other should behave in exactly predictable and consistent ways. One monk would closely observe the other's conduct, try to anticipate or control his movements, and then might easily succumb to sentiments of jealousy. One question put to an *abba* was: "If one lives with a brother and one sees someone talking to him, one becomes troubled, thinking: 'Why do you want to speak with others?' "[158] Here, the questioning monk assumes that the pair should be self-sufficient and their relationship exclusive of others. Furthermore, a monk who developed an affection (*schesis*) for a third monk would also spend a lot of time coming and going out of the abode he shared with his monastic partner, which the latter might find disruptive.[159]

Next, there is the concern about maintaining *homonoia*, unity of mind and spirit, which would be threatened by bickering and minor disagreements over matters of everyday life. One story reports how a monastic pair were the victims of a raid by Saracens. Utterly destitute, they roamed the desert in search of something edible. Sisoes managed to find two grains of barley in a heap of camel dung. His brother observed him putting something in his mouth and complained: "Is this your love [*agapê*], that you find something to eat, and don't call me?" Of course, Sisoes had carefully guarded the other grain in his hand to give to his brother.[160] Situations of disagreement or simply fatigue over sharing the same life were not uncommon. A story in the *Sayings of the Desert Fathers* describes two "brothers" of different age who came to an *abba*, apparently for the sole purpose of seeking his advice on their predicament. The older complained about the younger one, but the *abba* led them to

---

[156] John Cassian, *Conferences* 16. 3, ed. M. Petschenig, CSEL 13 (Vienna, 1886), 440–41. Trans. E. C. S. Gibson, consulted at http://www.osb.org/lectio/cassian/conf/book2/conf16.html#16.1.

[157] John Cassian, *Conferences* 16. 28, ed. Petschenig, 462.

[158] Nau 427.

[159] *AP* Poimen 2, PG 65, col. 317 B.

[160] *AP* Sisoes 31, PG 65, 401C–D.

reconciliation.[161] The ordeal of sharing living quarters, whether as "brothers" or as teacher and disciple, must have been so substantial that one brother posed the question to *abba* Poimen: "How can a man live in peace with the brother who shares his habitation?"[162]

The same problems of incompatibility of character or complaints about annoying habits occurred also between teachers and disciples, who—depending on the viewer's perspective—might also appear as a pair. Paul of Cappadocia, for instance, had fled from the Persian invasions to Constantinople, and from there to Nitria, where he "shares accommodation with an elder." After living with the elder for a year and three months, he went to the "*hegoumenos* of the mountain [of Nitria]" to complain that the elder did not observe very strict asceticism and did not allow him to chant the usual psalms. The terse response of the *hegoumenos* was to tell him to stick it out.[163] Not only were disciples annoyed at their *abba*; sometimes the elder found his disciple's habits hard to bear. Even trivial matters, such as a young man's thoughtlessness in placing his feet on the table while eating, could become a cause of annoyance.[164]

The antidote to disagreement and to willfulness is the virtue of humility: two "brothers" decided to live together, each determined to subject himself to the other's will. But after many years, the devil managed to get them to quarrel over the appearance of a bird. One thought he had seen a dove, the other insisted that it was a crow. But after spending three days apart, they came to their senses again, agreed that they had seen an animal with wings, asked for each other's forgiveness and lived happily ever after.[165]

Negative emotions such as jealousy and annoyance may have been the cause of potential friction, but could also become an occasion to demonstrate love, support, or humility. A lovely example is the story of two "brothers" engaged in handiwork. The tool of one brother broke, while the other's remained intact. In order to prevent his brother from succumbing to anger derived from competitiveness, the other brother now also broke his own tool.[166] Other stories report how a monk turned a deaf ear to his brother's tendency to gossip, in order to bring him to compunction.[167]

Disagreements between brothers, whether biological or monastic, were sometimes of such severity and duration that they were taken to the grave. In such cases, posthumous reconciliation could be achieved only with great difficulty, with the intervention of a pious intermediary who would provide the

---

[161] *AP* Regnault, 151–52, Nau 638.
[162] *AP* Regnault, 312–13, Ethiopic Coll. 14. 2.
[163] *AP* Regnault, 176–77, Paul Evergetinos II 19.5.
[164] *AP* Regnault, 229–30, Butler, *Paradise* II 64.
[165] *AP Alphabetical*: Niketas 1, PG 65, 312B–C.
[166] *AP* Regnault, 189, Paul Evergetinos III 39, 5–6.
[167] *AP* Regnault, 260, Armenian II 76 (3) A.

certainty that the deceased no longer held a grudge against the living partner.[168] One story is interesting in its application of the language of affection, even within an urban setting and between clergy of different rank. A presbyter and a deacon were of one accord and held great love of divine origin for one another, but the presbyter died while the deacon still held a grudge against him. The deacon was finally released from his bad conscience by visiting a pious *chartophylax* in Constantinople who allowed him a vision of Heaven (which looks like the imperial chancery) that included the priest so that the two were able reconcile.[169]

Mutual suspicion after long years of cohabitation could also be expressed in sexual terms, when one partner's straying from the ascetic purpose was interpreted by the other as an act of alienation, with the same emotional effect as infidelity. We will encounter more such stories in the context of penitential assistance below. A curious story that deserves to be mentioned here is preserved in the Georgian hagiographical tradition, known as the *Life of Stepanes and Nikon*, although the original version may well have been composed in Greek. It is full of commonplaces and exaggerations, and thus should not be read as a historical document, but the message it conveys remains relevant: the relationship of two men who agreed to pursue the monastic life together was prone to tensions even after many decades.

Nikon is said to have come from "the great city of Rome," perhaps meaning Constantinople. He met Stepanes while they were both on pilgrimage to Jerusalem and shared the same accommodation for a whole month. They agreed to move to the desert together, where they lived in separate cells, but in close proximity. Only during Easter did they open their doors, and thus it happened that after forty-seven years of tranquil existence, as Stepanes was reading the *Life of Anthony,* Nikon perceived that he was tempted by a woman, while Stepanes had the same impression of Nikon. Outraged, they seized upon each other and began a fight—perhaps the only physical contact they had had in decades? Stepanes fled in outrage and sought adjudication from the monastic fathers in Egypt as well as Athanasius of Alexandria. Eventually, Stepanes submitted himself to a trial by fire to prove the truth of his accusation. When he remained unscathed, Nikon joined him in the fire to prove his own innocence. The story ends in ambiguity regarding the guilt of one or the other of the partners, but on a conciliatory note, with the image of both of them resisting the flames of sinful desire together, and the hagiographical happy end of a shared death three days later.[170]

---

[168] H. Delehaye, "Un groupe de récits 'utiles à l'âme,'" *Annuaire de l'Institut de philologie et d'histoire orientales* 2 (1934 = Mélanges Bidez), 255–66. A similar story is reported by Paul of Monembasia, *BHG* 1318y (trans. Wortley, 156–60).

[169] F. Halkin, "Un diacre réconcilié avec son ami défunt (*BHG* 1322d)," *RSBN* n.s. 26 (1989), 197–202.

[170] I am grateful to Bernard Outtier for bringing this story to my attention and for sharing his unpublished English translation with me. The story existed in a Greek version, but is now extant

Sexual temptations are one way of expressing the danger of emotional estrangement or deviation from the shared purpose of monastic living. At the same time, temptations of the flesh are often depicted as obstacles that can be surmounted through a joint effort of the two men. They become tests of loyalty and of mutual support. When successfully mastered, they are extolled in tales of strengthened commitment that usually conclude with a harmonious, often synchronized death and joint burial, as the next chapter will show. But first, it is necessary to address the issue of male-male attraction within the context of paired monasticism.

The Ambiguity of Male-Male Attraction

Competition, anger, and nagging grudges were the negative consequences of living together, following the daily rhythms of life in unison, sharing meals, and perhaps sleeping under the same roof. On the positive side, emotional attachment and affection might eventually result from the pairing, if it had not already been the cause of it. This brings us to the vast gray zone of male-male attraction, where homosociability may easily find articulation in homoeroticism and lead to male-male sexual activity. It is only the latter that is castigated by Christian authors, often to the extent that they aim to establish a *cordon sanitaire* around it in order to quell its causes by extensive and detailed prohibitions of the former. Recent studies by Rebecca Krawiec, Albrecht Diem, David Brakke, Caroline Schroeder, Cristian Gaspar, and Derek Krueger have greatly contributed to our understanding of the sexual desire of men and women in the monastic contexts of Late Antiquity, from Egypt to Gaul, how it was experienced and articulated, and how monastic leaders attempted to control it by one of three means: first, through general advice, personal admonition, and punishment; second, by the enforcement of avoidance of physical contact between monastics in the course of the movements of daily life; or, third, through the elimination of external opportunities by claustration from the outside world.[171]

Since brotherhood language was also used as code for sexual relationships, the possibility of sexual relations can never be excluded. The ambiguity

only in an Arabic translation from the year 902 (ms. Sinai Arabic NF 66), as well as two Georgian versions from the tenth and eleventh centuries, respectively.

[171] R. Krawiec, *Shenoute and the Women of the White Monastery: Egyptian Monasticism in Late Antiquity* (Oxford, 2002); A. Diem, *Das monastische Experiment: Die Rolle der Keuschheit bei der Entstehung des westlichen Klosterwesens* (Münster, 2005); D. Brakke, *Demons and the Making of the Monk: Spiritual Combat in Early Christianity* (Cambridge, MA, 2006); C. T. Schroeder, *Monastic Bodies: Discipline and Salvation in Shenoute of Atripe* (Philadelphia, PA, 2007); C. Gaspar, "'The Spirit of Fornication, whom the Children of the Hellenes Used to Call Eros': Male Homoeroticism and the Rhetoric of Christianity in the Letters of Nilus of Ancyra," in *Chastity: A Study in Perception, Ideals, Opposition*, ed. N. van Deusen, 151–83 (Leiden and Boston, 2008), with extensive bibliography; Krueger, "Between Monks."

of language always permits multiple interpretations, depending on context. The *Regula Isaiae abbatis* of the fifth century, an Arabic text (probably based on a Greek or Coptic original) that was translated into Latin in the seventeenth century, prohibited monks from sharing a meal with women, entering *fraternitas* (whatever that is supposed to mean) with a boy, sleeping with an adolescent young man under the same blanket, and looking at their own naked body.[172] A council of bishops in Tours in 567 was anxious to preempt suspicions about sexual improprieties in monasteries through a series of measures: no priest or monk was allowed to receive another man in his bed, and monks were prohibited from sharing cells where two of them could be together or deposit private belongings.[173] Male-male associations could not only pose dangers to those involved, but also affect suspicious observers, in a process that modern psychology would perhaps recognize as "transference," the projection of one's own fears and anxieties onto another person. In one story reported in the *Systematic Collection* of the *Sayings of the Desert Fathers*, which has a separate section on "Lust," a man "attacked by a demon" accused two men who were living in close association of sleeping together (i.e., having sex), until he was reprimanded by a wise *abba*.[174]

In some instances, our sources are quite explicit about the attraction of male beauty, carnal longings, and sexual contact, whether they occur between men of the same age or between an older and a younger man. There is the enigmatic story of "two brothers" who have to flee from the monastic settlement in Scetis "because the enemies are chasing them." God must have been on their side, however, since they were miraculously able to cross a river on foot.[175] But the cause of their flight, as well as the nature of their relationship, remains obscure. Could it be that the larger monastic community looked askance at their association? Indeed, in at least one story, two brothers were accused of cohabiting, presumably in the carnal sense, but then cleared of suspicion.[176] In a similar story, two brothers were given a penance for something they were suspected of doing, and accepted the punishment with great humility, even though they had been wrongly accused.[177]

In comparison to the love between fathers and sons, which is devoid of any physical aspect, the love between brothers was treated with suspicion, in a letter by Barsanuphius and John: "The father's love for his children is

---

[172] *Regula Isaiae abbatis*, ch. 1, PL 103, col. 429 A. See also Diem, *Monastische Experiment*, 42–43.

[173] Council of Tours (567), CCSL 148 A, col. 15, p. 181. On the significance of the introduction of communal dormitories in Western monasteries, see A. Diem, "Organisierte Keuschheit. Sexualprävention im Mönchtum der Spätantike und des frühen Mittelalters," *Invertito* 3 (2001), 8–37, http://www.invertito.de/en/annual/invo3_o2en.html.

[174] Nau 181, trans. Ward, *Wisdom*, no. 49, 15–16.

[175] *AP* Regnault, 295, Ethiopic Coll. 13. 35.

[176] *AP Systematic* 5.33= Nau 181.

[177] *AP Alphabetical*: Macarius 21, PG 65, col. 269D–272A.

one thing, the brother's love for his brothers another. The spiritual father's love for his children is not at all carnal or harmful, for he is secure in his spirituality and, by either deeds or words, he is always attentive to the young, whatever their needs may be."[178] Youth was a particularly dangerous time of life for either experiencing sexual desires or causing them in others—both of which ought to be avoided within a monastic context. An elder thus gave the following advice: "Do not sleep on the same mat, while you are young, with anyone, except with your brother or your *synabba* (the one who is an *abba* with you)."[179]

In a story that confirms the ubiquity of domestic arrangements *à deux* between father and disciple and attests to the need to seek another person's blessing for such an undertaking, *abba* Makarios dispensed unveiled advice. The occasion was the visit by an old man with a younger "brother," who declared to him: "We wish to live together as one, our father." This may well have been a request to receive the permission and blessing of Makarios, who was renowned as one of the great ascetic leaders of his time. In his response, he reminded them of the different roles they played according to their age and seniority. The older man was admonished to "Act first like a shepherd. If an ox-fly infects a sheep with worms, the shepherd treats it until he has killed the worms. If the sheep begins festering with worms, he rinses it until the infestation is removed." Makarios then explained that the ox-fly signifies the devil, the sheep the companion brother who is with you. "The worms are the passions and the pleasures of the demons who live in the soul, that swarm about in the heart, like the worms who are in the wounds of the body. The remedy that cleanses the wound that is festering with worms, is progress, abstinence, and the salutary teaching of God. These are the things that purify the soul, render it clean from any passion and of all evil of the bad enemies, the demons." The sheep metaphor is significant. While Makarios encouraged the older man to act like a shepherd, he invited the younger to assume the role of a sacrificial lamb: "Act like Isaac, who obeyed his father to the point of making a sacrifice that is agreeable to God." The identification of the younger man as the "sheep" that is attacked by demons, seems to suggest that the older man has a responsibility for the cleanliness and purity of his younger companion.[180]

Paired monks attracted a certain amount of attention in monastic and hagiographical writing, as the stories throughout this chapter show. This is not mere curiosity, even less salacious interest. Their joint life is treated

---

[178] Barsanuphius and John, *Ep.* 342.
[179] *AP Systematic* 5.53.
[180] *Vertus de Saint Macaire*, ed. Amélineau, *Histoire*, 155–56; trans. Vivian, *Saint Macarius*, 113–14.

as a form of monastic cohabitation that is perfectly legitimate, normal, and accepted within the spectrum of living arrangements available to ascetics and monks. The most extreme form of ascetic living was that of the grazers or gyrovagues, men and very occasionally women who roamed the desert and shunned all human contact. They neither engaged in any kind of productive labor nor interacted with disciples or visitors. They had neither disciples nor pious visitors to promote their fame during their lifetime. In hagiographical stories, they are discovered shortly before or after their death by a chance traveler who marvels at the sight of their emaciated naked body and their ability to adapt to nature in such a radical way. Even within this setting, whether real or imagined, paired monks make their appearance.

The remoteness of the location, the fact that the protagonists are unobserved by others and thus free to follow their own inclinations, lends to some of these stories a certain touch of romantic hyperreality.[181] They depict monastic pairs in a paradisiacal setting, in prelapsarian nakedness and perfect innocence where sexual temptation has no place. The narrator himself is allowed only a brief glimpse of this idealized state of being, and that only after he has put some distance between himself and the world through travel, while the audience is treated to these refractured stories of male intimacy as if glimpsing down a telescope, depending on the narrator for explanations.

In one story, Makarios, whom we encountered earlier as the spiritual father of the Roman Brothers, is said to have encountered such a pair on an island in a lake in the middle of the desert, where wild animals came to drink. They explained that one of them was from Egypt, the other from Libya, that they had met in the same monastery and then came to an agreement to pursue this particular way of life together, which they had now maintained for forty years.[182] The *Spiritual Meadow* of the early seventh century tells the story of two naked anchorites who paid a surprise visit to a church on Mount Sinai.[183] This story isolates the motif of nakedness, while the previous story combines this motif with that of a hidden paradise where man and beast live in perfect harmony with nature.[184]

The practice of two monks living together as a recognized pair seems to have been such a common phenomenon by the sixth century that it became the hook for novelistic treatment in hagiography. In this regard, it is interesting

---

[181] On such narratives within the larger framework of male-male companionship and desire, see also Krueger, "Between Monks."

[182] *Apophthegmes sur Saint Macaire*, ed. Amélineau, *Histoire*, 218, trans. Vivian, *Saint Macarius*, 66–67, with ref. to *AP Alphabetic*: Macarius 2, trans. Ward, 125–6; *AP Systematic*: 20.4.

[183] *Pratum Spirituale* 122, trans. Wortley, 99–100.

[184] Such hidden paradise is not exclusive to Christian monks. Two Egyptian magicians, Jannes and Jambres, also created a paradise garden that is accidentally discovered: *Historia Monachorum* 21.5–8, ed. Schulz-Flügel, 369–70, trans. Russell, 108–09.

to follow the development of the story of Andronikos and Athanasia that was first developed at that time.

Both from prosperous families in Antioch, they married to please their parents, and after the birth of their two children decided to live a "chaste marriage" and to dedicate themselves to works of charity. After the death of both children, Athanasia was overcome first by grief, then by the desire to pursue a strict monastic life. Both spouses left for Egypt, where Andronikos became a disciple of Daniel of Scetis, whom we encountered above, after entrusting his wife to a group of elderly virgins in Tabennisi. After many years, they met again as they were both traveling to Jerusalem. Athanasia recognized her husband, but due to her emaciated ascetic appearance was not recognized by him. Now their relationship advanced through the usual stages of monastic companionship: initially travel companions for practical reasons, they shared the pilgrimage experience to Jerusalem. This led to an agreement to continue to live together as cell mates, but only after the prayer of blessing from *Abba* Daniel had been obtained. Prior to death, "Athanasios" (as she now appeared to her husband-companion) promised his companion that they would soon be reunited in Heaven. After her death and the revelation of her true identity thanks to a written declaration she had left under her pillow, her husband behaved in the true manner of a monastic companion: he refused to leave the abode where they had lived together and died not much later. The ambiguity of their relation is brought to the fore in the concluding struggle over Andronikos's burial place: some of his fellow monks claimed his body for their community in Scetis, others were ready to honor his primary commitment to his companion of many years and wished to bury him next to Athanasia.[185]

This tale is remarkable for its approximation of chaste marriage and monastic coupledom, here packaged within the romance-like tale of reunited lovers. The premise works only because of the emphatic exclusion of any sexual element in the relationship between the two protagonists. The message of this tale seems clear: life as a monastic pair is to be considered far superior to marriage. Both are based on a mutual agreement to share house and hearth, but only within the framework of Christian asceticism can both partners fulfill their true calling to live a life of mutual spiritual support. The best advertisement for chaste marriage seems to be the model of monastic pairs.

---

[185] This story is told in the cycle of narratives around Daniel of Sketis, ed. B. Dahlman, *Saint Daniel of Sketis: A Group of Hagiographic Texts* (Uppsala, 2007), 166–79. These date from the sixth century. Several centuries later, this story is embroidered. This version (*BHG* 123a) is edited by A. Alwis, *Celibate Marriages in Late Antique and Byzantine Hagiography: The Lives of Saints Julian and Basilissa, Andronikos and Athanasia, and Galaktion and Episteme* (London and New York, 2011), 249–77.

In two particularly curious stories, paired monasticism was a kind of happy end to a relation that had its beginning in the world. The first is set in sixth-century Edessa and involves a priest and a construction worker; the second takes place in Egypt and involves a hermit and a pimp. In both stories, the established social phenomenon of paired monasticism allows the narrators to play with appearance, disguise, and reality.

Some time in the early fifth century, a unique association between two ascetically inclined men in Syria is reported. The earliest extant manuscripts of the Syriac version of this text date from the sixth century, and it is not clear whether an original Greek version preceded it. In any case, *The History of the Great Deeds of Bishop Paul of Qentos and Priest John of Edessa* takes us to the ascetic milieu of the city of Edessa in the bicultural zone between Greek and Syriac. This is a curious text on many accounts. In a noticeable departure from hagiographic convention, the title mentions not one but two protagonists. And the text seems to fizzle out at the end, with the disappearance of Paul and the briefest of mentions of the death of John, but without the customary mention of posthumous miracles. The story it tells is no less unusual, in that it pairs two men of different ascetic lifestyles and inclination, whereas usually the obligation to mutual support between two men presupposes that they intend to act in synchrony in pursuing the same rhythms of life.

These two were even of different social background. Their acquaintance begins when John, a pious man who had been ordained to the priesthood, hired Paul, a day laborer who had escaped from the burdens of his previous life as a bishop of "Qentos" in Italy (an unknown toponym), for some work on his house. John invited him to share his table and found ways to extend the labor contract, in the secret hope that this might lead to a permanent association: "Even if by these means, I will make him acquainted with me and he will become a brother to me forever."[186] Perhaps he had already discovered his attraction to Paul? One evening, John began to stalk Paul as the latter went up to pray at a mountainside cave a short distance from the city. This cave holds a special role in the narrative. It is a mysterious place where pretenses no longer exist and truths become known. It is also a place that instilled fear at first, in the form of visions of poisonous creepy animals and ferocious beasts of prey. Eventually, it offered a refuge and a second home to the two, as they became acquainted with a small group of men who lived there. Here, John and Paul experienced the freedom from the city below and received divine approval from above that allowed them to enter into a close and lifelong relationship that extended beyond death. They recognized the hidden spiritual qualifications of each other, that Paul was really a bishop and that John had the power

---

[186] *The History of the Great Deeds of Bishop Paul of Qentos and Priest John of Edessa*, trans. H. Arneson et al., Texts from Christian Late Antiquity 29 (Piscataway, NJ, 2010), ch. 10, p. 36.

of prayer and was well known among the group of twelve other men who lived in the cave. Could this be a community of likeminded men who preferred each other's company to the ties of social obligations including the expectation of married life that prevailed in the city below? This curious group is never called anything else but "blessed men."

The joy of Paul and John after this first visit to the cave was palpable, as their life now took a different direction: "So they praised and glorified God, and they went down from there, requesting oaths from one another that these secrets would not be uttered in the world until one of them was separated from the other, either by death or by departure from that place. Blessed John asked blessed Paul to live with him, but Paul was not to be persuaded. Instead, he said to him: 'When you permit me to attend to my former ways, I will be your beloved.' "[187] They then agreed on the terms of their relationship. John suggested that Paul would continue in his work as a day laborer, but return to John's house in the evening, unless they both preferred to spend the night in the mysterious cave or in prayer in the church. Paul's plan was different. It provided for an alternation between the winter months "with the blessed men in the cave," and the summer months when he "would return to his previous ways," so that, after receiving the approval of Bishop Rabbula (a well-known historical figure associated also with a famous illuminated manuscript now in the British Library), "John could accommodate Paul's wish in every way."[188]

In the visible social hierarchy of Edessa, Paul may have been inferior, but in the internal emotional dynamics of the relationship with John, he definitely had the upper hand. This becomes clear when the two of them returned from a long journey to Mount Sinai, only to find merely five of the cave companions still alive. John made his wishes clear: "My brother Paul, from now on I will never leave you. If you want to come to my house, then come. If you want for us to go up to the blessed men, then let us go up." Paul, however, insisted on continuing in his daily labor. At this emotional moment, the narrative changes to a first-person account in the voice of John: "In order not to lose him and be deprived of his companionship, I let him proceed as he wanted. This became his practice."[189] Soon, Paul became known in the city for his miraculous abilities and fled his new-found prominence by secretly escaping to the city of Nisibis. Like the cave, this is a liminal place, described as "Nisibis of the border region" and "Nisibis, which is in the borderlands between the Persians and the Romans."[190] The topical ambiguity functions as a mirror for

---

[187] Ibid., chs. 18–19, p. 44. Does this erotically charged language contain a *double entendre* to the passive role of the *erômenos* during male-male intercourse?

[188] Ibid., chs. 19–20, p. 46.

[189] Ibid., ch. 36, p. 68.

[190] Ibid., chs. 42–43, p. 76.

the ambiguity, uncertainty, and inherent element of danger in their relationship. In great distress, John went in search of his companion, wandering far and wide for six months until he reached Nisibis. When he finally set eyes on him, Paul was on a ladder, carrying a vessel of water. He shouted up to him, but although Paul recognized him, he did not slow his step, but climbed even higher, put down his vessel, and then disappeared from sight without a further trace. "No one ever heard anything about him again."[191] By now, the narrative has returned to the third person. John is suffering unspeakable "sadness and distress," and barely has the energy to seek shelter among the poor in a church-operated hospice. During the night, Paul appears to him in a dream, insisting as he had done throughout on setting his own terms: "My brother, John! Do not trouble yourself to seek me, because you will not again see my face in this bodily life. I will not give up the very reason why I left my city only to give you peace. So, stand up, go home, and go up to stay with the blessed men in the cave, and await God's deliverance with them. For we will shortly depart from this world, and in the company of our Lord we will forever rejoice with one another."[192] John followed Paul's instructions and died after spending eight months with the men in the cave. The narration ends with a glorification of John's deeds, but no further mention is made of Paul until the last sentence: "The history of the great deeds and the noble conduct of the saints, bishop Paul and priest John, has come to an end."[193] This is a strange tale of one-sided emotional attachment, secrets that are shared and mutual promises that are broken, the evocation of a muscular male body engaged in sweaty labor, a low-key community of cave-dwelling men on the fringes of society—all of it sprinkled with anecdotes of prayer, miracles, conversions, and built into a narrative framework of travel and movement. The hagiographical mode is here employed to convey not the usual model of an individual engaged in the pursuit of personal sanctification, but as a story of a complex relationship between two men, both of them ordained clergy, whose relationship constitutes the central point of the narrative.

An interesting version of the formation of emotional attachments, but with the distinct buzz of homo- and heterosexuality in the background, is offered in a story that centers on the pimp who controls prostitution in all of Alexandria, a man by the name of Sergios. It results in three years of paired ascetic life in the desert. This is an elaborate tale, refractured and blurred through several lenses as it anticipates the incredulity and resistance of the audience. It is recorded in Greek in the tenth-century collection of edifying

---

[191] Ibid., ch. 43, p. 78.

[192] Ibid., ch. 44, p. 78.

[193] Ibid., ch. 45, p. 80. For a slightly different ending, of a later date and poorly attested, see 14–15.

tales by Paul of Monembasia, which is based on earlier materials. It also circulated in a Georgian and an Arabic version.[194]

The story, we are told, was encountered by the monk Ambakoum (Habakuk?) in "an ancient book." Its first protagonist is the monk Elpidius who leaves his monastic cell, plagued by the demon of boredom, and wanders in the desert, where he encounters "a naked man with white hair." This hermit then tells his story in the first person. He, too, had been plagued by boredom and had gone in search of someone who would be his equal in ascetic accomplishments. Divinely instructed, he went to Alexandria to seek out Sergios, who was "the supervisor and director of all the prostitutes." At an inn, the hermit broke with his ascetic habits and partook of all the foods that were put in front of him. He then insisted on going to Sergios's house with him. At this suggestion coming from an older monk, the hermit proceeds to tell Elpidius, the brothel owner, "was secretly scandalized, thinking that perhaps I had been besieged by the adversary and that I wanted to sin." Homosexual contact initiated by a desert hermit on a city break is here considered a definite possibility. The hermit's advances were not rejected, although the circumlocutions ("scandal," "sin") that are used have negative connotations.

But the story takes a different turn and leads to a very different union between the two men, when the hermit remained true to his initial purpose and insisted on hearing what good deeds Sergios had done. Reluctantly, Sergios admitted to having saved a noble woman from debt bondage and prostitution by giving her 100 gold pieces to release her husband and two children from the governor of the city of Alexandria. Encouraged by his listener's eager response, Sergios added another story of how he had saved seventy nuns from losing their virginity to the rapacious demands of another governor of Alexandria. In keeping with Sergios's line of business, this story, too, has sexual overtones. Sergios had prevented the rape of these chaste women by dressing up prostitutes as nuns and cutting their hair, then sending them out as substitutes. Not only that, Sergios explained that he spent "all my modest savings" to pay these pretended nuns for their services. Once the horny governor had left and the real nuns had regained the safety of their convent, the prostitutes refused to return to their old ways and insisted instead on remaining in the monastic state. This is an interesting application of the hagiographical topos of the make-believe religious action (often the child's play of baptism, sometimes liturgical play-acting on a stage) that then turns out to have been accomplished for real.

---

[194] *BHG* 1449i, by Paul of Monembasia, trans. Wortley, 119–26, who probably wrote in Constantinople around 960–980, based largely on earlier materials. See G. Garitte, "'Histoires édifiantes' géorgiennes," *Byzantion* 36 (1966), 396–423, at 396ff. for the Georgian translation of an Arabic version of this story, from an appendix to the *Pratum Spirituale* in ms. Iviron Georgian 9, copied in 977.

After hearing Sergios's stories, the hermit declared himself greatly edified to have found his equal or even his superior in holiness. This is another hagiographical topos: the accomplished ascetic who goes in search of his equal, and is then humbled when he finds someone in a most unlikely place whose good deeds surpass his own. But now the tale takes a remarkable departure from hagiographical convention. Sergios refused to let the hermit depart and instead insisted that they remain united in life and death: "I have been ranked with you, I will not be separated from you, but I will come with you." It is not clear what prompted this sudden and radical attachment. But as a result of Sergios's decision (we are not told about the hermit's reaction), the two of them lived together for three years. The hermit concludes his tale by mentioning that Sergios died four years ago, then instructs his visitor to pay him a second visit three days later. Upon his return, the narrator Elpidius found the man dead, and then "buried him next to *abba* Sergios as he had directed me."

Within the narrative, Sergios's decision to become the saint that the hermit already saw in him mirrors the prostitutes who turn their initial pretense to be nuns into reality. The relationship between the hermit and Sergios oscillates between appearance and reality. The hermit had gone to the city in search of hidden sanctity, while the pimp's initial response gave in to appearances in suspecting his visitor of sexual intentions. The story's *dénouement* consists of the recognition of the true nature of both men. By the end of their storytelling, Sergios the do-good pimp declares that he and the desert hermit are equals in good deeds. This seems to be reason enough for him to decide to attach himself to the hermit for the rest of his life. Their equality in virtue would have lost in relevance as they moved from the urban environment, where Sergios was at home, to the desert, which was the accustomed surrounding for the hermit. Once there, the hermit as the more experienced in the ways of asceticism would have provided guidance for his new companion. Sergios's intention was to forge a lasting relationship that would extend beyond the grave. And indeed, although the two did not die at the same time, they were still buried in the same tomb thanks to the timely arrival of the narrator of this colorful tale.

Like the story of Paul of Qentos and John of Edessa, the story of the hermit and Sergios tells of an attachment that was formed in the world, but then articulated and enacted within the framework of asceticism. Whether this is a narrative device or based on actual occurrences, the fact remains that paired monasticism was able to lend respectability to male-male relations, regardless of the impetus that led to their formation. Hagiographical tales of sexual relations are a way of expressing the danger of emotional estrangement or the peril of deviation from the shared purpose of monastic living. Such fraught relations are often depicted as obstacles that can be surmounted through a joint effort of the two men. They become tests of loyalty and of mutual support. When successfully mastered, they function as tales of strengthened commitment that usually conclude with the monastic happy end of a harmonious, often synchronized death and joint burial, as the following chapters will show.

E. Sharing Spiritual Capital and the Same Tomb

Given that paired monasticism was common in Egypt, Palestine, and Syria, among hermits and cenobites, among men and—rarely—women, and that the emotional challenges this life represented are sometimes addressed in the written sources, it is now time to pay closer attention to the positive enactment of these relationships. The establishment of a phenomenology of the code of conduct within these close relationships will facilitate the recognition of brother-making relationships on the basis of these indicators, even if they are not labeled as such. Most relevant for the purposes of this study is any evidence for the contractual nature of paired relationships and the possibility of a ritual, perhaps as simple as a prayer, that underscores this commitment.

It is in those kinds of narratives where support is offered, expected, or demanded that the mechanisms of paired relationships are most clearly articulated and their contractual nature comes to the fore. These narratives usually take as their starting point one partner's desire to have sex with a woman, while in the town or city. They signal the danger of multiple threats to the relationship: the abandonment of the ideal of monastic chastity, the departure from the accustomed isolation of the pair in the desert and exposure to other social contacts in the city, and perhaps the threat of heterosexual yearnings to a close, affective male-male relationship that may or may not have been expressed sexually. In these tales, all these perils are overcome and conquered by an increased emotional and ascetic investment of one partner in order to compensate for the failings of the other. At the end of the day, their joint balance sheet comes out even. This element of expectation and obligation points to the contractual nature of these relationships.

"Vicarious penance" is the designation that scholars have given to the sharing of the burden of someone else's sins. It was generally assumed that a spiritually more advanced man had the ability not only to pray for, but also to absorb the weight of the sins of others. In a manner of speaking, he had laid up a heavenly bank account of good deeds which was large enough to share with others.[195] This ability was one of the great qualifications that disciples sought in a spiritual father. It was also something that spiritual fathers themselves offered to those for whom they felt a special responsibility, as I have

---

[195] See also B. Bitton-Ashkelony, "Penitence in Late Antique Monastic Literature," in *Transformations of the Inner Self in Ancient Religions*, ed. J. Assman and G. Stroumsa, 179–94 (Leiden, 1999), at 188–89.

shown elsewhere.[196] Although the basic pattern of vicarious penance applies to hierarchical father-son or elder-disciple relationships, it is also attested among paired monks.

One version of the basic story goes as follows. Two monastic brothers leave the desert and go into the city to sell their handicraft. One falls into fornication with a woman and confesses to his brother who immediately "admits" to have done the same. As one does his penance on behalf of the other, God recognizes "the toil of their love" and reveals it to their elders. The story concludes with the comment: "Truly, this is what it means to offer one's soul on behalf of one's brother."[197] In these tales, sex with a woman represents the worst imaginable transgression for a monk, and the town or city features as a very dangerous location that is best avoided. Accordingly, the vast majority of these stories presuppose an anchoritic or semi-anchoritic setting.[198] In this and similar stories, the tempted brother is rescued by the timely intervention of his partner. He may be brought to reason by the other's entreaties or saved by his prayers.[199] He may also find his partner pretending to experience the same yearnings, in an ultimate display of self-sacrifice for the sake of maintaining their unity of purpose. Sometimes, the yearning is simply for a return to the world.[200] Indeed, it might be argued that within the discourse of monasticism, this is what sex with a woman and its association with an urban setting are intended to signify.

These moments of crisis are played out in both kinds of monastic pairs, whether "father-son" or "brothers." Take, for example, the following story in the *Sayings of the Desert Fathers*. Two men who lived together were brothers, although one of them was a hermit, the other his servant. The latter sold their handiwork in the town and squandered some of the money in an "indecent place." The hermit pretended to go there too, and when the two of them exited together, asked his servant to pray for him. This went on for quite a while, until the hermit confessed on his deathbed that he had only pretended to engage in these activities in order to bring the servant to repentance. After his death, the sinning brother applied himself to the asceticism of penance.[201]

---

[196] Some of the following is a further elaboration of C. Rapp, "Spiritual Guarantors at Penance, Baptism and Ordination in the Late Antique East," in *A New History of Penance*, ed. A. Firey, 121–48 (Leiden, 2008).

[197] *AP Systematic*: 5.31 and 5.32, ed. Guy, 1: 268–72; 5.31 corresponds to Nau 179, and was popularized in Latin in the *Vitae Patrum* 5.27, PL 73, col. 880 C–D. Also Nau 346, p. 297–98. In one story of a monastic pair making its way to town, the troubled monk himself used the journey for intensive prayer to find relief from his sinful purpose: *AP Systematic*: 5.52 = Nau 454b.

[198] One exception is the tale of the "brother" who falls into fornication with the servant woman who comes to their remote dwelling and brings them what they need, and who is eventually saved by the continuous prayers of his partner. *AP* Regnault, 139, Nau 608B.

[199] *AP Systematic*: 5.32 = Nau 180.

[200] *AP* Regnault 139, Nau 609; see also Nau 5: Two brothers live together in desert; one of them leaves on his own, followed by the other who asks: "are you the only one to have sinned in the world?"

[201] *AP* Regnault 138–39, Nau 608A.

One particularly dramatic story is set in Palestine and reported in the seventh-century *Spiritual Meadow*.[202] It indicates clearly the extreme to which mutual obligation under oath could be carried. Two men "had sworn an oath to each other that they would never be separated from each other, either in life or in death." They lived as monastic brothers until one of them experienced sexual yearnings so strong that they could no longer be suppressed. The afflicted brother gave his partner a choice: either to be released from their joint commitment to the monastic life together, or to be joined by him in visiting a brothel. The second brother, rather than allowing their commitment to be dissolved, chose to maintain it by following his brother to the city, where he stood outside the "house of fornication" while his brother fulfilled his desires. Now the story takes an unexpected turn. Despite the entreaties of his more ascetic partner, the first brother deemed it impossible, after this experience, to return to the monastery. And so both of them remained together in the world, supporting themselves as laborers by seeking employment in "the Monastery of the Byzantines" on the Mount of Olives just outside Jerusalem. They formed an economic unit, pooling their wages, which the first brother spent on "riotous living" in the city, while the second one maintained a continuous fast and remained in "profound silence." This setup allowed each of them to pursue his own path: they lived as laymen, but earned their living in a monastery which was perched on the border between city and desert. The abbot of the monastery eventually pried the story out of the second, ascetic brother who avowed that he was performing his acts of asceticism not just for himself, but also on behalf of his partner: "It is because of my brother that I put up with all this, in the hope that God will look upon my affliction and save my brother." The wise abbot responded by giving him reassurance that the soul of his brother has been saved, and indeed, the profligate brother at just that instance made a turnaround and asked to be taken back to the desert for the sake of his own salvation. They both went to the desert and locked themselves up in a cave: physical barriers were still necessary to contain the worldly minded brother. The wayward monk was the first to die, and did so in a state of grace. His ascetic brother ended his days in the same location.

This story affirms that some brothers were joined by an oath in a lifelong association and introduces a contractual element to the description of paired monasticism.[203] The intention of these tales of vicarious penance in the face

---

[202] For a discussion of this and other monastic pairings in the *Spiritual Meadow*, see also Krueger, "Between Monks."

[203] A variant of this type of narration that is told only in the Syriac version of the *Sayings of the Desert Fathers* emphasizes the enormous potential of extended vicarious penance, even though the two men involved are not explicitly said to be a pair or to have a long-standing acquaintance. One very ascetic brother went to town to sell his goods and asked another brother to go with him. The ascetic was seduced by a rich woman and lived with her in luxury for seven years while the brother who accompanied him remained in the same spot to pray for his brother, living in a continuous fast and exposed to elements. After the woman's death, the fallen brother repented and they both

of the danger of women and of the city is to teach their audience a lesson in the importance of mutual support in the pursuit of Christian asceticism. It is remarkable that the ideal social setting to illustrate such support in action is the one-on-one relationship of paired monks. This is reminiscent of the limestone ostrakon with the joint declaration of Peter and Solomon as they sought admission to the Monastery of Phoibammon which included an explicit statement of their willingness to take responsibility and be held accountable for each other's infringements.[204] Between monastic brothers, the willingness to perform penance for and with another is the result not only of a general Christian motivation, but also of a contractual obligation. One story in the *Apophthegmata* hints at this: Two monastic brothers, accomplished ascetics both, lived together in a *koinobion*, and each was able to see the grace of God in the other. When the first one harshly criticized a third monk for his lack of fasting, his brother immediately noticed the absence of grace in him. The harsh monk realized what he had done: "That is my sin, but toil with me for two weeks and we will beseech God that he forgives me."[205] This story shows that vicarious penance between two monastic partners was not only offered freely, as in the other cases discussed above, but could even be demanded and taken for granted. The narrators of these tales assume the widespread existence of monastic pairs, and expect their audience to be familiar with the phenomenon. Pairs of "brothers" in this context represent the ideal of a monastic relationship, an ideal that can teach an important lesson even to those who live in different circumstances.

Vicarious penance also had a place in larger monastic communities, when the obligation of mutual support was not personal, but collective. John Climacus suggests that this might have been done within the ideal monastic community which he sketches in his *Ladder of Divine Ascent*: "If one of them committed a fault, many of the brothers would seek his permission to take the matter to the shepherd [i.e., the spiritual leader] and to accept both the responsibility and the punishment."[206] Carrying the sins of others and shouldering the punishment for their misdeeds could become a lifetime vocation for some. One monk in a *koinobion* decided to carry all the weight of the sin of others, even to the point of falsely accusing himself of fornication. The other

---

returned to the monastery. There is no mention of any further association of the two. The explicit morale of the tale is to demonstrate how the patience of one man can save another. *AP* Regnault 224–25, Butler, *Paradise* 1.395.

[204] British Museum 8, in Biedenkopf-Ziehner, *Koptische Ostraka*, 1: 120–25. This kind of promise, analogous to standing surety for a loan, was also common in the process of recommending someone for ordination to the clergy, and is known by the German term "Ordinationsbitten."

[205] *AP Systematic* 9.18, Guy, 440–42. This is, to the best of my knowledge, the only instance where the occasion for fraternal vicarious penance is a sin other than fornication.

[206] John of the Ladder, *Ladder of Divine Ascent*, Step 4, PG 88, col. 685D, trans. Luibheid, 96.

monks ridiculed his apparently excessive sinfulness, but the abbot knew of his practice and took this as an opportunity to teach his monks a lesson.[207]

Joined in Death and Burial

The committed nature of the relationship of paired monks is evident especially at the end of their lives. It was not uncommon for spiritual fathers to promise to their disciples that they would be reunited in Heaven and that the younger one would be assured a resting place in his elder's tomb. In this aspect, too, monastic relations mirrored those of biological families. Family tombs for successive generations were, in fact, the common pattern of burial in the Roman and Late Roman Empire. A touching example that combines both elements is Gregory of Nyssa's report on the death of his sister Makrina, who represented for him a model of asceticism, which she practiced along with their mother, Emmelia, by transforming their household into a monastic community.[208] Makrina was laid in the same grave as her mother: "They had both with one voice prayed to God their entire lives, that after their death their bodies should be mingled together so that their experience of community [tên kata ton bion koinônia] during their lifetime should not even in death be undone [diazeuchthênai]."[209] Even outside the monastic setting, there is the occasional glimpse of a close friendship that is expected to transcend the boundary between life and death, as happens at the end of the adventuresome tale of Barlaam and Joasaph, when both were buried together "for it was appropriate that their bodies should rest together, since their souls were meant to live in eternity [syndiaiônizein] together."[210]

But our focus here is on paired monks, and among them we encounter not only the intention to be buried in the same tomb, but also to share the experience of death and make the transition to the afterlife together. Several stories describe this lifelong commitment that does not end with death as one of the declared intentions at the beginning of a paired relationship. Many more report the death of paired monks one after the other, within a close sequence of weeks or days, sometimes just a few hours.[211]

A story told with striking narrative detail is reported by Anastasius Sinaites about twin brothers who also became monks together as disciples of the same *abba*, near the Holy Mountain of Sinai. The twin brothers died together and were buried in the same cave. Their *abba* died shortly after. When the *abba's*

---

[207] AP Anonymous, Nau 328, p. 209.

[208] S. Elm, *"Virgins" of God: The Making of Asceticism in Late Antiquity* (Oxford, 1994), 64–105.

[209] Gregory of Nyssa, *Life of Makrina* 35, 16–20.

[210] John of Damascus, *Barlaam and Joasaph*, ed. R. Volk, *Historia animae utilis de Barlaam et Ioasaph (spuria)*, Die Schriften des Johannes von Damaskus 6 (Berlin, 2006), 606, lines 16–18.

[211] A few more examples of joined death are found in the list of hagiographical tales assembled by John Wortley: AP Anonymous, Nau 622, *BHG* 1448mb, *BHG* 1444m.

surviving disciple went to place his body in the same cave, the bodies of the two brothers refused to accommodate him between them. Instead, they appeared to the disciple together in a dream, to chide him: "how have you not understood that we have been born together, have been in the military service of the king on earth together, have left the world together, were buried together and have stood before Christ together, and yet you have separated us and placed another one between us?"

Here we have the clearly expressed view that those who engaged in the common pursuit of monasticism were not only joined in the timing of their death and in the location of their burial, but that all those components were the essential prelude to being joined in the afterlife. The brotherhood bond between these two monks receives narrative reinforcement by the insistence that they are not just monks, but biological brothers, and not just any kind of brothers, but twins—the closest approximation of equality to which an idealized brotherhood relationship can aspire.

Paisios, a hermit who is well represented in the *Sayings of the Desert Fathers*, was united in death with a certain Paul. It had been Paisios who had pursued their relationship after seeking out Paul because of his reputation as a forceful supplicant. "[H]e went to meet him, and they became good friends. Inseparable, helping each other, they were as a mighty fortress and acquired happily the gifts of *hesychia*." After Paisios died, Paul soon followed him. When a certain abbot from Pisidia, Isidore, made an attempt to transfer the relics of Paisios to his own monastery, a series of miraculous events forestalled their removal until the remains of Paul were brought along as well from their own resting place in the desert. The hagiographer John, who was a member of this same community, comments: "Not only are their souls united in Heaven, but also their bodies."[212]

In contrast to this literary motif, descriptions of actual burials, especially those of paired monks, are rare in the monastic literature of fourth- to sixth-century Egypt. The archaeological record, discussed below, yields only meager results. This picture changes by the seventh century, when Egypt is no longer the sole focus of monastic living and the monastic movement has taken root in the regions of Palestine and Syria.[213] The *Spiritual Meadow* by Sophronius is remarkably detailed in its description of burial sites of monastic founders and other celebrities of the monastic life. This is due to an increased institutionalization of monasticism, eager to preserve its collective memory by making its founding fathers or famous figures the focal point of each monastery, thereby assigning to an establishment a distinct flavor and identity that would attract pious visitors and future members.

---

[212] John the Little, *Life of Paisios*, trans. Papadopoulos and Lizardos, 44–47.
[213] For parallels in Anglo-Saxon England, see Krueger, "Between Monks," 58.

Written and Archaeological Evidence for Joint Monastic Burials

A Syriac text published by J.-B. Chabot in 1896 under the title *Le livre de la chasteté composé par Jésusdenah, évêque de Baçrah* contains what might be best described as a "monastic genealogy" of Mar Eugenius (Awgin). He was the progenitor of a very influential monastic community on Mount Izla whose monks became monastic founders in their own right. The *Book of Chastity* may well have been composed in the eighth century as a way to establish an authoritative lineage of well-respected ascetics.[214] Whatever its purpose or authenticity, the work shows that in Syria, too, monastic pairs were assumed to be a common phenomenon and that the monastic tradition of Egypt was held in high regard.

A total of 140 individuals are listed in this text, some of them with little more than their name and location, others with more elaborate stories. Special emphasis is placed on the social and religious origin of the monks when they come from a wealthy background or convert from Zoroastrianism. Many of them are reported to have spent time in Egypt, at Scetis, or at Sinai. Their educational achievements, their place of study, the books they read, and the works they composed are also highlighted. Whenever a monk's place of burial is recorded, it is located either in the church of the monastery that he founded or next to his monastic teacher. Just like in the Egyptian cases, these pairs could consist of either a teacher-disciple team, or a teacher and two disciples, or two men by themselves, perhaps former co-disciples after their teacher's death.

Even rarer than written reports of monastic burials is actual archaeological evidence for monastic burials in general, and even more so for the burial of two people in the same tomb, within a short time span—the kind of joint burial that many of the paired monks so fervently hoped for, according to the monastic sources. A papyrus, perhaps from the sixth century, perhaps a century or two earlier, attests to the concerns of Christians about their burial place. It records the result of arbitration by a certain Leontius regarding the future occupation of two tombs. The agreement stipulates that the three parties involved, Didymos, John, and Eusebios, have equal shares of the "small tomb," while Didymos alone may make use of the "great tomb" for "his corpses." This papyrus is interesting not only for demonstrating that individual Christians took forethought about the use of tombs and were anticipating shared use, but also for the fact that the judicial hearing is recorded as ending

---

    [214] J.-B. Chabot, "Le livre de la chasteté composé par Jésusdenah, évêque de Baçrah," *Mélanges d'archéologie et d'histoire de l'École française de Rome* 16 (1896), fasc. 3–4, 1–80, and 225–91. For a recent discussion of this text, see F. Jullien, "Aux sources du monachisme oriental: Abraham de Kashkar et le développement de la légende de Mar Awgin," *Revue de l'histoire des réligions* 225, no. 1 (2008), 37–52. I am grateful to Vicenzo Ruggieri for bringing this source to my attention.

with a ritual moment: "they left me compliantly and prayed for one another this very day, no one of them showing any signs of annoyance."[215]

Archaeology yields little evidence in general for monastic burials in Egypt, but some evidence is beginning to come to light.[216] From one of the Christian cemeteries in the town of Arsinoe, in the Fayum Oasis, comes a limestone tombstone, probably from around 700, inscribed in Greek, that has the successive funerary inscriptions of Menas, son of Timotheos, and of Gerontios, son of Marnitas the *praepositus*, who was a priest of the cathedral church at Arsinoe. Based on the indiction dates, it seems that Gerontios died first, followed in the next year by Menas. These two are, admittedly, not monks, but at least one of them is identified as a member of the clergy, and thus may fit our pattern. A similar gravestone comes from the Fayum, now in Berlin, dated to 703. It invokes God's blessing for "Pousei and Kosmas," and asks that "they" be taken up to the bosom of Abraham.[217] A double burial of anchorites was discovered in 1998 in the "Monastery of Cyriacus" in Thebes by a Hungarian mission of the Eötvös Loránd University in Budapest. This is an extension of the site known as the Monastery of Epiphanius at Thebes excavated by Herbert Winlock and others in 1914. The two tombs were side by side, separated by a low wall of bricks, and one of the bodies was found undisturbed, wrapped in a linen shroud with leather fastenings. The site suggests a monastic community of moderate size and high economic level.[218]

Concrete evidence for the joint burial of two or more individuals is difficult to find under any circumstances. It is thus even the more precious to come across a group of six tombstones from a cemetery outside the city of Edessa in Macedonia, on the Via Egnatia, that not only record joint burials, but attest to this practice among celibate women. As Carolyn Snively proposes, these inscriptions suggest a community of religious women and "that the women had been living together and were buried together." The six inscriptions mention a total of ten names, and it is not clear whether the three inscriptions in that group which duplicate names refer to the same individuals or attest to the continuity of monastic naming practices.

> Tomb of the deaconess Theodosia and of Aspilia and Agathoklia virgins.
> Tomb of Agathoklia virgin and deaconess.
> Tomb of Theodosia and Aspilia virgins.

---

[215] J. G. Keenan, "A Christian Letter from the Michigan Collection," *ZPE* 75 (1988), 267–71.

[216] A great rarity is the dated tombstones of the sixth century from Dekhelah, the western necropolis in Alexandria. They specify not only the name of the deceased, but also his immediate spiritual "family" relation, whether brother, father, or monastery. M. G. Lefebvre, *Recueil des inscriptions grecques-chrétiennes d'Égypte* (Cairo, 1907), 1–3. For further additions, see A. Latjar, "Minima epigraphica: Aus dem christlichen Ägypten," *Journal of Juristic Papyrology* 26 (1996), 65–71.

[217] Lefebvre, *Recueil*, no. 790; *Aegypten. Schätze aus dem Wüstensand*, no. 67.

[218] T. Bács, "The So-Called 'Monastery of Cyriacus' at Thebes," *Egyptian Archaeology. The Bulletin of the Egypt Exploration Society* 17 (Autumn 2000), 34–36.

Tomb of Kalimera and Akulina and Apantia ever virgins.
Tomb of . . . and of Theodoule a virgin.[219]

In yet a different region, this time Lycia in Asia Minor, a monastic complex of the sixth century has been identified on a hillside in a river valley. It consists of several rooms, a cistern, and two small churches. Remains of frescoes adorn the walls and there are some fragments of relief sculpture. The settlement probably served as a focal point for individual hermits who lived in the surrounding hillsides. At a short walking distance from it was a separate burial structure, in the shape of a "tomba a camera" that was typical for the region, with the significant exception that the interior arrangement here provided for the separate deposition of bodies to the left and right of a central area.[220] This communal burial arrangement may have been intended to replicate relations between the members of this monastic settlement.

Further afield, in Constantinople, written sources report the joint burial near the relics of martyrs of two women who had shared the same dedication to a life of Christian piety. Interestingly, this happened at the instigation of the widower of one of them. The two women are mentioned by the fifth-century church historian Sozomenos in the context of the report of the discovery of the relics of the Forty Martyrs of Sebaste by Pulcheria, the pious sister of the emperor Theodosius II. The first known owner of the relics had been Eusebia, a "deaconess of the Macedonians," that is, the followers of Makedonios, an Arian and bishop of Constantinople from 342 to 346 and from 351 to 360. She had built a repository for them on her extramural property, next to which she intended to be buried. She was very close to the wife of the former consul and prefect Kaisarios. Their attachment was characterized by *charis* and adherence to the same dogma and worship, and they wished to be buried together. Kaisarios honored this arrangement at the time of his wife's death, and later purchased the plot of land so that he, too, could be close to his wife in burial. A generation later, this burial complex was in ruins and the location of the martyrs' relics unknown until their rediscovery by Pulcheria. Its original purpose could be recalled only at the instigation of divine visions and with the help of the recollections of an old monk who remembered the burial of Kaisarios's wife.[221] It is not clear whether Eusebia was married, but it is worthy of note that the two women's decision about their joint burial was respected by the husband of one of them. Sozomenos's phrasing suggests that

---

[219] C. Sniveley, "Invisible in the Community? The Evidence for Early Womens' Monasticism in the Balkan Peninsula," in *Shaping Community: The Art and Archaeology of Monasticism*, ed. S. McNally, 57–68, BAR International Series 941 (Oxford, 2001), quotations at 63, 62.

[220] V. Ruggieri and G. C. Zaffanella, "La valle degli eremiti nel canyon del Koça Çay a Kizilbel in Licia," *OCP* 66 (2000), 69–88, at 79–82.

[221] Sozomenos, *Historia Ecclesiastica* 9.2; *AASS* March 10; Basil of Caesarea, *Oratio in laudem ss. Quadraginta martyrum* 7.749.

this decision was motivated as much by a desire to remain connected in death as by the perceived need to maintain a distance from those who did not share their dogma and worship. Perhaps this is also the reason why in 516 during the reign of Anastasius, also in Constantinople, two bishops were laid in the same tomb.[222]

The sharing of spiritual capital and the promise to be united in death underline the intended permanence and stability of committed relationships between monks. These features belong to the phenomenology of paired monasticism along with vicarious penance, mutual promises, and a ritual moment that affirms their intentions. These elements are not always present at the same time in our written sources. This is especially true for the edifying literature of Egyptian monasticism that offers snapshots of significant "teachable moments," but has no interest in providing further context. Taken together, however, these writings, augmented by other sources, offer an aggregate picture of paired monasticism as a widespread, respected, and respectable option within the spectrum of monastic living arrangements. For the description of the evolution of such relationships over many years we have to turn to biographical narratives in hagiography or historiography. For this purpose, case studies will be interspersed into the historical discussion that occupies the remainder of this book.

F. Case Study: Symeon the Fool and John and Other Examples from Hagiography

The earliest detailed hagiographical description of a monastic pair is in the *Life of Symeon the Fool*, composed by Leontius of Neapolis around 640. It describes how he met John, how they became monastic companions in the desert and how they remained connected, even though Symeon lived out the final years of his life as a saint in disguise in the city. This story is rife with complex emotions, a heady mix of personal attraction and attachment, sudden monastic conversion, hidden jealousies, disappointed hopes, and a long period of separation culminating, in monastic fashion, in reunification in the afterlife. It also contains a decisive reference to a prayer ritual that consecrates a fraternal bond between two monks. Because descriptions of male-male attachments, or indeed of any emotional Odysseys, are rare in Greek literature of the time, this tale has generated a certain amount of interest among scholars.

Leontius, its author, was a key figure in the history of Byzantine hagiography. He was bishop of Neapolis (Limassol) in Cyprus in the mid-seventh century, at a time when Arabs first established their presence on the island and when its

---

[222] Marcellinus Comes, *Chronicle*, s.a. 516, ed. T. Mommsen, in MGH, Auctores Antiquissimi 11 (1894).

church became involved in the Monothelete controversy. In addition to the *Life of Symeon the Fool*, Leontius also composed a *Life of John the Almsgiver*, a further work of relevance to the practice of *adelphopoiesis* to be discussed below. A third hagiographical work from his pen was a *Life of Spyridon*, the fourth-century shepherd who became bishop of Trimithous on Cyprus, a text which is no longer extant. Finally, he is known as the author of a *Dialogue against the Jews*, which survives only in later quotations.

Cyprus belonged to the cultural zone that extended from Egypt to the Holy Land and the southern shores of Asia Minor, and all of Leontius's saintly protagonists were active within this radius. The story of Symeon and John is set in Jerusalem, the Jordan Valley, and finally in Emesa (Homs) in Syria. Leontius is our only source of information on Symeon, apart from a brief mention in the *Church History* of Evagrius Scholasticus that places the saint's activity at the end of the sixth century, and does not mention John.[223] How Leontius acquired this information is not known, although there is some speculation about an earlier written version of at least part of the account, and the possibility of an oral informant.

Symeon is the earliest holy fool (Greek: *salos*) celebrated in hagiography, a humble saint in disguise who performed outrageous and provocative acts that were intended to hide his true nature as a miracle worker.[224] He acquired his reputation as a holy fool because he acted like a madman among the city dwellers of Emesa in Syria for several decades. But before his re-entry into urban society, he had lived as a monk together with his "brother" John for thirty years. Although the main focus of Leontius's narrative is Symeon's miracle-working life as a madman in a prosperous Syrian city, he tells the story of the two men's association with great care and loving attention to detail.

The two met as young men, as each was traveling from Syria with his relatives on a pilgrimage to Jerusalem—John with his newly wedded wife and his old father, Symeon with his old mother. They became acquainted in Jerusalem, in a displaced location of heightened expectations and intense spirituality, while they made their prayer rounds of the Holy City—similar to the relations discussed earlier that were forged between students and co-disciples of the same *abba* who become close friends after sharing the formative experience of pilgrimage. This is the beginning of the lifelong association of Symeon and John, as Leontius explains: "Since the two young men had spent time together and had become friends, they would no longer part from each

---

[223] Evagrius Scholasticus, *Historia Ecclesiastica* 4.32–34.

[224] On Symeon and the phenomenon of holy foolery, see S. A. Ivanov, *Holy Fools in Byzantium and Beyond* (Oxford, 2006), and C. Ludwig, *Sonderformen byzantinischer Hagiographie und ihr literarisches Vorbild: Untersuchungen zu den Viten des Äsop, des Philaretos, des Symeon Salos und des Andreas Salos* (Frankfurt, 1997).

other."[225] When it was time to leave Jerusalem, Symeon and John decided to travel some of their way home together, along with their relatives. At a certain point, as they looked east toward the Jordan, they made a sudden and spontaneous decision to abandon their families and join a monastery in the valley. In the description of Leontius, it is both their desire to be together and the magnetism of the monastic life that prompts their decision, and it is easy to imagine that after their pilgrimage experience, they had lost interest in a return to their old ways and established family relationships.

At the monastery, the abbot Nikon who received them recognized the love and affection (*storgê* and *agapê*) they had for each other. They did everything in unison: they received tonsure and new garments in the monastery and experienced the same visions. A charmingly realistic note is added when Symeon and John displayed some signs of naïve anxiety over receiving new white garments, which they initially misconstrued as a second baptism.[226]

After only a few days, they decided to leave the monastic community and to live together as hermits in the desert. As they prepared to depart from the monastery, an interesting prayer session took place: the abbot Nikon "knelt down, placing Symeon on his right and John on his left,"[227] and prayed to God for help in fulfilling their ascetic purpose. This kind of prayer, I like to suggest, is the origin of the blessing of *adelphopoiesis* as we know it.

While all of this was going on, each of the two young men secretly feared that the other would be held back from continuing on this path, John by love for his wife, Symeon by affection for his mother. For more than two decades, they lived in close proximity in the area near the Dead Sea, but under separate roofs. They took responsibility for each other's spiritual progress and often prayed for one another's concerns—the same pattern of sharing spiritual capital that has been noted before.

Eventually, Symeon was divinely inspired to continue his saintly life in the city. John, however, was not ready to take this step and wished to remain in the desert. His beseeching words to his long-standing companion are significant:

> for the sake of Him who joined us, do not wish to be parted from your brother. You know that, after God, I have no one except you, my brother, but I renounced all and was bound to you. . . . Remember that day when . . . we agreed not to be separated from each other. Remember

---

[225] *Life of Symeon the Fool*, ed. A.-J. Festugière and L. Rydén, *Léontios de Néapolis, Vie de Syméon le Fou, Vie de Jean de Chypre* (Paris, 1974), trans. D. Krueger, *Symeon the Holy Fool: Leontius' Life and the Late Antique City* (Berkeley, CA, 1996), 124.

[226] L. Rydén, *Bemerkungen zum Leben des heiligen Narren Symeon von Leontios von Neapolis* (Uppsala, 1970), 58–64. That baptism and monastic initiation are similar in intent and share similar liturgical features has already been noted in conjunction with the placement of the *adelphopoiesis* ritual in the manuscripts, where it often appears in proximity to either or both.

[227] *Life of Symeon the Fool*, trans. Krueger, 134.

the fearful hour when we were clothed in the holy habit, and we two were as one soul, so that all were astonished at our love. . . . Please don't, lest I die and God demands an account of my soul from you.

The story continues:

When brother John saw that he [Symeon] was persistent, he knew that he had been convinced by God to do this, since nothing would separate them except death, and perhaps not even that. For they had often prayed to God, that he would take the two of them together, and they knew that the Lord heard them in this as in all things.[228]

When they finally parted, John felt "as though a sword had separated him from his body." Symeon tried to assuage him by repeating his earlier promise that they would be united in death. And indeed, a few days before his own death, Symeon appeared to John in a vision to call and embrace him, and John died a few days later. Although not deposited in the same tomb, the two were united in death, in the same way as many of the paired monks we encountered earlier.

Theirs was a typical relationship of paired monasticism, complete with a joint purpose, shared living arrangements, mutual spiritual support, and the expectation that their bond would last into the afterlife. What makes it particularly relevant for the present study is the mention of a prayer and blessing by the abbot to mark this initial moment of commitment. Here, finally, is a clear description of how we should imagine the beginning of many of the monastic pairings we have encountered in the previous pages. And it may not be too far-fetched to imagine that the good abbot used words in his blessing ceremony similar to those in the *adelphopoiesis* prayers that are transmitted in the *euchologia*.

A parallel tale is reported by Theodoret of Cyrrhus in the mid-fifth century. He recounts a story told by another Symeon, also known as Symeon the Elder, one of the pioneers of monasticism in northern Syria in the late fourth century. While on a pilgrimage to Mount Sinai with some companions, he passed through the "desert of Sodom," in the area close to the Dead Sea where Symeon the Fool and John would also have established their residence. There, Symeon the Elder and his companion met an old and shriveled-up hermit who lived in a tomb-like cave. After some prodding, the hermit was willing to share his story: "'I too had the same longing,' he said, 'that makes you depart. I had made a friend share this journey who was like-minded and had the same goal as I did; we had bound each other with an oath to let not even death break up our fellowship. Now it happened that he came to the end of life on the journey, in this place. Bound by the oath, I dug as well as I could, and

---

[228] Ibid., trans. Krueger, 142–43.

committed his body to burial; by his grave I dug another tomb for myself, and here I await the end of life and offer to the Master the customary liturgy.'"[229] The features are recognizable: the location in the desert just east of the road that leads from Syria to the Sinai, with Jerusalem as a central destination; two like-minded men on pilgrimage; the oath; and the promise to remain united throughout life and into death. It is quite possible that this brief and touching tale, or events like it, might have inspired Leontius's account of the first half of the *Life of Symeon the Fool*.

What prompted Leontius to report this tale of a close companionship between Symeon and John? It is, after all, not essential to his plot. The omission of this first part of the *Life* would not have detracted from his purpose of presenting "a nourishment which does not perish but which leads our souls to life everlasting."[230] An exclusive focus on Symeon's time in Emesa would still have allowed him to depict the saint as "most pure, just as a pearl which has traveled through time unsullied." Several stories of Symeon's indifference to women, even naked women whom he surprised by "streaking" through the bath house, are intended to illustrate this. Perhaps Leontius describes Symeon's relationship with John in such detail to demonstrate that the holy man is equally immune from same-sex temptations, even and especially when the opportunity would offer itself at close quarters? Or does Leontius perhaps himself reveal a particular personal interest in close male-male relations? He was certainly not alone in this. Leontius was part of a whole cluster of men with monastic leanings and literary skills who showed an interest in the concept of spiritual brotherhood and its potential application in the public realm, as a later section will show.

G. Byzantine Continuations of Paired Monasticism

A father living with one or more disciples in a remote location, monks living in pairs of two either by themselves or within large communal monasteries—all of these possibilities that were established in the formative phase of the monastic movement continued to be options in the Byzantine period. Our sources are not consistent either in their reporting or in their evaluation of these options. There remained considerable fluidity in the size and organization of monastic establishments, from hermitages for individuals or groups of varying size gathered around a spiritual father to large communal monasteries.[231]

---

[229] Theodoret of Cyrrhus, *Historia Religiosa* 6.9, ed. Canivet, Leroy-Molinghen, 1: 358, 10–20, trans. Price, 66.

[230] *Life of Symeon the Fool*, trans. Krueger, 132.

[231] D. Papachryssanthou, "La vie monastique dans les campagnes byzantines du VIIIe au XIe siècle," *Byzantion* 43 (1973), 158–80; D. Krausmüller, "Byzantine Monastic Communities: Alternative

In later Byzantine writing, monastic pairings are usually mentioned in three contexts: either in a matter-of-fact disquisition on living and sleeping arrangements; in stern admonitions against special friendships between two monks that would be a distraction to them and to the community; or in narratives of a close relation between two specific individuals. We encounter the former two in monastic foundation documents (*typika*, sing. *typikon*) and the last in hagiography. Special friendships remain a concern in Orthodox monasticism to the present day. During the service of monastic tonsure, the abbot's admonition to the postulant includes in the list of sentiments or behaviors to be shunned, along with envy, gluttony, and other distractions, also "special friendships." Relationships that are disruptive to the community are clearly to be avoided. *Adelphopoiesis*, by contrast, had the positive effect of providing two men with mutual support on their spiritual journey.

After the *Rules of Pachomius* and the *Catecheses* of Basil, no monastic rules are attested until the ninth-century reform of monasticism initiated by Theodore the Stoudite, with the exception of a *typikon* of the late eighth century from the Monastery of St. John Prodromos in Pantelleria, a small island southwest of Sicily, which survives only in a translation into Old Church Slavonic. The rules established by the founder John for his monastic establishment are remarkable for their enforcement of strict discipline not just in diet and daily routine, but also regarding the social interaction and conduct of the monks. Infringements would incur harsh punishment. A repeated concern that is spelled out in great detail is the avoidance of close contact, physical and otherwise, of two monks. Yet, it seems to be taken for granted that two monks share the same cell, although the possibility that discord may arise between them is so strong that a procedure for the resolution of such situations is established:

> Should a brother declare: "I cannot stay with this brother in the same cell or [sit] at the same table," let him be asked on account of what sin does he do [it]. Should he answer [that it is] owing to extreme weakness, lest his brother cause scandal, we exact that an inquiry be made into this matter. Should the latter state: "[Yes], I am causing scandal," and this being the reason why he separates himself from the proper order of the brethren, and [why also he] says: "I wish to sit alone in my cell," let them bring the church priests to him and let him be instructed amidst the brethren. Should he still not hearken, let them take off his

---

Families?" in *Approaches to the Byzantine Family*, ed. L. Brubaker and S. Tougher, 345–58 (Farnham 2013), suggests that these relationships mirror those vertical family relationships that are not parental, but for example between uncles and nephews. He also observes that this practice is in striking contrast to Western monasticism, where novices are grouped together, away from the core community of the monastery.

monastic garments in front of the church and then expel·him from the monastery.[232]

The reference to the "scandal" that might arise between two monks is tantalizingly oblique. Are these annoying habits? Incompatible personalities? Sexual temptations? The determination to avoid such a situation or to resolve it expeditiously resonates with the phrase in the prayer for *adelphopoiesis* that enjoins the two brothers to avoid causing "scandal" to each other, and generally reinforces the notion of brotherhood as an assumed absence of strife.

The chronological framework and geographical origin of this rule position it in close proximity to the first attestation of the prayers for *adelphopoiesis* in the *Barberini Euchologion*, which was most likely copied in Calabria in the late eighth century. It seems that the monastic prototype of paired monasticism that inspired the prayers for *adelphopoiesis* remained a viable option even as the ritual was, as shall be seen below, increasingly pressed into service as a way to soften the boundaries between monastics and laymen and eventually between laymen of different status.

Theodore the Stoudite

A significant milestone in the development of monastic organization in Byzantium occurred in the early ninth century, under the leadership of Theodore the Stoudite (759–826).[233] He began his monastic life at the age of twenty-one, when the entire family decided to dedicate themselves to monastic pursuits. As his father had been a high official in the imperial financial administration, the family had considerable wealth and social standing. Their estates were sold, and the male and female members settled in separate communities on their one remaining property, in Sakkoudion in Bithynia, under the spiritual guidance of Theodore's maternal uncle Plato. Their enthusiastic embrace of strict poverty and the adoption of social and economic equality within the monastic community went contrary to the ingrained practices of the day and soon attracted large numbers of followers. During his long life, Theodore became a prominent public figure, not least because of his criticism of Constantine VI in the Moechian Controversy. For failure to produce a male heir, the emperor had divorced his wife, Maria of Amnia, whom we will encounter again later as one of the rare examples of a woman proposing

---

[232] *Typikon of John for the Monastery of St. John the Forerunner on Pantelleria*, ch. 20, trans. G. Fiaccadori, in *Byzantine Monastic Foundation Documents*, 65.

[233] For details on Theodore's life, see G. A. Schneider, "Der hl. Theodor von Studion. Sein Leben und Wirken: Ein Beitrag zur byzantinischen Mönchsgeschichte," PhD diss., Münster, 1900; and most recently T. Pratsch, *Theodoros Studites (759–826)—zwischen Dogma und Pragma: Der Abt des Stoudiosklosters von Konstantinopel im Spannungsfeld von Patriarch, Kaiser und eigenem Anspruch*, Berliner Byzantinistische Studien 4 (Frankfurt, 1998).

"ritual sisterhood." Theodore also adamantly resisted the iconoclast policies of Emperor Leo V, and in consequence was subjected to periods of confinement and exile. In 799, during the reign of the iconophile empress Irene, he was given the opportunity to revive a fledgling community of monks on the estate adjacent to the Church of St. John the Forerunner in Stoudiou. This property on the southwestern edge of Constantinople had been dedicated to this purpose in the fifth century by its eponymous founder Stoudios, but had since fallen into disrepair. Theodore and his monks reestablished a community there that followed strict rules of liturgical observance, maintained a highly differentiated organization of labor, prized the practice of poverty and the eradication of social distinctions, and emphasized spiritual discipline.[234]

Several sets of prescriptions for his monks are attributed to Theodore. Some of them exhibit a concern for special friendships between two monks, or for displays of favoritism out of affection.[235] "If someone whispers affectionately with a brother, both should be separated, so that they desist from each other."[236] The overseer of the Stoudite monastery was advised to nip such relationships in the bud. His task was to keep watch on discipline day and night to prevent several undesirable outcomes: that two young men should be together, that "fraternizations" (*phatriai* or *syskêniai*) are formed; and the opportunity for pernicious bold language (*parrhêsia*), the unruliness of arrogance (*hybris*), and laughter.[237] Theodore was not only weary of the possibility of personal attachments within the monastery, he also counseled great caution regarding the monks' relations with people outside. For this reason, he issued the prohibitions against his monks entering into *adelphopoiesis* with laymen that will be discussed below in chapter 4.

Symeon the Stoudite and Symeon the New Theologian

The Stoudite monastery provided a fertile seedbed for monastic leaders in subsequent generations. In the late tenth century, Symeon the Stoudite (ca. 918 to ca. 987) was to acquire fame as the spiritual father of Symeon the New Theologian. Symeon the Stoudite's *Ascetical Discourse* emphasizes the importance of daily examination of conscience and confession of sins to one's spiritual father. It is also at pains to ensure that monks keep to themselves and avoid unnecessary contact with others. They slept in individual cells and were not allowed not visit the cells of other monks, except on rare occasions that

---

[234] J. Leroy, "La vie quotidienne du moine stoudite," *Irénikon* 27 (1954), 21–50, at 30–31.

[235] Theodore the Stoudite, *Poenae monasteriales* 101, PG 99, col. 1745 D.

[236] Theodore the Stoudite, *Monachorum poenae quotidianae* 32, PG 99, col. 1753 A.

[237] Theodore the Stoudite, *Poem* 9, ed. P. Speck, *Theodoros Stoudites, Jamben auf verschiedene Gegenstände* (Berlin, 1968), 131–32. D. Krausmüller, "Abbots and Monks in Eleventh-Century Stoudios: An Analysis of Rituals of Installation and Their Depictions in Illuminated Manuscripts," *REB* 65 (2007), 255–82.

of their spiritual father. Special friendships (the Greek expression is *agapên idikên*, "love apart") with other monks were to be avoided, and one was especially to refrain from idle conversation and from befriending a newcomer, because this may arouse suspicions. "For in most cases, it will shift your focus from a spiritual to a passionate [love], and you will fall into useless troubles." In short, the monk should keep himself aloof, as if he were a stranger, from his fellow monks.[238]

These preventative measures were not always successful, however, and it could happen that two monks developed particular affection for each other. Symeon's advice for such a case was measured and sagacious. He did not criticize, condemn, or chastise. Even his word choice is cautious. He calls this "an innocent, simple love" (*agapên en haplotêti*) and assumes that it is most likely to arise between young monks. Symeon's advice is directed to their spiritual father, who is encouraged to intervene once other monks in the monastery take notice, in order to prevent a situation where the two might cause offense (*mê skandalizesthai tinas*). Compassionate words of encouragement should be applied, along with very gentle pressure, to persuade each one to spend less time in the other's presence. "Watch yourself and abstain from a merging of minds and from partial friendship and from familiarity of intercourse."[239]

How Symeon the Stoudite put his own advice to spiritual fathers into practice can be seen in his relationship to another Symeon, about three decades his junior, who would outgrow him in fame and become known as Symeon the New Theologian (ca. 949 to ca. 1022). The latter exerted great influence as a mystic. His visionary theology of divine light and its activity in the human soul later became the intellectual foundation of Hesychasm. At least three decades after the saint's death, Niketas Stethatos composed a biography of Symeon the New Theologian. This *Life* describes how Symeon arrived at the Stoudiou monastery in Constantinople as a very young man, and immediately made contact with his spiritual adviser of many years, Symeon Eulabes ("the Pious"), also known as Symeon the Stoudite. The new novice was presented to the abbot Peter and since there was a shortage of available cells, he was assigned to live in the same cell as his spiritual father. The space was clearly not set up to accommodate more than one person, so Symeon the Stoudite directed his new charge to sleep under the stairs of his cell—a suitable location to contemplate the narrow upward path of virtue that he had chosen.[240] Symeon the Stoudite trained the young novice to abandon his

---

[238] Symeon the Stoudite, *Ascetical Discourse*, 9–11, ed. and trans. H. Alfeyev and L. Neyrand, *Syméon le Stoudite: Discours ascétique*, SC 460 (Paris, 2001), 80–84.

[239] Symeon the Stoudite, *Oratio ascetica* 39, ed. Alfeyev and Neyrand, 124–26.

[240] Niketas Stethatos, *Life of Symeon the New Theologian* 11, ed. I. Hausherr, *Vie de Syméon le Nouveau Théologien par Nicétas Stéthatos (949–1022)*, Orientalia Christiana 12 (Rome, 1928), 18–20; trans. R. P. H. Greenfield, *Niketas Stethatos: The Life of Saint Symeon the New Theologian*, Dumbarton Oaks Medieval Library (Cambridge, MA, and London, 2013), 29.

own will through rigorous demands of total obedience, while the aspiring monk developed such a strong attachment to his instructor that eventually the abbot of the monastery expelled him. There are no reports of further contact between the two in this life, but the disciple retained a strong—detractors would say excessive—attachment to his teacher until his dying day.

The younger Symeon found admission in another monastery in Constantinople, that of St. Mamas, and soon thereafter, in the year 980, became its abbot. Twenty-five years later, he withdrew to the eremitic life, entrusting the community to this disciple Arsenios. Symeon's farewell speech to his community is interesting for its application of kinship terms to denote a carefully calibrated hierarchy of familiarity and rank: his monks are his "children and brothers,"[241] or even "children, brothers, and fathers,"[242] while his disciple Arsenios is "father, brother, and *hegoumenos* [abbot]."[243]

Still, the disciple's attachment to his spiritual father in the Stoudite monastery remained strong, even at a distance. After the latter's death, Symeon composed hymns of praise in verse and a hagiographical biography in prose and had his teacher's portrait painted. Every year, on the anniversary of his death, a lavish feast was celebrated that attracted large crowds because of the distribution of charity to the poor on that occasion.[244] The extravagance and popularity of these celebrations, combined with the unusual presence of an icon image of a recently deceased monk, raised the suspicion and jealousy of the church leaders in the capital. A synod was convened to condemn him and in 1009, Symeon the New Theologian was sent into exile.[245] Accompanied by only one disciple, he found a ruined church, dedicated to St. Marina, which he was able to restore with the help of local donors. It soon became the focal point of a growing monastic community, so that the lavish celebrations in honor of Symeon the Elder (i.e. the Stoudite) could be resumed.

According to the hagiographical account, the two Symeons were even believed to work miracles together. Anna, the abbess of the convent at Bardaine, was on the point of death from a violent fever, attended only by her spiritual mother, when she had a vision of Symeon the New Theologian who was holding Symeon the Elder by the right hand. The former asked what was wrong with her, "since you are not speaking to your mother nor to us who are your friends." When she murmured that she was *in extremis*, Symeon the Elder turned to his disciple, instructing him: "Get going, master Symeon. Take her by the hand and give her something to eat." Anna then continued her reminiscences of this miraculous appearance: "He then did

---

[241] Ibid., 60, ed. Hausherr, 80, trans. Greenfield, 135. Cf. 67, ed. Hausherr, 90, trans. Greenfield, 153.

[242] Ibid., 64, ed. Hausherr, 86, trans. Greenfield, 145.

[243] Ibid., 63, ed. Hausherr, 86, trans. Greenfield, 145.

[244] Ibid., 72–73, ed. Hausherr, 98–100, trans. Greenfield, 163–67.

[245] Ibid., 100, ed. Hausherr, 138, trans. Greenfield, 231–33.

this, and it seemed to me that he was giving me to eat, having asked for food from my mother." Immediately after she had been nourished "by these holy hands," Anna came to, and asked her mother for food, which she ate with great gusto.[246] This story of a nun who received life-sustaining nourishment from her spiritual mother mirrors the relationship between Symeon the New Theologian and his spiritual father, which was—earlier in the *Life*—also conceptualized in terms of feeding and physical sustenance.

Discipleship led to strong identification with the teacher. Later in life, Symeon the New Theologian had a disciple of the same name, resulting in three monastic generations of Symeons.[247] The new disciple's original name had been Nikephoros, but at the age of fourteen he was offered to the monastery by his parents to be educated by Symeon the New Theologian. He eventually took monastic vows in the Monastery of St. Marina, and assumed the name Symeon, after his spiritual father.[248] This Symeon "the third" as we might call him, enjoyed a unique position as the only favorite disciple of Symeon the New Theologian in his old age. The expressions used in the *Life* to denote their connection are significant: the disciple becomes "familiar more than all others" with the saint, and finds himself the recipient of "much love and affection" (*agapê kai prospatheia*). He alone was permitted to remain in the saint's cell, sleeping on the floor—a privilege that had not been granted to anyone previously.[249] Later, he became the sole caretaker of the holy man in his final illness, and was even permitted to sleep next to him.[250]

A further close disciple was—by his own telling—Niketas Stethatos, the narrator of the *Life*, who reminisces about their relation in his closing chapters. Symeon, we are told, addressed him as "my spiritual child" and regarded him as Christ would have considered the apostles, close associates and carriers of the good news of the Gospel into posterity. Symeon reminded him in a written letter that he regarded him as his legitimate heir: "I have on one occasion agreed to hold you as myself, and have entrusted to you all that is mine." Symeon, Niketas reports, then continued to admonish him in his younger years to adhere closely to charity which encourages forgiveness of others and discourages suspicion, "so that you will always remain, in everything and in the eyes of everyone, without causing scandal, neither to us nor to anyone else."[251] The narrator does, in fact, present himself as Symeon's exclusive and authorized literary executor. But more so, there are hints here of a formalized relationship that has as one of its defining characteristics the avoidance of

---

[246] Ibid., 115, ed. Hausherr, 160–162 trans. Greenfield, 269–71. Translation mine.

[247] Ibid., 112, ed. Hausherr, 156, trans. Greenfield, 261.

[248] Ibid., 116, ed. Hausherr, 162, trans. Greenfield, 273.

[249] Ibid., 117, ed. Hausherr, 164–66, trans. Greenfield, 275–77. Translation mine.

[250] Ibid., 125–27, ed. Hausherr, 180–82, trans. Greenfield, 301–07.

[251] Ibid., 132, ed. Hausherr, 190–92, trans. Greenfield, 321. Translation mine.

"offense" (*skandalon*) among the partners within the relationship and in the eyes of outside observers. Niketas relates how he found himself in an ecstatic vision of his spiritual father, recalling, among a long list of virtuous char-acteristics and spiritual achievements, his "love without suspicion" (*agapên anhypokriton*) and his "brotherly love" (*philadelphian*)—the same expressions used in the *adelphopoiesis* prayers.[252]

We know from other sources that Symeon had a further close attachment to Antony, whose peaceful death he commemorated in one of his *Discourses*. According to the title of this *Discourse*, Antony was "his brother."[253] Symeon's affection for him was evident: he called him "beloved brother" and referred to him as "sweetest brother." Yet in the end, Antony on his part displayed remarkable detachment from all personal relations. Symeon reports that on his deathbed, "He did not remember any of his relatives, nor did he name any friend in this life." Symeon here seems to suggest that it would not have been uncommon, even for an accomplished monk like Antony, to show concern for one's kin as well as for one particular person who had the status of "friend." In his description of the death of a favored disciple, Symeon shows him as conforming to the ideal of distance from other monks that he himself had established for his followers—although not always practiced himself.

For all his ascetic seclusion and visionary abilities, Symeon the New Theologian was well connected in the society of his day. He was acquainted with powerful people in Constantinople, who came to his support when he fell under suspicion and was exiled. Among these loyal acquaintances, one man stands out in the hagiographical account by Niketas Stethatos: Orestes, a well-to-do merchant who lived with his wife and children in Chrysopolis. He is introduced as a "friend" of the saint and their relation of friendship is repeatedly emphasized by the narrator. Orestes suffered a sudden stroke and was brought home on a litter. His wife and children "together with all the friends who were present" began to lament his imminent death. At just this moment, Symeon saw in a vision that "his friend Orestes" was at the point of death. He decided to pay him a visit "so that I, coming as a friend, may see my friend, and that I may be seen by him." When he arrived at the house of "the friend," the wife welcomed him with the words: "Look, father: the friend whom you have loved and by whom you were eagerly loved is fading." Symeon shed tears of *sympatheia* at the sight of his "friend" in such a grave state, then restored him to health through his prayers. The story is now extended

---

[252] Ibid., 134, ed. Hausherr, 194–96, trans. Greenfield, 327–29. Symeon's spiritual fatherhood of the narrator is reaffirmed in ch. 137, p. 200, trans. Greenfield, 335.

[253] Symeon the New Theologian, *Catecheses* 21, ed. B. Krivochéine and J. Paramelle, *Symeon le Nouveau Théologien: Catéchèses 6–22*, SC 104 (Paris, 1964), 350–62. *Vita*, ch. 58. There is no record of a biological brother of Symeon in his monastery, but his *Life* includes a monk of this name among his closest disciples.

in an interesting way, as the narrator explains that "the friend" henceforth continued to produce expressions of his gratitude toward the holy man in the form of offerings. Symeon is said to have accepted the presents because of love (*agapên*), but also to have seized this opportunity to remind Orestes, who is now twice addressed as "brother," of the omnipotence of God.[254] The word choice here may be significant. Orestes is not addressed as a "son," as would be fitting for a layperson or spiritual junior, but the author is at pains to present him as a friend of the holy man, in a relationship that is mutual and equal.[255] A relationship that is marked by the exchange of gifts and favors, prayers in return for donations, and sustained over a long period of time fits the pattern of friendship. It also invites speculation about whether their association would in other circumstances have been recognized as one of *adelphopoiesis* between a monk and a layman.

Philotheos and John

Niketas Stethatos, the hagiographer of Symeon the New Theologian, was quite familiar with hagiographical conventions that required the mention of at least one posthumous miracle in order to prove intercessory powers as a sign of a saint's proximity to God after death. He took this as an opportunity to introduce a digression about a remarkable couple of monks. Among the early adaptors of Symeon's posthumous cult were two men who are represented acting as a pair.[256] "Two pious men, one of them called John, the other Philotheos, had come to an agreement in the world, according to the divine commandment and decree of the Lord. And after they wisely left the world together, they put on the holy garb of monasticism and retreated independently to engage in ascetic pursuits." They were able to build a beautiful and richly decorated "holy monastery for ascetics" at the entrance of the Propontis to Byzantium, "although they lived together in poverty." Upon completion of the building, Philotheos shut himself in a cell to live an ascetic life in total seclusion, while John, who was a eunuch, became the *oikonomos* of the monastery.

Philotheos and John were acting in unison and, it seems, initially independently from other circles. Although they agreed to leave the world together, there is no mention of a monastic community that they joined, or a spiritual father who directed them. Instead, they simply and "on their own initiative" put on monastic clothing and went about their business. They pooled their

---

[254] Niketas Stethatos, *Life of Symeon*, 121–22, ed. Hausherr, 172–74, trans. Greenfield, 289–93. Translation mine.

[255] But note that he also calls his detractors "brothers," ch. 123.

[256] Niketas Stethatos, *Life of Symeon*, 145–48, ed. Hausherr, 214–20, trans. Greenfield, 359–71. Translations mine.

financial resources—however meager they may have been—and succeed in completing an ambitious building project without outside assistance. Once this was achieved, Philotheos and John remained in the same household, as it were, but each inhabiting a different sphere: Philotheos living in ascetic seclusion, John tending to the financial administration of the establishment that now attracted others. It was only at this point that they sought outside advice. Philotheos visited Constantinople on a pilgrimage to the holy sites and in order to consult with spiritual men. His conversation with Niketas Stethatos, one of the most ardent followers of Symeon the New Theologian, made a deep impression on him, and he departed not only inspired by stories about Symeon but also equipped with a book of his teachings.

This fledgling community of John and Philotheos became part of the large circle of followers of Symeon the New Theologian, sharing in the possession of his writings, of his icon portrait, and in the observation of his feast day on the anniversary of his death. The hagiographer makes it abundantly clear that Symeon himself gave his approval. For the deceased saint appeared in a vision to Philotheos to offer assurances of the hermit's ability to fulfill his ascetic purpose. He achieved this through the comfort of physical contact, placing his hand inside Philotheos's garments, on his bare stomach to make it shrink. This happens in a vision, but the visions of Symeon, the hagiographer insists, are real, not like dreams, as if the saint reached down from Heaven. Philotheos was graced with such a special vision where Symeon appeared to him as a beautiful angel, with a luminous face, and wearing the distinguished garment of a high-ranking eunuch. This is odd. While the eunuchs who served as attendants at the Byzantine court are often invoked in literary representations to imagine the youthful, prepubescent beauty of angels surrounding the King of Heaven, Symeon is nowhere else referred to in this role. But Philotheos's companion John had been a eunuch prior to becoming a monk. Is it possible that this identification of Symeon as a eunuch carries a double meaning within this story, affording special validation to John's physical state? Or did it perhaps confirm that whatever was attractive about Symeon in his transformed state was also attractive about John, at least in the eyes of Philotheos? The close association between Philotheos and John certainly receives Symeon's approval, when he announces "I have come to be here and to live with you [pl.]."

The writings associated with Symeon the New Theologian, whether his own *Discourses* or the hagiographical account of his life by Niketas Stethatos, offer a full view of the entire range of possibilities for monks to conduct their personal relations: from special friendships that ought to be avoided to shared roofs and shared purses in the case of Philotheos and John, and from dearly beloved spiritual teachers to laymen who enjoy the special status of friend. Symeon the New Theologian may have been unusual not just among Byzantine theologians and mystics, but also among Byzantine authors for the remarkable degree of self-awareness and interiority that he reveals. His affections may appear to the modern reader as too numerous and too demonstrative. They take us into a monastic world that had undergone profound changes since Antony, Pachomius, and numerous others who first followed the call of the desert to devote their lives to the pursuit of virtue. By the tenth century, monasticism was no longer a utopian experiment based on a radical eschatological hope, but one possible form of articulation of Christian piety. Instead of being a flight from the demands and duties of the world and a clean break with family life, middle Byzantine monasteries perpetuated the social structures that prevailed outside. The enclosure of a monastery served as a boundary marker, not as a protective wall. Monks, by consequence, did not exclusively keep to themselves, but maintained close relations with men and women outside. This was acceptable only under the guise of kinship relations. The creation of ritual kinship found ready application by monks, who used this guise as a way to maintain connections with those "outside." As shall be seen below, one of the main functions of *adelphopoiesis* was the softening of boundaries between the monastery and the world or, as time went by, between people of different gender, ethnicity, or religion.

Monasticism on Mount Athos

Stoudite monasticism exerted its influence on subsequent generations and radiated far from the capital. The Stoudite *typikon* served as an inspiration for other foundations. Outside Constantinople, at Mount Athos on the easternmost peninsula of the Chalkidiki in northern Greece, the tenth century saw the consolidation of earlier, scattered monastic settlements. This was due to the initiative of Athanasius the Athonite who managed to secure imperial patronage for his enterprise. The future emperor Nikephoros II Phokas (r. 963–69) is said to have harbored such close affection for him that the hagiographical rendition of their relation has "the character of a little love story, of divine love."[257] The *typikon* that was created some time between 970 and 972 owes its existence to a behest by the following emperor, John Tsimiskes (r. 969–76), to Euthymios, a monk of the Stoudiou monastery, to intervene in serious dissent (*skandalon* is one of the words used, along with *philoneikia*, "competitive quarrelsomeness") among the different monastic groups on the mountain. This *typikon* reiterates the same concern that Theodore the Stoudite had expressed for his monastery in Constantinople, the avoidance of *adelphopoiesis* with laypeople.

---

[257] P. Odorico, "Le saint amour: Introduction au colloque," in *Corrispondenza d'amorosi sensi: L'omoerotismo nella letteratura medievale*, ed. P. Odorico and N. Pasero (Alessandria, 2008), vii–xi, p. x. Some aspects of their relation fit the pattern of spiritual kinship that we have observed between monks: the desire to be with the other, the joining of right hands to confirm their bond, a prayer by one for the other. In this instance, it is clear that Nikephoros desires to be accepted as a spiritual son: *Vita A*, ch. 30, ed. J. Noret, *Vitae duae antiquae sancti Athanasii Athonitae*, CCh, ser. gr. 9 (Turnhout, 1982), 15; *Vita B*, ch. 11, ed. Noret, 137–38.

The most objectionable feature of relations with laymen was the conviviality that accompanied feasting and alcohol consumption. *Synteknia* and *adelphopoiesis* from this point of view represented comparable dangers to the monk, as he would be invited to family feasts in his role as spiritual kin. This was to be avoided at all cost. Even though existing relationships were honored, they ought to be avoided in the future.

"None of the brothers shall [henceforth] be permitted to leave the mountain and to conclude *synteknia* or *adelphopoiia* with laymen. If some should have done such a thing already, then they shall no longer go to their houses, or have lunch or dinner with them, or in general feast and drink with them."[258]

On the Holy Mountain of Athos, it was (and still is) possible for men to live the monastic life in a large organized community *(laura)*, or in a smaller family-like setting *(skêtê)* where three generations lived under one roof: an elder, his disciple, and a young apprentice-servant, with the expectation that after the death of the elder, the next generation would move on to the next higher position of seniority and a new servant would be recruited. Equally possible is the arrangement of two monks living together, or indeed the isolated existence of a solitary hermit, a practice which some cenobites adopted for a limited period of time during Lent.

From tenth-century Athos, we have confirmation of a ritual gesture of joined hands for two monks who seek a blessing for their relationship of mutual support. It is Athanasios the Athonite himself who performs this blessing in his role as spiritual father, according to the *Life* that was composed in his honor not long after his death. According to this text, two biological brothers became monks together. They received Athanasios's blessing by putting their hands into his. He also advised them that from now on, they ought to recognize one another as "father"; in other words, that their relationship was to be on equal terms, infused with mutual respect.[259]

There is even rare documentary evidence for small-group monasticism on Mount Athos, in the form of a dotation document of about 1000, issued by the monk Euthymios on behalf of his disciple John. John had been entrusted to him, we learn from this document, at a young age by his biological father, and Euthymios now takes care of his future. He has purchased a piece of land which he deeds to John for his future use. He even specifies that John may eventually wish to live with two or three disciples, but limits their maximum number to seven, perhaps because the land would not suffice to sustain more people. Eventually, it is expected that John will designate his own heir from among his monks or at least those of the *laura*. Here, as in the monastic arrangements half a millennium away in Egypt, we notice the same

---

[258] *Actes du Prôtaton*, ed. D. Papachryssanthou, Archives de l'Athos, 7 (Paris, 1975), 212.
[259] Athanasius the Athonite, *Vita B*, 11.3.

features of a monastic father taking responsibility for his "son" who becomes the heir of his cell, and the expectation that monks should live in groups of varying size, in this instance counting at least two and at most seven members.[260] Paired monastic relations existed at the time also in other regions. In Calabria, Nikephoros lived a shared ascetic life together with Phantinos, until the former was divinely inspired to leave for Mount Athos, and the latter for Thessaloniki.[261]

Evidence for this kind of committed monastic brotherhood pairing on Mount Athos continues throughout the centuries. In the middle of the fourteenth century, the *Life of Niphon Kausokalybites* ("the hut-burner") addresses with remarkable precision the hierarchical nuances of monastic living arrangements. After leaving his relatives in his native village in the Despotate of Epiros, where he also achieved his first monastic training, Niphon traveled to Athos and apprenticed himself to Theognostos in the humble role of disciple. But once Theognostos found out that Niphon held the rank of a priest and had already had some experience as a monk, the dynamics of their relationship changed. Now the elder insisted that they live together as brothers and "drive the golden chariot of virtue" together—a suggestion that Niphon found too constraining and therefore left.[262] The chariot expression is used again later, when after several years of living in complete solitude Niphon escaped his growing popularity and took up residence with Maximos the Hut-Burner, another of the great elders on the Holy Mountain. The two recognized each other as kindred spirits who are "bound together" in love. Now it was with Maximos that Niphon was "driving the golden chariot of virtue together."[263] This is a charming elaboration of the more down-to-earth image of spiritual brothers as a yoke-pair (*syzygos*), usually of oxen, that was present in some of the earlier monastic writings. Instead of being metaphorical beasts of burden that are yoked together, the two are now in the driver's seat, like ancient Helios, the sun god, guiding the gleaming and shining chariot of monastic virtues toward the highest Heaven.

The Model Established by the Monastery of the Theotokos Evergetis

The Stoudite model of internal organization and spiritual direction exerted a strong influence on the subsequent development of monasticism in

---

[260] *Actes de Lavra 14, Archives de l'Athos*, vol. 1, ed. G. Rouillard and P. Collomp (Paris, 1937), 38–40.

[261] Athanasius the Athonite, Vita B, 43.23–29 (*syndiatômenos, syndiagontes*). The parallel passage in Vita A is less expressive.

[262] *Life of Niphon*, ch. 2, ed. F. Halkin, "La vie de saint Niphon," *AB* 58 (1940), 12–27, at 14.

[263] Ibid., ch. 4, ed. Halkin, 16.

Byzantium, not only on Mount Athos. Many other monasteries adopted and adapted the Stoudite model, and it served as an inspiration for the next wave of monastic revival in the eleventh century that originated from the Monastery of the Theotokos Evergetis ("Mother of God the Benefactress") in Constantinople. The *typikon* of the Monastery of the Theotokos Evergetis spells out clearly what kind of assistance a monk should be able to expect. It was composed by its abbot Timothy in the years following the death of Paul, the original founder of the monastery, in 1054. Later abbots reshaped the work and added to it. Chapter 24 is entitled "Concerning the fact that the brothers are not allowed to have servants," and explains:

> It will not be possible for you to have servants, but it is very good that there should be two of you in your cells united by the law of spiritual love, being of the same mind and really living together as brothers in harmony, bearing the same yoke of Our Lord wholeheartedly, being subservient to one another in peace, proper care and reverence so that you will have the opportunity to fulfill the word of David, "See now! what is so good, or what so pleasant, as for brethren to dwell together?" (Ps. 132 [133]:1). But in this matter also, it is necessary to make specific distinctions, namely, that the novice should defer to the one who is more advanced, the more unlearned to the more educated, the more uncouth to the more sophisticated, and the younger to the older. But if the superior should decide that some should be alone in their cells, he himself may sanction the arrangement.[264]

In this text, harmonious fraternal relations, again imagined as a yoke-pair, are here for the first time undergirded with words from the Psalms of David.

Several monastic foundations of the late eleventh and twelfth centuries, perhaps as many as eight establishments, drew their inspiration from the spiritual and organizational tradition of the Evergetis monastery. Most of them, however, assumed that the monks would live, and presumably sleep, in a large community. Only three of the Evergetis-inspired monasteries followed its lead in allowing monks to live in smaller groups of two or three. First among them is the small Monastery of St. John the Forerunner at Phoberos, a location that has been identified as lying near the entrance to the Bosphorus on the Asian side opposite Constantinople. In language that closely resembles

---

[264] *Typikon of Timothy for the Monastery of Theotokos Evergetis*, ch. 24, trans. R. Jordan, *Byzantine Monastic Foundation Documents*, vol. 2 (Washington, DC, 2000), 490; ed. P. Gautier, "Le typikon de la Théotokos Évergétis," *REB* 40 (1982), 5–101, at 67. A similar arrangement was envisaged by Francis of Assisi, who advised that a hermit should have at least one, possibly two disciples as assistants, or that two hermits should have two assistants, for a maximum of four people in such a nuclear monastic family. Their relation is conceptualized as that of a mother and her sons: Francis of Assisi, *De religiosa habitatione in eremis*, ed. H. Boehmer, rev. F. Wiegand, *Analekten zur Geschichte des Franziskus von Assisi*, 2nd ed. (Tübingen, 1930).

that of the Evergetis *typikon*, John, the founder of this monastery, assumes that the most beneficial living arrangement should be in groups of three, presumably representing three generations in replication of a family: an older experienced monk, his immediate disciple of middle age, and a younger novice monk who would serve and assist them as part of his training.[265]

This regulation partially replicated the phrasing of the Evergetis *Typikon*, but with the significant alteration of the living arrangement from two to three monks per cell. While the number of inhabitants was increased, the monastic virtues that they were expected to practice remain the same: spiritual love, harmony, and peace. Although this arrangement that facilitated the training of novice monks and alleviated the burdens of age for older monks was clearly inspired by practical considerations, it is nonetheless couched in language of unanimity, concord, and brotherhood.

The second monastery to have adapted the living arrangements of Evergetis is the Monastery of the Theotokos Kosmosoteira ("Mother of God Who Saves the World") near Bera in Thrace. It was founded by the *sebastokrator* Isaac Komnenos, the sixth child and second son of the emperor Alexios I Komnenos, as a place for this burial after he had seen his hopes for the throne thwarted on several occasions. He stipulated in his *typikon* of 1152: "It is very useful and appropriate for the monks to live two in each cell, and to conduct themselves in it as brothers one in soul, in agreement with each other. But there are certain occasions, that the superior would recognize, when he might want perhaps to have certain monks alone in the cells."[266] Noteworthy here is the distant reminiscence of the ancient ideal of friendship as "one soul in two bodies" and the assumption that two brothers sharing a cell is the norm.

The founder of the third monastic settlement of the twelfth century that advocates small-scale living arrangements was Savas, son of the Serbian king Stephen Nemanja, who retreated to the monastic life on Mount Athos and became the first archbishop of Serbia. There, he generously endowed the large Monastery of Hilandar, which remains an important stronghold of the Serbian Orthodox tradition to the present day. If monks needed to be closer to the administrative center of the Holy Mountain, the Protaton at Karyes, Savas also founded a small monastery (referred to as *kellion*) in 1197 or 1199, whose *typikon* survives in medieval Serbian and in Greek. Savas points out

---

[265] *Rule of John for the Monastery of St. John the Forerunner of Phoberos*, ch. 43, trans. R. Jordan, in *Byzantine Monastic Foundation Documents*, vol. 3 (Washington, DC, 2000), 924; ed. A. I. Papadopoulos-Kerameus, *Noctes Petropolitanae* (St. Petersburg, 1913; repr. Leipzig, 1976), 58.

[266] L. Petit, "Typikon du monastère de la Kosmosotira près d'Aenos (1152)," *Bulletin de l'Institut d'Archéologie Russe à Constantinople / Izvestiia Russago Archeologicheskago Instituta v Konstantinople* 13 (1908), 11–77, at 45; *Typikon of the Sebastokrator Isaac Komnenos for the Monastery of the Mother of God Kosmosoteira near Bera*, ch. 51, trans. N. P. Ševčenko, in *Byzantine Monastic Foundation Documents*, vol. 2 (Washington, DC, 2000), 822.

that this establishment was purpose-driven and an interim solution, not a permanent setup.

> In like manner I managed to acquire a number of cells in Karyes so the monks coming from the monastery on some service would have a place to rest. In addition, there in Karyes I have set up a distinctive form of the solitary life. I constructed a *kellion* and a church in the name of our holy, God-bearing and sanctified father Sabbas, as a dwelling for two or three brothers (cf. Matt. 18:20), as the Lord says.[267]

The invocation of Matthew 18:20, "For where two or three are gathered in my name, I am there among them," suggests that such an arrangement was considered of special value in securing the power of the prayers of its inhabitants—a consideration that would be of concrete relevance for a community in this temporary abode for monks who were acting as lobbyists on behalf of the mother house at Hilandar. All four of these eleventh- and twelfth-century sets of monastic rules, beginning with the Evergetis *typikon*, make a special effort to explain and justify the small-group living arrangements they stipulate.

Even outside the Evergetis tradition, the sharing of a monastic residence by two or three monks was not unheard of in the late Byzantine period. A throwaway phrase in the *typikon* of Nikon of the Black Mountain (ca. 1025–1100) indicates that this also entailed inheritance rights. Nikon was well known for his interest in monastic traditions. Originally from the Black Mountain near Antioch, he composed a *florilegium* of edifying texts for the benefit of monks when they were displaced during the onslaught of Seljuk invasions and the arrival of the Crusaders. Nikon was charged by the Patriarch of Antioch to exert control over and instate reform measures in the Monastery of the Mother of God *tou Roidiou* ("of the pomegranate"), which was located in territory in Asia Minor that had come under Armenian rule. Like many monasteries, this establishment seems to have degenerated into a comfortable place of retirement for wealthy aristocrats who had no desire to be deprived of their accustomed luxuries or to abandon possession of their personal effects. Nikon's rules regarding the inheritance of such objects after their owner's death are quite detailed. It is in this context that the assumption is made that monks lived two to a roof: "If, however, a fellow brother also cohabits with [the dying man], he has authority over whatever belongs to [the dying monk's] lot. But if his [spiritual] father cohabits with him, let what is fitting and pleasing to God

---

[267] *Typikon of Sabbas the Serbian for the Kellion of St. Sabbas at Karyes on Mount Athos*, ch. 2, trans. G. Dennis, in *Byzantine Monastic Foundation Documents*, vol. 4 (Washington, DC, 2000), 1333–34.

prevail."[268] This regulation seems to imply that a monk would either live with a monastic brother or with his spiritual father, but firmly grants inheritance rights only to the former.

The three great reform efforts in the history of Byzantine monasticism, those that originated with the Stoudite monastery, with Mount Athos, and with the Monastery of the Theotokos Evergetis, all encouraged monks to share their cells either in pairs or in groups of three, in the latter instance representing different generations—the same arrangements that were present in the original formative phase of monasticism. The perils of property disputes and personal disagreements remained the same. If sexual temptation was mentioned, it occurred only as an afterthought. The language in which these relations are couched leaves no doubt: these men represented one spiritual unit; they depended on one another in their spiritual progress. Whether as oxen yoked together, or as chariot drivers holding the reigns, their task of pulling the metaphorical plough or driving the chariot of virtue could only be achieved if they avoided the disruptions of causing offense and acted in unison, living in spiritual love. The success of his association was of vital importance for a monk's spiritual progress as an individual, and hence it is not surprising that we continue to hear reports of a blessing through prayers to confirm such a pairing.

The Kievan Caves *Paterikon*

Brother-making was so essential to Byzantine monasticism that it was exported along with other monastic practices outside the Byzantine Empire, such as those adopted by the Kievan Caves Monastery when it was established on the banks of the Dnieper river in the eleventh century. From small beginnings, it grew into a large foundation of cenobites, hermits, and semi-anchorites that soon enjoyed the patronage of Russian nobility. The people, events, and lore associated with it are particularly well documented for the twelfth and early thirteenth centuries in the *Paterikon*, which records the history of the foundation and preserves the wisdom and teaching of its most prominent members, in conscious imitation of the *Apophthegmata* of Egyptian monasticism. The Kievan Caves *Paterikon* mentions two instances of monastic brother-making which show the same features that have been identified for the paired monks in Egypt. One story regards the emotional challenge of anger, the other burial in the same tomb, and there are several examples of vicarious penance.[269] The first story begins: "There were two spiritual brothers,

---

[268] *Typikon of Nikon of the Black Mountain for the Monastery and Hospice of the Mother of God tou Roidiou*, ch. 11, trans. R. Allison, in *Byzantine Monastic Foundation Documents*, vol. 1 (Washington, DC, 2000), 434.

[269] *Kievan Caves Paterikon*, Discourse 8 and Discourse 12, trans. M. Heppell, *The Paterik of the Kievan Caves Monastery* (Cambridge, MA, 1989), 83 and 108.

the deacon Evagrij and the priest Tit. They loved each other deeply and sincerely, so that everybody marveled at their harmony and boundless mutual affection. But the devil, that hater of good who is always roaring like a lion seeking someone to devour, made enmity between them and instilled such hatred that they would not look at each other."[270] The story then elaborates on Evagrij's failure to accept reconciliation and his punishment by sudden death. The characterization of their relationship in its initial stages is strongly reminiscent of the phraseology that accompanies *adelphopoiesis* in the Byzantine tradition. The morale of the story underlines the expectation of constant and enduring harmony that is characteristic of such monastic pairings.

The second story is equally redolent of the language of monastic friendship. "There were two brothers in this great Caves Monastery who had been united by a sincere love from their youth, and who had one mind and one will towards God. They begged the blessed Marko to dig a grave for the two of them, so that they might both be buried there when the Lord commanded it." This relationship seems to have had an equally strong emotional component, yet it unraveled posthumously, when the younger one died and was buried in the designated tomb, but in the higher position which the older wished to claim for himself. The remainder of the story deals with the senior monk's fierce grudge against Marko, who had performed the burial, and his subsequent punishment and remorse. His reward came at the time of his death when he was buried, not next to his brother, but to the elder, Marko, "as was fitting."[271] Upon second glance, this story reveals a strong sense of hierarchy that is only thinly disguised by the assumption of brotherhood. These are hierarchies coupled with affective attachments and the possibility of realignment. Whereas the cantankerous monk was initially insistent on his seniority to his spiritual brother, he learned to accept Marko as senior to himself.

This chapter has shown that among the many different living arrangements that developed over time in Byzantine monasticism, the one constant that abides is the pairing of two monks, whether elder-disciple or brother-brother. This tradition continues in Orthodox monasticism to the present day. The relations among the monastic pairs that are described in the middle and late Byzantine sources correspond to the phenomenology of the prototypical relations of *adelphopoiesis* that are reported from late antique Egypt, Palestine, and Syria. It is rarely spelled out that monks received the ritual blessing of *adelphopoiesis*, but our medieval authorities usually see no reason to report the obvious. The fact that the prayers for *adelphopoiesis* are contained in a large number of manuscripts that were in monastic use speaks for itself. By the middle Byzantine period, *adelphopoiesis* had already expanded beyond

---

[270] Ibid., Discourse 23, trans. Heppell, 140–41.
[271] Ibid., Discourse 32, trans. Heppell, 177–81.

its original scope. It began, as the term suggests, as an equal relation between like and like, people who were of the same societal status. In the seventh century, its application was extended, without ever losing its original meaning, to connect unlike and unlike in such a way as to allow them to conduct themselves as if theirs was a relation between equals, and especially between family members. In this way, *adelphopoiesis* developed into a boundary-crossing strategy that was a convenient social tool for monks and laymen, for men and women, for people of different socioeconomic status, and even for people of different ethnicity or religion. These are the developments that will concern us in the next chapters, as brother-making moves to lay society.

The Social Practice of Brother-Making in Byzantium

A. Seventh-Century Transitions

Male-Male Affective Relations and *Adelphopoiesis* in Seventh-Century Hagiography

The previous chapter used scattered evidence and the occasional casual remark in monastic and hagiographical literature to illustrate the phenomenology of paired monasticism: two (sometimes more) men in the joint pursuit of the ascetic ideal, sharing the same conditions of life (sometimes the same roof), and the same spiritual capital (sometimes on the basis of a firm mutual agreement, occasionally affirmed by a prayer). These attestations were interpreted as attestations *avant la lettre*, as it were, of *adelphopoiesis*. This changes with the seventh century, when the authors of saints' *Lives* began to be more outspoken about male-male affective bonds. The language of friendship was now infused with expressions of emotion. In this context, the expression of *adelphopoiesis* and its cognates in the specific social sense of "brother-making" made their first appearance in Byzantine Greek. In this period, brother-making developed into a strategy of boundary crossing that allowed monks and monasteries a legitimate pathway of communication with the outside world. As we shall see below, it was a pathway that eventually was closely monitored by ecclesiastical and imperial authorities.

Leontius of Neapolis painted a convincing and indeed gripping picture of a relation of spiritual friendship and emotional closeness between Symeon the Fool and John, a relation that showed all the features of paired monasticism, as has been seen above. With the mention of a prayer of blessing for their bond, this description produced in the 640s also provides an important link to the *adelphopoiesis* prayers that are preserved in the *euchologia* beginning in the late eighth century. Leontius was not the only seventh-century author to display a keen interest in a spiritual bond with an emotional component and social consequences. There is a whole cluster of authors and literary figures associated with Cyprus that shares an interest in close monastic friendships and *adelphopoiesis*.

Peter and Paul, Cyrus and John

About twenty years before Leontius composed his *Life of Symeon the Fool*, two men from Palestine, both of them monks, both of them united in close friendship from early youth, made a pilgrimage together. They not only visited the holy sites associated with the life of Christ, but also traveled to the holy men in the Jordan valley and the Judean Desert. They even went to Egypt to seek out the monks and monasteries there, just like John Cassian and his friend Germanus had done in the late fourth century. Their names were Sophronius and John, the account of their travels was the *Spiritual Meadow*. It was composed by John Moschus not long before he died in Rome, either in 619 or in 634. Sophronius would hold the Patriarchal See of Jerusalem from 634 to 638.[1] At some point before that, John and Sophronius had lived for a decade at Mount Sinai where they were part of the same community that John Climacus describes in his *Spiritual Ladder*.

Based on their own experience, the concept of a shared spiritual life must have held great appeal for them. Perhaps this contributed to the impetus for Sophronius to compose three texts on two saintly pairs, Peter and Paul, and Cyrus and John. In a festal speech in honor of Peter and Paul, Sophronius introduced them as a yoke-pair (*syzygia*), and praised them for their close relation, for doing everything in unison, even being celebrated at the same festival. Theirs was a friendship grounded in Christ and they held each other in "genuine, heartfelt brotherly love [*philadelphian anhypokriton ek kardias*]." This is the brotherly love "without shame" that is mentioned in some of the prayers for the *adelphopoiesis* ritual and is so difficult to understand without further explanation. In commenting on 1 Peter 2:17 ("love the brotherhood"), Sophronius also explained that "love makes us brothers [*adelphopoiein*]."[2] He displayed a clear predilection for the language and concept of "brother-making" that is firmly anchored in the theological realm—the result of Christ's love shared with others.

---

[1] H. Chadwick, "John Moschus and his Friend Sophronius the Sophist," *JThSt* n.s. 25 (1974), 41–74, repr. in Chadwick, *History and Thought of the Early Church* (London, 1982). See also H. Usener, *Der heilige Tychon* (Leipzig and Berlin, 1907), 80–107; and V. Deroche, *Études sur Léontios de Néapolis*, Acta Universitatis Upsaliensis, Studia Byzantina Upsaliensia 3 (Uppsala, 1995), 31–36.

[2] Sophronius of Jerusalem, *In SS. Apost. Petrum et Paulum*, PG 87, cols. 3335–64, at col. 3360 A–C.

Also from Sophronius's pen survive two works in praise of a further saintly pair, Cyrus and John. They were martyred in the Great Persecution under Diocletian, but soon acquired a reputation as miracle-working saints, known as *anargyroi*, physicians who offered healing without a fee. The popularity of Cyrus and John was such that they feature among the pairs of martyrs invoked as models in the earliest attested ritual prayer (Prayer A) for *adelphopoiesis*. At their shrine in Menuthis, near Canopus in Egypt, a large cult site was constructed in the fifth century, to which people flocked from far and wide to seek relief and healing. Sophronius himself had received a miraculous cure from an eye problem there. As an expression of gratitude, not long after 610, he composed a work *In Praise of Cyrus and John* and later an account called the *Miracles of Cyrus and John*. While the latter focuses on the beneficiaries of the miracles and their ailments, the former work elaborates on the relationship between the two saints. In the gushing tones typical for an *encomium*, Sophronius marvels at their relation as a twosome (*dyas*), and as a yoke-pair (*syzygia*). He explains that they received their unity of mind (*homonoia*) and affinity (*synapheia*) for one another as a divine gift, and anticipated their joint reward as "one glory" and "one crown," referring to the crown of martyrdom. Their burial in the same tomb was praised as evidence of their unity of thought and purpose that could not be dissolved by "conduct, place, tomb, time, or suffering."[3] This rhetorical celebration emphasizes that the close relation between Cyrus and John was not merely an external result of spiritual need and social convention, but that it was an essential constituent of their inner identity. In the veneration of posterity that kept their memory alive, these two holy men existed not as individuals, but only inasmuch as they were a pair. There may be a further theological dimension to this, as Phil Booth has plausibly suggested. Sophronius was writing in the extended aftermath of the Council of Chalcedon, at a time of high religious anxiety, when debates about the separate yet united divine and human nature of Christ brought disunity to the churches and monasteries in the region. Against this background, Sophronius may well have celebrated the yoke-pair of Cyrus and John as a marvelous paradox for God's ability to unite two distinct entities.[4]

---

[3] Sophronius, *In Praise of Saints Cyrus and John*, chs. 11–12, and ch. 27, intr., ed., and French trans. P. Bringel *Sophrone de Jérusalem. Panégyrique des saints Cyr et Jean. Réédition d'après de nouveaux manuscrits*, PO 51/1, no. 226 (Turnhout, 2008). The text is also available online: http://halshs.archives-ouvertes.fr/halshs-00003975/en/. There is the possibility of marital imagery here, in the mention of a yoke-pair (*syzygos*, "the one to whom one is yoked," being one of the regular words for marital partner, usually the wife).

[4] P. Booth, "Saints and Soteriology in Sophronius Sophista's Miracles of Cyrus and John," in *The Church, the Afterlife, and the Fate of the Soul*, ed. P. Clarke and T. Claydon, 52–63, Studies in Church History, 45 (Oxford, 2009), esp. 56–57.

John the Almsgiver, Patriarch of Alexandria, and Niketas, Governor of Egypt

There is good reason to believe, although it cannot be proved with certainty, that Sophronius and John stopped in Cyprus on their way to Egypt. On the island, they would have made the acquaintance of Leontius, who, as the bishop of the prosperous city of Neapolis, would have been in a position to offer them hospitality. Perhaps their own relationship or the stories of their home region later inspired Leontius to tell his own tale of Symeon the Fool and John. Sophronius and John definitely shared with Leontius an interest in another figure who would be made famous through Leontius's pen, John the Almsgiver, the Chalcedonian Patriarch of Alexandria from 610 to 620 who was linked by close ties of friendship and ritual kinship to the Heraclian dynasty.[5]

The hagiographical dossier on John the Almsgiver (or "the Merciful") consists of several texts which complement and support one another. John Moschus and Sophronius were the first to compose an account in his praise, but this covered only the events prior to his appointment as patriarch. It was continued by Leontius of Neapolis, the same author who wrote the *Life of Symeon the Fool*. Leontius's text, clearly labeled as a sequel to a previous work, circulated independently in three slightly different redactions (BHG 886b, 886c, 886d).[6] The account by Sophronius and John no longer survives in its original form, but the entire sequence (Sophronius and John, followed by Leontius) was used by later epitomators. One abbreviated version was edited by Hippolyte Delehaye (BHG 887v). It was paraphrased in the tenth century by Symeon Metaphrastes.[7] Independent of that is a second, much shorter *synaxarion* entry edited by Euridice Lappa-Zizicas (BHG 887w).[8]

John's appointment in the year 610 to the patriarchal throne of Alexandria, where he subsequently gained a saintly reputation because of his charitable works, was not an obvious choice. He came from a prominent family, was married, the father of several children, and had no previous involvement in matters religious or ecclesiastical. But he was on intimate terms with

---

[5] The following is based on C. Rapp, "All in the Family: John the Almsgiver, Niketas and Heraclius," *Nea Rhome: Rivista di ricerche bizantinistiche* 1 (2004 = *Studi in onore di Vera von Falkenhausen*), 121–34.

[6] Festugière and Rydén, *Léontios de Néapolis*; H. Gelzer, *Leontios' von Neapolis Leben des heiligen Iohannes des Barmherzigen, Erzbischofs von Alexandrien* (Freiburg and Leipzig, 1893); C. Mango, "A Byzantine Hagiographer at Work: Leontios of Neapolis," in *Byzanz und der Westen. Studien zur Kunst des europäischen Mittelalters*, ed. I. Hutter, 24–41, SB Österreichische Akademie der Wissenschaften, Philosophisch-historische Klasse, 432 (Vienna, 1984); Deroche, *Études sur Léontios de Néapolis*.

[7] H. Delehaye, "Une vie inédite de saint Jean l'Aumônier," *AB* 45 (1927), 5–74.

[8] E. Lappa-Zizicas, ed., "Un épitomé inédit de la vie de s. Jean l'Aumônier par Jean et Sophronios," *AB* 88 (1970), 265–78.

Niketas, the cousin and supporter of Heraclius in the latter's quest to overthrow the emperor Phokas. The three of them in fact hailed from the same social class: John was the son of the governor of Cyprus, Heraclius the son of the governor of North Africa, while Niketas's father (and Heraclius's uncle) was a high-ranking general. After the successful *coup d'état* that ended with the brutal murder of Phokas in 610, they seem to have divided their tasks. Heraclius became emperor in Constantinople, Niketas was appointed governor of Egypt, and John was persuaded to accept the position of patriarch in this strategically important province, which provided grain for the capital but also was a hotbed of religious dissent.

Some time before these events, and therefore presumably covered in the lost account by Sophronius and John, Niketas and John had apparently been joined in ritual brotherhood and it was probably by invoking this relation that Niketas was able to compel John to take his office. The expression used in the original seventh-century account cannot be known, as this episode is accessible to us only in later redactions. In the Anonymous Delehaye, John's appointment to the patriarchal see is attributed to the people of Alexandria, and also to Heraclius and Niketas. The emperor strongly urged John to take this position, but the driving force was Niketas, "who had at that time been honored with the rank of *patricius*, who was ruling alongside Heraclius, and who had become the ritual brother [*adelphopoiêtos*] of the blessed [John]."[9] The later paraphrase of the Anonymous Delehaye by Symeon Metaphrastes avoids the use of the word *adelphopoiêtos*, using a circumlocution instead. According to this rendition, John owed his patriarchal appointment to the emperor's decision to yield to the demand of the Alexandrians, but especially to Niketas, the patrician, who had great influence with the emperor, and who was "a brother in the spirit [*adelphos kata pneuma*] to the blessed [John] and strongly bound to him by bonds of friendship [*desmois philias*]."[10] The condensed version published by Lappa-Zizicas echoes the Anonymous Delehaye. According to this text, John was appointed to the patriarchal throne of Alexandria with the consent of the people of the city and especially at the initiative of the emperor Heraclius and of Niketas "his comrade-in-arms and ritual brother [*tou symmachou kai adelphopoiêtou autou*]."[11]

These variants in expression reveal the flexibility of authors between the seventh century (the date of the original version) and the tenth century (the latest possible date of the various paraphrases) in their choice of expressions

---

[9] Delehaye, "Vie inédite," ch. 2, p. 20, line 36, to 21, line 1.

[10] Gelzer, *Leontios' von Neapolis*, Anhang II, p. 110, lines 8–9.

[11] Lappa-Zizicas, "Un épitomé inédit," ch. 4, p. 274. She seeks to improve the meaning by attributing the ritual brotherhood bond to Niketas and Heraclius, instead of John and Niketas. In my view, one does not need to preclude the other. Ritual brotherhood need not have been "monogamous." Sidéris, "L'*adelphopoièsis* aux VIIe–Xe siècles à Byzance," considers this a key passage for his argument that *adelphopoiesis* had its origin in the military milieu.

to interpret a close association between two men. The same relationship could be described as spiritual brotherhood, as the bonds of friendship, or as being comrades-in-arms. In the experience of these middle Byzantine authors, the practical dimension of *adelphopoiesis* could take on all these shades of meaning. Whether or not the later paraphrases based themselves on the original seventh-century texts when they employed the adjective *adelphopoiêtos* must remain an open question, however.

How did the relation between John the Almsgiver and Niketas play out? Again, different authors use different expressions. Once John had been appointed at Niketas's urging, the latter assumed that he was at liberty to demand favors and cooperation from John as one might expect from an *adelphopoiêtos*. Hard pressed by the catastrophic effects of the Persian invasions, Niketas requested financial assistance from the church's ample funds. John, however, responded in a manner that befitted his new status as a bishop. He reacted to Niketas's bold demands with the meekness and generosity befitting a holy man. His actions were promptly rewarded by the miraculous arrival of jars filled with coins, which brought Niketas to compunction. Their relationship now assumed a new dimension. The Anonymous Delehaye (who depends on Leontius in this part) is most explicit in his choice of words: "From then on, they were thus bound to one another in spiritual love, so that the god-inspired shepherd received him [Niketas] and became the *synteknos* [godfather] of the frequently remembered most illustrious man."[12] Niketas thus introduced the new relation of *synteknia* to cement his existing bond of friendship and loyalty with John as his ritual brother. The multiplication of ritual kinship relations to reinforce personal ties would become, as we shall see, typical among lay society in the middle and late Byzantine periods.

The nature of their relationship is underscored later in the account of John's life. The Anonymous Delehaye emphasizes that they were "bound together by a relationship of spiritual disposition [*syndethênai pneumatikês diatheseôs schesin*]," while Leontius even speaks of a "strong bond of spiritual love [*pollên syndethênai pneumatikên agapên*]"[13] The expressions "disposition" (*schesis*) and "bond" (*syndesmos*) are often used in Byzantine literature to characterize the emotional ties between friends and especially between ritual brothers.

Niketas and John remained intimately connected. When Alexandria was threatened by the advancing Persians, they agreed to leave the city together

---

[12] Delehaye, "Vie inedite," ch. 25, p. 36, lines 9–12. Leontius of Neapolis uses the word *agapê* and also mentions the bond of *synteknia*: Gelzer, *Leontios' von Neapolis*, ch. 12, p. 25, lines 12–14; Festugière and Rydén, *Léontios de Néapolis*, ch. 10, p. 357, lines 74–76.

[13] Delehaye, "Vie inedite," 47, p. 67, lines 22–23: *syndethênai pneumatikês diatheseôs schesin*; Festugière and Rydén, *Léontios de Néapolis*, ch. 52, p. 402, lines 7–10; Gelzer, *Leontios' von Neapolis*, ch. 44b, p. 90, lines 21–23: *pollên sundethênai pneumatikên agapên*.

and planned to make their way to Constantinople where, Niketas insisted, the emperor was in need of John's prayers and blessings. During the journey, however, John received a premonition of his death and parted ways with Niketas so that he could end his life in his native Cyprus. His farewell to Niketas included ample blessings for the latter, along with the assurance of further blessings for the imperial family.[14] On an earlier visit to the capital, Niketas had made the acquaintance of a further holy man, Theodore of Sykeon, who will concern us again soon.

Antony of Choziba and the Men in his Affection

Cyprus was a point of convergence for authors and men of the church in the first half of the seventh century. The island became a gathering point for the opposition to the imperially sanctioned doctrines of Monoenergism and Monotheletism. They were joined by refugees from Palestine and Syria who sought safety from the Sasanian and Arab invasions.[15] As has been noted, the hagiographer Leontius was bishop of Neapolis, John the Almsgiver—a native of the island—found his final resting place in Amathus, and Sophronius and John probably passed through on their journey to Egypt. In their turn, many Cypriots joined the monasteries in Palestine. Set in the same monastic milieu in the Judean Desert near the Jordan valley as Leontius's tale of Symeon and John is another text that is especially valuable because Antony, the hagiographer, speaks without artifice and in clear emotional terms about his own close attachments. Antony hailed from Cyprus and eventually found a monastic home at the Laura of Choziba in the Jordan valley, where he would later encounter his future spiritual father George, a fellow Cypriot and the protagonist of the *Life*.

Antony begins his *Life of George of Choziba* with autobiographical reminiscences. After a dissolute youth in Cyprus, he secretly left his paternal home, together with "one of my *sympaktorôn*"—a reference to an agreement (*pactum*) between several young men. Their plan to go to Raithou in northern Egypt was cut short by the Sasanian invasions, so that they went to Choziba in the Judean Desert instead. They were received into the monastery there and tonsured shortly thereafter—a familiar pattern of friendship that carries over into the monastic life. But not for long. Antony continues: "I do not know what came into the mind of my *sympaktôr*. He went to the Holy City together

---

[14] Festugière and Rydén, *Léontios de Néapolis*, ch. 52, p. 402, lines 13–403, line 52; Gelzer, *Leontios' von Neapolis*, ch. 44b, pp. 91–92; Delehaye, "Vie inedite," ch. 47, pp. 67–68.

[15] A. Cameron, "Cyprus at the Time of the Arab Conquests," *Cyprus Historical Review* 1 (1992), 27–49, repr. in Cameron, *Changing Cultures in Early Byzantium* (Aldershot, 1996); C. Rapp, "Christianity in Cyprus in the Fourth to Seventh Centuries: Chronological and Geographical Frameworks," in *Cyprus and the Balance of Empires: Art and Archaeology from Justinian I to the Coeur de Lion*, ed. C. A. Stewart, T. W. Davis, and A. Weyl Carr, 29–38 (Boston, 2014).

with the Hegoumenos and then secretly stole himself away to go to Raithou. But I was in grief and pain for being deprived of my companion [*hetairos*], and wanted to catch up with him." Antony had now lost one of his companions, who had decided to break their agreement—thus adding insult to injury. His sense of bereavement recalls the depth of sadness that John experienced when his companion Symeon the Fool left for Edessa. Eventually, Antony found consolation for his loss with the arrival of George at the monastery, who was not only a fellow Cypriot but also more advanced in age and in spiritual experience.[16] The beginning of their relationship is described in telling terms. After hearing George's admonition that, as a monk, he no longer ought to pursue "worldly association, friendship and familiarity [*etaireian . . . kosmikên kai philian kai synêtheian*]," Antony formally subjected himself to George as his spiritual father with the words: "I give myself over to you [*soi paratithêmi emauton*]."[17] This marks the transfer of Antony's allegiance from a strong homosocial bond with his "buddy" that had its origin in the world to a formalized filial relationship within the monastery. This allegiance would be tested later, when a new monk from Rhaitou arrived at the monastery and tried to "attach himself [*kollasthai*]" to Antony who was clearly flattered by his attentions. True to his role as a spiritual father, however, George saw to it that he never gave the two youngsters an opportunity to be alone—much to the professed annoyance of Antony, who only later understood the wisdom of his spiritual father's intervention when it became clear that this newcomer was a heretic.[18] Read between the lines, the *Life of George of Choziba* is an autobiographical account of a series of emotional attachments. It throws into sharper relief the emotional landscape of the youthful spirit of adventure in combination with the spiritual yearning for monastic vocation that must have formed the background to some of the monastic pairs that have been presented on the foregoing pages.

All of these hagiographical stories indicate the presence around the middle of the seventh century of a distinct group of authors who share the same interests in close emotional relations between men, their articulation within a monastic framework, and the practice of *adelphopoiesis*. Perhaps these authors and the men whose stories they told formed an "emotional community," analogous to those that Barbara Rosenwein has identified in the early medieval West: clusters of authors who belonged to the same social circle and used the same language to describe the display of emotions.[19] The geographical node that connects Leontius of Neapolis, Sophronius of Jerusalem, and

---

[16] [C. Houze], "Sancti Georgii Chozebitae confessoris et monachi Vita auctore Antonio eius discipulo," *AB* 7 (1888), 95–144, ch. 8, pp. 130–33.

[17] Ibid., chs. 32–33, pp. 131–33.

[18] Ibid., ch. 41, pp. 142–43.

[19] B. Rosenwein, *Emotional Communities in the Early Middle Ages* (Ithaca, NY, 2006).

Antony of Choziba and several of the characters in their stories is the island of Cyprus. They were all writing under the Heraclian dynasty that dominated much of the seventh century. In the hagiography of this period, including the next text to be discussed, *adelphopoiesis* makes its first literary appearance under this name.

Theodore, Bishop of Sykeon, and Thomas, Patriarch of Constantinople

The same Niketas who was joined to John the Almsgiver as a ritual brother also benefited from a connection to the holy man Theodore, who was bishop of Sykeon in Galatia. This happened in 612 after Niketas had traveled to Constantinople to attend the baptism of Heraclius Constantine, Heraclius's son and designated successor. On this occasion, Heraclius invited his cousin Niketas to also become his *synteknos*, displaying the same desire to reinforce existing family ties—this time biological, not ritual—that had prompted John the Almsgiver's *synteknia* with Niketas. During his visit, the presence and the prayers of the great miracle-working bishop Theodore brought Niketas healing from a severe illness.[20] Theodore was aligned with the forces that welcomed the downfall of the emperor Phokas and brought Heraclius to the throne. In anticipation of these events, he himself had concluded *adelphopoiesis* with Thomas, the Patriarch of Constantinople, according to an elaborate hagiographical story.

The *Life of Theodore of Sykeon*, composed by his disciple George some time after the saint's death in 613, can with some justification be considered part of Heraclius's propaganda campaign to tarnish the memory of his predecessor Phokas. It is the earliest text of which we know with certainty that it uses the word *adelphopoiesis*. The *Vita* describes in colorful detail the evolution of an *adelphopoiesis* relationship between two men of the church where patronage, prophesy, and prayer are goods that can be exchanged, expected, and claimed. Its geographical focus encompasses Galatia, a core region of Asia Minor, as well as the imperial capital of Constantinople.

The first contact between the patriarch and the holy man was indirect. Thomas in Constantinople heard about Theodore's miraculous powers from Domnitziolos, the nephew of the emperor Phokas and his *curopalates* (head of the palace), who had earlier profited from the saint's prophetic assurances and prayers when he was leading the Byzantine army in a campaign against Persia. Ever since that time, he had shown his gratitude in personal visits to the saint, support for his charitable work, and donations for the adornment of Theodore's monastery. He even commissioned a processional cross to be

---

[20] *Life of Theodore of Sykeon*, 154, ed. and trans. A.-J. Festugière, *Vie de Théodore of Sykéôn*, *Subsidia hagiographica*, 48 (Brussels, 1970), 1: 124–25.

made of gold. After hearing further reports of the saint's astounding powers of foreknowledge, the patriarch in a letter invited Theodore to the capital. Before he even set eyes on him, the patriarch had thus succeeded in obliging the holy man through his generosity.

Upon his arrival, Theodore was received by the patriarch with the customary friendly welcome, and then paid a visit to the emperor Phokas in the course of which he prophesied that the emperor would be visited by the wrath of God unless he mended his ways. This audience was immediately followed by a second reception by the patriarch.

On this occasion, prompted by "a friendly attachment [*schesis*] and confidence toward him, with many pleas [Thomas] persuaded" Theodore to enter into ritual brotherhood (*adelphopoiesis*) with him. Analogous to the monastic pairs united unto death, the Patriarch asked to be "with" the holy man also in the life to come. Theodore was clearly reluctant to accept this proposal, while Thomas, as the continuation of the narrative shows, was interested in acquiring a share of the saint's intercessory powers and especially in his gift of prophesy. As soon as they were "brothers," he demanded from Theodore an interpretation of the strange portent of shaking processional crosses that had occurred in Sykeon, and then learned from the saint about the sorrows and upheavals that would soon afflict the empire—a reference to the imminent overthrow of the emperor Phokas.

This is an important passage. *Adelphopoiesis* here appears as an agreement that requires the explicit consent of both partners. In this as in many other cases, the person who hopes to gain the most is also the one who initiates the proposal in anticipation of concrete benefits deriving from this association. We are not informed about the way in which this particular relation of *adelphopoiesis* was confirmed. It would be interesting to know if one or the other of the liturgical prayers included in the *euchologia* were used on this occasion, and if so, who would have been qualified to perform this ritual that joined the highest dignitary of the Byzantine church and a saintly bishop in this bond of spiritual brotherhood.

The patriarch's aim in gaining the holy man as his spiritual kin is obvious. He wanted to be assured of his prayers as an intercessor in this life and in the next. The continuation of the story bears this out. When Theodore prophesied the future calamities that would befall the empire, Thomas implored him with tears to pray to God for his timely demise so that he may be spared from witnessing these horrors. He lent force to his request by reminding the bishop of his obligation to pray for him because of their bond of brotherhood and friendship.

The narrative continues with Theodore's desire to depart from Constantinople. The patriarch, however, refused to give his leave, pointing out that the good bishop's prayers on behalf of the city would be required in the upcoming turmoil. Not much later, the patriarch fell seriously ill and again asked for prayers for his demise. Theodore tenaciously refused to coop-erate and prayed for his recovery instead. The patriarch then repeated his entreaty, this time appealing to their bond of brotherhood and now "without hesitation" the holy man complied with this "order" (*keleusis*), as he called it. The patriarch died the same day.

This is a significant episode that illustrates the obligations associated with brother-making, even among monks and clerics. The relation between patriarch and holy man was understood as having a contractual character. Mutual support—here in the form of prayer assistance; in earlier instances in chapter 3 in the form of vicarious penance—was not only freely given, it was expected and, if necessary, could also be demanded.

The enactment of *adelphopoiesis* in this hagiographical narrative dem-onstrates that the patriarch proposed this relationship in the anticipation of profiting from the holy man's intercessory powers. Whatever personal attach-ment there could have developed in the short time that the patriarch had per-sonally known his visitor in Constantinople may possibly have played a role, but that alone cannot have been the determining factor. Sergios, Thomas's successor on the patriarchal throne, had "even more desire for and confidence in" Theodore than his predecessor, yet did not ask to forge a formal bond of brotherhood with the saint.[21]

Conclusion

Several reasons come to mind to explain the greater visibility of *adelpho-poiesis* in the sources of the seventh century. In times of permanent threat by external enemies along the eastern and northern frontiers—Persians, Arabs, Slavs, Avars—and in a period of unstable social structures, there was a heightened need to secure support by whatever means.[22] In the fourth cen-tury, the extended kin group had offered strong horizontal ties and a wide maneuvering space for the individual. By the seventh century, it was replaced by the nuclear family unit and more restricted options to forge relations.[23] It fell to each individual to take the initiative to generate his personal network of alliances. By this time, too, monasticism and its teachings had gained a firm foothold in Byzantine society. The confluence of kinship concepts with monastic values opened new opportunities to articulate and expand one's range of personal relations, through the extension of brother-making beyond the confines of the monastery.

---

[21] Ibid., ch. 136, ed. Festugière, 1: 109.

[22] J. F. Haldon, *Byzantium in the Seventh Century: The Transformation of a Culture* (Cambridge, 1990), 376–87.

[23] K. Cooper, *The Fall of the Roman Household* (Cambridge, 2007).

After more than three centuries of collusion with the empire, Christianity had not only shaped the values and worldview of Byzantine society, but also generated an array of possibilities for the construction of social alliances and networks. Expressions of Christian piety took firm hold in public life, where the veneration of relics and of religious images became noticeably more pronounced and where monks and monasteries became forces to be reckoned with. It was in this context that godparenthood (*synteknia*) and brother-making (*adelphopoiesis*) acquired greater public visibility as they were used to strengthen associations between laymen and monks or, as shall be seen in the next chapter, bonds between laymen. What results is a reciprocal relation between the secular and the religious realm, as the individual's social needs were met in rituals sanctioned by the Church and dispensed by priests.

B. Spiritual Brotherhood beyond the Monastery

Brother-making had the potential not only to join like with like, but also like and unlike, to borrow a phrase from Wendy Bracewell.[24] This extraordinary flexibility explains why *adelphopoiesis* retained its original value within monastic communities, while the radius of its application in the social world of middle and high society saw a gradual expansion. The first step in this development occurred when monks agreed to enter brother-making with laymen. The boundaries between the monastic and the secular world were not an obstacle to contact or communication. To the contrary. The tendency of monks and monasteries to generate a network of relations cast in kinship terms has been observed by Peter Hatlie who remarks that "a spiritual relationship could easily become a functional or instrumental relationship."[25] In Byzantium, laymen and laywomen chose monks as their spiritual advisers. It was monks, not priests, whom they would seek out in search of spiritual guidance, prayers, and blessings or to unburden their conscience. Often, these would be treated as members of the extended family and their spiritual efforts would be recompensed with donations of a material kind.[26]

From its beginnings in the early centuries of Byzantium, monasticism developed into a major force in society. By the middle Byzantine period, after the political upheaval of the Arab invasions and the religious turmoil

---

[24] W. Bracewell, "Friends, Lovers, Rivals, Enemies: Blood-Brotherhood on an Early-Modern Balkan Frontier," *Caiete de antropolgie istorica* 2, nos. 1–3 (2003), 103–30.

[25] P. Hatlie, *The Monks and Monasteries of Constantinople, ca. 350–850* (Cambridge and New York, 2007), 289–311, quote at 299.

[26] R. Morris, "Spiritual Fathers and Temporal Patrons: Logic and Contradiction in Byzantine Monasticism in the Tenth Century," in *Le monachisme à Byzance et en Occident du VIIIe au Xe siècle*, ed. A. Dierkens, D. Missone, and J.-M. Sansterre, 273–88, *Revue Bénédictine* 103 (1993).

of iconoclasm, monasteries emerged as a mainstay of society. They continued to be places of notional retreat, but their locations were not only in the
desert, on the fringe of village society, or at major pilgrimage sites, but also
in or near urban centers. Many of these were founded at the initiative of
women and men of the aristocracy to secure a place for themselves, their
offspring, and their kin, where they could spend their declining years in
tranquility and be assured of the prayers of the monastic community over
their tombs. This trend to create and endow monastic foundations as family
institutions became especially pronounced among male and female members of the Komnenian dynasty in the late eleventh and twelfth centuries.
Other monasteries owed their existence to a spiritual leader who had gathered a group of followers around him, and depended for their support on
wealthy and influential laymen, whether aristocrats or even the emperor
himself, as in the case of John I Tsimiskes (r. 969–76) who sponsored the
foundation of the Great Lavra on Mount Athos.

Large organized communities could count as many as several hundred
members. Through inheritance and donations, monasteries acquired large
amounts of property and thus became not just treasure-houses of valuable
objects for devotional use, but also major property owners with economic
interests in land development and the rural labor force. This translated into
real political power, far beyond the care of souls. Capable and eloquent monastic leaders could easily mobilize great numbers of men and women for their
cause. When this cause was resistance against religious or family politics at
the court, monasteries posed a direct challenge to the throne. Emperors trod
more or less carefully in their relations with monasteries, depending on their
personal inclination and their political backbone. Some sought to curry favors
by granting tax exemption and administrative independence, others attempted
to channel at least part of the material wealth of monasteries into the state's cof-
fers by revoking earlier privileges.

These developments were not without consequence for the monks, their
tranquility, and focus on a life of prayer. By tradition, there were legitimate
practical reasons to leave the monastery, either to conduct business, to discharge spiritual responsibilities or to visit relatives. Such outings could harbor
their own dangers, as demonstrated by the stories mentioned in chapter 3 of
vicarious penance after a monk had fallen into sin with a woman while on
business outside the monastery. In order to avoid even the thought of temptation, some monks refused to set eyes on female relatives who came to see
them, in extreme cases rejecting even the sight of their own mothers. Yet the
monks' status as spiritual experts in prayer and the guidance of souls meant
that lay people were eager to gain access to them, preferably in an association
of assured duration. As Rosemary Morris observed: "It was, in fact, to monks
that Byzantines of all ranks turned in times of crisis, when self-help or existing
communal and kinship structures were of no avail and when the officials of

the state seemed powerless to intervene or were, themselves, the cause of the problem."[27]

Spiritual kinship offered the possibility of an extension of family relations across the monastic-lay boundary in a way that could be regarded as legitimate because it involved an ecclesiastical ritual. Both sides could profit from such relations. The layman could expect to gain access to the monk's spiritual expertise and the power of his prayers, perhaps even to increase his own social standing through this association, while the monk would receive expressions of gratitude in the form of gifts and donations, either to himself or to the monastery, along with legitimate reasons to venture outside the confines of monastery on occasion.

Such relations between monks and laymen became an increasing concern for monastic leaders who expressed their reservations in no uncertain terms. For sixty-one monasteries, ranging in date from the seventh to the fifteenth centuries, the expressed wishes of their founders survive, whether in foundation charters (*typika*) or in testaments. Together with other prescriptive works aimed at regulating the life of individual communities, such sources convey a monastic perspective on *adelphopoiesis*.[28] By the turn of the ninth century, extramural *adelphopoiesis* between monks and laymen became a major issue in these texts. Whenever it was mentioned, it was presented as one of several options of spiritual kinship, along with *synteknia* (godparenthood) and the participation at weddings as a best man, that is, holding the wedding crowns in the marital ritual, a role that usually fell to the godparent later in life.[29]

The great reformer of monasticism in Constantinople at the turn of the ninth century, Theodore the Stoudite (759–826), whom we have already encountered in chapter 3, did not allow any infringements to strict claustration. He frowned upon the relation of monks to lay people outside the community, whether family members or others. Theodore issued punitive regulations against monks who attended *symposia*, drinking parties, with laymen.[30] And in his *Testament* that functioned as a monastic rule, issued shortly before his death, he firmly admonished: "You who have fled from the world and from marriage, do not maintain relations of *adelphopoiia* or *synteknia* with lay people. For this is not found in the Fathers. And even if it is

---

[27] R. Morris, *Monks and Laymen in Byzantium, 843–1118* (Cambridge, 1995), 110.

[28] For the treatment of *adelphopoiesis* in the *typika*, see the remarks by I. M. Konidarês in Konidarês and K. A. Manaphês, *Nomikê theôrêsê tôn monastêriakôn typikôn* (Athens, 1984), 138–43.

[29] Attempts to prevent monks from becoming godparents of laypeople are also known from Syriac monasticism. See W. Selb, *Orientalisches Kirchenrecht*, vol. 2: *Die Geschichte des Kirchenrechts der Westsyrer (von den Anfängen bis zur Mongolenzeit)*, Österreichische Akademie der Wissenschaften, Philosophisch-historische Klasse, Sitzungsberichte, 543 (Vienna, 1989), 276.

[30] Theodore the Stoudite, *Monachorum poenae quotidianae* 53, PG 99, cols. 1748–57, at col. 1755 B. For an aspect of his views of temptation, sexual and theological, see P. Hatlie, "The City a Desert: Theodore of Stoudios on *porneia*," in *Desire and Denial*, ed. James, 67–74.

found, then only rarely, and this is not the rule [*ou nomos*]." The dangers of such associations are implied in the next paragraph: "Do not share a meal with women, whether they are under monastic orders or lay women, except your mother or sister according to the flesh."[31] Indeed, one of the radical measures Theodore introduced to the Stoudiou monastery was the exclusion of all female creatures, not just women, but also animals. With this comment, Theodore seems to suggest that the most perilous effect of brother-making for a monk would be the close contact with the opposite sex that feasts and shared meals would easily entail. At the same time, he reluctantly admitted that there was precedent for *adelphopoiesis* relations between monks and laypeople, rare as it may have been, although such relations were not the norm or, according to an alternative translation, "not the law."

Roughly a century after the *Life of Theodore of Sykeon* first used the word *adelphopoiesis*, Theodore the Stoudite provides the earliest firmly datable indication of the extended application of *adelphopoiesis* beyond monastic circles, to lay society. The spiritual origin of the monastic relationship was still present, but its practice was now receiving a different interpretation as an option to bridge the divide between the secular and the monastic world. From now on, *typika* sporadically addressed this issue. The severity of the rejection of kinship and other relations to the outside world depended to a large extent on the origin and nature of the monastery itself. Foundations by a spiritual leader for his disciples and followers would tend to be stricter, while monasteries that owed their existence to an aristocratic founder or foundress were more open to the possibility of allowing access to the original benefactor's kin group, as Catia Galatariotou has demonstrated. In addition to affecting the financial organization of the monastery, this distinction between aristocratic and nonaristocratic foundations had pronounced repercussions for the regulation of contact with outside society. The nonaristocratic foundations tended to establish strict rules that protected the claustration of the monks, while the family foundations by aristocrats had a greater stake in keeping the boundaries between the inside and the outside of the monastery somewhat permeable, albeit in a monitored way.[32]

---

[31] This injunction appears first in Theodore's letter of advice to his disciple Nikolaos, who had recently become abbot: *Ep.* 10, ed. G. Fatouros, *Theodori Studitae Epistulae*, 2 vols. (Berlin and New York, 1992), 1: 32, lines 33–36, with commentary, 152*. It is repeated verbatim in Theodore's *Testament*, which was probably composed between 806 and 809: Theodoros Stoudites, *Testamentum*, PG 99, cols. 1813–24, at col. 1820 B. Translation mine. See also the translation and commentary by T. Miller, *Byzantine Monastic Foundation Documents*, 5 vols. (Washington, DC, 2000), 1: 67–83.

Already Jerome (ca. 347–420) was complaining that the relation of spiritual parenthood between older women and younger men often degenerated into one of "marital license": Jerome, *Ep.* 125.6.2, ed. I. Hilberg, *Sancti Eusebii Hieronymi Epistulae*, part 3, CSEL 56 (Vienna and Leipzig, 1868), 123, lines 15–18.

[32] C. Galatariotou, "Byzantine *ktetorika typika*: A Comparative Study," *REB* 45 (1987), 77–138, at 95–101 and 109–13.

To counteract an uncontrolled proliferation of such relations, *adelphopoiesis* and *synteknia*, as well as acting as a best man at a wedding ("holding the wedding crowns"), became the target of monastic regulations. The greatest concern was not the participation in the ecclesiastical ritual of brother-making in and of itself, but the social consequences that the relationship entailed: familiarity, ease of access, and the opportunity for socializing, especially at feasts that involve drinking—a chemically induced way of lowering the threshold for the transgression of boundaries of socially acceptable behavior. In an intoxicated state or under the pretext of it, and in company that included women, monks would have felt at liberty to say and do things that were otherwise not permitted.

In the late tenth century, Athanasios imposed a cohesive organization on monastic life on Mount Athos, not least thanks to imperial support. In his *Typikon* of 973 to 975 for the Great Lavra, he repeated the prohibition of Theodore the Stoudite.[33] Elsewhere, he expressed grave concern that the monks should abstain from contact with the outside, especially from opportunities for feasting, drinking, and contact with women. Even on their way to the monastery, monks and laymen were to observe proper restraint in their comportment. They should avoid speaking in a loud voice, shouting, using foul language, or joking.[34] In another *typikon* for the Athos monasteries, dated to the year 971 or 972 and signed by the emperor John Tsimiskes, Athanasios included among the regulations for monks the prohibition against making bonds of *synteknia* and *adelphopoiesis* with lay people. Even pre-existing relations of this kind should not be maintained. "None of the brothers is to be allowed to leave the mountain to form a bond of *synteknia* or *adelphopoiesis* with laymen. If some of them have already concluded a bond of this sort for themselves, they must still not go off to their houses or have lunch or dinner with them or join them at all in drinking."[35]

The second great reform wave in Byzantine monasticism originated in the eleventh century with the Monastery of the Theotokos Evergetis in Constantinople. In these circles, it was generally assumed that monks would live in pairs, as has been noted before. It was also taken for granted that the abbot should set an example of strict claustration and of avoidance of any contact—whether personal or business-related—with the outside world, so that warning of the danger of *adelphopoiesis* with laymen was not even an

---

[33] *Typikon of Athanasios the Athonite for the Lavra Monastery* 32, ed. P. Meyer, *Die Haupturkunden der Athosklöster* (Leipzig, 1894; repr. Amsterdam, 1965), 112f.; trans. G. Dennis, *Byzantine Monastic Foundation Documents*, 1: 258f.

[34] P. Meyer, *Haupturkunden der Athosklöster*, 113, esp. lines 21–22; trans. Dennis, 1: 259.

[35] *Typikon of the Emperor John Tzimiskes* 14, ed. D. Papachryssanthou, *Actes du Prôtaton*, Archives de l'Athos, 7 (Paris, 1975), p. 212, lines 92–93; op.cit., p. 260, lines 60–62. trans. G. Dennis, *Byzantine Monastic Foundation Documents*, 1: 238 (translation slightly altered).

issue in this rule or other rules inspired by it.[36] Not all monasteries adopted such strictures, however, and several legal experts of the eleventh century stated emphatically that monks were prohibited from forming ritual kinship relations with laypeople. Nikephoros Chartophylax, in a letter of response to various questions posed to him by Theodosios, a monk and hermit in Corinth, not only issued the usual prohibitions for monks regarding *adelphopoiesis* with laypeople, but added that such relations did not enjoy legal recognition. He was the first author to introduce a legal angle, presumably with an eye to relations between laypeople, when he addressed the issue of *adelphopoiesis* following the topics of second marriage, illicit sexual relations, and penitence, and before dealing with abortion, asserting that: "It is forbidden to monks to enter into relationships of [baptismal] co-parenthood or *adelphopoiesis*. And the church enjoins this [prohibition], by way of commandment, to the abbots and supervisors of monasteries. For the law does absolutely not recognize the so-called 'brother-makings.'"[37] Around the same period, Peter Chartophylax responded to a query whether monks were allowed to become godfathers, to enter into brother-making, or to hold wedding crowns, in no uncertain terms: "These are against the canons (of the church) and prohibited."[38]

Peter Chartophylax's recommendation would become something of a yardstick for future authors. In the early fourteenth century, it was cited in Constantine Harmenopoulos's summary of canon law. Harmenopoulos begins by invoking canon twenty-two of the seventh session of the Council in Trullo, which prescribed that when laymen sit at the table with women, they should behave graciously and abstain from "joking" with them, while monks or priests should sit by themselves, shunning the presence even of female relatives, unless they are in the company of pious and religious men and women. To reinforce this code of conduct, he then refers to Peter Chartophylax's observation that monks are not permitted to become *synteknoi* (godfathers), to act as best man at a wedding, or to conclude *adelphopoiesis*.[39]

In later Byzantine centuries, as has been noted, the walls of monastic enclosures became more permeable for movement in both directions. It was thus not uncommon for prominent men and women to return to secular affairs

---

[36] *Typikon of Timothy for the Monastery of the Theotokos Evergetis* 13, ed. Gautier, "Typikon de la Théotokos Évergétis," 49, trans. Jordan, *Byzantine Monastic Foundation Documents*, 2: 483; see also 18, ed. Gautier, 61, trans. Jordan, 2: 488.

[37] P. Gautier, "Le chartophylax Nicéphore," *REB* 27 (1969): 159–95, at 172. Compare G. A. Rhalles and M. Potles, *Syntagma tôn theiôn kai hierôn kanonôn tôn te hagiôn kai paneuphêmôn apostolôn, kai tôn hierôn oikoumenikôn kai topikôn synodôn, kai tôn kata meros hagiôn paterôn*, vol. 5 (Athens, 1855), 400.

[38] Petros Chartophylax, in Rhalles and Potles, *Syntagma*, 5: 370.

[39] M. T. Fögen, "Harmenopoulos, Constantine," *ODB*, 2: 902. Constantine Harmenopoulos, *Epitome canonum*, PG 150, cols. 45–168, at col. 124 D. Even though it does not correspond verbatim, Harmenopoulos probably refers to the passage by Peter Chartophylax cited above.

after spending time in a monastery, only eventually to retire to the relative quiet of the monastic life at the end of their lives. Relations with one's kin remained strong, especially in the aristocratic family foundations, to the point of eroding the spirit of monastic seclusion. Under the Palaiologan dynasty, a renewed reform attempt was made by Athanasius I, who was Patriarch of Constantinople from 1289 to 1293 and again from 1303 to 1309. His attempts to curb the lavish lifestyle and the liberties taken by monks of certain social status did not have lasting success.[40] His monastic rule was addressed to all the monks throughout the *oikoumene*. It speaks of the brotherhood of all in Christ and the brotherly love that issues from it, where there is no space for friendly disposition (*schesis*) toward relatives or for personal friendships (*philia*). All monks, and especially heads of monasteries, were expected to exercise restraint in their comportment, especially during the liturgy (no leaning against the walls) and during meals (no idle talk), but also while going about their work inside the monastery (no laughter and definitely no women). In the same breath, the patriarch added: "More generally, let the superior guard himself and the brotherhood from sworn associations [*synômosiai*] and drinking parties [*symposia*] during the day or night, also from special friendships [*philia merikê*] with a few or many, either within or outside the monastery."[41] In the ruling of the stern patriarch, there should no longer be any consideration for any ties of kinship or friendship, no preferential treatment in the process of admission, and absolutely no visits to the outside. His prohibition for monks not only regarded the cultivation of relations outside the monastery as an objectionable offense, but also encompassed the formation of cliques and their convivialities, on whatever side of the monastic enclosure they occurred. The earliest such prohibition had been issued at the Council of Chalcedon in 451, where canon 18 addressed the destabilizing potential of such group formations in no uncertain terms: "Secret unions [*synômosiai*] and associations [*phratriai*] are forbidden even by the secular laws; and much more is it becoming that they should be forbidden in the Church of God. If, then, clerics or monks are found to conspire or to combine or to make intrigues against their bishops or their brother clerics, they shall certainly lose their office."[42] Later repeated at the Council in Trullo, this regulation speaks to the fear of the destabilizing potential of groups or associations that employ fraternal language and model their conduct on sibling relations.

---

[40] T. S. Miller and J. Thomas, "The Monastic Rule of Patriarch Athanasios I: An Edition, Translation and Commentary," *OCP* 62 (1996), 353–71.

[41] Ibid., ch. 4, p. 361.

[42] *Acts of the Council of Chalcedon*, canon 18, ed. P. P. Joannou, *Discipline générale antique*, vol. 2: *Les canons des Pères Grecs* (Grottaferrata, 1962), 84; trans. C. J. Hefele, *A History of the Councils of the Church* (Edinburgh, 1883), 3: 404. This was repeated as canon 34 at the Council in Trullo; ed. Joannou, *Discipline générale antique*, 2: 168.

The basic prohibition of *adelphopoiesis* and *synteknia* for Athos monks was repeated in the year 1406 in a chrysobull of Manuel II Palaiologos as part of a renewed attempt to reform the lassitude of the monks on the peninsula. This time, the regulation was accompanied by further explanations: "No monk of the Holy Mountain should go out and make *synteknia* or *adelphopoiia* with laypeople. For this is unseemly for monks who have foresworn children, fathers and all blood relations altogether. And if some have already transgressed in this way, they shall no longer go to their houses, nor take lunch or dinner with them, or indeed join in drinking parties with them, nor should they leave anything to them as their heirs."[43] This spells out for the first time an additional aspect of the perceived peril of ritual kinship relations between monks and laypeople, namely the danger of the alienation of a monk's personal property to an outside heir that would otherwise pass into the ownership of the monastery.[44] The emperor is remarkably lenient in his prescription, simply curtailing the monks' future actions, while accepting existing *adelphopoiesis* relations as valid, and without threatening punishment.

Concerns of an economic nature continued to be voiced in conjunction with brother-making across lay-monastic boundaries. Following in the same vein as Patriarch Athanasios I, two generations later Patriarch Matthew I (1397–1410) issued general advice to the monks under his authority. Under the general heading of the avoidance of issuing privileges to individual monks or of forging connections to lay people, the summary of the patriarch's rules by the monk Markos includes the following prohibition: "(It is not permitted) under the pretext of supporting the monastery, to make friends with people outside the monastery, especially not with laypeople, and to conclude friendships, *adelphopoiia*, or the so-called *synteknia* with them, and to conduct business in the form of loans, worldly exchanges, and trade."[45] This is followed by prohibitions of profit-making trading enterprises, even for the benefit of the monastery. In this perspective, *adelphopoiesis* appears as one of several social setups that would facilitate profitable economic interaction. This mention of what in modern fundraising jargon might be called "cultivating the donor base" offers an indication of the potential motivation for a monastery or its members as they actively pursued relations with lay people.

The way in which monastic reformers and regulators addressed *adelphopoiesis* involving monks reveals how the relationship could be put to use as a

---

[43] Chrysobull-Typikon of Manuel II Palaiologos 10, *Actes du Prôtaton*, ed. D. Papachryssanthou, Archives de l'Athos, 7 (Paris, 1975), 260, lines 59–62. My translation.

[44] For an emphasis on this aspect of *adelphopoiesis*, on the basis of patchy and thus inconclusive evidence, see Bébén, "Frères et membres du corps du Christ."

[45] I. M. Konidarês and K. A. Manaphês, "Epiteuleutios boulêsis kai didaskalia tou oikoumenikou patriarchou Matthaiou A' (1397–1410)," *EEBS* 45 (1981–82), 462–515, at 496–97, lines 906–10. For the historical background, see also H. Hunger, "Das Testament des Patriarchen Matthaios I (1397–1410)," *BZ* 51 (1958), 288–309.

boundary-crossing strategy to join like and unlike, monk and layman. This entailed dangers and temptations especially for the monk: his ascetic self-control was compromised by the feasting and drinking that accompanied such relations, his commitment to chastity was threatened by the contact with women outside the monastery, while his obligation to Christian love of one's neighbor was imperiled by his close association with special individuals. As the earliest regulations show, *adelphopoiesis* was from the beginning contextualized and interpreted as one option among the other forms of kinship generated by church rituals: co-godparenthood (*synteknia*) and holding wedding crowns (i.e., acting as a best man). It harbored the same danger of fomenting unrest as all small, closed groups such as sworn associations or drinking clubs. In later centuries, the origin of ritual kinship in a spiritual bond was overshadowed by social practice and *adelphopoiesis* was used to create a framework for the transaction of business and as a way to pass on inheritance—a confusion that would also become a concern in the brother-making relations between laymen.

The attempts to regulate the conduct of monks with regard to *adelphopoiesis* with laypeople span the early ninth to the early fifteenth centuries. The first regulations thus coincide roughly with the earliest manuscript attestation of the ritual prayers in the *Barberini Euchologium*. In these texts, brother-making is treated so matter-of-factly that we may assume that it was fast becoming a mainstay of society. Although the individual stepping stones along this way are not traceable, and although our gaze is always dependent on the pattern of the production and survival of the sources, the main trajectory seems clear: it begins with small-group and paired monasticism in the fourth century, continues with the earliest allusions to prayers that join two monks, affirms the practice of *adelphopoiesis* (now under this name) among monks, clerics, and laymen in the hagiography of the seventh century, and steps onto the scene of widespread social practice in the late eighth and ninth centuries, when monks begin to employ it as a way to negotiate their distance from lay society. As the historical sources discussed next will show, this was also the time when men and women of the world put this strategy to good use among themselves in the hope of advancing their interests and status.

A Word of Caution

Since the focus of this investigation is on the ritual of *adelphopoiesis* and its application, I consider only those instances where *adelphopoiesis* is either strongly implied or explicitly mentioned by that word. The story of the emperor Basil and John, the son of Danelis, which will be discussed next, for example, speaks only of "spiritual brotherhood." Yet we are justified in treating it as an example for *adelphopoiesis*, not only because these expressions were used interchangeably in the legal sources, but also because the context makes it clear that this was a formalized fraternal bond concluded between two men. The same values of harmony, unity of purpose, loyalty, assistance, and support also characterize the language of friendship, so that there is a strong tendency for close friends to address one another as "brothers." These characteristics also apply to the relationship between Basil's son, the future emperor Leo VI, and his school-mate, the future patriarch Nikolaos Mystikos, that will concern us again soon, which is called by the legal term "brother-hood by arrangement."

The conservative approach to handling the sources has the advantage of assembling watertight evidence, but the disadvantage of covering only a small catchment area. A more inclusive study of social relations in Byzantium than can be attempted here would pay due attention to the language of friend-ship, the use of kinship designations for close associates or as honorific titles, and reference to oaths that confirm agreements between two people. All of these could be, and often were, part and parcel of the practice and enactment of individual brother-making relations, so that we may safely assume that the evidence for *adelphopoiesis* presented here is only the tip of a very large iceberg.

A further pitfall in interpreting the sources is anachronism in expression. One indication that *adelphopoiesis* had entered into the mainstream of social relations was the use of the term by later authors to describe relations that preceded them by centuries. This is the case in the *Story of the Construction of Hagia Sophia*, which dates from the second half of the ninth century—the same period when Basil's story demonstrates a heightened social presence of *adelphopoiesis*.[46] According to this legendary account, the emperor Justinian had entered into a formal relation of brotherhood with Strategios, the min-ister of finance (*comes sacrarum largitionum*) from 535 to about 538, who played an important role in the building works.[47] On one occasion, Strategios is called the emperor's *adelphopoiêtos*;[48] later in the text, he is referred to as the "spiritual brother" of Justinian.[49] In a similar context, Severus, a man of patrician rank, is mentioned as the *adelphopoiêtos* of the emperor Constans II (r. 641–68), the grandson of Heraclius.[50] The *Patria of Constantinople*, a

---

[46] On this text, see G. Dagron, *Constantinople imaginaire: Étude sur le recueil des "Patria"* (Paris, 1984), 265–69.

[47] Strategios's career is well documented in the sources: see A. H. M. Jones, J. R. Martindale, and J. Morris, *Prosopography of the Later Roman Empire*, vol. 2: *395–527* (Cambridge, 1980), 1034–36; and Jones, Martindale, and Morris, *Prosopography of the Later Roman Empire*, vol. 3: *527–641* (Cambridge, 1992), 1200–01.

[48] *Narratio de aedificatione templi s. Sophiae*, ch. 4; ed. T. Preger, *Scriptores originum Constantinopolitanum*, vol. 1 (Leipzig, 1901), 78, 13–79, 1.

[49] Ibid., ch. 9, ed. Preger, 85, 1. Boswell's quotation in *Same-Sex Unions*, 229n56 of this passage is an error.

[50] *Scriptores originum Constantinopolitanarum*, ed. Preger, 10: 251–52; Pseudo-Codinus, *De aedificiis Constantinopolitanis* 107, PG 157, cols. 515–612, at col. 585D–588A (where *adelphopoiêtos*

document attributed to the sixth-century author Hesychius of Miletos that was revised in the tenth century, credits Severus with the construction of a home for the aged.[51] Whether these passages by later authors offer sixth- or seventh-century evidence for *adelphopoiesis* involving emperors is difficult to say, although they certainly have been interpreted as such. At the very least, they should be regarded as anachronistic retrojections reflecting the lived reality of their ninth- and tenth-century authors, similar to the use of the term in the later paraphrases of the *Life of John the Almsgiver*.

Cautious as my approach may be, it still yields firm evidence for brother-making relations between identifiable individuals at the rate of at least one pairing per century. Combined with further literary references and prescriptive sources that regulate brother-making for monks and for laymen, this is sufficient evidence to affirm the importance of *adelphopoiesis* throughout the Byzantine Empire.

C. Case Study: Emperor Basil I and John, the Son of Danelis

The most prominent person who is attested to have entered into brother-making is the future emperor Basil I (867–86), the founder of the Macedonian dynasty.[52] Like no other, he made judicious use of the potential for political and economic alliance that brotherhood by arrangement offered. This strategy facilitated his meteoric rise, which brought the country lad from Macedonia to Constantinople to make his fortune and ultimately—after the murders of a rival at court and of his erstwhile benefactor and predecessor, Michael III—to the imperial throne, which he held for nearly two decades until his death as the result of a hunting accident.

There are no contemporary sources for Basil's reign; those that survive date from at least a century later, sometimes present a confused chronology, and often disagree with one another.[53] The events that interest us are

---

is rendered into Latin as *frater adoptivus*). Although the text has only "Konsta," the identity of the emperor is quite clear from the context: he is a descendant of the emperor Heraclius and was murdered in his bath in Sicily, whereupon Severus led the fleet safely back to the East. Boswell, *Same-Sex Unions*, 229 and n. 58, however, confesses his inability to identify the emperor in question, whom he assigns to the sixth (!) century.

[51] *Patria Konstantinoupoleôs* 3.108, *Scriptores originum Constantinopolitanarum*, ed. Preger, 2: 251, 18–252, 4.

[52] The following is an expanded and partially revised version of Rapp, "Ritual Brotherhood in Byzantium." For a detailed evaluation of the sources, see also S. Tougher, "Michael III and Basil the Macedonian: Just Good Friends?" in *Desire and Denial in Byzantium*, ed. James, 149–58; and Tougher, "Imperial Families: The Case of the Macedonians (867–1025)," in *Approaches to the Byzantine Family*, ed. Brubaker and Tougher, 303–26.

[53] For an overview of these sources, their historical value and their interrelations, see J. Karayannopoulos and G. Weiss, *Quellenkunde zur Geschichte von Byzanz*, 2 vols. (Wiesbaden,

no exception: The best-known version is told in the *Life of Basil (Vita Basilii)*, according to which Basil entered into brotherhood with John, the son of the fabulously wealthy widow Danelis who lived in the Peloponnese. The other tradition is represented by the chronicles of Symeon Magister, Leo the Grammarian, and George the Monk, which ultimately go back to a common source. According to their account, Basil contracted brotherhood with Nikolaos, a man associated with the Monastery of Diomedes in Constantinople.

The story about Danelis and her son is told in the *Life of Basil (Vita Basilii)*, an official biography written by an anonymous "ghost writer" at the instigation of Basil's grandson, the emperor Constantine VII Porphyrogennetos, and preserved as book 6 of the so-called *Theophanes Continuatus* in a manuscript of the early eleventh century.[54] In this account, Basil was an upstart from Macedonia who made his way to the capital and received a helping hand from the abbot of the Monastery of Diomedes, eventually entered the service of the wealthy and well-connected Theophilos as chief of his stable (*protostrator*), and accompanied his master on imperial business to the city of Patras in the Peloponnese.[55] When the master and later his servant visited a local church, a monk, to whom Basil's future as emperor had been revealed, paid no attention to Theophilos, but later received Basil with great honors. The lady Danelis, a widow of great power and wealth, heard about this incident and demanded an explanation from the monk, complaining—with barely concealed ambition— that he had never shown such honor to herself or her own family.[56] On learning the reason, she waited for the right moment to invite Basil to her house, showered him with presents of immense value, and, "for the time being," asked from him only that he enter into a bond of spiritual brotherhood (*pneumatikês*

1982), 2: 368–72. For the legendary character of the sources on Basil, see G. Moravcsik, "Sagen und Legenden über Kaiser Basilieios I," *DOP* 15 (1951), 59–126; for their ideological slant, see A. Markopoulos, "Oi metamorphôseis tês 'mythologias' tou Basileiou A'," in *Antecessor: Festschrift für Spyros N. Troianos zum 80. Geburtstag*, ed. V. A. Leontaritou, K. A. Bourdara, and E. S. Papagianni, 947–70 (Athens, 2013). For the cultural context of the *Vita Basilii*, see P. Magdalino, "Knowledge in Authority and Authorized History: The Intellectual Programme of Leo VI and Constantine VII," in *Authority in Byzantium*, ed. P. Armstrong, 187–209 (Farnham, 2013). Here and in the following, I am indebted to Claudia Ludwig and Thomas Pratsch for their advice on prosopographical matters.

[54] The *Vita Basilii* was edited by I. Ševčenko, *Chronographiae quae Theophanis Continuati nomine fertur Liber quo Vita Basilii imperatoris amplectitur*, CFHB 42 (Berlin, 2011). This supersedes the text in *Theophanes continuatus*, ed. I. Bekker, *Theophanes Continuatus, Ioannes Cameniata, Symeon Magister, Georgius Monachus*, CSHB (Bonn, 1838), 3–481, at 211–353. For an annotated translation into modern Greek, see C. Sidere, *Bios Basileiou: Hê biographia tu autokratora Basileiu I. tu Makedonos apo ton estemmeno engono tu* (Athens, 2010).

[55] *Vita Basilii* ch. 11, ed. Ševčenko, 40–46. "Theophilos," PMBZ 1, no. 8221.

[56] "Danelis," PMBZ I, no. 1215. On this wealthy and powerful widow, see S. Runciman, "The Widow Danelis," in *Etudes dediées à la mémoire d'André Andréadès* (Athens, 1940), 425–31; I. Ševčenko, "Re-reading Constantine Porphyrogenitus," in *Byzantine Diplomacy: Papers from the Twenty-Fourth Spring Symposium of Byzantine Studies, Cambridge, March 1990*, ed. J. Shepard and S. Franklin, 167–95 (Aldershot, 1992), 192–93.

adelphotêtos syndesmon) with her son John (see Figures 4.1 and 4.2).[57] Basil at first refused because of the inequality in their status, but finally yielded to her continued insistence. Only then did Danelis explain the monk's prophesy to Basil and requested that he show love and compassion "to us." Basil in return promised that if and when he had the power to do so, he would make Danelis the mistress (*kyrian*) over all this country.[58] Clearly, the instigator of this bond of brotherhood is an ambitious mother. The narrator, well aware of the central importance of Danelis's first generous gift in creating a future obligation on the part of the recipient, compared this act to sowing seed in fertile soil in anticipation of a manifold harvest.[59] This part of the story owes its inspiration to a scene in the *Alexander Romance*, when the fabulously wealthy Queen Kandake recognized the young Alexander, despite his disguise, as the real king. She showered him with lavish gifts and wished to make him her son. Such literary borrowing may cast doubt on the veracity of the description of the encounter between Basil and Danelis in the *Life of Basil*. But even if the details are adopted from another source, they provide a contemporary view of how an *adelphopoiesis* relation could be enacted.[60]

The narrative continues with Basil's career under the emperor Michael III (842–67). He was made *protostrator* (chief of the stable), given a beautiful wife, and eventually became Michael's adopted son and finally co-emperor. As Michael's extravagant taste for drinking and partying was threatening to ruin the state, the story goes, he was eventually killed in his sleep at the instigation of a group of conspirators. Basil, who is conspicuously absent during the narration of Michael's demise, became emperor soon thereafter. There follows an extensive treatment of his virtues and accomplishments on the battlefield and at home. To illustrate Basil's generosity toward those who helped him before his rise to power, our source gives two examples: the abbot of the Monastery of Diomedes, who now received lavish imperial donations for his monastery in return for his assistance to Basil when the latter first set foot in the capital, and the lady Danelis.[61] Immediately after his accession, the new emperor made good on his earlier promise and called Danelis's son John to the capital, appointed him to the prestigious rank of senior sword-bearer (*prôtospatharios*), and granted him *parrhêsia* (a complex term meaning freedom of access and of speech with someone of higher position) "on account of the bond of spiritual brotherhood by which they had been previously

---

[57] "Ioannes," PMBZ 1, no. 3328.

[58] *Vita Basilii* 11, ed. Ševčenko, 44, lines 56–57.

[59] Ibid. 11, ed. Ševčenko, 44, lines 43–44.

[60] E. Anagnostakes, "To epeisodio tês Daniêlidas: Plêrophories kathêmerinou biou ê mythoplastika stoichei?" in *Hê kathêmerinê zôê sto Byzantio: Praktika tou a' diethnous symposiou*, ed. C. Angelidi, 375–90 (Athens, 1989); Magdalino, "Knowledge in Authority."

[61] *Vita Basilii* 74, ed. Ševčenko, 252, lines 7–17. According to this source, however, the abbot does not become Basil's "brother by arrangement."

united."[62] Even more important in the eyes of the historiographer was the relation with Danelis. Desirous to see Basil and in expectation of "greater honors," she followed the imperial invitation and despite her old age made the journey to Constantinople, carried on a litter. She was welcomed like royalty and brought such a stupendous array of gifts as no foreign ruler had ever presented before.[63] Scholars have speculated whether this part of the Danelis story was perhaps inspired by the biblical story of the visit of the Queen of Sheba, who brought exorbitant gifts from Africa to King Solomon which were then used for the adornment of the newly built Temple in Jerusalem. At the time when the Danelis story was committed to writing, this would have had rich resonances, since Basil had also been a temple builder (the lavishly decorated Nea Church was the first major church to be built in the capital after Justinian's Hagia Sophia), and his son and successor Leo VI "the Wise" liked to see himself compared to Solomon.[64]

In return for her gifts, Danelis received many honors and titles, including that of "mother of the emperor" (*mêter basileôs*)—part of a trend toward the use of kinship designations as titles.[65] Then the gift-giving escalated: Danelis decided that these rich rewards were more than an equitable return for her offerings, and therefore ceded to Basil, "her son and emperor" (*tô huiô kai basilei*),[66] a substantial part of the Peloponnese. She returned to Greece holding a more elevated rank and greater authority than before, "as if she were the sovereign empress of those dwelling there,"[67] perhaps an allusion to Basil's earlier promise to make her "mistress," of her possessions.

As time went by, Danelis outlived both Basil and her son John. But her attachment to the imperial family continued. She made another journey to the capital to visit Basil's son and successor Leo VI, and—despite the fact that she had at least one grandson by the name of Daniel[68]—named Leo as

---

[62] Ibid. 74, ed. Ševčenko, 252, lines 3–254, line 4.

[63] Ibid. 74, ed. Ševčenko, 254, lines 5–256, line 37.

[64] Anagnostakes, "To epeisodio tês Daniêlidas." I am grateful to Christina Angelidi for this reference. See most recently, S. Tougher, *The Reign of Leo VI (886–912): Politics and People* (Leiden, 1997), 122–32.

[65] *Vita Basilii* 75, ed. Ševčenko, 258, lines 1–14. It is commonly held that "Father of the Emperor" (*basileôpatôr*) was granted as an official title for the first time by Basil's son Leo VI to his father-in-law Stylianos Zaoutzes. See A. Kazhdan, "Basileopator," *ODB* 1: 263–64; and P. Karlin-Hayter, "The Title or Office of Basileopator," *Byzantion* 38 (1968), 278–80. This passage can be taken as evidence that Danelis was the first woman to be honored with a kinship designation as a title. An earlier example is Philaretos the Merciful, whose daughter was chosen to become the wife of Constantine VI (r. 780–97). According to his hagiographer, Philaretos rejected all the gifts and honors that the Emperor lavished upon him, and wished to be called only "grandfather of the emperor" (*pappos tou basileôs*): M.-H. Fourmy and M. Leroy, "La Vie de S. Philarète," *Byzantion* 4 (1934), 85–170, at 151, line 13.

[66] Thus also the translation of Ševčenko, 259. Boswell, *Same-Sex Unions*, 235, thinks that this expression refers to a gift made jointly to her biological son and the emperor. But in that case, the Greek would have to read *tô huiô kai tô basilei*.

[67] *Vita Basilii*, ch. 75, ed. Ševčenko, 258, lines 11–12.

[68] Ibid., ch. 77, ed. Ševčenko, 262, line 4.

FIGURE 4.1 *Left: Danelis dines with John and the future emperor Basil I; right: Basil and John are united in brotherhood through a priest's prayers in a church. Illuminated Chronicle of Skylitzes, twelfth century, Escurial, ms. graecus Vitr. 26–2, folio 85 recto*
Source: V. Tsamakda, The Illustrated Chronicle of Ioannes Skylitzes in Madrid *(Leiden, 2002), no. 206.*

the heir to her possessions. There is good reason to assume, as Cyril Mango has suggested, that her wealth—the gifts she gave to the court on her visit to Constantinople, the gifts that she sent every year to Basil, and her possessions at home, which she bequeathed to Leo—was so significant that these transactions were recorded in the imperial archives, which then became the source of information for the author of the *Life of Basil*.[69]

According to the story of "spiritual brotherhood" (*pneumatikos adelphos* is the term that is used; *adelphopoiesis* or related words are not mentioned) between Basil and John as it is told in the *Life of Basil*, the instigator and main beneficiary of this relation was Danelis: she forged a lasting relation with the imperial throne, her de facto rule over large parts of Greece received imperial recognition, and her association with the Emperor translated into a position of enhanced authority and honor. The relation is interpreted as creating obligations as well as ties of property and inheritance that extend over three generations, from Danelis to Basil and on to Leo.

The second group of sources, none of which mentions Danelis or her son, describes Basil's "brotherhood" with a man from the Monastery of St. Diomedes in Constantinople.[70] The alternative story is told in most detail in the chronicle of George the Monk, which I follow here: Basil came from

---

[69] C. Mango, "Introduction," in I. Ševčenko, ed., *Chronographiae quae Theophanis Continuati nomine fertur Liber quo Vita Basilii imperatoris amplectitur*, CFHB 42 (Berlin, 2011), 11*–12*.

[70] The *Vita Basilii* in Theophanes Continuatus also includes this story, with the abbot of the monastery as the protagonist, but significantly omits the "brotherhood" bond. *Theophanes Continuatus*, ed. Bekker, 223, lines 10–225, 1, and 316, lines 19–317, 7.

FIGURE 4.2 *Top: Danelis travels to Constantinople; bottom: Danelis brings presents to Emperor Basil I. Illuminated Chronicle of Skylitzes, twelfth century, Escurial, ms. graecus Vitr. 26–2, folio 102 recto*

Source: V. Tsamakda, The Illustrated Chronicle of Ioannes Skylitzes in Madrid *(Leiden, 2002), no. 229.*

his native Macedonia to the capital to seek employment. Exhausted from the journey, he fell asleep on the steps of the monastery dedicated to the martyr Diomedes that was conveniently located just inside the Golden Gate to the city. That night, Diomedes appeared in a dream to Nikolaos, the caretaker (*prosmonarios*) of the church,[71] instructing him to look after Basil who would one day become emperor. The next day, he took Basil to the baths, clothed him, and concluded "brotherhood" with him. He also succeeded in securing a position for Basil in the stables of Theophilos. Just like Danelis, Nikolaos converted his knowledge of the future success of Basil into political currency, by first creating an obligation through bene-factions, then suggesting the brotherhood relation. And the strategy paid off: soon after his accession to the throne, Basil appointed Nikolaos to the

---

[71] According to Theophanes Continuatus, *Chronicle*, 223, 15, the man in question (who is never identified by name) was the abbot of the monastery. Genesius, ed. A. Lesmüller-Werner and J. Thurn, *Iosephi Genesii regum libri quattuor*, CFHB 14 (Berlin and New York, 1978), 77, reports that some of his sources mention a monk and others an abbot.

highest ecclesiastical office after the Patriarch of Constantinople, that of *synkellos*, and also to the office of financial administrator of the patriarchate (*oikonomos*).[72]

Whether these two stories of Basil's brother-making, either with Danelis's son John or with Nikolaos of the Monastery of Diomedes, are narrative duplicates of the same event, or whether they relate to two different events, we will never know. Obviously, the chroniclers were more concerned to record the fact that Basil had entered into a brotherhood relation before his reign than with the identity of his "brother."[73] In both traditions, the story serves a double purpose: to illustrate the prophesies about Basil's future ascent to the imperial throne that were revealed to others, and to underscore Basil's moral integrity when after his accession he showed his gratitude to his earlier benefactors.

Both source traditions agree on the central role of Theophilos (also called by the diminutive Theophilitzes, "little Theophilos") for Basil's rise to power. Theophilos maintained a *hetaireia*, or boys' club, which the *Life of Basil* describes in colorful detail:

> As it happened, this little Theophilos was a man of high spirit, nor was he devoid of pride: the therefore strove to surround himself with men of excellence, handsome and tall in stature, men above all outstanding in courage and strength of body; and he derived a great deal of pride and satisfaction from these people: thus, to give an example, one could see them decked out in silken robes, and being conspicuous on account of other apparel. The young newcomer Basil was enlisted among these, and since he was found to be far superior to others, both in the strength of his body and in the manliness of his soul, Theophilos made him his *protostrator*.[74]

This group was in friendly competition with a similar posse that the emperor Michael III had gathered around himself and sometimes participated in joint events. On various such occasions, Basil had the opportunity to display his good looks, imposing stature, and athletic prowess in front of the emperor Michael and other admirers, and it was not long until the emperor "took him over from little Theophilos, to enroll him among the imperial *stratores*."[75] This is a rare glimpse of the formation of homosocial groups in Byzantium, based on physical attributes and personal skill.

---

[72] George the Monk, ed. I. Bekker, *Theophanes Continuatus, Ioannes Cameniata, Symeon Magister, Georgius Monachus*, CSHB (Bonn, 1838), 842, lines 19–20.

[73] Boswell, *Same-Sex Unions*, 236–37, admits that there may be only one original story, but prefers the possibility that Basil was joined in brotherhood with two men.

[74] *Vita Basilii*, ch. 9, ed. Ševčenko, 38–39.

[75] Ibid., ch. 13, ed. Ševčenko, 52–53.

The second narrative tradition represented by George the Monk also leaves ample room for speculation about Basil's social success in the context of male bonding. It is tempting to associate Nikolaos of the Diomedes monastery with one of the pious confraternities associated with baths and bathing that are attested in Constantinople from the sixth century. This would fit well with the fact that Nikolaos also has a brother (perhaps a *confrère*) who is a physician and who brokers Basil's introduction to Theophilitzes. This takes us into the world of bathing culture and its erotic and sexual possibilities for male-male relations. It has even been suggested that Nikolaos may have been particularly impressed with the sight of Basil's "knapsack" and "staff," here understood as a *double entendre* for male genitals.[76] The story of Basil and those in other sources relating to this phenomenon of closely knit male groups was the subject in 1965 of the seminal study "Byzantinisches Gefolgschaftswesen" by Hans-Georg Beck. He gave a brilliant analysis of the intricate and complex relations of friendship, patronage, and political alliance that Basil and other ambitious men who were lacking in family pedigree, education, and wealth cultivated to foster their social advancement.[77]

Basil was extraordinarily successful in exploiting the bond of spiritual brotherhood for his own political purposes. An attentive reading of the second group of sources on the reign of Basil, that is, those that mention his brotherhood with Nikolaos, opens up the possibility that he had contracted an additional number of such relations. In three chronicles,[78] the passage discussing Basil's advancement of the career of the monastic caretaker Nikolaos continues with a list of other "brothers" whom he placed in positions of power and influence. The chronicles of George the Monk and Leo the Grammarian,[79] which belong to the same textual tradition, are most revealing in their phrasing. The chronicle of Symeon the Logothete presents a more straightforward version of a list of four "brothers," which is therefore suspicious as the *lectio facilior*.[80] George the Monk, after pointing out that Basil made Nikolaos finance minister and right hand of the

---

[76] *Chronika Georgija Amartola*, ed. Istrin, 2: 5, line 35. For such charitable lay associations, see chapter 1 and P. Magdalino, "Church, Bath and Diakonia"; Tougher, "Michael III and Basil the Macedonian," 155–56. On the Monastery of Diomedes, see Janin, *Les églises et les monastères*, 100–02.

[77] Beck, "Byzantinisches Gefolgschaftswesen." Boswell, *Same-Sex Unions*, does not note this work. Beck seems to accept that Basil entered into spiritual brotherhood with both Nikolaos and the son of Danelis. He then carries his observations further to point out several other close relationships that Basil forged in the course of his career at the court of Michael III.

[78] Genesius omits this list.

[79] Leo the Grammarian, ed. I. Bekker, *Leonis Grammatici chronographia*, CSHB (Bonn, 1842), 256, lines 13–21.

[80] Symeon the Logothete, ed. I. Bekker, *Theophanes Continuatus, Ioannes Cameniata, Symeon Magister, Georgius Monachus*, CSHB (Bonn, 1838), 691, lines 10–14.

patriarch, continues by saying that the emperor made "his *other* brother John" chief of the imperial guard (*droungarios tês viglas*),[81] placed "*their* other brother" Paul in charge of the imperial treasury (*tou sakelliou*), while "the other brother Constantine" (Leo the Grammarian has merely "the fourth") became head of the internal revenue service (*logothetês tou genikou*).[82] Since Nikolaos was, as these same sources inform us, Basil's "brother by arrangement," his "other brother John" must also have also been joined to him in this relation of ritualized kinship, and the same must apply to Paul and probably also to Constantine.[83]

These passages raise the question of the exact extent of the "brotherhood" thus concluded: was each of these individuals joined in brother-making with Basil only, or did their individual relations with Basil amount to lateral relations of brotherhood between the "siblings" thus created? We know that "brotherhoods" (*phratriai*), especially for religious and military purposes, existed in Byzantium, and it is possible that our texts refer to just such a social grouping, formed to consolidate Basil's power in his quest for the throne. We have no knowledge as to the exact procedure to gain membership in such a group, but it is conceivable that the prayers for *adelphopoiesis* could have been adjusted for this kind of brother-making. There was also the possibility of creating close ties through oath taking. Basil, we are told, forged such a connection with Symbatios,[84] an important man at the court of Michael III who was married to the daughter of the caesar Bardas, the emperor's close associate. Basil gained him as an ally in his quest to secure the emperor's favor: "through oaths they assured each other of being in harmony and lasting love."[85] Whether this report, preserved in only one of the two narrative traditions, is intended to hint at an *adelphopoiesis* relation, must remain open.

---

[81] It is unlikely that this John is identical with the son of Danelis of the same name.

[82] George the Monk, ed. Bekker, 842, 13–843, 2. The version of George the Monk published by Istrin, 21, lines 27–31, mentions the advancement of Nikolaos, of "his brother" John, and "from among his other brothers," the advancement of Paul and Constantine.

[83] It is attractive to identify our John and Constantine with John *ho Chaldos* and Konstantinos *ho Toxaras*, associates of Basil who assisted him in his plot against the caesar Bardas and in the murder of Michael III: George the Monk, ed. Bekker, 830, 837; Leo the Grammarian, ed. Bekker, 244, 51; Symeon the Logothete, ed. Bekker, 678, 685 (without mentioning John *ho Chaldos*). There is a slight problem in the sequence of the narrative: long before the promotion of "John" and "Konstantinos" is discussed, the chronicles describe how "John *ho Chaldos*" and "Konstantinos *ho Toxaras*," along with several others, meet an untimely death by way of divine punishment: George the Monk, 839; Leo the Grammarian, 253; Symeon the Logothete, 687–88. But this need not be an obstacle: the sources for this period are notorious for their confusion of the chronographic sequence, and it would make perfect sense for the chroniclers to mention the death of the assassins immediately after the murder, and to discuss Basil's generosity in promoting his friends later in the narrative about his reign.

[84] "Symbatios," PMBZ 1, no. 7169.

[85] George the Monk, ed. Bekker, 828, lines 15–16; cf. the version of George the Monk, ed. Istrin, 11, 35–36. See also Leo the Grammarian, ed. Bekker, 242, lines 17–18; and Symeon the Logothete,

The case of Basil offers detailed and colorful insight into the potential for brother-making in the orbit of the imperial court. By the late ninth century, men with ambitions, but lacking in family networks, wealth, or status, turned to brother-making for the sake of political and social advancement. The chronicles also show what was involved in such relations: shared ambitions and interests were more important than the compatibility of financial means or status at the moment when they were affirmed. In both versions, it was the socially superior who initiated the brotherhood relation by granting gifts and favors in the expectation of future recompense after a reversal of fortunes. Brother-making was not a fleeting sentiment or a spur-of-the-moment decision, it was for the long haul. In this way, it replicated the feature of diachronic reciprocity that typically characterizes relations within the kingroup, where favors bestowed in the present are expected to pay dividends in the future.

D. Brother-Making in Practice: Middle and High Society

In the early eleventh century, a former courtier explained how an individual might imagine to be invited into the emperor's favor:

> I ask you to suppose that the Emperor on earth sent one of the least important of his servants to you, wearing shabby clothing and not riding a horse or a mule, but carrying only a written document with the imperial seal and signed by the Emperor's own hand. Suppose that in the text of this document the Emperor declared you to be his true brother and friend, that he promised that he would soon proclaim you a joint-ruler of his empire, that he desired to place a crown on your head, and that he was going to clothe you in imperial purple. How then should you behave towards the messenger?[86]

In this hypothetical scenario, the greatest conceivable honor that the emperor had to bestow is that of being considered "a true brother and friend." This declaration was not merely empty rhetoric (which may have its own worth in terms of enhancing one's reputation and social standing), but was accompanied by the promise of very concrete benefits, in the form of a share in power while the emperor was alive, and the prospect

---

ed. Bekker, 676, lines 2–4. According to this narrative, Basil depended on Symbatios in a crucial moment, when he incited him to murder his own father-in-law, who was Basil's greatest adversary at court. The *Vita Basilii* in *Theophanes Continuatus*, however, does not implicate its protagonist Basil in the murder of the caesar Bardas.

[86] Symeon the New Theologian, *Epistle* 3, ed. and trans. H. J. M. Turner, *The Epistles of Symeon the New Theologian* (Oxford, 2009), 713–21; trans. 135.

of inheriting it after his death. Such ample rewards must have been imagined by the wealthy widow Danelis for her son John when she urged the future emperor Basil to enter into brother-making with him. The author of this lovely passage was Symeon the New Theologian (949–1022), who left a promising future at the imperial court to pursue the monastic life and, as has been noted above, became an influential visionary and spiritual director to monks and laymen in and around Constantinople. He employed this imagery in one of his letters to a spiritual son as a way to explain that even monks and priests who appear to be unworthy of their calling because of their lax conduct should be considered valid mediators of God's grace.

Forms of familial address and titles, gifts, and favors were all part and parcel of the articulation of social relations in the middle and late Byzantine periods, whether in the imperial palace, in the large mansions of the wealthy and powerful, in monastic establishments, or in the imagined workings of God's court in Heaven.

From the ninth century, *adelphopoiesis* had a firm place in lay society. Beginning with the *Life of Basil* and all the way through to the demise of the Byzantine Empire in the fifteenth century, authors of chronicles, histories, and letters mention individual cases of brother-making or refer to *adelphopoiesis* in more general terms. These attestations are the subject of the following pages. They offer evidence for men and now, at last, also for women, their social context and motivations as they contracted ritual sibling relations.[87]

Kinship and Other Close Associations

The ground for these developments had been laid with the Macedonian dynasty founded in the ninth century by Basil I, who instrumentalized his close ties of "brotherhood" in order to gain the throne and stabilize his power. His son Leo VI followed in his footsteps, although his brother-making relation with the future patriarch Nikolaos—as shall be seen shortly—turned out to be less successful.

Although the foundation of the wealth and power of the families of the land-holding aristocracy lay in different regions of the empire, the focus of their political ambitions was Constantinople, where they established residences and vied for positions of influence at the imperial court.[88] Family ties

---

[87] C. Messis, "Des amitiés à l'institution d'un lien social," goes over much the same ground and offers significant additional material from post-Byzantine times.

[88] H. Köpstein and F. Winkelmann, eds., *Studien zum 8. und 9. Jahrhundert in Byzanz*, Berliner Byzantinistische Arbeiten 51 (Berlin, 1983); F. Winkelmann, *Quellenstudien zur herrschenden Klasse von Byzanz im 8. und 9. Jahrhundert* (Berlin, 1987); and the articles in J. Haldon, ed., *The Social History of Byzantium* (Oxford, 2009).

and lineage were important in the self-definition of the aristocratic houses, and it is no coincidence that the use of family names became customary in this period. This went hand in hand with an enhanced position of wives as conveyors of lineage. Designations of kinship, whether by blood or now also by marriage, came to such prominence in the ninth century that they carried the same weight as titles. Special titles were applied to male relations through marriage: The husband of someone's daughter, sister, or sister-in-law was a *gambros*, the father of the bride and the father of the groom were *sympentheroi* (literally: "co-fathers-in-law"). By the twelfth century, sons and daughters took to using the name of their mother's family alongside that of their father's.

In their competition for an ever greater share of wealth, influence, and power, these aristocratic families relied on the creation of kinship relations, especially through marriage, often combined with *synteknia* and *adelphopoi-esis*, in order to make alliances among themselves, or to forge highly coveted ties with the imperial family.

Kinship terms began to be employed in the late eighth and ninth centuries with the same function and with the same value as a title. An early example was the appellation "grandfather of the emperor" that Philaretos the Merciful received after his granddaughter Maria of Amnia married the future emperor Constantine VI. A few decades later, as we have seen, Danelis was awarded the designation "mother of the emperor" due to her son's ritual brotherhood with Emperor Basil I. Basil's son and successor Leo VI would later grant the title "father of the emperor" to his father-in-law Stylianos Zaoutzes.[89] The concept of kinship combined with the element of choice in conferring this honorific designation gained real purchase in ninth-century Byzantium. In keeping with the model of familial ties, a certain *decorum* attached to such kinship designations. The relatives were expected to be on friendly terms and mutually supportive in matters political, military, social, and financial.

From the late eighth century onwards, the documentation regarding the norms that govern social interactions becomes more extensive. The emperors begin to take an interest in regulating society within a firmly Christian value system. This trend is tangible in the legislative work of the emperor Leo III, the *Ekloga* of the year 741. It intends to advance the Christianization of society, especially in response to the shock of the Arab invasions, which Leo had effectively repulsed in the previous year. Compared with Justinan's legislation, which continued in the Roman tradition, Leo's codification was deeply steeped in Holy Scripture as justification and explanation. Karl Ubl thus speaks of a *Funktionswandel des Rechts* (functional change of the law).[90]

---

[89] See Kazhdan, "Basileopator," 1: 263–64; and Karlin-Hayter, "Title or Office of Basileopator."

[90] K. Ubl, *Inzestverbot und Gesetzgebung: Die Konstruktion eines Verbrechens (300–1100)*, Millennium Studies 20 (Berlin and New York, 2008), 484.

Imperial law and canon law address various aspects of marriage, from inheritance rights to appropriate partners. In the earlier centuries, the ancient tradition of marriage as a contract between two parties prevailed. Christians had the additional option to seek a blessing from a priest. It would take until the ninth century for the ritual for engagement and marriage to be attested in the liturgical manuscripts. The ecclesiastical ritual of marriage was recognized as having legal force surprisingly late, in a *Novella* of Emperor Leo VI, perhaps of the year 894. This declaration was one major step in the "Christianization" of marriage as a spiritual bond. By the end of the tenth century, the Church also claimed interpretive authority over the legal aspects of marriage.[91] And attempts at social engineering were made in the form of the *Tomos of Sissinos*, a ruling issued by the patriarch in 997 that specified that the marriage prohibitions up to the seventh degree of consanguinity also affected the ascendants of a person. This had the effect of prohibiting marriages between uncles and nieces, for example, and other marital strategies that would have consolidated the property of a large family. Exogamy was encouraged precisely to prevent the large land-holding families in the provinces from becoming too powerful. In the late eleventh century, with the beginning of the Komnenian dynasty, the foregrounding of familial ties as a model for social relations comes to the fore in the sources. The dynasty's founder, Alexios I Komnenos (1081–1118), conducted imperial politics on the model of the aristocratic household: a family whose membership could be extended through marriage, through kinship designations, and through the conferral of honors and titles, and where the bestowal of favors was reciprocated by the discharge of obligations.[92] The court was no longer the pinnacle of a pyramid of offices that allowed advancement through the ranks, but an extended family into whose household others could be co-opted at the emperor's wish and whim.

As a consequence of the expansive application of kinship designations in the middle and late Byzantine periods, kinship terms not only carried the same value as titles, but could also be applied to define a relationship of a specific degree of closeness with someone who was not actually one's kin. To call someone a "cousin," for example, would place him at

---

[91] Ibid., 485, 488. A. Schminck, "Kritik am Tomos des Sisinnios," in *Fontes Minores*, vol. 2, ed. D. Simon, 215–54 (Frankfurt, 1977), 215; K. G. Pitsakis, "Parentés en dehors de la parenté: Formes de parenté d'origine extra-législative en droit byzantin et post-byzantin," in *Parenté et société dans le monde grec de l'antiquité à l'âge moderne: Colloque international, Volos (Grèce), 19–21 juin 2003*, ed. A. Bresson et al., 297–325, Ausonius Éditions Études 12 (Paris and Bordeaux, 2006).

[92] M. Angold, *The Byzantine Empire, 1025–1204: A Political History* (London and New York, 1984), 212–20; P. Magdalino, "Innovations in Government," in *Alexios I Komnenos*, ed. M. Mullett and D. Smythe, 146–66, Belfast Byzantine Texts and Translations 4.1 (Belfast, 1996); J. Shepard, "'Father' or 'Scorpion'? Style and Substance in Alexios' Diplomacy," in *Alexios I Komnenos*, ed. Mullett and Smythe, 68–132.

a greater distance than a "brother." This was a common feature in epis-tolography and diplomatic exchange. In his letters to foreign rulers, the emperor addressed them according to a carefully calibrated hierarchy of proximity. This form of address was a typical way of Byzantine emperors to deal with high dignitaries both at home and abroad, which allowed the Byzantine emperor to claim for himself the supremacy of the paternal position.[93] Franz Dölger (1891–1968), a pioneering figure in the develop-ment of Byzantine studies in Germany, claimed this as a constitutional principle of Byzantine foreign politics, and in an influential article pub-lished in 1940 dubbed it the "Family of Kings"—a concept and term that continues to enjoy great currency in medieval scholarship. But a word of caution is in order. The meshing of Dölger's scholarly interests with the privileges he could claim in his role as head of the *Abteilung für deutsch-balkanische Beziehungen* of the *Deutsche Akademie zur wissenschaftlichen Erforschung und Pflege des Deutschtums* during the Second World War, especially in gaining access to ancient manuscripts on Mount Athos, has in recent years become the subject of scrutiny. What is more, Wolfram Brandes has convincingly argued that Dölger's concept of the *Familie der Könige* was ultimately inspired by his vision for a new, hierarchical world order with Germany at its center.[94]

Imperial foreign politics, like everything else in Byzantium, was infused with religious language. In the ninth century, emperors not only invoked fra-ternity or paternity in their relations to Western rulers, but also qualified their relation as a "spiritual" one.[95] In those instances where Christian mission and the urgent invitation to convert to Byzantine Christianity accompanied impe-rial relations with foreign peoples, the emperor was ready to act as godparent, and thus to establish a quasi-familial relation of spiritual parenthood with his counterpart. A famous example is the baptism of Olga, Queen of Rus', in Constantinople in 945 or 957. On this occasion, the emperor Constantine VII Porphyrogennetos became her godfather. He also granted her a title and rank in the court hierarchy, that of the "Lady with the Belt" (*zostê patrikia*).[96] Like the emperor, the Patriarch of Constantinople also employed terms of kinship

---

[93] F. Dölger, "Die Familie der Könige im Mittelalter," *Historisches Jahrbuch* 60 (1940), 397–420; reprinted in Dölger, *Byzanz und die europäische Staatenwelt* (Ettal, 1953); see also Dölger, "Brüderlichkeit der Fürsten," *Reallexikon für Antike und Christentum*, vol. 2 (Stuttgart, 1954), cols. 642–46.

[94] W. Brandes, "Die 'Familie der Könige' im Mittelalter: Ein Diskussionsbeitrag zur Kritik eines vermeintlichen Erkenntnismodells," *Rechtsgeschichte / Legal History* 21 (2013), 262–84, at 277–78 on Dölger's political role.

[95] C. Gastgeber, "Kaiserliche Schreiben des 9. Jahrhunderts in den Westen," *Quellen zur byzan-tinischen Rechtspraxis*, ed. C. Gastgeber, 89–106, Österreichische Akademie der Wissenschaften, Philosophisch-historische Klasse, Denkschriften, vol. 413 (Vienna, 2010), 98.

[96] J. Featherstone, "Olga's Visit to Constantinople in *De Ceremoniis*," *REB* 61 (2003), 241–51.

("son," "brother") in his correspondence with Orthodox and non-Orthodox Christian dignitaries, but only very rarely in his letters to Muslims.[97]

This tendency to extend the application of kinship designations to an expanding group of people is paralleled by an amplified interpretation of the *adelphopoiesis* relationship. In the Byzantine sources from the ninth century and later, "brothers" continue to play an important role. Although it is not always possible to determine whether or not the emperors were joined to those whom they call "brothers" through the ecclesiastical ritual of *adelphopoiesis*, the sources still afford important insight into the concrete implementation of brother-making for military, political, and social purposes. What sets the cases from these later periods apart from those discussed earlier is the fact that the original brotherhood relation is now often expected, at least by one of the parties involved, to carry over to the relatives of the two "brothers"—an issue that the normative texts discussed in chapter 5 attempt to clarify.

Even more frequent in the sources are references to close friendships that were strengthened by promises and oaths.[98] Affirmations of faithful service to the emperor or declarations of orthodox belief had been sporadically offered under oath in the early centuries of Byzantium. Beginning in the eighth century, oaths took on greater relevance in the political life of Byzantium, and laws issued by the empress Irene insist that for an oath to be legally valid, it must be taken in church, sworn on a Gospel book.[99] Beginning with the Komnenian dynasty in the late eleventh century, oaths became an important political tool as the emperor dealt with Crusaders who were passing through his lands, or with internal contestants to his throne. Extracting assurances under oath offered a way to confront conflict head-on, either as a promise of loyalty in anticipation of trouble or as a declaration of a change of heart after the fact. By the Palaiologan period in the late thirteenth century, oath taking had become such a regular feature of political life that Manuel Moschopoulos reflected on them in a short treatise. In this context, it is important to recall that the single liturgical gesture for *adelphopoiesis* mentioned repeatedly in the prayer books is also typical of an oath: the placing of the future "brothers" right hands, one upon the other, on a Gospel book. In distinction from an oath, however, in this instance the participants remained silent while the priest recited the prayers. Still, one of the enduring appeals of *adelphopoiesis* must have been its adaptability to the arena of personal and power politics,

---

[97] J. Preiser-Kapeller, "Eine 'Familie der Könige'? Anrede und Bezeichnung 'ausländischer' Machthaber in den Urkunden des Patriarchatsregisters von Konstantinopel im 14. Jahrhundert," in *Das Patriarchatsregister von Konstantinopel: Eine zentrale Quelle zur Geschichte und Kirche im späten Byzanz*, ed. C. Gastgeber, E. Mitsiou, and J. Preiser-Kapeller, 257–90, Denkschriften der philosophisch-historischen Klasse 457, Veröffentlichungen zur Byzanzforschung 32 (Vienna, 2013).

[98] The aspect of oath taking is highlighted in G. Sidéris, "L'*adelphopoièsis*."

[99] Nichanian, "Iconoclasme et prestation de serment à Byzance;" L. Burgmann, "Die Novellen der Kaiserin Eirene," in *Fontes Minores*, vol. 4, ed. D. Simon, 1–36 (Frankfurt, 1981).

where the ritual prayers were not only supported by the same ritual gesture, but offered with the same intent as an oath.[100]

Homosociability may also have gained a greater role in the public life of the middle Byzantine period, as the story of Basil I and his early years at the court of Michael III has shown. Michael III was not known as "the Drunkard" for nothing. He had a reputation for drinking and carousing with the boys, and Basil soon became one of them, joining one of the men's clubs that seem to have been popular at the time. In this period, two offices first appear that speak to the close ties of homosociability, both at court and in the church: the office of *parakoimomenos*, "the one who sleeps next" to the emperor, and the office of *synkellos*, the "cell-mate" of the Patriarch of Constantinople and his closest associate.

Maria of Amnia and a Suggested Pact of Sisterhood in the Late Eighth Century

Basil's was not the first sibling relation by arrangement that preceded a career at the imperial court. That distinction, interestingly enough, goes to the sisterhood proposal reported in the *Life of Philaretos the Merciful*, a hagiographical text composed around 822 by the saint's grandson Niketas. The events take us back to the year 788, when the empress Irene was searching for a suitable woman to become the wife of her son, the future emperor Constantine VI. In a Cinderella-like tale, the imperially appointed search committee scoured the Byzantine provinces until they reached Paphlagonia and the grand mansion where Philaretos lived with his wife, children, and grandchildren. Originally a wealthy man, Philaretos had become impoverished, the story goes, because of his saintly impulse to give away all his possessions to the poor, the needy, and those in distress. It was only because the neighbors brought foodstuffs to his back door that his wife was able to produce a suitable meal for the imperial delegation. But their fortune was about to change. The emissaries identified Philaretos's exquisitely beautiful granddaughter Maria as a possible candidate for the bridal contest, and thus the entire household, all thirty of them, departed for Constantinople.

During the waiting period prior to the final decision, Maria had a proposal for the ten other girls who were also bridal candidates: "Dear sisters, let us make a pact [*syndesmon*] between ourselves of the kind called sisterhood [*adelphosynê*] that she who becomes empress shall assist the others."[101] Nothing came of this, however, because Maria was reduced to silence by the haughty rebuke of another girl. The hagiographer tells this story to illustrate

---

[100] Svoronos, "Serment de fidelité."
[101] *The Life of Philaretos the Merciful*, ch. 4, ed. and trans. L. Rydén (Uppsala, 2002), 90–91.

Maria's gentle disposition and her innate generosity, a trait that she shared with her compassionate grandfather. But read in parallel with Basil's story, this tale reveals to us that networking was essential on the way to the imperial court. In an environment where backbiting and intrigues were not uncommon, it was advisable to secure a firm and binding commitment of support for one's way to the top. Once the goal was reached, the doling out of rewards was interpreted as a sign of honesty and virtue. This is how Basil acted once he was installed on the throne, and this is what Maria offered her co-contestants. And indeed, her family was soon in a position to extend generosity to others: her two sisters made advantageous marriages, the entire family received lavish gifts, and they were assigned large mansions close to the palace. Philaretos however refused all imperial offers of high office, regalia, or titles except one, "grandfather of the emperor," thus becoming the first recipient of a title based on kinship.[102]

This story need not be true to the letter, although the marriage of Maria of Amnia to Constantine VI in 788 is historical.[103] But it reveals the defining force of kinship relations within larger social structures, and enforces the impression that kinship by choice was one of the few available strategies for those eager to move up in the world to forge alliances with a common goal and in anticipation of common, or at least shared, gain.

Emperor Leo VI and Patriarch Nikolaos Mystikos

With Basil I, *adelphopoiesis* had gained a firm place in court circles. His son and successor, Leo VI (r. 886–912), was known for maintaining such a relationship with Nikolaos Mystikos, who became Patriarch of Constantinople in 901. The phrase that is used, however, is slightly different: "brother by arrangement," revealing a predominantly legal, rather than a ritual aspect in the interpretation of their bond.[104] The only source for this relationship is the so-called *Life of Euthymios*, a tendentious narrative aimed at glorifying Nikolaos's successor, Euthymios, a prominent abbot in Constantinople who had a reputation for saintliness and the gift of prophesy.[105]

---

[102] Ibid., ch. 7, ed. Rydén, 100–01, with note on 134, which explains that in one manuscript version, Philaretos asks for the designation as "father of the emperor."

[103] Bride shows are a popular motif in the historiography of the ninth century, and of debated historicity. See W. Treadgold, "The Bride-Shows of the Byzantine Emperors," *Byzantion* 49 (1979), 395–413; L. Rydén, "The Bride-Shows at the Byzantine Court: History or Fiction?" *Eranos* 83 (1985), 175–91.

[104] On the political career of Nikolaos, see J. Gay, "Le patriarche Nicolas le Mystique et son rôle politique," in *Mélanges Diehl*, vol. 1, 91–100 (Paris, 1930). For historical detail, see Tougher, *Reign of Leo VI, passim*. The legal sources for brother-making are discussed in chapter 5.

[105] *Life of Euthymios, Patriarch of Constantinople*, ed. and trans. P. Karlin-Hayter, *Vita Euthymii patriarchae Constantinopolitani*, Bibliothèque de Byzantion 3 (Brussels, 1970), 11, lines 30–32; 71,

Leo and Nikolaos were pals from their school days and knew each other very well.[106] As a close associate of the Patriarch Photios, who was deposed and banished at the beginning of Leo's reign, Nikolaos—fearing for his own safety—sought refuge in a monastery outside the capital and accepted tonsure. The hagiographer continues: "This Nicolas was later taken by the Emperor Leo, because they had been school-fellows and brothers by arrangement [*thetos adelphos*] and, because he made a great affair of the tonsure, honoured with the position of private secretary."[107] What happened is clear: just like his class-mate, the future emperor Leo, Nikolaos had obviously been groomed for a career in politics, but in a moment of political upheaval thought it advisable to embrace the safety of the monastic life, which disqualified him for a career at the court. It seems that he later reproached his old friend Leo for being instrumental in his premature and involuntary withdrawal from the life of Constantinopolitan society ("he made a great affair of the tonsure"). Leo was compelled to honor Nikolaos by granting him an important position, both because they were "brothers by arrangement" and because he felt the personal obligation to compensate Nikolaos for his loss of career opportunities. And ample compensation it was. As soon as the incumbent Anthony had passed away in 901, Nikolaos was appointed by Leo to the highest office to which a monk could aspire, that of Patriarch of Constantinople.

The intimacy of their relation found further expression in the fact that during the pregnancy of Leo's consort Zoe Karbonopsina, when she was carrying the future emperor Constantine VII, Nikolaos paid her daily visits and regularly sat at table with her.[108] As Leo's ritual brother, he enjoyed the same liberty with the women of the household as a family member. But soon after the birth of Leo's heir to the throne in 905, their relation turned sour over Nikolaos's refusal as Patriarch of Constantinople to consecrate and approve Leo's fourth (and uncanonical) marriage to the boy's mother. Leo reproached him with harsh words, recalling that already in their school days Nikolaos had been a "crafty schemer" (*mêchanorrhaphos*).[109] Two years later, the quarrel over Leo's fourth marriage, the so-called Tetragamy Affair, forced Nikolaos to resign

---

lines 5–6. The expression "brother by arrangement" (*thetos adelphos*) can refer to nonbiological brotherhood contracted in a variety of ways: (1) through adoption, (2) through godparenthood, (3) through *adelphopoiesis*. It is unlikely that Nikolaos was considered Leo's "brother by arrangement" because he had been adopted as a son by Leo's father, Basil. The prevailing application of the legal institution of adoption was either as an inheritance strategy or as an act of charity. It would have made no sense for Basil to engage in filial adoption when he was already blessed with ample male offspring in addition to Leo: Stephen, who became Patriarch of Constantinople, and Alexander, Leo's co-emperor and successor. For historical background, see Tougher, *Reign of Leo VI*.

[106] *Life of Euthymios*, ed. Karlin-Hayter, 11, lines 30–32; 71, lines 5–6; 85, lines 16–17.

[107] Ibid., 10.

[108] Ibid., 81, lines 15–17.

[109] Ibid., 85, lines 16–17.

from the patriarchal office. Most remarkable is the conciliatory tone of their exchanges at this point, each asserting the love (*agapê*) he held for the other.[110]

Indeed, Leo showed remarkable lenience when the patriarch's behavior on several occasions gave reason to suspect his loyalty. Nikolaos and his clergy failed to stand by Leo when he nearly fell victim to a vicious attack on his life in the Church of St. Mocius, and instead disappeared from the scene as fast as they could.[111] Not much later, a letter in the style and handwriting of Nikolaos suggested his involvement in a plot against the throne. Leo was so upset at this sudden discovery that he changed color and began to tremble.[112] Yet, because of their brotherhood relation and their friendship since childhood, he refrained from showing his grief to Nikolaos.[113] Even when Nikolaos's opposition to Leo's fourth marriage had become politically intolerable and plans were hatched for his demise from office, Leo refrained from using the incriminating letter except as a last resort to blackmail Nikolaos into resigning from the patriarchate.[114]

The *Life of Euthymios* which reports these events is a biased document, of course, aimed at exposing the faults of his predecessor Nikolaos. But read between the lines, it allows us to catch a glimpse of an *adelphopoiesis* relation concluded between two young men who anticipated a political career and for this reason promised each other mutual support in a relation of ritual kinship. Once he had entered the monastic state, Nikolaos could no longer be considered for promotion to an office in the imperial administration or in the emperor's household. But he nonetheless received his due when he was appointed patriarch and became a frequent guest in the palace. Most remarkable is Leo's lenience when confronted with Nikolaos's machinations, as reported in the *Life*. One reason for his ostensible gullibility must have been his continued expectation of loyalty and support on the basis of their *adelphopoiesis* relation. In the hagiographer's depiction of this relationship between patriarch and emperor, Nikolaos held the emotional and political upper hand over Leo, all on the basis of their compact of brotherhood.

Two Pairs among Tenth-Century Aristocrats

Under the Macedonian dynasty that began with Basil I, the same extended kinship strategies that emperors or future emperors employed to secure their position were also put to good use by aristocrats, among men of influence

---

[110] Ibid., 89, lines 5–6; 99, lines 24–25; 139, lines 4–5 (here the key concepts are *storgê* and *pothos*, which convey strong emotional affection).

[111] Ibid., 67, lines 21–23.

[112] Ibid., 69, lines 22–23.

[113] Ibid., 71, lines 5–6.

[114] Ibid., 91, lines 19–22.

and wealth. Most of what we know about this (and, for that matter, any other) period depends on the patterns of reporting that generate sources and the accidents of survival that preserve their manuscripts. This explains why in this part of our inquiry, we largely depend on historians who had an interest in or access to the imperial court and thus only report on the highest circles of society. But there are exceptions. Information on other segments of society in the form of narratives can be found in hagiography, as was the case with the *Life of Philaretos*, the grandfather of Maria of Amnia. A female counterpart to this generous head of household was Mary of Vizye in Thrace, who was celebrated in a saint's *Life* composed perhaps after 1025. She died at the hands of an irascible and violent husband, and acquired a reputation for sanctity in her role as wife and mother. She thus embodies a new type of female sanctity that was prominent in the late ninth and early tenth centuries, the pious housewife. After her death, Mary the Younger, as she is also called, worked such an abundance of miracles that her husband and sons felt compelled to provide a proper resting place for her remains, which grew into a popular cult site that attracted women and men from all walks of life and even protected the city of Vizye against Bulgarian attacks.

It is striking that Mary's hagiographer is at great pains to establish a strong connection to the reign of Basil I, including a vilification of the loose life of his predecessor, Michael III which has no purpose in the narrative. Mary's father, we are told, was among the "very powerful men of Greater Armenia who came to the great city of Constantine and appeared before the emperor Basil. He received them gladly, rewarded them with presents, raised them to high positions, and held them in the greatest honor."[115] These are suggestive words, indicating that Basil, like his benefactors Theophilos and Michael III, may have enjoyed surrounding himself with a select group of strong men. Who better to cultivate as loyal followers than ambitious men of similar background from the margins of the empire who were seeking their fortune in the capital, like Basil himself once had done? The phrasing of this passage is too vague to conclude, beyond mere suggestion, that this relation had been strengthened through brother-making. But it seems that both Mary's husband and her son maintained relations of this kind. Some time after her father's death, Mary's brother-in-law Bardas who was a landowner in Thrace suggested that she marry his friend Nikephoros, the commander of a regiment (*droungarios*). The exact words used to describe the development of the relationship between the two men are worth quoting in full. At the beginning, Nikephoros was referred to as "a friend and companion." As time went by and their friendship intensified, Bardas made the following proposal to Nikephoros: "Since, O dearest of men, we have been connected and bound

---

[115] *Life of Mary the Younger*, ch. 2, AASS Nov. IV (Brussels, 1925), 692–705, col. 692D, trans. A. Laiou, in *Holy Women of Byzantium*, ed. A.-M. Talbot (Washington, DC, 1996), 255.

together so intimately, I think it proper to make this bond of love [*ton desmon tês agapês*] more forceful and more perfect, by adding to it the ties of marriage alliance, so that we may be twice bound, adducing kinship to our acquaintance." Bardas then expressed his hope that through this marriage, "we shall preserve our love [*agapê*] unbroken."[116] This close and binding friendship between social equals in the provincial aristocracy, one a landowner, the other a military officer, fits the pattern of *adelphopoiesis*. They confirmed their affection for each other and strengthened their bond through the addition of marriage. The friendship between the two men may have prospered as a result; the marriage, however, was an unhappy one. While Mary gave away all her wealth to charitable causes, her husband gave in to suspicions about her fidelity and beat her to death. Her twin sons, however, took after their mother in the pursuit of virtue. Stephen, the younger one, became a monk, while Vaanes made an advantageous marriage, took up his father's profession, and also became a *droungarios*.

His generosity made him popular with the soldiers, and like his father before him, Vaanes cultivated a relationship with another man. The *Life* explains: "As his associate [*synasketên*] and helper in all <his> excellent exploits he had a certain Theodore, who succeeded his father as *tourmarches*, a man brave and robust in military matters but braver still in the ways of God. Vaanes was yoked to him [*syzeuchtheis*], like a pedigreed, powerful young bull, and together they plowed in themselves as though in fertile land, and they sowed the seeds of virtue like the best of farmers. In due season they cheerfully harvested, depositing the ripe fruit with God and in the divine vats, and received therefrom eternal joy."[117] It seems to be the military milieu in particular that fosters these homosocial affections in two generations of the same family. What exact actions and activities are intended by this flowery circumlocution, we will never know. Suffice it to note that we have already encountered the notion of the "yoke of virtue" in another eleventh-century text from the monastic milieu, the *Life of Symeon the New Theologian*, and that Basil's relation with John, the son of Danelis, was characterized as the sowing of seed. The *Life of Mary the Younger* thus features close male-male relationships in three generations of military men in Mary's family, beginning with her father's warm reception at the court of Basil.

This quartet of biographical texts, the *Vita Basilii, Life of Philaretos*, the *Life of Euthymios*, and the *Life of Mary the Younger*, were all created in the context of the Macedonian dynasty and its own self-promotion. This was an environment in which male-male bonding and female-female bonding were cultivated and became a recognizable part of the social fabric. We have

---

[116] Ibid., ch. 2, col. 692D, trans. Laiou, 256.
[117] Ibid., ch. 30, col. 704A, trans. Laiou, 284.

earlier encountered a cluster of hagiographical texts of the seventh century in which *adelphopoiesis* played an important role. There are parallels between the two clusters. Both were composed during uncertain times of political change. Revolutions from the social and geographical fringes of the Empire abruptly ended the existing reign and brought new emperors and their men to power. As new-comers to the pinnacle of power, both Heraclius and Basil I were regarded by their contemporaries as David-like figures. Instead of a Jonathan, they cultivated larger support groups. The coteries that formed around them shared not only the same political vision (evident especially in the prophesies of the *Life of Theodore of Sykeon*), but also a consensus regarding social values—all of this manifest in the same personal comportment, along with a familiar way of expressing closeness and emotions, analogous to the "emotional communities" identified by Barbara Rosenwein for the early medieval West. This was the basis for their interaction and explains the peak in authorial interest in *adelphopoiesis* relations at these times. These relations were described in the general language of friendship and siblinghood, but the mention of commitment, bonds, and yokes points more specifically to their affirmation through the prayers of *adelphopoiesis*.

Emperor Romanos IV Diogenes and Nikephoros Bryennios

In the eleventh century, we hear of yet another emperor who had acquired a "brother" for himself. According to the historical report of Anna Komnena, Romanos IV Diogenes (r. 1068–71) had asked Nikephoros Bryennios to be his "brother" because he held a brotherly disposition toward him, and because he valued his intellect, sound judgment, and honesty in word and deed. Anna consistently calls them brothers *ek prohaireseôs*, brothers "by choice."[118] As a *magistros* and general, Bryennios fought with Romanos in 1071 against the Seljuk Turks in the Battle of Mantzikert.[119] When in 1094/5 the Cumans threatened the Danube frontier, Alexios I Komnenos entrusted Bryennios with the defense of Adrianople. The Cumans were led by a rebel who claimed to be the son of the deceased Romanos Diogenes. The pretender was convinced that as soon as he met Nikephoros Bryennios, he would be received with open arms and showered with financial support and other favors on the grounds of his (supposed) father's relationship with the general. The historian Anna Komnena, who was married to the caesar Nikephoros Bryennios,

---

[118] Anna Komnena, *Alexias* 10.3.3, ed. D. R. Reinsch and A. Kambylis, *Annae Comnenae Alexias*, 2nd ed., CFHB 40, no. 1 (Berlin and New York, 2001), 288, lines 26–37; trans. E. A. S. Dawes, *The Alexiad of the Princess Anna Comnena being the History of the Reign of her Father, Alexius I, Emperor of the Romans, 1081–1118 A.D.* (London, 1928; repr. New York, 1978), 241; see also 10.3.4, p. 289, line 47, trans. Dawes, 241.

[119] See Kazhdan, "Bryennios, Nikephoros," *ODB* 1: 330–31.

the son or the grandson of the Nikephoros in this episode,[120] has only con-tempt for this ruse: "These facts are true and known as such by all, but the Pretender was so shameless that he actually called Bryennius 'uncle.'" A little later, Anna emphasized again that such relations are not uncommon.[121]

The pretender's intention was to claim, as the son of a "brother by arrange-ment," the obligation of support that would have been due his father. There could be no clearer indication that such "brotherhood" relationships, rooted as they probably often were in a friendly disposition, also required tangible proof of one's professed brotherly inclinations in the form of concrete support in the political arena or on the battlefield. Moreover, this story demonstrates that, at least in the minds of some Byzantines, "brotherhood by arrangement" between two men created ties of friendly obligation that devolved upon their sons. The potential for transgenerational obligations that are projected onto relations of ritual brotherhood by their practitioners was also a concern in the legal writings, as the following chapter will show.

It is easy to imagine how a close relation in the parents' generation would also lead to greater familiarity between the offspring of the two. It is equally conceivable that the two brothers would take responsibility for the welfare of each other's offspring, in the same way that godparents often did. One such case from Kievan Rus' is reported in the *Kievan Caves Paterikon* that reflects the life of this extensive monastery and of the laypeople associated with it in the twelfth and thirteenth centuries. "Among the city's powerful men there were two named Ioann and Sergij, who were good friends. These two came to the God-appointed church and saw on the miraculous icon of the Theotokos a light brighter than the sun, and they entered into spiritual brotherhood with each other." Shortly before his death, Ioann entrusted the inheritance for his five-year-old son to Sergij. Years later, when it was time to claim the inheri-tance, Sergij denied any knowledge of it. Only a miracle wrought by the icon forced him to reveal where he had hidden the money. In this story of two prominent men, a prior friendship was affirmed through the ecclesiastical ritual. Although it was expected to translate into an equally friendly rela-tion with the next generation, self-interest took over until divine intervention restored justice.[122]

Michael Psellos

One eleventh-century author who offers rich information about his own life across a wide variety of literary genres is Michael Psellos (1018–ca. 1081), the

---

[120] See Kazhdan, "Bryennios," *ODB* 1: 328–29.

[121] *Alexiad of the Princess Anna Comnena*, trans. Dawes, 241.

[122] *Kievan Caves Paterikon* 5, trans. M. Heppell, *The Paterika of the Kievan Caves Monastery* (Cambridge, MA, 1989), 14–15.

learned courtier, epistolographer, and historian whose career spanned the reign of seven emperors. In a letter, he addressed a friend as "dearest, most beloved cousin, godfather [*synteknos*], like-minded brother," piling up designations of biological and ritual kinship in order to convey closeness and affection.[123] A number of men in his circle were addressed as "brothers," and hence he also claimed to be connected to their sons as his "nephews."[124] In his *Chronographia*, he declared himself to have been a "spiritual brother" of the father of Eudokia Makrembolitissa his favorite empress, as a way of claiming paternal seniority to a woman whose benefactions he relied upon.[125] But his friendships were not merely rhetorical. As a young man, he had become a third party to a close friendship between two men of slightly more advanced age who remain anonymous. One of them must have been John Xiphilinos, the other perhaps John Mauropos or Christopher of Mytilene. Psellos later recalled that the two appeared to him "as a pair" but claimed that his attachment to them was equally strong, so that he could not countenance the thought of separation. The three of them decided to become monks together—perhaps on the assumption that a monastery was a suitable place where such an association would be recognized. In order to strengthen their bond and to make it indissoluble also by the most forceful outside intervention, even that of the emperor himself, they took an oath on this.[126] It is not inconceivable that they used the prayers for *adelphopoiesis* on this occasion.

Crossing Boundaries: Brother-Making in the Middle and Late Byzantine Period

In the middle Byzantine period, which was bracketed by the recovery from the Arab invasions, on the one hand, and by the capture of Constantinople by the Fourth Crusade in 1204, on the other, *adelphopoiesis* gained greater traction in society. It expanded beyond the monastery and found application among laypeople as one of several strategies to extend one's social network through kinship by arrangement and was for this reason often mentioned alongside *synteknia* and marriage. As a boundary-crossing strategy, it could

---

[123] Michael Psellos, *Ep.* 90, in *Michaelis Pselli scripta minora: Magnam partem huc inedita*, ed. E. Kurtz and F. Drexl, vol. 2 (Milan, 1941), 118, lines 26–119, line 1. F. Tinnefeld, "'Freundschaft' in den Briefen des Michael Psellos: Theorie und Wirklichkeit," *JÖB* 22 (1973), 151–68; S. Papaioannou, "Michael Psellos on Friendship and Love: Erotic Discourse in Eleventh-Century Constantinople," *Early Medieval Europe* 19, no. 1 (2011), 43–61.

[124] H. Ahrweiler, "Recherches sur la société byzantine au XIe siècle: Nouvelles hiérarchies et nouvelles solidarités," *TM* 6 (1976), 99–104, at 109.

[125] Michael Psellos, *Chronographia* 7.4, ed. É. Renauld, *Michel Psellos, Chronographie ou histoire d'un siècle de Byzance (976–1077)* (Paris, 1928), 2: 154.

[126] Ibid. 6.192–94, ed. Renauld, 65–66; cf. F. Lauritzen, "Christopher of Mytilene's Parody of the Haughty Mauropus," *BZ* 100, no. 1 (2007), 125–32, at 130–31.

be employed to turn enemies into friends, either preemptively or after a confrontation, as a peace-making gesture. This aspect of the reconciliation of enemies is also present in some of the Greek prayers of *adelphopoiesis*, as well as in the Church Slavonic *Euchologium Sinaiticum*. As the land-holding families in the provinces grew more powerful and clans were in competition with each other and vied for positions at the court,[127] brother-making was a readily available tool to secure support or at least to affirm the absence of hostile intentions.

A lead seal from the late tenth or early eleventh century offers intriguing possibilities along those lines. Small lead seals accompanied administrative documents or trade goods and have survived in the thousands from the middle Byzantine period. But bilingual seals are exceedingly rare. Even rarer are seals that carry the names of two people. This one carries the inscription "Lord, assist me Machetarios and Philip," written in Greek on the obverse, and "Of me, servant (of God), Mxit'ar, and of Philip" written in Armenian on the reverse.[128] Two men, who are not otherwise known but clearly of some social standing, hailing from different linguistic background and sharing the same seal—this invites speculation. The Armenian-speaking Machetarios is the one who gives his voice to the inscription. Was he in the service of the Byzantine Empire, as other men by this name? Or did he live in Armenia? Why is he the only one of the two to emphasize his religious devotion? What was their reason for sharing an official *carte de visite*, as it were? Was this a joint economic or administrative venture, or a relationship of a more personal nature? And in either case, could it have been affirmed by the prayers of *adelphopoiesis*?

The eleventh-century aristocrat Kekaumenos in his advice manual cautioned his son to be extremely wary of the obligations that he would be called upon to fulfill once he accepted gifts from others. He then went on to explain that "greedy and ambitious men also know to exploit other means to establish a relation of patronage and obligation with their betters, namely through *adelphopoiesis, synteknia*, and by offering their children as sons- or daughters-in-law."[129] The nuclear family was the only place that was considered to offer protection and

---

[127] For the social changes in the eleventh century and later, see Ahrweihler, "Recherches sur la societé byzantine"; A. P. Kazhdan and A. Wharton Epstein, *Change in Byzantine Culture in the Eleventh and Twelfth Centuries* (Berkeley, CA, 1985), 56–73; J.-C. Cheynet, *Pouvoirs et contestations à Byzance (963–1210)* (Paris, 1990).

[128] B. Coulie and J. W. Nesbitt, "A Bilingual Rarity in the Dumbarton Oaks Collection of Lead Seals: A Greek/Armenian Bulla of the Later 10th/Early 11th Centuries," *DOP* 43 (1989), 121–23. The Armenian background to many of the *adelphopoiesis* relations in the middle Byzantine period is intriguing and would repay further study.

[129] Kekaumenos, *Strategikon*, ed. B. Wassiliewsky and V. Jernstedt, *Cecaumeni strategicon et incerti scriptoris de officiis regiis libellus* (St. Petersburg, 1896; repr. Amsterdam, 1965), 49, lines 10–14. http://www.ancientwisdoms.ac.uk/library/kekaumenos-consilia-et-narrationes/

a place to prosper in safety.[130] Friendship in itself, although cherished and praised in letters, could be fickle and needed reinforcing through other ties of obligation.[131]

Once the Crusaders had established their presence as new neighbors especially in mainland Greece and the Peloponnese, the creation of a framework within which cooperation facilitated coexistence became a paramount concern. Brother-making, which had already proved to be a successful strategy for crossing the monastic-lay divide, offered a convenient mechanism to cross the boundary between Orthodox and Catholics, perhaps the more so because the Westerners were familiar with the gesture of oath taking. That *adelphopoiesis* could fulfill the purpose of turning potential political adversaries into allies is nowhere better expressed than in the fourteenth-century *Chronicle of the Morea*, which describes the conquest of this region by the Crusaders from a Frankish point of view. It comments on the defection of Michael, the Despot of Epirus, from the camp of William of Villehardouin on the eve of a battle of Pelagonia in 1259 with these words: "Never believe a Roman in whatever he may swear to you; when he wants and desires to betray you, then he makes you godfather of his child or his ritual brother [*adelphopoieton*] or he makes you an in-law so that he may exterminate you."[132] This is echoed in the advice to avoid contact with Catholic Latins given to the Orthodox faithful by Feodosij, the abbot of the Kievan Caves monastery, in the last decades of the eleventh century: "Christians should not give their daughters to them in marriage, nor receive them into their own homes, nor swear any oath of brotherhood with them, nor have them as godparents, nor exchange kisses with them, nor eat with them, nor drink from the same vessel."[133]

This application of *adelphopoiesis* with potential adversaries finds interesting confirmation in the *History* of Niketas Choniates, the eyewitness historian of the conquest of the Constantinople by the Fourth Crusade in 1204. He describes how just before the conquest of the city some high-ranking Byzantines sought to "become comrades"[134] of the Latins in order to avoid a military

---

[130] A. Kazhdan, "Small Social Groupings (Microstructures) in Byzantine Society," *XVI Internationaler Byzantinistenkongress, Wien, 4.–9. Oktober 1981, Akten II/2 = JÖB* 32, no. 2 (1982), 3–11; Kazhdan, "The Constantinopolitan Synaxarium as a Source for Social History of Byzantium," in *The Christian Near East, Its Institutions and Its Thought*, ed. R. F. Taft, 484–515, OCA 251 (Rome, 1996).

[131] Hatlie, "Friendship and the Byzantine Iconoclast Age"; A. Demosthenous, "The Power of Friendship in 11th and 12th Centuries [*sic*] Byzantium," in *Byzantium: Life and Fantasy*, 29–41 (Nicosia, 2008); E. Patlagean, "Self and Others," in *A History of Private Life*, ed. P. Veyne, vol. 1, 591–615 (London, 1987).

[132] *Crusaders as Conquerors: The Chronicle of Morea*, trans. H. E. Lurier (New York and London, 1964), 187. Greek text in *The Chronicle of Morea*, ed. J. Schmitt (London, 1904; repr. Groningen, 1967), 260, lines 3934–37. This passage is preserved in the codex Havniensis, but omitted in the Parisinus.

[133] *Kievan Caves Paterikon* 37, trans. Heppell, 212.

[134] *Nicetae Choniatae Historia*, ed. J. A. van Dieten, CFHB 11, no. 1 (Berlin and New York, 1975), 561, lines 19–20.

confrontation. The paraphrase of this work into a more colloquial register of Greek renders this expression in much more telling terms: "they made friends with the Franks and concluded brotherhoods [*adelphopoiêsias*]."[135]

Rituals that involved the church or that were accompanied by oaths had the power to create new social realities. People could be made brothers and sisters across the divides of politics, faith, and ethnicity, even across the divide of gender. The latter was an aspect of particular concern to monastic leaders, but not only to them. Stern advice was issued to laymen and laywomen of the middling strata of society in an apocalyptic vision of the punishments in Hell, the *Vision of Anastasia*, variously dated between the late tenth and the twelfth centuries. The list of sexual offenders who suffer next to a river of fire includes, according to one manuscript version, "the perjurers, those who swear wrongly, the false witnesses, ... and those who fabricate a fraternal relationship in order to commit adultery with respect to his wife."[136] That the ecclesiastical ritual of *adelphopoiesis* is intended becomes clear from the context, which also mentions oaths. In the twelfth century, the learned John Tzetzes, author of commentaries on Homer, in one of his letters listed among those responsible for a recent disturbance in Constantinople not only drunken men, but also women who were making bold "like *adelphopoietoi*."[137] A legal expert in the fourteenth century, John Pediasimos, commented in a matter-of-fact way that *adelphopoiesis* between a man and a woman does not represent an obstacle to their later marriage.[138] It would be interesting to know more about these male-female relations. Did women ever initiate them? In what social milieu was this deemed expedient? But besides these intriguing glimpses into the possibilities of crossing gender boundaries, our sources remain silent.

Imperial *Adelphopoiesis* in the Thirteenth and Fourteenth Centuries

The late Byzantine period, after the recovery of Constantinople from Latin rule in 1261 and prior to the final capture of the city by the Ottomans in 1453, saw the geographical extent of the emperor's power reduced to a fraction of its former glory. Inflation gripped not only the economy, but also the hierarchy of imperial offices, where new, ever more grandiose titles were bestowed on the emperor's favorites—a trend that had already begun with the Komnenian dynasty in the eleventh century. While in the middle Byzantine period

---

[135] This was noted by E. Hörandner in her review of Kretzenbacher, "Rituelle Wahlverbrüderung," *Byzantinische Zeitschrift* 67 (1974), 147–48.

[136] Baun, *Tales from Another Byzantium*, 407n16 (*Apocalypse of Anastasia*, Paris version).

[137] John Tzetzes, *Ep.* 14, in *Ioannis Tzetzae Epistulae*, ed. P. A. Leone (Leipzig, 1972), 26, lines 10–12.

[138] See below, chapter 5.

kinship terms became popular as honorific designations for select individuals, in the later centuries of Byzantium, they were used liberally to signal affection and affirm proximity. This is particularly evident in the genre of epistolography that flourished at the time, as scholars vied with each other in the composition of letters sparkling with rhetorical brilliance, each intended as a little gift for its recipient. The abundant employment of kinship terms in the literary sources of this period makes it difficult to distinguish between descriptions of historical reality, on the one hand, and rhetorical convention and literary taste, on the other. But perhaps this is asking too much and we should content ourselves with the observation that the extension of kinship by choice—whether for a fleeting moment through literary convention or through the conclusion of rituals with lasting effects—had become a pervasive mechanism to express and enforce the coherence of one's social group.

One telling example is John III Dukas Vatatzes, emperor of Nicaea from 1221 to 1254. He affectionately referred to his minister of finance Demetrios Tornikes as his "beloved brother,"[139] not merely when he addressed him directly in letters, but also when he mentioned him in official documents. Whether this means that they had indeed concluded *adelphopoiesis*, as Franz Dölger assumed, cannot be said with certainty, but it is clear that theirs was an association that was also honored by the next two generations.[140] When Tornikes's sons competed with the members of other aristocratic families for a social position at the court of the emperor John IV Laskaris (r. 1258–61), their claim to such a distinction was especially strong. This was, as the historian George Pachymeres explained at the end of the thirteenth century, because their father had enjoyed a certain familiarity with John Dukas Vatatzes, the grandfather of the young emperor, and in letters and documents had been addressed as his "brother."[141]

The intervening emperor of Nicaea, Theodoros II Laskaris (r. 1254–58), maintained a very close friendship with his adviser George Mouzalon, so close that he called him with the same term as that reserved for biological brothers, *autadelphos*. An annotation to a treatise that he dedicated to

---

[139] F. Miklosich and J. Müller, *Acta et diplomata graeca medii aevi*, vol. 4 (Vienna, 1871), 147, lines 9–10.

[140] F. Dölger, "Chronologisches und Prosopographisches zur byzantinischen Geschichte des 13. Jahrhunderts," *Byzantinische Zeitschrift* 27 (1927), 291–320, at 303n1; emphasized again in Dölger's brief report on K. Amantos, "Epitimion kata tês adelphopoiias," *EEBS* 4 (1927), 280–84, in *Byzantinische Zeitschrift* 28 (1928), 175; and finally in Dölger, "Johannes VI. Kantakuzenos as dynastischer Legitimist (1938)," in *Paraspora. 30 Aufsätze zur Geschichte, Kultur und Sprache des byzantinischen Reiches*, 194–207 (Ettal, 1961), 197f., n. 12.

[141] Georgios Pachymeres, *Historiai* 1.21, ed. A. Failler, French trans. V. Laurent, *Georges Pachymérès, Relations historiques* (Paris, 1984), 1: 91, lines 25–92. Compare also Georgios Akropolites, *Historia*, ed. A. Heisenberg, *Georgii Akropolitae Opera*, 2 vols. (Leipzig, 1903), reprinted with corrections by P. Wirth (Stuttgart, 1978), 1: 90, lines 19–24.

Mouzalon explained that "he deemed him worthy to be called his brother."[142] Honorifics, kinship designations, and expressions of friendship are here rolled into one.

In the fourteenth century, there is one firmly identifiable instance of imperial brother-making: John VI Kantakouzenos (r. 1347–54), who after the death of Andronikos III Palaiologos in 1341, claimed that theirs had been a close relation of "brotherhood," in order to position himself as the tutor and regent for the latter's young son, John V.[143] John Kantakouzenos's *History* abounds with references to his intimate relationship with Andronikos, including recourse to the friendship topos of "one soul in two bodies," even to the point where he was permitted to sleep in the emperor's bed.[144] In his desire to construct an enlarged familial network, Kantakouzenos employed a cross-generational application of brother-making to advance his own political legitimation that included even the ascendants in the family line.[145]

According to these descriptions of *adelphopoiesis* at the court and in its orbit, the relation had various facets: it could be concluded as a confirmation of genuine feelings of friendship or it could be initiated as a utilitarian alliance where one "brother" lent his loyalty and support in anticipation of a future reward by the other. Its contractual character was recognized by both "brothers" who were well aware of their obligation toward each other.[146] The assumption of affective closeness, loyalty, and the absence of strife that kinship relations entail also made *adelphopoiesis* a convenient tool to bridge the division of enmity and strife, or to cross boundaries of gender, ethnicity, and faith. In many instances, the associations between two men were expected by those involved to extend across the generations—an issue that the legal sources repeatedly address.

---

[142] Mentioned in Mullett, "Byzantium: A Friendly Society," 7n20.

[143] Dölger, "Johannes VI. Kantakuzenos," 197–99.

[144] *Ioannis Cantacuzeni eximperatoris Historiarum libri IV*, CSHB, ed. L. Schopen, 3 vols. (Bonn, 1828–32), 1.20 = Schopen, 1: 19; 2.9 = Schopen, 1: 369; 2.40 = Schopen, 1: 558; 3.24 = Schopen, 2: 150; 3.25 = Schopen, 2: 157. When Byzantine authors mentioned sleeping in the same bed, we must not be led into thinking that this carried any sexual innuendo. Beds were commonly shared by several people until the modern period. The woman Dionysia, who was married and had a daughter by the same name, is said to have had a bedmate (*sygkoitōn*) in a woman named Susanna: *Miracula Theclae* 46, ed. G. Dagron, *Vie et miracles de saint Thècle*, Subsidia hagiographica 62 (Brussels, 1978), 408.

[145] See also F. Kondyli, "Changes in the Structure of the Late Byzantine Family and Society," in *Approaches to the Byzantine Family*, ed. Brubaker and Tougher, 371–93.

[146] Compare this to the list by W. Puchner, "Griechisches zur 'Adoptio in fratrem,'" *Südost-Forschungen* 53 (1994), 187–224, at 189, of the different societal functions of *adelphopoiesis* in post-Byzantine Greece: as protection and support of those in need, the old, and the sick; as social advancement and assurance of protection by people of means and influence; as a psychological strategy of uniting fighters in times of crisis; as a strategy to supplement family relations in small communities; and as an expression of intimate friendship.

{ 5 }

Prescriptions and Restrictions in Byzantium

A. Rules and Regulations

Descriptions of *adelphopoiesis* relations in historical writing illustrate the practice in the highest echelons of society. Emperors and aristocrats entered into brother-making to cement friendships and secure the goodwill of allies who might otherwise be potential contenders. Casual remarks in other sources point to even more widespread use among the upper classes, where it found broad application, not only to join like with like, but also and especially to bind like and unlike. *Adelphopoiesis*, as we have seen, had the potential to join men and women, Orthodox and Catholic, and Greeks and Latins.

The similarity in social function—especially the opportunity for feasting and exposure to the other sex—between ritual brotherhood, *synteknia*, and marriage has already been noted in the discussion of the prohibitions for monks to enter into any relationship of ritual kinship. Now we encounter the same cautionary remarks not from the vantage point of monastic founders set on maintaining high moral standards in their communities, but from the viewpoint of legislators and jurisprudents eager to ensure that the original distinctions between *synteknia* and *adelphopoiesis*, the two kinship relations that adult men (and women) could enter by their own choice, would not be eroded by social practice.[1]

Many of these authors were men of the church. The boundaries between secular and ecclesiastical law were not sharply drawn in Byzantium, ever since

---

[1] J. Zhishman, *Das Eherecht der orientalischen Kirche* (Vienna, 1864), 285–89; K. E. Zachariä von Lingenthal, *Geschichte des griechisch-römischen Rechts*, 3rd ed. (Berlin, 1892; repr. Aalen, 1955), 118–19.

the emperor Justinian declared that canon law and imperial law had the same validity. The dispensation of justice, too, often fell to bishops and metropolitans, who offered the closest point of recourse for the men and women in the provinces, and frequently belonged to the educated classes. The legal literature of Byzantium consists not only of individual laws issued by emperors and their compilation in law codes, but also of legal commentaries and explanatory treatises on specific issues from the pen of jurisprudents, as well as rulings and legal advice dispensed by judicial authorities.[2] A particularly user-friendly genre is the question-and-answer format, in which legal advice was often couched. I employ it in the following for the sake of clarity and brevity.

Did It Make a Difference if Monks or Laymen Were Involved in Brother-Making?

Apparently, the most pressing concern was that of monks entering into brother-making with laypersons. Already in the ninth century, monastic rule-givers began their efforts to curb brother-making of monks with laymen, though it would take until the eleventh century for legislators to address the relation between men in secular society. *Adelphopoiesis* inside monasteries was never affected by any of these rulings, although "special friendships" between monks were occasionally frowned upon.

How Did Legislators Interpret the Brother-Making Relationship?

By the time that brother-making was addressed in eleventh-century legal writing, laypeople had used it for several centuries as a social networking strategy. In this, as in many other instances, theory and regulations followed social practice. As a kinship relation that also had its origin in a church rite, brother-making was most frequently interpreted in relation to godparenthood (*synteknia*).

How Did Brother-Making Relate to Godparenthood?

Lawgivers and legal commentators were at pains to explain the difference between *adelphopoiesis* and *synteknia*, and in doing so affirmed that these relations were employed for comparable social reasons. The greatest issues were marriage prohibitions based on incest taboos between the family members of the two men involved.

---

[2] For a good introduction to this body of texts, see the relevant articles in W. Hartmann and K. Pennington, eds., *The History of Byzantine and Eastern Canon Law to 1500* (Washington, DC, 2012).

An entire brand of explanatory literature was created to explain the marriage prohibitions. These texts are usually labeled "On the Degrees of Kinship" (*Peri bathmôn syggeneias*) or "On the Degrees of Marriage" (*Eis tous gamikous monous bathmous*). A few of these manuscripts are accompanied by tree-shaped diagrams that visualize the ascendants and descendants of husband and wife, a practice that had its origin in the West and reached Byzantium via Sicily, as Evelyne Patlagean has suggested (Figure 5.1).[3] The composition of these treatises occurred in the context of a general increase in the activities of jurisprudents and a wider dissemination of their works in manuscript form. There is to date no systematic study of these treatises, and their textual history is complex. In their simplest form, they are basic explanations about the degrees of consanguinity, as an explanatory aid to imperial and ecclesiastical laws. More elaborate treatises employ a wider definition of kinship, beginning with blood relations (agnatic), relations through marriage (cognatic), and extending to relations through spiritual kinship. A useful classification scheme is introduced by some texts that distinguish relations "by nature" (*physei*), such as siblings or children, from relations "by arrangement" (*thesei*). The latter include relations by filial adoption and relations by ritual brotherhood. In those instances, the practical advice is always the same: ritual brotherhood does not result in marriage prohibitions and does not enjoy legal recognition.

The earliest such treatise dates from roughly the same period as the first manuscript attestation of the ritual and the story of Basil's brother-making with John, the son of Danelis—evidence of the heightened relevance of family relations and kinship concepts in the middle Byzantine period. Some time in the eighth or ninth century, a commentary on the *Ekloga*, the law book of the Isaurian emperors of the first half of the eighth century, was put together, perhaps with recourse to the work of Theophilos the Antecessor.[4] This included a small treatise under the title *On the Degrees of Consanguinity* (*Peri bathmôn syggeneias*). This text proved so popular that modern editors of the Appendix to the *Ekloga* are reluctant even to attempt to identify and list the relevant manuscripts.[5] In this early form of the treatise *On the Degrees of Consanguinity*, there is no reference either to

---

[3] E. Patlagean, "Une représentation byzantine de la parenté et ses origines occidentales," *L'Homme* 6, no. 4 (1966), 59–83; repr. in Patlagean, *Structure sociale, famille, chrétienté à Byzance, IVe–XIe siècle* (London, 1981).

[4] D. Simon, "Zur Ehegesetzgebung der Isaurier," in *Fontes Minores*, vol. 1, ed. D. Simon, 16–43 (Frankfurt, 1976), assuming a date of March 726 for the publication of the *Ekloga*. For a revised date of 741 for the *Ekloga*, see O. Kresten, "Datierungsprobleme isaurischer Eherechtsnovellen. I. Coll. I 26," in *Fontes Minores*, vol. 4, ed. D. Simon, 37–106 (Frankfurt, 1981).

[5] L. Burgmann and S. Troianos, "Appendix Eclogae," in *Fontes Minores*, vol. 3, ed. D. Simon, 24–125 (Frankfurt, 1979), 56–57: "Von der Aufzählung dieser Handschriften nehmen wir Abstand." ("We refrain from listing these manuscripts."). The Greek text of the treatise (Ecloga Appendix IX, 1–8) is at 113–16.

FIGURE 5.1 *Diagram to illustrate the marriage prohibitions between ascendants and descendants within the same family. Manuscript copied in 1175, probably in Calabria*

Source: *Bibliotheca Marciana, Fondo greco antico 172, folio 27 verso.*

synteknia, or to *adelphopoiesis.* Although the spiritual relationship generated at baptism between individuals, and by extension their relatives, was recognized as an obstacle to marriage by imperial law from the sixth century and by ecclesiastical law from the seventh, it would take a time lag of several centuries until these issues were articulated in theoretical treatises regarding marriage prohibitions.[6]

A very influential version probably dates from the last decade of the eleventh century. It is anonymous and appears as an appendix to the *Synopsis Basilicorum maior*, offering supportive material to the *Basilika*, the collection of laws completed under Leo VI, probably in 888. Among the relations "by arrangement," only filial adoption is granted recognition. *Adelphopoiesis* is declared to be "against the law," the text continues, "and there is no good reason for it."[7]

In the early thirteenth century, Demetrios Chomatenos prepared a treatise on the topic of marriage prohibitions on the basis of consanguinity (see the next section), followed a few decades later by John Pediasimos. Like Demetrios Chomatenos, John Pediasimos held the office of *chartophylax* "of Bulgaria," with its location in the archbishopric of Ohrid. He made extensive use of Chomatenos's *Ponêmata diaphora* in his own works. Indeed, it is possible that John Pediasimos was the redactor responsible for circulating them in their present form.[8] He would certainly have had privileged access to the material in its original version. John Pediasimos had a distinguished record that spans the distance from Epiros to Constantinople: he held the rank of deacon, was known as a polyhistor and had at one time been the chief philosopher (*hypatos tôn philosophôn*) in Constantinople.[9]

Some time between 1275 and 1335, Pediasimos composed "On Marriages" (*Peri gamôn*). The work builds on earlier treatises that were designed to identify licit and illicit marriage partners depending on the degree of kinship. Pediasimos employed the conventional distinction between relationships "by nature" (*physei*) and relationships "by arrangement" (*thesei*), the latter further subdivided into relations through baptism and through filial adoption. *Adelphopoiesis* is addressed at the end of the discussion of relations "by arrangement." The author agrees with earlier jurisprudents that, as it was not legally recognized, *adelphopoiesis* presented no marriage impediments to other family members due to consanguinity. Even if a man and a woman had been joined in brother-making, this was not an obstacle to their marriage, unless it had been concluded secretly. Despite his acknowledgment of the practice of brother-making, even between men and women, Pediasimos is one of the few legal experts of the early fourteenth century who threatened punishment for the priests who performed the ritual.[10]

---

[6] Macrides, "Byzantine Godfather."

[7] I am greatly indebted to Andreas Schminck for sharing his expertise and his unpublished work on this treatise with me.

[8] Demetrios Chomatenos, *Ponêmata diaphora*, ed. G. Prinzing, CFHB 38 (Berlin and New York, 2002), 41*, 306*.

[9] P. Pieler, "Pediasimos, Johannes," in *Lexikon des Mittelalters*, vol. 6 (1993), col. 1850.

[10] A. Schminck, "Der Traktat *Peri gamôn* des Johannes Pediasimos," *Fontes Minores*, vol. 1, ed. D. Simon, 126–74 (Frankfurt, 1976), esp. 156, lines 375–82.

John Pediasimos's treatise served as an inspiration in the first half of the fourteenth century for several large compendia: the *Prochiron auctum*, and the works of Matthaios Blastares and Constantine Harmenopoulos. All of them insist that *adelphopoiesis* does not enjoy legal recognition. The *Prochiron auctum* is an expanded handbook of laws compiled in the fourteenth century. Under the heading of "brotherhood by arrangement," it lists fraternal adoption, which is without legal consequences. As an afterthought, *adelphopoiia* is mentioned as equally irrelevant to marital prohibitions.[11]

More detailed is the legal handbook compiled by Matthaios Blastares in Thessaloniki in 1335, which consists of a sequence of short explanations about the different constellations that result in marriage prohibitions. His treatment of relations "by arrangement" is followed by a separate heading *On adelphopoiia*, which affirms that is it not legal.[12] Indeed, Blastares went one step further and gave the reason for the lack of legal recognition, explaining that it is brought about by "no praiseworthy" motivation. The only legitimate purpose which he could imagine for *adelphopoiesis* would be to secure an heir, but, as he was quick to point out, the legal relationship that fulfills that function is filial adoption. It is left to our imagination what this "less than praiseworthy" motivation may have been. Illicit sex between women and men? Between men and men? The formation of secret confraternities or criminal gangs? All of these could and did happen without the cover of brother-making, but the public performance of the ritual would surely have given the men and women involved greater social and spatial mobility to pursue their intentions.

A decade later, around 1345, Constantine Harmenopoulos produced the *Hexabiblos*, a compilation of secular law. He reiterated the familiar statement that *adelphopoiesis* was not recognized by the law, and therefore did not pose a hindrance to marriage. He mentioned the relation a second time, in the context of inheritance rights and of fraternal adoption, where brother-making was equally declared to be without consequence.[13] Harmenopoulos's treatment of *adelphopoiesis* reveals the two areas where the relation was likely to generate confusion and which legal experts needed to address: marriage prohibitions and inheritance rights. These concerns show that the men who were joined by *adelphopoiesis* may have interpreted this relation as having consequences for their families, too. Although Harmenopoulos was clearly

---

[11] *Prochiron auctum* 8.85, ed. I. Zepos and P. Zepos, *Jus Graecoromanum*, vol. 7 (Athens, 1931; repr. Aalen, 1962), 71.

[12] Matthaios Blastares, *Syntagma kata stoicheion* 2.8, *Diaresis tês syggeneias*, Rhalles and Potles 6, 126–27. See also S. Troianos, "Byzantine Canon Law from the Twelfth to the Fifteenth Centuries," in *The History of Byzantine and Eastern Canon Law to 1500*, ed. W. Hartmann and K. Pennington, 170–214 (Washington, DC, 2012), 185–87.

[13] Constantine Harmenopoulos, *Hexabiblos* ed. G. E. Heimbach (Leipzig, 1851; repr. Aalen, 1969), 4.8.7, 514; 5.8.92, 660; Troianos, "Byzantine Canon Law," 188–90.

inspired by Pediasimos's treatise in his discussion of the degrees of relationships, he also used other sources.[14]

The inclusion of brother-making in several of the treatises *On the Degrees
of Consanguinity* poses interpretive challenges. Should this be understood as
an acknowledgment of the ubiquity of *adelphopoiesis* in late Byzantine society? Or would a systematic theoretical treatise on the topic simply have been
incomplete without the mention of this relationship, regardless of its social
relevance? Does this indicate a rise in popularity and a diffusion of the use of
brother-making at this time, or is it merely a result of the increased composition of such treatises and their subsequent dissemination? A firm answer to
these questions would have to begin by establishing the percentage of treatises *On the Degrees of Consaguinity* that mention *adelphopoiesis*—a task that
would go far beyond the scope of the present study.

How Did *Adelphopoiesis* Relate to Fraternal Adoption (*Adoptio in Fratrem*)?

The difference between fraternal adoption and *adelphopoiesis*, which is based
on a church ritual, cannot be emphasized enough, since the two are often
elided in modern scholarship.[15] The legal sources of the middle and late
Byzantine periods treat brother-making as distinct from fraternal adoption
(*adoptio in fratrem*). Diocletian had prohibited the latter, with specific reference to foreigners, in a law of 285.[16] It is depicted as an obscure practice on
the fringes of the empire that need not be of serious concern.[17] As kinship
relations "by arrangement," neither is found in nature—because one cannot
make a brother for oneself—and therefore both are declared to be devoid of
any legal recognition. As an inheritance strategy, filial adoption is recom-
mended instead.

Later legal literature makes a clear distinction between fraternal adoption
and *adelphopoiesis* based on the ecclesiastical origin of the latter. For this reason, *adelphopoiesis* is the only fraternal relationship that is also dubbed "spiritual" (*pneumatikê*), a feature it shares with ritual co-parenthood (*synteknia*).
This spiritual aspect is missing from any discussion of fraternal adoption and
reinforces the relevance of the ecclesiastical context for our understanding of
the long trajectory of *adelphopoiesis* in the history of Byzantine society.

---

[14] Schminck, "Der Traktat *Peri gamôn* des Johannes Pediasimos," 173, with n. 126.

[15] Shaw, "Ritual Brotherhood"; Pitsakis, "Parentés en dehors de la parenté," 322–23. Although
there is a church ritual for filial adoption, none exists for fraternal adoption.

[16] *Codex Iustinianus* 6.24.7.

[17] Discussed in detail by Shaw, "Ritual Brotherhood." *Codex Iustinianus* 23.2.67 dealt with a case
of marriage between the son and the daughter of two men joined in fraternal adoption. This ruling
was repeated in the *Basilika* 28.4.24, p. 1830.

Was Brother-Making an Exclusive Relationship between Two Men?

Although the ritual for *adelphopoiesis* mentions—with one exception—only two men, a wider application cannot be excluded. It would have been easy enough for the celebrant to adapt the text of the ritual as the situation required. All we can say is that the phrasing of the ritual gives no indication of its being *intended* to include more than two men. But the example of the emperor Basil I shows that a man could have several "brothers." The possibility of a wider application of the ritual for the formation of confraternities or other kinds of brotherhood associations definitely lurked in the background of some texts that discouraged *adelphopoiesis*.

Was *Adelphopoiesis* Open to Women?

The only indication of a bond of ritual sisterhood between women of which I am aware comes from hagiography: the proposed compact between Maria of Amnia and the other contestants in the bride show that would lead to her marriage to the future emperor Constantine VI, as told in the *Life of Philaretos* of the ninth century. But relations of ritual siblinghood between women and men seem to have been rather common. This is not only indicated in the literary sources, but also addressed in legal writing.

Was *Adelphopoiesis* Concluded between Women and Men?

The *Peira*, an eleventh-century collection of legal texts, seems to give an indication about this. It emphasizes that *adelphopoiesis* was a relation affecting only the two individuals involved and that marriage prohibitions resulting from this relation applied only to them, but not to their kin.[18] This is the earliest legal text to mention *adelphopoiesis*. It also raises the possibility of a man and a woman becoming ritual siblings, which would—at least according to some—constitute an obstacle to a later marriage. Two centuries later, John Pediasimos explicitly barred from marriage men and women who were joined in *adelphopoiesis* and who had engaged in sexual relations, unless they confessed to this infringement prior to the wedding.[19] This was not an uncommon occurrence: a poem of the early sixteenth century poked fun at women who attempted to disguise their love affairs under the cover of either *synteknia* or *adelphopoiesis*.[20] In the late sixteenth century, the legal scholar Manuel

---

[18] *Peira* 49, 11, ed. Zepos and Zepos, *Jus Graecoromanum*, 4: 201, lines 6–7.

[19] Schminck, "Der Traktat *Peri gamôn* des Johannes Pediasimos," 156, lines 375–81.

[20] K. Krumbacher, "Ein vulgärgriechischer Weiberspiegel," *Sb. Akad. Munich*, 1905, no. 1, 335–432, 412, lines 1199–1204.

Malaxos from Nauplio, who later worked as a scribe in Italy, explained that the frequent occurrence of subsequent marriage between a man and a woman who had previously contracted brother-making had led the church to prohibit the relation altogether. Any such existing relations should be regarded as null and void, and presented no obstacle to marriage. Whoever engaged in brother-making, including the priest who performed the prayers, should henceforth be punished.[21] In post-Byzantine times, the gender-crossing potential of the relation must have become so dominant as to dictate its abandonment altogether.[22] Implicitly, these condemnations confirm that sexual relations were not expected or intended to follow from the ritual, at least in the understanding of the priests who performed it.

What Were the Practical Dangers of Brother-Making in Secular Society?

The flexibility of the relation was its advantage and its detriment. It allowed ease of access to family and household of the ritual brother, and thus opened the possibility for the violation of privacy and sexual boundaries. A passage in the spurious canons that circulated under the name of John Chrysostom, but that are of uncertain date, mentions in the context of the punishments for adultery the possibilities of a man's intercourse with his *synteknissa* (co-godmother, and possibly also the wife of his co-godfather) and with the wife of his ritual brother (*adelphopoiêtos*). Such illicit relations were especially grave because they occurred between spiritual kin and thus also broke the incest taboo.[23]

Could Brother-Making Be Revoked?

Marriages can end in divorce, oaths can be broken, children can be disinherited. Was it possible to dissolve a relation of spiritual brotherhood? The closest analogy of a spiritual kinship relation, baptismal co-godparenthood (*synteknia*), does not seem to permit an annulment of this bond. There are only the faintest glimpses of such a possibility for brother-making. One is the quotation from an otherwise unidentified manuscript of Manuel Malaxos offered by Zachariä von Lingenthal in his encyclopedic history of Greco-Roman law.

---

[21] Manuel Malaxos, *Nomokanon*, ch. 502, ed. D. S. Gkines and N. I. Pantazopoulos (Thessaloniki, 1985), 330. See also G. de Gregorio, *Il copista greco Manuel Malaxos: Studio biografico e paleografico-codicologico* (Vatican City, 1991).

[22] L. Kretzenbacher, "Serbisch-orthodoxe 'Wahlverbrüderung' zwischen Gläubigenwunsch und Kirchenverbot von heute," *Südost-Forschungen* 38 (1979), 163–83.

[23] John Chrysostom, *Epitimia LXXIII*, no. 5, in J. B. Pitra, ed., *Spicilegium Solesmense*, vol. 4 (Paris, 1858; repr. Graz, 1963), 461.

It refers to the fact that some men had dissolved the brotherhood that they had sworn on a Gospel book and gives this as a reason for the fathers of the church to dismiss the relation altogether.[24] The second instance is based on documentary evidence from the chronological and regional border of our study: a sequence of two Latin documents in the archives of Ragusa (Dubrovnik) of the late fifteenth century speak first of a fraternal contract between two men, and a few years later refer to its dissolution.[25]

What Was the Legal Status of Brother-Making?

The jurisprudents of all periods insisted that the relation enjoyed no legal status and had no legal consequences. In the twelfth century, Niketas, metropolitan of Thessaloniki responded to the question by priests "If some wish to make *adelphopoiia*, should we make them, or not?" that it is superfluous and only leads to great sins, explaining that all mankind has been made brothers through baptism and that the only legitimate brotherhood relations either by nature or "by arrangement" are those involving a father.[26] What exactly the author intended by mentioning "great sins," whether these were infringements of a sexual, social, or political nature, escapes our knowledge. Although the statement is firm and anchored in a religious argument combined with legal knowledge, it refrains from uttering condemnations or threatening punishment.

Was Brother-Making between Lay Persons ever Prohibited?

Only beginning with the early fourteenth century were condemnations issued and efforts put into place to curb the practice. As has been noted in chapter 4, Patriarch Athanasius I (1303–09) insisted that monks should avoid such relations with laymen and declared them invalid. His strictures against brother-making between laymen were even more severe. On one occasion, he demanded that priests prohibit ritual brotherhood, requesting that they make known to the church those who refuse to abide by this. On another occasion, he ruled that priests should prevent the formation of "brotherhoods" (*adelphosynai*, plural) by imposing a penance. If penance could not be applied, he requested that the priests report such brotherhoods to the civil authority—possibly a reference to confraternities or other kinds of associations. Both these rulings, the principled patriarch explained, were part of

---

[24] Zachariä von Lingenthal, *Geschichte des griechisch-römischen Rechts*, 119n354.

[25] Discussed in detail above, chapter 1.

[26] *Erôtêseis diaphorôn nomimôn kai kanonikôn zêtêmatôn anenechtheisai Nikêta, tôi hagiôtatôi mêtropolitê Thessalonikês*, A. Pavlov, ed., "Kanonicheskie otviety Nikity, mitropolita Solunskago (XII vieka?)," *Vizantijskij Vremmenik* 2 (1895), 378–87, at 384.

his effort to remedy the dissolution of morals, especially among monks and priests.[27] Not only the ritual brothers themselves, also the priests who performed the ritual came under attack at this time. As has been noted, John Pediasimos declared in his treatise *On the Degrees of Consanguinity* that ritual brotherhood relations should not only be considered void, but that the priests who performed them should be subject to ecclesiastical discipline. We are not informed whether these rigorous demands were ever put into practice.

What Were the Effects of Brother-Making on Subsequent Generations?

The legal sources, with a single exception,[28] insisted that it was a lateral bond limited to the two men involved and that it carried no marriage prohibitions for the next generation. This feature distinguished it from the other relation of spiritual kinship, *synteknia*, which carried marriage prohibitions up to the seventh degree of consanguinity. At the same time, the frequent injunctions to refrain from brother-making as a means to pass on one's inheritance imply the possibility of a cross-generational extension of the original bond, from one's ritual brother to his son. Indeed, some of the narratives of *adelphopoiesis* in court circles that we encountered in chapter 4 confirm that such claims were not unusual.

What Do the Legal Sources Reveal about the Practical Benefits of Brother-Making?

The reasoning of Matthaios Blastares, who advocated filial adoption instead of *adelphopoiesis* as an inheritance strategy, suggests that brother-making could also have sprung from economic motivations. If other indications can serve as a guide, there may have been economic benefits to brother-making already for the generation that concluded the bond.

In the monastic environment that gave rise to the prayers for *adelphopoiesis*, the sharing of spiritual capital was an essential manifestation of these relationships. In the early modern cases of *affratellamento* known from Ragusa or from Southern France, the sharing of capital, of tools, and of skills enabled men and their families to improve their condition on a larger scale than they would have been able to afford as individuals. It is easy to imagine how the social advantages of such a brotherhood relation also translated

---

[27] V. Laurent, *Les regestes des actes du patriarcat du Constantinople*, vol. 1, pt. 4 (2nd rev. ed. Paris, 1972), no. 1762, p. 541; no. 1777, p. 554.

[28] Codex Parisinus graecus 1384, fol. 171r—quoted by Zachariä von Lingenthal, *Geschichte des griechisch-römischen Rechts*, 119n352—prohibits marriages between the sons and daughters of ritual brothers.

into economic benefits in the form of the exchange of gifts and favors and mutual assistance in business ventures. But the advantages did not stop there. Many people were of the opinion that the property of the two brothers was somehow held in common and passed on jointly to their heirs. In this way, it would have been possible to retain property within the "family" circle, and to counteract the imperial efforts from the late tenth century to discourage close marriage in order to prevent the land-holding aristocracy from becoming too powerful.[29] *Adelphopoiesis* between distant relatives might well have been employed as an antidote to the economic effects of exogamy.

What Can the Legal Documentation on Brother-Making Tell Us about Male-Male Relationships?

The existence of male-male relationships that were blessed and formalized through the brother-making ritual was clearly acknowledged by Byzantine legislators and legal commentators. Yet they were at pains to depict such relations as having no legal status, relegating them to the private sphere of social convention or the religious sphere of optional prayers. That they did so rather frequently, beginning in the eleventh century, points to a well-established practice. Moreover, their reasoning reveals that the ritual often joined not just men and men but also men and women. With very few exceptions, these people would have been married to other people. We will never be able to separate their motivations, whether the expansion of social networks, the affirmation of friendship, or the desire to add respectability to sexual relationships. In a society where women and men did not mix easily, brother-making offered a cover for extramarital sexual encounters. Men, by contrast, had frequent opportunities to mingle. And although sodomy between men was prohibited by the emperor Justinian, six centuries later it was possible for two men who were publicly recognized as a couple to inquire of the Patriarch Lukas Chrysoberges (1157–69/70) whether their relationship as lovers was an obstacle to the marriage of one with the sister of the other. The answer was negative.[30] We observe here the same layering of relationships between men that had prompted the brother of Mary of Vizye to marry her off to his ritual brother, which proved to be an unhappy marriage with a deadly outcome for the wife. Significant in the present case is the fact that in their inquiry to the patriarch, the male-male couple refer to each other as lovers. In other words, there was no need to employ brother-making to formalize their relationship.

---

[29] Laiou, "Family Structure." See also J.-C. Cheynet, "Aristocratie et héritage (XIe–XIIIe siècle)," in *La transmission du patrimoine: Byzance et l'aire méditéranée*, ed. J. Beaucamp and G. Dagron, 53–80 (Paris, 1998).

[30] V. Grumel and J. Darrouzès, *Les regestes des actes du patriarcat du Constantinople*, vols. 2–3 (Paris, 1989), no. 1087. 9, p. 528. For background, see Pitsakis, "Parentés en dehors de la parenté," 320.

What Is the Value of the Legal Evidence?

The forceful language with which the jurisprudents aimed to regulate, devaluate, or castigate it underscores the continued practice of *adelphopoiesis* in Byzantium. Throughout the Byzantine centuries, it was treated as a relation that was blessed by the church—a feature that sets it apart from blood brotherhood and from fraternal adoption.

Implicitly, the legal sources also reveal the reasons that might have prompted people to pursue this relationship: first and foremost to create a lasting association between two men, perhaps with an economic motive of joining property for the benefit not only of the current, but also of the next generation. Such an association could be further strengthened, depending on the availability of family members of the right age, by godparenthood and marriage. These were the scenarios that caused the greatest confusion and for which clarification was requested from the jurisprudents. On occasion, brother-making was employed to allow men and women freedom of contact with each other outside of the strictures of marriage.

Beginning with the earliest statement in the eleventh century, the validity of the relationship between laymen was constantly called into question, culminating in outright rejection and the threat of punishment for practitioners and celebrants in the early fourteenth century. This leaves ample room for speculation why the relation came under attack at that particular time. Was it the moral impropriety of hetero- or homosexual relations that might occur under the cover of ritual brotherhood? Was it the fear of secret associations that might threaten social stability and political order? Was it because the increased role of the church in defining social relationships had become objectionable to the state?

For all the references to *adelphopoiesis* as being unlawful, unrecognized, unreasonable, and altogether unnecessary, Byzantine legal authors were on the whole remarkably quiet about the potential of the relation to cover up or to legitimize male-male sexual relations or to facilitate larger associations of a subversive nature.[31] To the contrary, *adelphopoiesis* may have been relegated to the margins of legality, but it was an openly recognized mainstay of society.

B. Case Study: Demetrios Chomatenos, Legal Expert and Bishop in Thirteenth-Century Epiros

In the social world of the early thirteenth century, brother-making was a recurring feature. This is illustrated by the written record left by Demetrios

---

[31] *Pace* Pitsakis, "Parentés en dehors de la parenté," 323.

Chomatenos, archbishop of Ohrid from 1216 to at least 1236. His ecclesiastical career began as a delegate-secretary (*apokrisiarios*) in Constantinople, and after a brief stint as archivist-secretary (*chartophylax*) of the archbishopric of Ohrid, he soon held the see of that city himself. These were times of political turmoil: the Crusaders had captured Constantinople and installed a Latin emperor and a Latin patriarch there, while the ruling dynasty of the Laskarids had established a Byzantine government in exile in Nicaea. Other aristocratic families ruled over areas of mainland Greece and the Peloponnese. Ohrid was the main city of the Despotate of Epiros, which abutted the Serbian kingdom to the west and the Bulgarian kingdom to the north. The church provided a stable force and a point of recourse, especially when competent, educated, and well-connected men like Chomatenos were at its helm. His advice in legal and ecclesiastical matters was sought not only from the flock under his sway, but also from leaders beyond the borders. It comes as no surprise that he claimed for himself influence and honor on the same level as a patriarch, and that in 1227 he was ready to bestow both unction and imperial coronation on the ruler of Epiros, Theodoros Doukas in Thessaloniki, whose subsequent claim to the imperial throne, however, came to naught.[32]

In several of his writings, Demetrios Chomatenos mentions brother-making in a surprising variety of applications: between men and women, between monks and laypeople, among servants, and among military officers, within Byzantium and beyond the borders, in the kingdoms of Serbia and Bulgaria.[33]

A treatise *On the Degrees of Consanguinity* that was requested by a "most venerable *despotes*" is attributed to Demetrios Chomatenos in some manuscripts.[34] It is a systematic disquisition of moderate length, beginning with the marriage prohibitions on the basis of consanguinity. Then follows a section on marriage prohibitions as a result of spiritual kinship. Through the mediation of God and the process of holy baptism, Chomatenos explains, the godfather and the biological father become "one person" (*heis anthrôpos*), their children are called "brothers," they themselves "co-parents (*synteknoi*)," and all their offspring is considered to belong to the same family. A further relationship "by arrangement" (*dia theseôs*) is filial adoption, which has the same validity as blood or spiritual kin. He then adds: "But brotherhood by arrangement, which is of undetermined [*asystatos*] and unaffirmed [*abebaios*] status,

---

[32] On the author, see most recently G. Prinzing, "The Authority of the Church in Uneasy Times: The Example of Demetrios Chomatenos, Archbishop of Ohrid, in the State of Epiros 1216–1236," in *Authority in Byzantium*, ed. P. Armstrong, 137–50 (Farnham, 2013).

[33] For the Epirote context, see A. Kiousopoulou, *Ho thesmos tês oikgeneias stên Êpeiro kata ton 13o aiôna* (Athens, 1990), 162–64.

[34] Demetrios Chomatenos, *De gradibus*, ed. J. B. Pitra, *Analecta sacra et classica spicilegio Solesmensi parata*, vol. 6, pt. 2 (Paris and Rome, 1891), cols. 719–50 (= PG 119, cols. 937B–945D), at col. 726. .

does not correspond to nature, and is not recognized by the law, presents no obstacle to marriage whatsoever." The passage concludes with the affirmation that the only legitimate relations "by arrangement" are those that mirror nature, that is, godfatherhood and filial adoption.

The decisive stance that Chomatenos took in this systematic treatise was mellowed when he dispensed legal advice in response to queries. Asked by Stephen Doukas, King of Serbia, "If some want to conclude *adelphopoiias*, should we allow them?" his answer was laconic: "These are not recognized by the church."[35] In other words, Chomatenos refrained from issuing prohibitions or punishments for brother-making among laypeople, but was equally reluctant to encourage it.

With regard to monks, however, the archbishop's recommendation was firm: brother-making of monks with lay people should be avoided under any circumstance. This is the advice he dispenses in one of his letters, addressed to the abbot of the Monastery of Saint Demetrios at Glavenitza. The abbot's concern should be to ensure a uniformly virtuous way of life among all the monks, regardless of their difference in social status. Distance from the world and its temptations should at all times be maintained. "For this reason, you must under all circumstances prevent the monks from mingling with laymen or gathering with them at the wrong time; especially you must prevent brother-makings and everything else that would make them inclined toward the world."[36] In this way, Chomatenos joins other authors of monastic treatises in their warning of the moral dangers of crossing social boundaries when monks engage in quasi-familial relations with people outside.

Demetrios Chomatenos's *Ponêmata Diaphora* are a colorful source for the social life of his time. They comprise 152 items, letters, responses, judicial decisions, and reviews. The work survives in four main manuscripts, in addition to several others, from the middle of the sixteenth century.[37] The mere fact of their survival in this form, with thematic chapter headings, and roughly arranged by subject material, along with the fact that Chomatenos often refers to specific passages in imperial law and canon law, indicates that these texts were gathered with the purpose of assisting others in the dispensation of justice, as some kind of reference work or rule book. They preserve an accurate reflection of the archive of a large ecclesiastical province in a prosperous region, during a time of political instability.

The first thirty pieces in this work deal with marriage in the widest sense. The restrictions in the choice of partner imposed by imperial and ecclesiastical law are a recurring concern. Consanguinity, especially in complex cases that result from death and remarriage, appears to pose the most frequent need

---

[35] Demetrios Chomatenos, *Canonicae quaestiones*, ed. Pitra, Question 208, col. 713.

[36] Demetrios Chomatenos, *Ponêmata diaphora*, ed. Prinzing, no. 147, p. 428.

[37] Ibid., ed. Prinzing, pp. 308*–26*.

for clarification, although *synteknia* is also mentioned.[38] Among this rich documentation, there appear two cases of *adelphopoiesis*: the brother-making between two military men, and the *adelphopoiesis* relation involving a servant woman.

Perhaps around 1216 or 1217, Chomatenos's advice was requested regarding the legitimacy of a proposed marriage. Alexander of Neokastro, "the most manly warrior," had been joined to the now deceased Chydros in brother-hood by arrangement (*dia theseos adelphotês*). Basos, the brother of Chydros, had a daughter, whom Alexander intended to marry. Was this union with niece of one's *adelphopoiêtos* permitted? Chomatenos's answer is an implied yes to the intended marriage, on the grounds that brotherhood by arrange-ment is not recognized by the law, and thus has no legal consequences. As precedent, the archbishop cited the law of Diocletian of the year 285, which prohibited fraternal adoption and then explained that the only consanguin-ity relations by arrangement that are recognized by the law are those that arise from godparenthood and filial adoption, because they imitate nature in bringing forth sons, while it is not possible to create a brother for oneself. The others, he continued, "we cast aside as relations that must be rejected and are not admissible."[39]

The case of Alexander and Chydros shows the possibilities for the multiple application of marriage and ritual kinship relations in order to forge ties between families that outlast the initial pairing of brothers, similar to the case of Mary of Vizye before. Alexander probably entered into brother-hood with Chydros because they were both military men, for the purposes of mutual succor on the battlefield. The army, like the monastery or institutions of higher learning, constituted a quintessentially homosocial environment, in which it was easy to form and articulate male-male attachments. Alexander sought to maintain his relation to Chydros's family even after Chydros's death, through a marriage alliance with the next generation. Or perhaps he felt obligated to take responsibility for his "brother's" niece by offering her a livelihood in his household, with the prospect of creating offspring that would result in an extension into future generations of the relation between to two families.

Demetrios Chomatenos's correspondence also preserves the record of an interesting court case that was heard before the archbishop of All Bulgaria, in which a man and a woman joined in brother-making play a supporting role: the soldier Rados accused his wife Slava of having committed adultery while he was away on a military campaign. The broker of this illicit relation-ship had been the maidservant Kale, who had acted on behalf of her "brother

[38] *Synteknia* as an obstacle to marriage: ibid., ed. Prinzing, no. 16, pp. 67–69.

[39] Ibid., ed. Prinzing, no. 5, p. 41, with commentary on pp. 67*–68*, and p. 304*. For a similar statement, see no. 140, p. 415.

by arrangement."[40] Such relations are otherwise only referred to summarily, but this is one of the very few cases of brother-making between a man and a woman where the individuals are known. As this instance shows, brotherhood arrangements would have facilitated the crossing of many boundaries—gender, social status, privacy of the home—and could thus pave the way for a violation of the threshold of immorality and illegality.

Chomatenos's extensive oeuvre offers a detailed picture of the concerns of a thirteenth-century metropolitan bishop on the fringes of the empire and at a time of political upheavals. By far the most common theme that occupies him in his function as administrator of legal advice is the entire gamut of issues relating to marriage: the appropriate choice of partner that does not violate marriage prohibitions, as well as engagements, divorce, legitimate offspring, and inheritance rights. A few of the cases on his desk resulted from *synteknia*, and even fewer were the consequence of "brotherhood by arrangement." The men involved lived in the borderlands of the empire, were of relatively high social status and served in the military. Beyond that, it would seem that Chomatenos's correspondence offers a reflection of the role of *adelphopoiesis* in late Byzantine society: it was present, although to a limited degree, and enjoyed social, but not legal recognition.

---

[40] Ibid., ed. Prinzing, no. 139, pp. 413–14.

{6}

Beyond Byzantium

The year 1453 and the end of Byzantine rule in Constantinople do not spell the end of *adelphopoiesis*. With the collapse of the power structure of the empire, the religious traditions and social practices of Byzantium were carried on within the framework of the church. As an ecclesiastical ritual, it continued to be a concern to the Orthodox church. *Euchologia* that contained the prayers were still copied, priests still performed the prayers, and bishops and patriarchs on occasion still attempted to restrict the implementation of the relationship to its original intention as a spiritual bond between two people (Figure 6.1). The anecdotal evidence becomes more frequent, offering nameless cases and stories of practices that are reported on good authority, but that cannot be traced with certainty. Taken together, these indications can complete our picture of *adelphopoiesis*. They throw especially vivid light on the contexts and motivations of the people who practice it. Some of that light may also help to illuminate, in retrospect, the practice of brother-making in earlier centuries.

Ritual brotherhood was extremely malleable to people's needs. It could be employed to strengthen ties within the extended kin group, or to broaden the kin group through the inclusion of outsiders. This applies to the close relations between two monks within a monastery that we have encountered on the previous pages just as much as to the practice of the Don Cossacks in the nineteenth century, who are reported as having contracted sworn brotherhood within a Christian ritual framework, often involving a church liturgy, in order to strengthen group cohesion.[1]

---

[1] S. O'Rourke, *Warriors and Peasants: The Don Cossacks in Late Imperial Russia* (Basingstoke and New York, 2000), 168.

FIGURE 6.1 *Saints George and Demetrios, sixteenth-century icon, Church of Hagios Nikolaos, Makrino in Zagori, Greece*
Source: *Christos Stavrakos.*

Indeed, the most striking defining feature is the function of *adelphopoiesis* to facilitate the crossing of boundaries. This has been observed already as a central motivation in the use of brother-making between monks and laymen that became so popular on a large scale that monastic leaders attempted to control it beginning in the ninth century. As a religiously permitted kinship strategy, brother-making could also bridge the boundaries between the sexes, and the indications of its use for this purpose become frequent from the thirteenth century. After the Crusades had brought neighbors of Western origin and Catholic observance into the towns and villages of formerly Byzantine territory in Greece, the Peloponnese, and elsewhere, *adelphopoiesis* was also employed to cross ethnic and religious boundaries.

Among the Orthodox Christians of post-Byzantine times, kin groups gained in social and political importance, and ethnicity and religion held special value as identity markers. In this environment, the practice of brother-making afforded a welcome measure of flexibility in a context where otherwise divisions had hardened. Once two people had agreed to become "brothers," all that was required was a church and a priest in order to conduct the *adelphopoiesis* ritual in the way prescribed by the *euchologia*, and perhaps not even that. Whether the church ritual was always observed in practice when two men wished to form a publicly recognized and divinely sanctioned bond is not entirely clear, especially when one of the two partners did not belong to Orthodox Christianity, but was Catholic, or even Muslim. In such instances, we may assume that other strong ritual gestures came into play, such as the exchange of blood,[2] or—in substitution—the drinking of red wine from a shared cup. The large feast that often followed the ritual act made the relationship public and allowed associates, friends, and kin to take a stake in it. The value of these relations lay precisely in the fact that they were known and recognized, adding an element of social control as a stabilizing factor.

A. Case Study: Kapetan Michalis and Nuri Bey

Modern Greek literature romanticizes such relationships, celebrating them as displays of strong masculinity that either encourage a spirit of mutual support in a time of crisis, or neutralize the potential for conflict. In the first sense, the concept is invoked by Dionysios Solomos in his epic poem *The Free Besieged* (*Eleutheri Poliorkimeni*), which describes the Siege of Messolonghi by the Turkish army in 1825–26 that ended in the heroic death of the entire population as they preferred to perish rather than surrender. Solomos, an Italian-speaking native of the island of Zakynthos, worked on *The Free Besieged* in three drafts, in both Italian and Greek, that were

---

[2] There is a single instance in a post-Byzantine *euchologion* where the mingling of blood is mentioned. Manuscript Athos Laura, Theta 91 contains on fol. 94 recto prayers *peri haimomixias*, and following that, on fol. 95 recto *peri pneumatikês haimomixias*. C. N. Constantinides and R. Browning, eds., *Dated Greek Manuscripts from Cyprus to the Year 1570* (Washington, DC, 1993), no. 82, pp. 287–93 (I have not seen the full text of the prayers). The manuscript was copied in 1536 by the monk Loukianos and dedicated to the Church of the Laura Phanêromenê in Paphos, Cyprus. Throughout Byzantine times, the "mingling of blood" referred to miscegenation and incest, but when qualified as "spiritual," it may well refer to prayers that were accompanied by the ritual exchange of blood.

never completed. In one scene, one of the fighting men encourages another to confide in him by calling him an *adelphopoiêtos*—here used as a form of address to invoke a relationship of comradery, familiarity, and trust.[3]

The potential of *adelphopoiesis* in the second sense, the diffusion of tension, is dramatized in Nikos Kazantzakis's novel *Kapetan Michalis*. Also set in the context of resistance against the Ottomans, this time in Crete in 1889, the novel begins in peaceful times. Kapetan Michalis, a Greek, and Nuri Bey, a Turk, personify the great powers. Their story demonstrates the interplay and tension between the larger forces of political and social constellations that conspire to determine the fate of the individual, and the individual's attempts to devise mechanisms for his own independent agency.

Kapetan Michalis is a strong man, fierce and irascible, whose father had been killed by Nuri Bey's brother, leaving him with a simmering grudge against the world in general and a hatred just below boiling point against the Turks in particular. The story begins with a tense encounter between the two, when Nuri Bey, who is in charge of the village, summons Michalis to his house because he wants to ask him a favor. A little earlier, Kapetan Michalis's brother had taken a donkey into the mosque. This provocation harbored the potential for escalating violence. In this highly charged situation, the two come together for an ostensibly amiable meeting, during which they measure their strength through gestures and carefully calibrated displays of anger. All the while, they continue drinking and conversing, and at a certain moment, both have flashbacks to their youth, when they had concluded a pact of brotherhood.

Their social position could not have been more different: the Turk born to wealth and power; the Greek "an underdog," whose family was subjected to daily humiliations.[4] Yet, in character, they were in similar: strong and proud young men raised to fight for honor, family, and tradition. As children, they had grown up playing together; as young men, their mutual respect oscillated between admiring love and murderous hatred, until one day, Nuri Bey declared: "We ought to mingle our blood, but in a different way." He cut Michalis's arm to draw blood, bound the incision with his own

[3] Solomos worked on the poem between 1833 and 1849. The passage in question is found only in the second of three drafts, Draft 2, section 7. D. Solomos, *The Free Besieged and Other Poems*, ed. and intr. P. Mackridge, trans. P. Thompson et al. (Nottingham, 2000), text and translation, 22–23, historical background, xiv–xxi. It seems that Solomos was rather taken by the idea of brotherhood, because he also worked on a poem or section of a longer poetic work which he entitled, in Italian, "La fratellanza," and in Greek, "Adelphopoietoi." E. Tsantsanoglu, "Hoi adelphopoitoi [*sic*]: Hena metakinoumeno Solômiko thema," in *Aphierôma ston Kathêgetê Lino Politê* (Thessaloniki, 1979), 145–51.

[4] Nikos Kazantzakis, *Freedom or Death, a Novel*, trans. J. Griffin (London 1956; repr. 1966; first published in Greek, 1950), 25.

hairband, and then Michalis did the same to him. They drank the com-mingled blood from a cup, accompanied by a solemn oath: "In the names of Mohammed and Christ . . . I drink to your health, Captain Michalis, my blood brother! I swear—yes, by Mohammed, that I will never harm you; not with word and not with deed, whether in war or in good times. Honour for honour, manhood for manhood, loyalty for loyalty! I have more than enough Greeks, you have more than enough Turks—take your vengeance among them!"[5] Then they shared a festive meal and went to sleep in the same bed—specially made ready with silk sheets at Nuri Bey's orders. Their relation became common knowledge among the villagers. Now, as they are sitting, smoking, and drinking, the intense memory of this moment floods through them both. The effect of this reminiscence on Nuri Bey is his desire to share a valuable gift with his guest, and the most precious possession he can think of is his newly wedded wife, who is promptly summoned to per-form a song on the mandolin for them. Michalis is both touched and upset by this extravagant gesture, and the scene ends in violence, with Michalis breaking a glass and Nuri Bey smashing the mandolin to pieces. But in the end, the entire performance of masculinity, honor, and strength serves its purpose, as Michalis announces at his departure that he will indeed grant Nuri Bey the favor he had asked: to prevail on his own brother to stop pro-voking the Turks.

Kazantzakis calls them *aderphochtoi*, a word I have not been able to find in any dictionary, although it may well be Cretan dialect. The author is well known for the liberty he took with the Greek language. The situation described in this novelistic fashion is rife with the potential for competi-tion and conflict that can be averted only by something stronger: a mutual promise, an oath according to their respective religious traditions, and the exchange of blood. Their new-found *détente* is enacted and reinforced by the performance of what a brotherly relation should entail: the sharing of a meal, access to the private part of the household, and a certain degree of intimacy—here indicated by sleeping in the same bed for one night, and the bestowal of generous gifts. This is taken to an extreme when Nuri Bey removes the veil of privacy by exposing his own wife and her musical tal-ents to the eyes of Michalis—a gesture that brings to mind the occasional warnings of Byzantine authors against the potentially pernicious effect of brother-making on the virtue of the women of the household. Most impor-tantly, the entire event achieves its intended effect: to avert a conflict between Greeks and Turks, Christians and Muslims on a larger scale, by compel-ling both leaders to adhere to the same rules without losing face, without demeaning their masculinity or compromising their honor. In the end, this

---

[5] Ibid., 27–28.

newly forged relation of brotherhood enables the Turk to ask a favor which he knows the Greek cannot refuse.

The potential of *adelphopoiesis* in the world of lay relations could not be clearer than in this story: where larger power structures draw sharp and often inhibiting lines of division based on ethnicity, religion, and, in other cases, social class and gender, brother-making offers a well-trodden dirt path (as conveyed by the colloquial German word *Trampelpfad*) to perforate those boundaries in order to achieve personal interests. It may not be part of the official road map, but is nonetheless (or perhaps just for this reason) well known and well traveled by those who know how to use it.

The story of Kapetan Michalis and Nuri Bey may be fictional, but its plausibility makes it gripping and convincing. In the early modern period throughout the Balkan regions and further east into Russia and even Mongolia, among Slavs, South Slavs, and Greeks, whether Orthodox Christians or Muslims, brother-making by various means—not all of them liturgical—was a commonly employed fraternization strategy for the extension of kinship, and found frequent reflection in works of literature.[6]

The Practice of *Adelphopoiesis* among Greeks and the Legal Situation after 1453

At various times, the Orthodox church made an effort to declare *adelphopoiesis* invalid, or even to curb the practice altogether by threatening punishment for the priests who performed the prayers. Like the prohibitions uttered in the Byzantine Empire, these seem to have had no effect and there are no known cases of priests being defrocked on these grounds. To the contrary, the regularity with which the relation of *adelphopoiesis* was addressed and the fact that the prayers were available in print confirms its persistence.

Agreements of brotherhood and oaths of friendship and support were flexible in their application, in Byzantine times and beyond. Among Greeks under the Turkokratia, *adelphopoiesis* found application both to facilitate interaction with the other side on an individual basis, as Kapetan Michalis and Nuri Bey had done, and to bring together several men in a club or association for the purpose of mutual assistance or even rebellion against the representatives of Ottoman rule. In Byzantium, the label of *adelphopoiesis* is not normally attached to such larger associations, but in later centuries this usage seems to become more prevalent in admonitions or prohibitions issued by the church. In the eighteenth century, for example, a condemnation was issued

---

[6] L. Kretzenbacher, "Rituelle Wahlverbrüderung in Südosteuropa: Erlebniswirklichkeit und Erzählmotiv," Bayerische Akademie der Wissenschaften, Philosophisch-historische Klasse, Sitzungsberichte 1971, no. 1 (Munich, 1971), 3–32.

in vernacular Greek, perhaps a paraphrase for the sake of publication of an original document by the Patriarchal Synod: the occasion was the formation of a brotherhood in the town of Karpenisi at the foot of the Pidnus Mountains in Central Greece. This led to an outright condemnation of *adelphopoiesis* on the grounds that it was not part of the ecclesiastical tradition. No priests or laymen should be part of it, the document declared, and any priests who performed prayers for it were to be defrocked, and laymen who participated in it were to be excommunicated.[7]

Adelphopoiesis came to the fore in the early decades of the nineteenth century when nationalist feelings were on the rise in the build-up to the Greek War of Independence. The "Society of Friends" (*Philikê Hetairia*) was formed as a secret organization among the Greeks of the Diaspora, with a wide net of membership from Iasi to the Mani and from Odessa to Constantinople, Vienna, and Moscow. Modeled on the Freemasons, it involved four levels of membership, beginning with the *adelphopoiêtoi*. True to the nature of the organization as a secret society that was fomenting military action with revolutionary aims, new members were co-opted on a one-on-one basis in a sequence of ritualized moments spread out over several days. First, *adelphopoiesis* was concluded between the old and the new member, by swearing on the Gospel, preferably in the presence of a priest. This established a basis of mutual trust and a safeguard against the betrayal of the more secret steps that followed. Next, the new member swore a first oath to affirm that the statements regarding his person were true and that his intentions were genuine. This was done before a priest, who was not, however, supposed to notice that the words of the oath were dictated by the old member. The second oath was a secret ceremony of the two men in private. The new member had to kneel on one knee while swearing on an icon the oath of membership and commitment to the cause, which he confirmed "with my own tears," before the old member officially acknowledged his acceptance into the society by placing his hand on the neophyte's shoulder. All this was done to the light of a yellow candle that the neophyte kept as a reminder of the oath.[8] The careful choreography of this process of initiation was designed to generate strong emotions and a tight bond between the two men, a bond that increased over the course of several days as their interaction moved from the public to the private sphere. What makes it interesting for our present study is the easy recourse to *adelphopoiesis*—as a term, as a concept, and as a ritual affirmation

---

[7] Amantos, "Epitimion kata tês adelphopoiias."

[8] The initiation is described in a document of 1815, translated in R. Clogg, *The Movement for Greek Independence, 1770–1821: A Collection of Documents* (London, 1976), 175–82; see also I. Philemon, *Dokimion historikon peri tês Philikês Hetairias* (Nauplio, 1834; available on Google Books), 144–46; and G. D. Frangos, "The *Philike Etaireia*, 1814–1821: A Social and Historical Analysis," PhD diss., Columbia University, 1971, 69–72.

through an oath—with its full range of associations as a male-male bond and as an ecclesiastically sanctioned relation. *Adelphopoiesis* remained flexible enough in its application to be of enduring appeal.

Studies of Greek folkways and customs tend to present a long historical trajectory in the practice of *adelphopoiesis*, from ancient Greece through Byzantium to more recent times. In many of these overview studies, the subtle but essential distinctions between fraternal adoption, blood brotherhood, and declarations of friendship are sacrificed for the sake of establishing a historical continuum that reaches to the classical past.[9] Anthropological and ethnographic studies point to an essential difficulty in the interpretation of customs and rituals by outside observers, who must balance their own observation and judgment with the explanations offered by the practitioners. Anastasios Georgopapadakis has offered a largely descriptive study of *adelphopoiia* in the Mani in the early decades of the twentieth century. In this remote area of the Peloponnese which prided itself on maintaining its own traditions, it was not uncommon for two men (more rarely two women) who usually had been friends for a long time to conclude brother-making with each other. The brother-making itself involved a retreat to the mountains for several days, where the two men would hunt for their own food. In the privacy of a mountain cave, they cut their wrists or their chests with a black knife to draw blood, which they then mingled and then sealed their relationship with a "hot embrace." Afterwards, it was possible, but not required, to ask for the priest's prayer, which was freely formulated, not recited from the prayer book. The resulting relationship had wide social ramifications. The two men usually came from different villages or at least from different households and their brother-making required prior permission by the elders of each family and was accompanied by the exchange of gifts, such as pistols, knives, or belts. The consequences of the relation were extensive: not only were the "brothers," their families, and descendants barred from intermarriage, but the two families were now expected to jointly extract revenge in blood feuds.[10]

Spiritual Friendship

The ritual of *adelphopoiesis* is, to the best of my knowledge, not currently performed for laymen or women by Greek Orthodox priests, either in the

---

[9] S. Kypriakides, "Adelphopoiia (kai adelphopoiesis)," in *Megalê Hellênikê Engkyklopaideia*, ed. P. Drandakes, vol. 1, 569–71 (Athens 1927; repr. 1963). A similar romanticizing retrojection of modern pratice to ancient precedent is the Chinese "Oath of the Peach Garden," when three friends in the context of a rebellion at the end of the Eastern Han Dynasty in the 180s are depicted as swearing to regard each other as brothers and express the hope to find their death on the same day. This story was first popularized in the fourteenth-century *Romance of Three Kingdoms*, but continues to serve as an inspiration for secret societies in present-day China.

[10] A. M. Georgopapadakis, "Hê adelphopoiia eis tên Manên," *Laographia* 13 (1951), 28–32.

United States or in the United Kingdom, or in Greece. Yet, monks and nuns will sometimes talk about strong spiritual bonds between two people within a monastic community, in a relationship that is known and recognized by others. That men and women in the monasteries of Orthodox Christianity still today find one partner with whom they share their spiritual journey in a special way, by mutual commitment, attests to the enduring appeal of the human need for support and friendship sublimated within a framework of active spirituality and confirmed by a ritual moment. It is also confirmation of the argument presented here that seeks the origin of the *adelphopoiesis* ritual in the early monastic movement.

A beautiful short story by the Russian novelist Antonin Chekhov, *On Easter Eve*, first published in 1887, offers through the eyes of the first-person narrator a glimpse of a monk's friendship with a ferryman outside the monastery. During the lonely passage across a dark river to reach the monastery for a light-filled and crowded Easter liturgy, the narrator listens to the ferryman's tender reminiscences of his deceased "fellow monk," as he calls him, although he is himself a lay person. The man remembers with gratitude the monk's motherly kindness, dreamily seeks his gaze in the face of a young woman, and fondly recalls the shared moments in the monk's cell when he listened in rapture to the flowery mystical language of the liturgical poetry that flowed from his pen. The setting of a river crossing at the break of dawn evokes the boundary between the monastery and the outside world. As the narrator walks away from his conversation with the ferryman, we share his impression that the mystery of enduring love and eternal life is more palpable in this simple tale of a deep spiritual friendship than in the liturgical pageantry of Easter.[11]

In Russia in the early twentieth century, there was also the remarkable case of Father Pavel Florensky (1882–1937). Originally from the Caucasus area, he spent most of his life in Moscow. Raised in a nonreligious environment, a mystical experience at the age of seventeen set him on a path to explore spiritual reality and to experience the divine cohesion of the cosmos. Gifted as a scientist, he went in search of a mathematical formula for infinity, while at the same time seeking ordination to the priesthood and a teaching position at the Moscow Theological Academy. Despite his continued contributions to science and engineering, in 1933 he came into conflict with the Soviet authorities and was sent to a prison camp in Siberia, where he died four years later. His seminal work, *The Pillar and Ground of Truth* (1914), is influenced by Russian Symbolism, but even more so rooted in the spiritual tradition of the desert fathers. His understanding of a divine love

---

[11] I am grateful to Michael Heim for sharing his translation of Chekhov's story with me. It was printed in a limited artist's edition by Shackman Press in a volume entitled *Anton Chekhov, Easter Week*.

that animates and permeates everything is expressed in letters addressed to an unidentified "brother," "friend," "elder," or "guardian." This love or "friendship" needs a counterpart, an Other, to be activated and articulated. In order to explain this concept, Florensky invokes the Orthodox tradition of *adelphopoiesis* (*pobratimstvo, bratotvorenje*). The liturgical office for brother-making, he explains, expresses and sublimates the human desire for a deep friendship and imbues it with a new sacrality, thus opening the path to an experience of the sacred in the community of others, in an idealized form of the church as a communal, human articulation of divine love whose nature it is to communicate itself.[12] The spiritual benefits and theological underpinnings of *adelphopoiesis* were not lost on Russian intellectuals of the late nineteenth and early twentieth centuries, and Florensky saw clearly that this was a tradition that reached back to the times of the desert fathers.

Slavs and South Slavs

The Balkan region and its peoples have attracted a great many travelers and observers in the nineteenth century, resulting in a great deal of writing that offers anthropological insights, with varying degrees of completeness and even greater variation in analytical rigor.[13] In this context, artificial or ritual kinship played a major role. The basic and strongest social unit was the family and, after that, the extended family in the form of the tribe (*zadruga*). A whole arsenal of kinship relations, in addition to marriage and co-godparenthood, was available to extend one's kin group and to forge friendly relations marked by an obligation of mutual support. Blood-brotherhood (*pobratimstvo* or *bratotvorenje*), involving the exchange of a drop of blood that was ingested (either from a pierced fingertip or arm, applied to a sugar cube, or mixed into a cup of red wine), was especially common between men, accompanied by solemn promises in the form of an oath. Already in the fifteenth century, the Serbian theologian Constantine Kostenencki ("the Philosopher") condemned the exchange of blood, especially between Christians and Muslims, as a heresy.[14] The prevalence of blood brotherhood from well before the seventeenth century in these regions raises interesting questions with regard to the ecclesiastical ritual of brother-making, which was practiced alongside and sometimes in conjunction with it.

---

[12] P. Florensky, *The Pillar and Ground of the Truth: An Essay in Orthodox Theodicy in Twelve Letters*, trans. B. Jakim (Princeton, NJ, 1997), 328–30. For context and background, see L. Graham and J.-M. Kantor, *Naming Infinity: A True Story of Religious Mysticism and Mathematical Creativity* (Cambridge, MA, and London, 2009).

[13] My own reading on this subject has been opportunistic, following leads that opened up at various moments in my research, but without aiming for a comprehensive or complete treatment.

[14] Mentioned in N. F. Pavkovic, "Pobratimstvo," in *The Lexicon of Serbian Middle Ages*, ed. S. Cirkovic and R. Mihaljcic (Belgrade, 1999), 526–27, which also offers details on the practice in medieval Serbia, sometimes supplemented by later anthropological observations.

Edith Durham, an intrepid frequent traveler and astute observer in the Balkans in the early decades of the twentieth century, who had a special fondness for Albania, recounts a lovely scene that is reminiscent of the motivation that drove the contract of *adelphopoiesis* between the son of Danelis and the future emperor Basil I. "The old bairaktar[15] of Nikaj heard that I was sister to the King of England and believed a blood alliance with me would be for the good of the tribe. The priest at whose house I was, however, laughed at him uproariously and he was hurt; so I never took part in the ritual."[16] What is interesting here, besides the case of mistaken identity, is that the priest is expected to have a say in this matter. Perhaps he had assumed that he would be requested to play a role in the ceremony.

In the regions of Serbia and Montenegro, Edith Durham and other observers from earlier periods note two kinds of brother-making, depending on their origin: "communion *pobratimstvo*" and "brotherhood of misfortune."[17] The latter was the result of an appeal, in a moment of great personal danger or need, to any man or woman who happened to chance by and who would be addressed as "brother" or "sister." That person would then rise to the challenge, offer assistance at a critical moment, and later reap the rewards in the form of a lasting relationship. The appeal was uttered in the name of God and of St. John the Baptist, the patron saint of all godfathers and godmothers. Such urgent pleas for help are reported especially from the battlefield in times of war, by prisoners of war in captivity, or by travelers who encountered sudden misfortune. They were directed at the enemy, appealing to common humanity, and begging for mercy, to be spared one's life or to be released from captivity, but not without the prospect of a divine reward for a righteous and merciful deed and the promise of reciprocity if an analogous situation should arise. There was a firm expectation that the other side would be compelled to respond positively to such a plea—an indication of a shared value system across political divisions and enemy lines. Another application of ritual brotherhood was after a murder had occurred, when a male member of the offended family was co-opted into the family of the culprit, thus eliminating the need to extract blood vengeance and avoiding an escalating spiral of blood feud between families.

The description of communion *pobratimstvo* offered by Edith Durham is in some aspects remarkably close to the ritual of *adelphopoiesis*, but with the addition of the shared cup and bread. Whether or not these were the consecrated elements of the Eucharist or the symbolic sharing of a meal remains unclear from her description: "The ritual for pobratimstvo, so far as I could

---

[15] The *bajraktar* in Albania was a tribal chieftain.

[16] M. E. Durham, *Some Tribal Origins, Laws and Customs of the Balkans* (London, 1928), 156.

[17] Ibid., 156–58. M. S. Filipovic, "Forms and Function of Ritual Kinship among South Slavs," in *VIe Congrès international des sciences anthropologiques et ethnologiques*, vol. 3, 77–80 (Paris, 1963).

learn, was as follows: The two parties went together to church. The pope[18] read a prayer. The two then took a large goblet full of wine, and both, setting their lips to it, sipped at once. They then broke bread and each ate a piece. They sipped and ate together thus three times and then kissed the cross, the Gospels, and the ikon, and lastly each other."[19] The symbolic sharing of food as part of the ritual would later be followed, we can assume, by a large feast.

Brotherhood bonds and brotherhood language were especially frequent in the heroic poems or frontier songs, first written down in the eighteenth century, that celebrate the deeds of the *hajduks*, social outcasts who lived as bandits and gained legendary status among rural society as freedom fighters against the Ottomans. In this social world, where status was affirmed through the display of strength and masculinity, by wielding weapons, stealing sheep, and executing blood feuds, *pobratimstvo*—in whichever way it was concluded—offered the chance of avoiding further bloodshed without tarnishing one's honor. It was also frequently concluded across the religious and political divide, between Muslim and Christian military men. These close homosocial bonds were not merely a form of military camaraderie, with the added possibility of an emotional attachment, between two fighters who respected one another, but had further value because the expectation of support, loyalty, and nonaggression extended to their families.[20] This dimension was enforced through the generally accepted rule that marriage between the children of ritual brothers was prohibited. As the two families remained distinct, more individuals stood to benefit from this arrangement.

A broader way of analyzing *pobratimstvo* is not by the ritual through which it is concluded or the specific situation that occasions it, but with reference to the regional and historical context in which it was employed, in order to elucidate further aspects of its practice. Wendy Bracewell has studied what she aptly terms "frontier *pobratimstvo*" in the Balkan region, where between the seventeenth and nineteenth centuries the Venetian republic, the Habsburg monarchy, and the Ottoman Empire exerted their political interests, often couched in religious language or implemented through religious institutions. This made for a tight web of boundaries and the creation of exclusionary mechanisms between spheres of political influence, and according to language, religion, social status—boundaries that were both enforced by the ruling powers and, she notes, willingly enacted by the men and women in towns, villages, and countryside. Disentanglement from these restrictions was possible through recourse to a common code of conduct and morality that extended to both sides of political fault lines and which included a high value

---

[18] That is, priest.

[19] Durham, *Some Tribal Origins*, 156.

[20] Bracewell, "Friends, Lovers, Rivals, Enemies," 113–16. See also Bracewell, "Frontier Blood-Brotherhood." I am grateful to Wendy Bracewell for sharing her insights with me.

placed on the family or clan. In this environment, the extension of kinship was an essential tool to secure the well-being and prosperity of a man and his family. *Pobratimstvo* was one such tool, along with *kumstvo*, co-parenthood (similar to the Greek *synteknia*), which was affirmed by standing witness at important ritual moments, marriage, baptism, circumcision, or first haircut.[21] Bracewell's study draws attention to the frequency of such relations between Catholics and Orthodox, and between Christians and Muslims, and underlines the fact that "individuals persisted in seeking religious sanction."[22] The different religious authorities responded in different ways. The Orthodox registered faint disapproval, but continued to print the ritual for the use of priests. The Catholic side, by contrast, intent on bolstering confessional identity to the exclusion of others, showed no ambivalence. Prohibitions from Dalmatia and Bosnia in the sixteenth, seventeenth, and eighteenth centuries are directed at Catholic priests, warning them against participating in ceremonies of ritual brotherhood between men and women, between Catholics and "Greek schismatics," and between Turks and Christians.[23]

Women only rarely appear in this context, most often as a man's "ritual sister," either in narratives or in ecclesiastical prohibitions that point to the difficulties of maintaining the original intent of the relation as excluding sexual contact. One form of ritual siblinghood practiced in Serbia, *pobratimstvo pricestno*, between a woman and a man, is reported as having its origin with a young woman who had fallen gravely ill and requested a young man's help "as a brother" as they visited a church or a monastery—perhaps a means to attain travel assistance on a desperate pilgrimage?[24] *Posestrimstvo*, sworn sisterhood between two women, is also attested, but does not seem to be of concern to the authorities and the fear of sexual relations is never articulated in this context.[25]

The application of the bond between a man and a woman in contravention of its original intent eventually led to the suspension of the church ritual in the Serbian Orthodox Church in the year 1975. A man and a woman had concluded ritual siblinghood, and later sought to be married. Their original spiritual relationship which explicitly excluded any possibility for sexual union was, however, considered an irrevocable obstacle—an echo of the ecclesiastical prohibitions of Byzantine times. As a consequence of this scandal, priests were forbidden to conduct such liturgies, and the ritual prayers were removed

---

[21] Bracewell, "Friends, Lovers, Rivals, Enemies," 105.

[22] Ibid., 111.

[23] References in ibid., 109.

[24] G. Castellan, *La vie quotidienne en Serbie au seuil de l'Indépendance, 1815–1839* (Paris, 1967), 239. Also mentioned by V. S. Karadzic, *Srpski rjecnik*, 4th ed. (Belgrade, 1935; first published Vienna, 1818), 528, who speculates that this custom is especially popular in Bulgaria. The Serbian word for ritual brotherhood is *bratotvorenje*.

[25] Bracewell, "Friends, Lovers, Rivals, Enemies," 115.

from the printed prayer book.[26] Leopold Kretzenbacher, an anthropologist and experienced traveler to the Balkans, reports this in a detailed study that treats *pobratimstvo* as a people's practice popular at all levels of society. Its appeal was such that it survived even under the pressure of Communist rule as an ecclesiastical ritual that Orthodox priests were willing to perform out of pastoral concern regardless of official prohibitions.[27] In addition to providing descriptions of brother-making rituals that he himself observed between a young woman and a young man in 1966 and between two men in 1977 and offering details about the liturgical tradition in Serbian prayer books since the fourteenth century, Kretzenbacher also notes, without attempting an explanation, that in modern times, *pobratimstvo* has been a much more important part of social relations in the Slavic world than *adelphopoiesis* among Greeks, despite the Byzantine origin of the ritual (Figure 6.2).

In most of the travelers' reports and anthropologists' studies, there is no clear distinction between blood-brotherhood and the ecclesiastical ritual of *adelphopoiesis*. The two could be performed individually, or in combination, but always to the same effect of absorbing potential or real conflict or of securing assistance.[28] Edith Durham calls it "a curious example of a pagan rite transformed into a parody of the Communion."[29] Observers note with puzzlement the ambivalence of the church, as its priests performed the prayers, while its leaders made repeated efforts at prohibiting the ritual. This raises a possible scenario: what if *adelphopoiesis* was in its origin a variant of blood brotherhood, perhaps cultivated in a military context,[30] that was Christianized, spiritualized, and thus sanitized? This cannot be excluded, but lack of evidence for anything but the ecclesiastical ritual in Byzantine times makes it unlikely. Indeed, the

---

[26] L. Kretzenbacher, "Gegenwartsformen der Wahlverwandtschaft pobratimstvo bei den Serben und im übrigen Südosteuropa," in *Beiträge zu Kenntnis Südosteuropas und des Nahen Orients*, vol. 2, 167–82 (Munich, 1967); Kretzenbacher, "Serbisch-orthodoxe 'Wahlverbrüderung,'" 167.

[27] Kretzenbacher, "Serbisch-orthodoxe 'Wahlverbrüderung,'" passim. He treats the suggestion that this is a pagan rite in Christian guise with great skepticism, and thus also plays down any possible connection to blood brotherhood. For a recent treatment in Serbian, see Pavkovic, "Pobratimstvo." I am grateful to Dejan Delebdzic for providing me with this article and a translation.

[28] A further way of generating a brotherhood relationship is milk kinship, based on being suckled by the same woman. The study of this phenomenon—which can be detected in the Hebrew Scriptures, is not uncommon in Islam, and is well attested in the Caucasus—is still in its infancy. A. Giladi, *Infants, Parents and Wet Nurses: Medieval Islamic Views on Breastfeeding and their Social Implications* (Leiden, 1999); P. Parkes, "Milk Kinship in Southeast Europe: Alternative Social Structures and Foster Relations in the Caucasus and the Balkans," *Social Anthropology* 12, no. 3 (2004), 341–58. C. R. Chapman, "'Oh that You Were Like a Brother to Me, One Who Had Nursed at My Mother's Breasts': Breast Milk as a Kinship-Forging Substance," *Journal of Hebrew Scriptures* 12 (2012), article 7.

[29] Durham, *Some Tribal Origins*, 156–57.

[30] See for example S. L. E. Lazarovich-Hrebelianovich, *The Servian People: Their Past Glory and Their Destiny* (New York, 1910), 73.

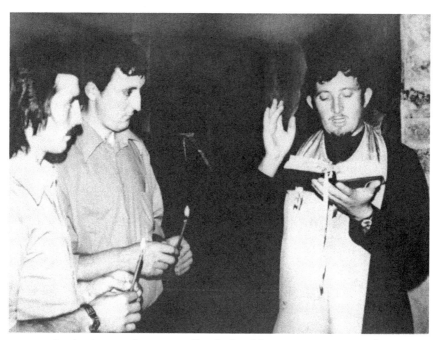

FIGURE 6.2 *A priest says the prayers of brotherhood for two young men in Serbia, 1977*

Source: L. Kretzenbacher, "Serbisch-orthodoxe 'Wahlverbrüderung' zwischen Gläubigenwunsch und Kirchenverbot von heute," Südost-Forschungen 38 (1979), 163–83.

absence of any attestation of an exchange of blood in conjunction with *adelphopoiesis* in Byzantine times makes this a moot point.

The composite picture that emerges from these pages is like a mosaic in which the tesserae are not fitting tightly. There are two primary colors that prevail throughout: the family and Christianity. The family provides the model of kinship as the basic structure for the assurance of loyalty, assistance, and support, especially in the notion of brotherhood as a relation between equals. Christianity offers a variation on this theme with its appropriation of the family model for other kinds of relation that are recast within the theological framework generated by the Incarnation. Monasticism is an attempt to infuse the social model of kinship and brotherhood with Christian ideals. This fusion of colors gives rise to *adelphopoiesis* as a recognized social bond that is blessed by prayers. Like a recurring ornament, brother-making remains in the picture throughout Byzantine history. It is a continued presence in the monastic tradition and also adorns the rich landscape of social relations among men and women of the world. In the process of its application, its contours may change shape, according to historical circumstance and concrete purpose: gaining access to spiritual or financial resources, upward social mobility, the neutralization of enemies, the crossing of boundaries of gender, ethnicity, and religion. It is not possible to see smooth transitions between these elements, and there are gaps in our knowledge. Still, the pieces fit together well enough to offer an impression of the flexibility and resourcefulness of the men and women of Byzantium to adapt existing social structures and the Christian interpretive framework that supports them to their own needs.

Appendix 1

Table of Manuscripts

Below is a list of sixty-six manuscripts that contain prayers for *adelphopoi-esis*. Only Greek manuscripts where the prayers are known to be present carry a number. The manuscripts that I was able to study in the original or in reproduction are marked with an asterisk. In those cases where a more recent, specialized study is available, earlier manuscript catalogs are not mentioned consistently. For the dating of the Sinai manuscripts, I have followed Gardthausen rather than Dmitrievskij.

Boswell offers a list of sixty-two "manuscripts consulted," which largely takes its lead from Dmitrievskij's list of prayer books and their content (here indicated as D). Boswell does not indicate which of these manuscripts he studied in the original. I have found a number of errors in Dmitrievskij's information (which is not surprising), which are repeated in Boswell (which is surprising, considering that in the preface, he gives the impression of having worked his way through the manuscript tradition, from London and Paris, to points further East).[1] Panagou identifies four additional manuscripts that had not previously been known to contain *adelphopoiesis* prayers, due to insufficient information in the printed catalogs. He does not include in his discussion sixteen manuscripts that were listed by Boswell.

Further manuscripts that contain the *adelphophoiesis* ritual will no doubt be identified in the future. I will strive to maintain an updated list online.[2]

---

[1] Boswell, *Same-Sex Unions*, 372–74 and ix–x. I have not been able to check on Boswell, 374, note 19, which refers to an article by Sreckovic who mentions two fifteenth-century manuscripts in Belgrade, Serbia.

[2] An updated list of manuscripts containing the prayers for *adelphopoiesis* can be found on my website at http://www.byzneo.univie.ac.at/mitarbeiter/akademisches-personal/rapp-claudia/ and on academia.edu.

Manuscript	Century, Region, Use	Folia	Prayer	Edition	Preceded by	Followed by
1	Vatican, Barb. gr. 336* (Barberinum Sancti Marci)	8; Southern Italy; Constantinopolitan rite of the pre-iconoclast period[1]	204v–205v	*Euchē eis adelphopoiēsin* —Kyrie ho theos ho pantokratōr ho poiēsas anthrōpon	Jacob[2] Strittmatter[3] Parenti[4]	Cutting of beard	Hair clipping of child
2	Sinai, gr. 957*	9–10[5]	20v–21r	*Euchē eis adelphopoiēsin* —Ho panta pros sōtērian	D 4 Gardthausen[6]	Hairclipping of child	Betrothal
3	Grottaferrata, Gamma beta VII*	first half 10[7] Calabria; monastic use	87r–90v	*Euchē epi adelphopoiēsin* —Ho poiēsas ton anthrōpon *Euchē allē tēs adelphopoiēsias* —Ho endoxazomenos en boulē agiōn *Euchē allē eis adelphopoiēsin* —Anthēron hēmin kai polypothēton hē tēs agapēs euodia	Passarelli[8]	Reconciliation of enemies	Revocation of an oath
4	Grottaferrata, Gamma beta IV*	10 (975–1000); copied near Monte Cassino; monastic use	125v–126v	*Euchē eis adelphopoiēsian* Those who want to become brothers enter behind the priest, place their hands on the Gospel, chant Psalm 23; the deacon says prayers for peace, "for the servants of God NN and NN, and for their love in Christ and their well-being," that their love and brotherhood may remain "without scandal," that the Lord God may forgive them every transgression, that we may be saved from all affliction. —Ho poiēsas ton anthrōpon —Ho panta pros sōtērian The priest embraces them and gives the dismissal.	Parenti[9]	For the afflicted	Unction of the sick

(*continued*)

#	Manuscript	Date/Origin	Folios	Text	Reference		
5	Grottaferrata, Gamma beta X	10	97r–98v	*Euchē eis adelphopoiēsin* —*Ho poiēsas ton anthrōpon* —*Ho panta pros sōtērian*	Panagou Rocchi[10]		Churching of woman
6	Sinai, gr. 958*	10	87r–87v[11]	*Euchē eis adelphopoiēsin* —*Ho panta pros sōtērian* —*Ho poiēsas ton anthrōpon*	D 31–32 Gardthausen[12]	Removal of wedding crowns	
7	St. Petersburg, gr. 226 (Euchologium Uspenskij)*	10; Italo-Greek; not monastic	114r–115r	—*Ho poiēsas ton anthrōpon* —*Ho panta pros to sympheron*	Koumarianos[13]	Veiling of a woman	Revocation of an oath
8	Paris, BN, Coislin 213*	1027; for the priest Strategios,[14] Constantinople	41r–41v	*Euchē eis adelphopoiēsin* —*Ho panta pros sōtērian* —*Ho ton chorōn tōn agiōn sou apostolōn*	Duncan[15] Arranz[16] D 998	Filial adoption	Cutting of beard or hair
9	Grottaferrata, Gamma beta II*	11; Southern Italy[17]	86v–87v	*Akolouthia eis adelphopoiēsin* The priest places the Gospel on the *analogion*; the brothers place their hands on it, holding lit candles in their left hands; he censes them. Invocations by deacon. Prayers by priest: —*Ho poiēsas ton anthrōpon* *Euchē etera eis adelphopoiēsin* —*Ho panta pros sōtērian* They bow to the Gospel, to the priest and to each other, and he says the dismissal.	Rocchi[18]	Hairclipping of child	Marriage
10	Sinai, gr. 959*	11; Palestino-Syrian ritual	100v–101r	*Euchē eis adelphopoiēsin* —*Ho panta pros sōtērian*	D 56 Gardthausen[19] Jacob[20]	Cutting of hair of a woman	Unction of the sick

	Manuscript	Century, Region, Use	Folia	Prayer	Edition	Preceded by	Followed by
	Sinai, glag. 37, "Euchologium Sinaiticum"[21]	late 11; Old Church Slavonic	9r–11v	—Ho panta pros sōtērian —Ho poiēsas ton anthrōpon —Ho tēs agapēs phytourgos (NB this prayer is not used in the Greek adelphopoiesis ritual)	Frček 658–668 Nahtigal 20[22]	First cutting of beard	Sowing
11	Sinai, gr. 961*	11–12?	86r–86v	Euchē eis adelphopoiēsin —Ho panta pros sōtērian	D 82 Gardthausen[23]	Hairclipping of child	Commemoration of the dead
12	Sinai, gr. 962*	11–12[24]	127r–128r	Euchē eis adelphopoiian (sic) —Ho panta pros sōtērian	D 71 Gardthausen[25]	Prayer for the sick	Commemoration of the dead
13	Vatican, gr. 1811*	1147 by scribe Petros; Italo-Greek[26]	52r–54r	Akolouthia eis adelphopoiēsin Priest places Gospel on analogion; two men place their hands on Gospel, holding lit candles in the right hand; they are censed by deacon; several introductory prayers —Ho poiēsas ton anthrōpon Euchē deutera —Ho enteilamenos hēmin They kiss the Gospel, the priest, and each other. Priest dismisses them with a blessing.	Canart[27]	Blessing of a vine	Adoption
14	Sinai, gr. 973*	1153; copied by the priest Auxentios; paper	112v–113v	Euchē epi adelphopoiias They put their hands upon one another, priest places a cross on them, chants Psalm 133; —Ho panta pros to sympheron charisamenos tois anthrōpois kai pneumatikēn adelphotēta systēsamenos —Hē tachinē akoē, ta tachina splagchna	D 122–123 Gardthausen[28]	Adoption	Stauropēgia

				Title	Ref.		
15	Vatican, Ottob. gr. 434*	1172/1173?[29]	61r–61v	*Euchê eis adelphopoiêsin* —*Ho panta pros sôtêrian*	Thiermeyer[30]	Harvest	After pollution
16	Bodleian, Auct. E.5.13*	12; originally at the Monastery of the Holy Savior, Messina	165v–166r	*Euchê eis adelphopoiêsin* —*Ho panta pros sôtêrian*[31]	Cf. Jacob[32]	Adoption	After a meal
17	Escurial, X.IV.13 (=408)	12; Salento, Southern Italy[33]	48v–50v	*Akolouthia eis adelphopoiêsin* priest, Gospel on stand, first brother, second brother, candles, sign of cross —*Ho poiêsas ton anthrôpon* —*Ho dia tês sês aphatou oikonomias* —*Ho eipôn tois hagiois sou mathêtais kai apostolois: eirênên tên emên didômi hymin*[34]	Andrés[35] Parenti[36]	Hairclipping	Adoption
18	Paris, BN, Coislin 214*	12	68v	*Euchê eis adelphopoiêsin* —*Ho panta pros sôtêrian*	Devreesse[37]	Wine harvest	Revocation of an oath
19	Paris, BN, gr. 330*	12	173–175v[38]	*Euchê eis adelphopoiêsin* —*Ho poiêsas ... ton anthrôpon*	Omont[39]	For the dead	First cutting of beard
20	Paris, BN, gr. 392*	12	113v–114r	*Euchê eis adelphopoiêsin* —*Ho panta pros sôtêrian*	Omont[40]	After a meal	For the dead
21	Vatican, Barb. gr. 329* "Barberinum secundum"[41]	12; Italo-Greek script; origin of prayers Calabria	116v–118r	unidentified first prayer[42] —*Ho poiêsas ton anthrôpon* —*Ho enteilamenos hêmin*	Jacob[43]	Adoption	Absence of rain
22	Vatican, Barb. gr. 345*	12; Southern Italian script	64r–65v	*Taxis eis to poiêsai adelphous* They enter, place their hands on Gospel	Jacob[44]	Adoption	Benediction of eggs and cheese at Easter

(continued)

	Manuscript	Century, Region, Use	Folia	Prayer	Edition	Preceded by	Followed by
				—Ho en hypsistois katoikôn *Etera euchê* —Ho poiêsas ton anthrôpon —Ho einteilamenos hêmin			
23	Vatican, Barb. gr. 431*	12; Southern Italian script	97r–98r	*Akolouthia eis adelphopoiêsin* Priest places the Gospel on a stand; the brothers place their right hands on it, lit candles in left hand, censing and invocations by deacon, introductory prayers —Ho poiêsas ton anthrôpon They bow to the Gospel and the priest. Dismissal.	Jacob[45]	Exorcism	Dedication of a church
24	Vatican, gr. 1552*	12	30v–31r	*Euchê eis adelphopoiêsin* —Ho en tê kata sarka sou oikonomia —Ho panta pros sôtêrian They kiss the Gospel, each other, and leave.	Giannelli[46]	Wedding	If something impure has fallen into wine or oil
25	Vatican, gr. 1554*	12; Italo-Greek[47]	111v–112v	*Akolouthia eis adelphôpiisian* (sic) They enter, carrying candles, they stand until the liturgy is completed, priest asks them to come to the bema with lit candles, censes them; speaks prayers for peace from above, for this holy house, for the two men —Ho en hypsêlois katoikôn —Ho poiêsas ton anthrôpon —Ho einteilamenos hêmin Priest makes an invocation over them and dismisses them.	Giannelli[48]	Prayer when hermit enters a cell	Adoption

	Manuscript	Date	Folios	Text	Reference		
26	Vatican, gr. 1872*	12; Italo-Greek	141r–142v	*Euchē eis adelphopoiēsin* / —*Ho panta pros sōtērian* / —*Ho en hypsēlois katoikon*	Canart[49]	Blessing of oil for the sick	Prayer for the dead
27	Vatican, gr. 1875*	12; Italo-Greek[50]	100v–102r	*Akolouthia eis adelphopoiēsin* / Priest places the Gospel on the *analogion*; they place their hands on the Gospel, hold lit candles, are censed by priest and deacon, introductory prayers.[51] / —*Ho poiēsas ton anthrōpon* / They kiss the Gospel, the priest, each other.	Canart[52]	Service for kneeling after Pentecost[53]	Vespers
28	Sinai, gr. 1036*	12–13	56v–57v	—*Ho poiēsas ton anthrōpon*	D 147 Gardthausen[54]	Blessing of a house	For the penitent
29a	Patmos, 104[55]	1234	30v	*Euchē etera (1) eis adelphopoiēsin* / —*Kyrie ho theos hēmōn ho en tē kata sarka sou oikonomia*	D 156	Wedding	Hagiasma tōn agiōn Theophanōn
29b	Patmos, 104 (bis)	1234	53r–54r, second time in same ms	*Euchē eis adelphopoiēsin* / —*Ho panta pros sōtērian* / Priest says *ektenē*, admonishes them, says prayer and blessing. They kiss the Gospel and each other.	D 157	After pollution	NT readings (?)
30	Athens, Ethnikē Bibliothēkē, 662*	12[56] or 13; several hands associated with Constantinople; paper	174v–175r	*Euchē eis adelphopoiēsin* / —*Ho panta pros sōtērian* / —*Ho ton choron tōn hagiōn sou apostolōn*	Kalaitzidis[57]	Departure of a battle ship	Reconciliation of enemies
31	Athens, Ethnikē Bibliothēkē 2795	ca. 13	83r–83v	*Euchē eis adelphopoiēsin* / —*Ho panta pros sōtērian*	Panagou[58]		

(continued)

	Manuscript	Century, Region, Use	Folia	Prayer	Edition	Preceded by	Followed by
32	Athos, Laura 189	13	17r–17v	*Euchē eis adelphopoiēsin* Invocation —*Despota kyrie ho theos hēmôn ho kataxiôsas dia tēs epiphaneias tou agiou sou pneumatos synaphthēnai tous agious sou apostolous Petrou kai Paulou* —*Ho panta pros sōtērian* —*Ho poiēsas ton anthrôpon*	D 179–180[59]	Theophany	Eating prohibited foods
33	Grottaferrata, Gamma beta I* (Euchologion "of Bessarion")	13;[60] associated with Constantinople	128r–128v	*Euchē eis adelphopoiēsin* —*Ho panta pros sōtērian* Invocation by the priest —*Ho ton choron ton agiôn sou apostolôn eklexamenos*	Arranz[61] Stassi[62] Parenti and Velkovska[63]	Departure of a battle ship	Reconciliation of enemies
34	Patmos, 105	13	4r–4v	*Euchē eis adelphopoiēsin* —*Ho poiēsas ton anthrôpon*	D 160	Baptism	Liturgy of Saint Basil
35	St. Petersburg, National Library, gr. 559*	13; Palestine?	26v–28r	*Akolouthia eis adelphopoiēsin* They approach the stand, invocations, *hyper ton doulon tou theou … kai tēs en Christôi adelphotētos hyper tou amisētous kai askandalistous …* —*Ho panta pros sōtērian* bow to Gospel and kiss it, the priest, each other —*Despota kyrie ho theos hēmôn ho ton choron tôn agiôn sou mathētôn kai apostolon*	D 190[64]	Hairclipping of child	Prayer for those who have polluted themselves in contact with infidels, esp. Muslims
36	Vatican, Barb. gr. 293*	13; Calabria	51v–55r	*Taxis kai akolouthia eis adelphopoiēsin* —*Ho panta pros sōtērian*	Jacob[65]	Release from an oath	Officium in ponderatione

(continued)

				Euchē etera —*Ho kataxiōsas dia tēs epiphaneias*			
37	Vatican, Barb. gr. 443*	13; Otranto	155v	*Akolouthia eis adelphopoiēsin* Invocations —*Ho poiēsas ton anthrōpon*[66]	Jacob[67]	Before a meal	Fragment of Vita of Andrew the Apostle
38	Vatican, gr. 1840*	13; Southern Italy	3r–3v	*Euchē eis adelphopoiēsin* —*Ho panta pros sōtērian* —*Ho poiēsas ton anthrōpon*	Canart[68]	Blessing of a house	Adoption
39	Grottaferrata, Gamma beta VI*	13 or 14	101r	*Euchē eis adelphopoiēsin* —*Kyrie ho theos hēmon ... tous agious sou mathētous kai apostolous krinein .... homonian dōrise tous doulous sou tonde kai tonde*	Rocchi[69]	Gospel of John in Latin	
40	Sinai, gr. 960*	13–14	39r	*Euchē eis adelphopoiēsin* —*Ho panta pros sōtērian*	D 196 Gardthausen[70]	Blessing of a house	Adoption
41	Sinai, gr. 966*	13 or 14; Southern Italy[71]	82v–84v	*Akolouthia kai taxis eis adelphopoiēsin* Those who wish to become brothers walk up to the priest. He places the Gospel on the stand. The first brother places his hand on the Gospel, and the second on the hand of the brother. The priest signs them with the sign of the cross. Invocation. —*Ho poiēsas ton anthrōpon* —*Ho panta pros sōtērian* —*Ho dia tēs aphatou sou oikonomias kataxiōsas adelphous kalesai* —*Ho endoxazomenos en boulē agiōn* —*Ho en hypsēlois katoikōn* They kiss the Gospel and one another.	D 215 Gardthausen[72]	Prayer for second marriage	Pentecost

	Manuscript	Century, Region, Use	Folia	Prayer	Edition	Preceded by	Followed by
42	Sinai, gr. 971*	13–14; paper	97r–100r[73]	*Euchai eis adelphou poiēsin* —*Ho poiēsas ton anthrōpon* —*Ho panta pros sōtērian* —*Ho en hypsēlois katoikōn*	D 251 Gardthausen[74]	Veiling of a nun	Adoption
43	Sinai, gr. 982*	13 or 14; Eastern paper, different hands, including one dated 1470	64v[75]	*Taxis ginomenē eis adelphopoiēsian* Priest brings them to the cancella, places the right hand of the younger on the Gospel book, then right hand of the older, they hold lit candles, invocations[76]	D 237 Gardthausen[77]	Reopening of a church after use by heretics	Prayers for emperors and empire
44	Grottaferrata, Gamma beta III*	14 (after 1347); Calabria	159v–16v	Taxis, invocations —*Ho en hypsistois katoikōn* —*Ho poiēsas ton anthrōpon* —*Ho panta pros sōtērian*	Rocchi[78]	Purification	Adoption
	St. John, Trogir, Croatia	1394, Latin			Bray 126–133[79]		
45	Athos, Laura Beta 7 (127)	13 or 14	73v	*Euchē eis adelphopoiēsin*	D 365 Eustratiades[80]	Hair clipping of child	Pollution of holy wine or oil
46	Sinai, gr. 981*	14? 16?; paper	205v–206v[81]	*Euchē eis adelphopoiēsin* —*Ho panta pros sōtērian* —*Ho en tē kata sarka sou oikonomia* They embrace each other and depart.	D 343 Gardthausen[82]	Wedding	Hairclipping of child
47	Paris, BN, gr. 324*	14–15	108v–109v	*Euchē eis adelphopoiēsin* —*Ho panta pros sōtērian* —*Ho ton choron tōn agiōn sou apostolōn* *Euchē allē* —*Ho poiēsas ton anthrōpon*	Omont[83]	Woman in childbed	Sowing seed

No.	Library	Date; material	Contents	Folios	Source	Rite type	Notes
48	Athens, Ethnikē Bibliothēkē, 2724	14–15	*Euchē eis adelphopoiían* Priest places Gospel book on the cancella; one brother, then the other place their hands on it; priests makes the sign of the cross over their heads; —*Ho panta pros sōtērian* —*Ho enischysas tois hagiois sou mathētais kai apostolois* —*Ho poiēsas ton anthrōpon*	104v–106v	Panagou[84]		
49	Athos, Konstamonites, 19 (20)	14 or 15; paper	*Euchē eis adelphopoiēsin* —*Ho panta pros sōtērian*	106r	D 498 Lampros[85]	Adoption	Prayer of John Chrysostom, before reading or listening to a reading
50	Athos, Panteleemon, 364	15; paper	*Akolouthia eis adelphopoiēsin* Extensive prayers; NT readings —*Ho poiēsas ton anthrōpon* —*Ho synathroisas tous agious sou mathētas* Priest makes them join hands —*Ho en tē kata sarka sou oikonomia* —*Ho panta pros sōtērian* Blessing, they kiss	15r–17v	D 569 Lampros[86]	Wedding	Churching of a woman
51	Athos, Pantokrator, 149	15; paper	*Akolouthia eis adelphopoiēsin*	97v–99v	D 489 Lampros[87]	Second marriage	Pollution of holy wine or oil
52	Athos, Xeropotamou, 51	15 or 16	*Eis adelphopoiēsin*	79r	D 659 Lampros[88]	Prayer for kneeling	None (last entry in ms)
53	Jerusalem, Metochion tou Taphou, 182 (8), now in Athens[89]	15	*Akolouthia eis adelphopoiēsin* Admonitions from NT; invocations for the two —*Ho poiēsas ton anthrōpon*	57–58	D 466–67 Papadopoulos-Kerameus[90]	Wedding	Pollution of holy wine or oil

(continued)

	Manuscript	Century, Region, Use	Folia	Prayer	Edition	Preceded by	Followed by
54	Patmos, 703		20v–23r	They join right hands —*Ho en tē kata sarka sou oikonomia* —*Ho synathroisas tous agious sou apostolous* —*Ho panta pros sōtērian* They kiss the Gospel and one another, then leave, after admonishments by the priest. *Akolouthia eis adelphopoiēsin*	D 920	Theophany	
55	Sinai, gr. 972*	15; paper	420v–421r	*Euchē eis adelphopoiēsin* —*Ho panta pros sōtērian*	D 578 Gardthausen[91]	After eating polluted food	Prayer for penitent
56	Athos, Philotheou, 164	15 or 16; paper	173r–174v	*Euchē eis adelphopoiēsin*	D 661 Lampros[92]	Hairclipping of child	Baptism of child
57	Sinai, gr. 977*	before 1516; paper; bilingual Greek and Arabic[93]	276r–277r[94]	*Euchē eis adelphou poiesin* —*Ho poiēsas ton ouranon … kai ton anthrōpon*[95]	D 710 Gardthausen[96]	Prayers during a procession out of fear	Sickbed
58	Athos, Laura, Omega 129 (1941)	1522; copied by Petros, priest and *protopapas*, of Karpasia (Karpathios); paper	63r–64v	*Akolouthia eis to poiēsai adelphopoiēsin*	D 747 Eustratiades[97]	Second marriage	Adoption
59	Jerusalem, Metochion tou panagiou taphou, 789 (615, 757), now in Athens[98]	1522; copied by monk Manuel from Chandax in Crete, offered to Andrew, cleric at Hagia Sophia; paper	293v–296v	*Akolouthia eis adelphopoiēsin* Priest places the Gospel on the stand, three (!) men place hands on Gospel, priest binds them (with a stole), they carry lit candles —*Ho panta pros sōtērian* —*Ho poiēsas ton ouranon*[99] —*Ho ton choron tōn agiōn sou apostolōn*	D 743–744	Second marriage	Prayer before someone takes communion

60	Karditsa, Monastery of Korone, 8	1563; Leukara, Cyprus; lay congregation	195v–197v	The brothers kiss, and receive communion. After the Gospel reading, the liturgy may be celebrated, if the brothers request it. In this case, the "recently made brothers" should be mentioned in the invocation. *Euché eis adelphopoiian* —*Ho panta pros sōtérian*	Constantinides-Browning[100]	Names of 24 Elders before the Throne of Christ	Readmission of those who had been forced to apostatize
61	Athens, Ethnikē Bibliothēkē, 2064	16; formerly in the library of the Gymnasium in Thessaloniki; prior owners included a priest and a *psaltēs*; paper	243v–244v	*Euché eis adelphopoiēsin* —*Ho panta pros sōtérian* —*Ho poiēsas ton ouranon kai tēn gēn kat'eikona sou kai homoiōsin*[101] Dismissal, they kiss the Gospel book	Panagou Politis[102]	Last rites (to f. 240), ff. 241–242 are empty	Blessing of a House
62	Athos, Panteleemon, 780	16	60r–62r	*Akolouthia eis adelphopoiēsin*	D 831 Lampros[103]	Wedding	Commemoration of the dead
63	Athos, Konstamonites, 60 (63)	16; paper	71v–72v	*Akolouthia eis adelphopoiēsin* Introductory prayers —*Ho panta pros sōtérian* —*Ho poiēsas ton anthrōpon* —*Kyrie ho dia stomatos lalēsas Dauid tō doulō sou: idou de ti terpnon* They kiss each other. Dismissal.	D 854–855 Lampros[104]	On a woman who has had a miscarriage	Engagement
64	Athos Kutlumousiou, 341	16; paper	160v–163v	*Akolouthia eis adelphopoiēsin*	D 953 Lampros[105]	Service of Holy Water at Epiphany	Virgin voyage of a ship
65	Athos Kutlumousiou, 358	16; paper	57r–72v	*Akolouthia eis adelphopoiēsin* —*Ho panta pros sōtérian* —*Ho poiēsas ton anthrōpon* —*Ho dia stomatos Dauid*	D 925 Lampros[106]	Second marriage	Burial of a priest

(continued)

Manuscript	Century, Region, Use	Folia	Prayer	Edition	Preceded by	Followed by
66 Sinai, gr. 989*	before 1554: monastic use; paper[107]	303r–305v[108]	*Taxis ginominē* [sic] *eis adelphopoiēsin* Invocation —*Ho kataxiōsas dia tēs epiphoitēseos tou agiou sou pneumatos sunaphthēnai tous agiou sou apostolous* —*Ho panta pros sōtērian* —*Ho en tē kata sarka sou oikonomia* Invocations. They kiss the Gospel and each another.	D 897 Gardthausen[109]	Death of a priest	Prayers of a spiritual father for a deceased
SPURIOUS						
Athens, National Library, 94	1542 (dated by colophon)	25r–25v	*Euché eis adelphopoiēsin*	D 787–88[110]		Holy Oil
Jerusalem, Patriarchal Library, 568[111]	17–18	224v–225r	*Euché eis adelphopoiēsin*	D 948	Blessing of wine	Beginning of sowing season
PRINTED						
Euchologion, Rome	1873	482–484	*Akolouthia eis adelphopoiian pneumatikén*			

[1] The manuscript once belonged to the Dominican Convent of San Marco in Florence.

[2] A. Jacob, "Les euchologes du fonds Barberini grec de la Bibliothèque Vaticane," *Didaskalia* 4 (1974), 131–222, at 154–57, for a description of the ms. For content, he refers to Strittmatter.

[3] Strittmatter, "The 'Barberinum S. Marci' of Jacques Goar," 331. See also G. Baldanza, "Il rito del matrimonio nell'Euchologio Barberini 366: Analisi della sua visione teologica," *Ephemerides liturgicae* 93 (1979), 316–51.

[4] Parenti and Velkovska, *L'eucologio Barberini gr.* 336, 199–200.

[5] Even at a very cursory glance, this manuscript seems to represent the tradition of the Patriarchal Church in Constantinople. One prayer on fol. 31v bears the marginal annotation "of Patriarch Germanos." Another prayer on fol. 38v is for the occasion "when the Patriarch blesses the waters in the palace." It is classified as representing "eastern origin," by G. Baldanza, "Rito del matrimonio," 317.

[6] V. Gardthausen, *Catalogus codicum graecorum Sinaiticorum* (Oxford, 1886), 204.

[7] The manuscript is composed of three parts of different *euchologia* of the tenth century.

8 Passarelli, *L'eucologio cryptense Gamma beta VII*, 130–33.

9 S. Parenti, *L'eucologio manoscritto Gamma beta IV della Biblioteca di Grottaferrata* (Rome, 1994), 55–56.

10 Panagou, *Hē adelphopoiēsē*, 121; A. Rocchi, *Codices Cryptenses seu Abbatiae Cryptae Ferratae* (Tusculo, 1883), 262–63 (has a description of the codex, without mention of the *adelphopoiesis* ritual).

11 Dmitrievskij, 31, erroneously states that the prayer begins on fol. 85r.

12 Gardthausen, *Catalogus*, 205; Baldanza, "Rito del matrimonio," 317, identifies the liturgical content as being of Palestinian origin with Constantinopolitan sources.

13 This manuscript was taken from the library of the Monastery of St. Catherine in the Sinai in 1850 by Porphyrios Uspenskij. A. Jacob, "L'euchologe de Porphyre Uspenski;" Koumarianos, *Il codice 226*, 101.

14 Jacob, "Prière pour les troupeaux de l'Euchologe Barberini," 11ff, note 43, on the role of Strategios as the patron of the manuscript.

15 J. Duncan, *Coislin 213: Euchologe de la Grande Eglise* (Rome, 1983), 60–61. Dated 1027, and owned by Strategios, priest at Hagia Sophia in Constantinople and in the patriarchal chapels, this is the earliest *euchologion* that carries a date. Duncan asserts (xvii–xviii) that it ranks in importance after Barb. gr. 336, but before the "codex Bessarionis" (Grottaferrata Gamma beta 1) of the eleventh century. For a partial edition of the second half of the manuscript, see J. M. Maj, SJ, "Coislin 213: Eucologio della grande chiesa," PhD diss., Pontificio Istituto Orientale, Rome, 1995.

16 Arranz, *L'eucologio costantinopolitano*, 355–56.

17 Jacob, "Prière pour les troupeaux," 1, for the regional origin, and assuming a twelfth-century date.

18 Rocchi, *Codices Cryptenses*, 244–49.

19 Gardthausen, *Catalogus*, 205.

20 A. Jacob, "Les sacraments de l'ancien euchologe constantinopolitain (1)," *OCP* 48 (1982), 284–335, at 305–09, argues that some prayers in this manuscript are of Constantinopolitan origin, although the simple script seems to indicate that it was produced for either an individual or a church of meager means.

21 On the complex issue of the origin of the prayers in this manuscript, whether Italo-Greek or Constantinopolitan, and the scholarly disagreements on this question, see Jacob, "Prière pour les troupeaux," 15, notes 57 and 58.

22 R. Nahtigal, *Euchologium Sinaiticum* (Ljubljana, 1941–42), 20. Nahtigal's study includes comparison material of several manuscripts in Serbia. I am grateful to Georgi Parpulov for his assistance with this part of my study.

23 Gardthausen, *Catalogus*, 205, with a thirteenth-century date. Dmitrievskij dates the codex to the eleventh or twelfth century.

24 Baldanza, "Rito del matrimonio," 317, identifies the liturgical content as being of "Eastern" origin with Constantinopolitan sources.

25 Gardthausen, *Catalogus*, 206.

26 P. Canart, *Codices Vaticani graeci: Codices 1745–1962* (Vatican City, 1970), 189–90: there are commemorations on several fols. (83v, 84v, 96v, 99v) of living and dead people, men and women. Some of them were priests, others officials in Apulia and Sicily, including, according to Canart, King Roger of Sicily.

27 Ibid., 182–90. Canart indicates an Italo-Greek origin for the script, while Strittmatter asserts that the codex is of Constantinopolitan origin. At a certain point in its history, it must have been accessible to Westerners, as suggested by the marginal annotations of names in Latin and Greek script on fol. 124v. The liturgy of John Chrysostom in this codex is similar to that in Grottaferrata Gamma beta II and Bod. Auct. E 5.13 (Canart, *Codices Vaticani graeci*, 182).

28 Gardthausen, *Catalogus*, 208–09.

29 There are several marginal annotations in Arabic. A.-A. Thiermeyer, "Das Euchologion Ottoboni gr. 434 (12. Jahrhundert)," PhD diss. (Thesis ad lauream), Pontificio Istituto Orientale, Rome, 1992, 56, suggests a provenance from a Palestinian colony in South Italy. For the date, see p. 57. There are marginal invocations by bishop Abraam on fols. 12v and 21v.

30 Thiermeyer, "Euchologion Ottoboni gr. 434," Greek text, 376–77. For a dating to the thirteenth century, see A. Feron and F. Battaglini, *Codices manuscripti graeci Ottoboniani Bibliothecae Vaticanae* (Rome, 1903), 240–41.

(continued)

31 Fol. 165r has three crosses above the line, indicating for ritual gestures for the priest: *eulogēson.... charisai.... pistin.*

32 A. Jacob, "Un euchologe du Saint-Sauveur 'in lingua Phari' de Messine: Le Bodleianus Auct. E.5.13," *Bulletin de l'institut historique belge de Rome* 50 (1980), 283–364. The manuscript is datable, on paleographical grounds, to the first half of the twelfth century; in the decades after Roger II of Sicily founded the monastery (288).

33 For the date, see S. Parenti, "Un eucologio poco noto del Salento El Escorial X.IV.13," *Studi sull'Oriente Cristiano* 15 (2011), 157–97, at 158, who follows the dating by André Jacob.

34 This prayer for peace, love, and unanimity "in this spiritual brotherhood" between two men, is not attested elsewhere.

35 G. de Andrés, *Catálogo de los códices griegos de la Real Biblioteca de El Escorial*, vol. 2: *Códices 179–420* (Madrid, 1965), 344–46.

36 Parenti, "Un eucologio poco noto," 181–82. He identifies Sinai 966 as a close parallel in content to this manuscript.

37 R. Devreesse, *Catalogue des manuscrits grecs*, vol. 2: *Le fonds Coislin* (Paris, 1945), 195–96.

38 In this manuscript, both the recto and the verso of a folio carry their own number.

39 H. Omont, *Inventaire sommaire des manuscrits grecs de la Bibliothèque Nationale* (Paris, 1898), 34.

40 Ibid., 40.

41 The prayers printed in Goar, *Euchologion*, 708–09, derive from this codex, but are not rendered with great accuracy.

42 The first prayer is not preserved in its entirety, as fol. 116 is cut off. The subsequent prayers carry the numbers 2 and 3.

43 A. Jacob, "Les euchologes du fonds Barberini," 131–222, at 153. This is Goar's "Barberinum secundum," ibid., 154.

44 Ibid., 159. Some of these folia are palimpsests.

45 Ibid., 185. The manuscript has several marginal annotations of names in Greek and Latin (Lukas the monk inscribes himself in Latin, fol. 30r, and in Greek, fol. 66v). On fol. 22r there is an invocation by a monk of the community of Elias Spelaitoes (in Greek: *monachos tou osiou patros hēmōn ilia tou spēleou*).

46 C. Giannelli, *Codices Vaticani graeci: Codices 1485–1683* (Vatican City, 1950), 131–34.

47 Ibid., 139: many prayers are accompanied by marginal annotations in Italian written in Greek letters. The prayers for *adelphopoiesis* are identified thus: *ouphisziou kouandou se phannou plīrati szourati* (i.e., *officio quando si fanno frati giurati*), referring to the office for making "sworn brothers." According to the notice on f. IIr, this manuscript was a gift of the Cardinal of Ascoli.

48 Ibid., 135–44.

49 Canart, *Codices Vaticani graeci*, p. 422–6.

50 Baldanza, "Rito del matrimonio," 317.

51 The introductory invocations end by asking God "That your servants, NN and NN, be blessed with a blessing of the spirit, let us pray to the Lord. That their love be preserved without hatred and without scandal, throughout their life, let us pray to the Lord. That they may be granted all that they ask towards their salvation and that they may receive the enjoyment of the eternal good things, let us pray to the Lord. That the Lord may grant them faith without shame, love without deceit, so that they and all of us may be saved from all sorrow and anger: may God have mercy on us."

52 Canart, *Codices Vaticani graeci*, 431–34.

53 Ibid., 432, indicates that the preceding prayers are those found in Goar, *Euchologion*, 597–604, which is the liturgy for Pentecost.

54 Gardthausen, *Catalogus*, 219.

55 Although, according to Dmitrievskij, this is a dated codex, it does not appear in A. D. Kominis, *Pinakes chronologēmenōn Patmiakōn kodikōn* (Athens, 1968).

56 A. I. Sakkelion, *Katalogos tōn cheirographōn tēs ethnikēs bibliothēkēs tēs Hellados* (Athens, 1892), 123.

57 P. L. Kalaitzidis, "To hyp" arithm. 662 cheirografo-euchologio tēs Ethnikēs Bibliothēkēs tēs Hellados," 51, mentions the prayer for *adelphopoiesis*, but does not provide the text.

58 Panagou, *Hē adelphopoiēsē*, 188. This manuscript is not covered in any printed catalog.

59 Information based on Dmitrievskij. A search for this shelf mark in Eustratiades's catalog turns up no result. S. Eustratiades, *Katalogos tōn kodikōn tēs megistēs Lauras* (Paris, 1925), 32, does, however, mention manuscript Gamma 7, of the twelfth century, which has the same number of folia as Dmitrievskij's Laura 189. Eustratiades further notes that the prayers and rituals in this manuscript differ significantly from the printed versions.

60 S. Parenti and E. Velkovska, "A Thirteenth-Century Manuscript of the Constantinopolitan Euchology: Grottaferrata I, Alias of Cardinal Bessarion," *Bollettino della Badia Greca di Grottaferrata* 3, no. 4 (2007): 175–96, at 187, advocate a thirteenth-century date for the script of the codex and the prayers it contains.

61 Arranz, *L'eucologio costantinopolitano*, 355–56.

62 Stassi, "L'eucologio Gamma beta 1," 127.

63 Parenti and Velkovska, "Thirteenth-Century Manuscript of the Constantinopolitan Euchology," prove that the association of this manuscript with Cardinal Bessarion and the Council of Florence is not attested prior to the seventeenth century.

64 In 1901, Dmitrievskij noted that the manuscript was owned by the head of the Russian mission in Jerusalem. It must since then have been moved to St. Petersburg. Dmitrievskij's notice may point to a Palestinian origin of the manuscript. This is confirmed by the notes kept in the National Library of Russia in St. Petersburg, according to which the manuscript was found by Kapustin in Palestine, then presented to St. Petersburg.

65 Jacob, "Les euchologes du fonds Barberini," 143. This codex is of very small size and the script poorly legible. The entire codex is a palimpsest.

66 This is added in a later, more cursive hand, at the end of a quire, so that the text ends abruptly at the bottom of the folic. It is possible that these prayers are a later addition, since they are not included in the index on two paper leaves (fols. Ir–IIr) that end with a dedication by "the most humble and useless servant Franciscus ho Arkoudios" to Cardinal Franciscus Barberini.

67 Jacob, "Les euchologes du fonds Barberini," 192.

68 Canart, *Codices Vaticani graeci*, 294–7.

69 Rocchi, *Codices Cryptenses*, 255–57. The text is on the bottom half of a fly-leaf.

70 Gardthausen, *Catalogus*, 205. Dmitrievskij dates this codex to the thirteenth century. Baldanza, "Rito del matrimonio," 317, identifies its content as being of "eastern origin."

71 The southern Italian origin of the manuscript is evident from the presence of the liturgy for the commemoration of King Roger (Robert) of Sicily (1101–1154) and his successor, King William. The manuscript is partly palimpsest, partly double-palimpsest.

72 Gardthausen, *Catalogus*, 206. Dmitrievskij dates this codex to the thirteenth century.

73 Dmitrievskij, 251, erroneously states that the prayer is found on fols. 93–96v.

74 Gardthausen, *Catalogus*, 208.

75 Dmitrievskij erroneously states that the prayers for *adelphopoiesis* are found on fol. 61v.

76 This is the end of a quire, and the text of the prayer(s) is missing. The text on the next folio begins acephalous.

77 Gardthausen, *Catalogus*, 213. Dmitrievskij dates this codex to the thirteenth century.

78 Rocchi, *Codices Cryptenses*, 249–51. This manuscript is the *euchologion Cryptoferrantense Falascae* used by Goar. On its date see S. Parenti, "Per la datazione dell' Eucologio Gamma beta III di Grottaferrata," *Segno e Testo* 7 (2009), 239–43.

79 O. A. Zaninović, "Dva latinska spomenika," 713–24. This was unavailable to me.

80 Eustratiades, *Katalogos tōn kōdikōn*, 13.

81 Dmitrievskij, 343, states that the prayer begins on fol. 203v, but this is an error.

82 Gardthausen, *Catalogus*, 213. Dmitrievskij dates this codex to the fourteenth century.

(continued)

83 Omont, *Inventaire sommaire*, 33.

84 Panagou, *Hē adelphopoiēsē*, 190. This manuscript is not covered in any printed catalog.

85 S. P. Lampros, *Catalogue of the Greek Manuscripts on Mount Athos*, vol. 1 (Cambridge, 1895), 38.

86 S. P. Lampros, *Catalogue of the Greek Manuscripts on Mount Athos*, vol. 2 (Cambridge, 1900), 365, who notes that the ritual following that of *adelphopoiesis*, beginning on fol. 18v, is for the blessing and naming of a child on the day of his or her birth.

87 Lampros, *Catalogue*, 1: 108.

88 Ibid., 202.

89 On the history of this collection and the difficulty of identifying manuscripts in their current location, see D. Reinsch, in P. Moraux, D. Harlfinger, D. Reinsch, J. Wiesner, *Aristoteles Graecus. Die griechischen Manuskripte des Aristoteles*, Peripatoi 8 (Berlin, 1976), 12–13.

90 A. Papadopoulos-Kerameus, *Hierosolymitikē Bibliothēkē ētoi katalogos tōn en tais Bibliothēkais tou agiōtatou apostolikou te kai katholikou orthodoxou patriarchikou thronou tōn Hierosolymōn kai pasēs Palaistinēs apokeimenōn hellenikōn cheirographōn* (St. Petersburg, 1899; repr. Brussels, 1963), 4: 152, referring to folia 56r to 58r.

91 Gardthausen, *Catalogus*, 208.

92 Lampros, *Catalogue*, 1: 162.

93 According to the colophon on f. 477v, dated 1516, the hieromonk Arsenios the Syrian, of the Holy Mountain of Sinai, stipulated that, after his death, this manuscript should become the possession of the monastery. The manuscript was designed for bi-lingual use in Greek and Arabic, arranged in two columns.

94 Dmitrievskij, p. 710, erroneously states that the prayer begins on f. 277r.

95 For a very similar text of the prayer, see Jerusalem, Metochion tou panagiou taphou 789 (no. 59) and Athens, Ethnikē Bibliothēkē 2064 (no. 61), below. I suspect that this is simply a variant of Prayer A, *Ho poiēsas ton anthrōpon kat'eikona sou kai homoiōsin* ("Who created man in your image and likeness"), as it continues with the same words. The scribe must have misread the *nomen sacrum* for *anthrōpon (anon)* as the *nomen sacrum* for *ouranon (ounon)* and then augmented it with the familiar formula *kai tēn gēn*, to generate the non-sensical formula *Ho poiēsas ton ouranon kai tēn gēn kat'eikona sou kai homoiōsin* ("Who made heaven and earth in your image and likeness").

96 Gardthausen, *Catalogus*, p. 211–2.

97 Lampros, *Catalogue*, 2: 358.

98 No. 789 in the catalog of Papadopoulos-Kerameus, *Hierosolymitikē Bibliothēkē*, vol. 5 (St. Petersburg, 1915; repr. Brussels, 1963), 278, with reference to fols. 291v–294v.

99 An additional invocation of George, Demetrius, Theodore, perhaps reflecting that this is a ritual for three men? For a very similar text of this prayer, see Sinai, gr. 977 (no. 57) and Athens, National Library, 2064 (no. 61).

100 Constantinides and Browning, *Dated Greek Manuscripts from Cyprus*, 346. The manuscript was copied on November 26, 1563 by the priest Georgios Nikephoros, son of the priest Chariton, in a village in the bishopric of Leukara in Cyprus. I have not seen the text of this prayer, which strikes me as unusually long in this manuscript.

101 Panagou, *Hē adelphopoiēsē*, does not give the text of this prayer. His reference on 194, n. 407, to Goar, 707, is an error. Compare the similar formula in Sin. gr. 977 (no. 57) and Jerusalem, Metochion to panagiou taphou, 789 (no. 59).

102 Panagou, *Hē adelphopoiēsē*, 193–94; L. Politēs, *Katalogos cheirographōn tēs Ethnikēs Bibliothēkēs tēs Hellados, ar. 1857–2500* (Athens, 1991), 104–05.

103 Lampros, *Catalogue*, 2: 432.

104 Lampros, *Catalogue*, 1: 40.

105 Ibid., 1: 311.

106 Ibid., 1: 312.

[107] According to the colophon on fol. 315r, this *euchologion* was bequeathed to the Monastery of Mount Sinai by the hieromonk Ioannikios, who died on September 24, 1554.

[108] Dmitrievskij's statement that the prayers for *adelphopoiesis* are found on fols. 311r–313v is an error.

[109] Gardthausen, *Catalogus*, p. 215.

[110] Dmitrievskij, no. 103, p. 787–8, refers to Athens, National Library 94. This is an error, as I found out during a visit to the Manuscript Reading Room of the Ethnikē Bibliothēkē in Athens, November 2010. The codex that is currently labeled as number 94 is a lectionary, and does not contain an *euchologion*. The catalog by I. Sakkelion, *Katalogos tōn cheirographōn*, 153 indicates that ms. 848 formerly had the number 94. But this manuscript is equally disappointing, as it contains largely sacramental liturgies and lessons from the New Testament, and no prayers for *adelphopoiesis*.

[111] Cod. 568 of the Library of the Greek Orthodox Patriarchate in Jerusalem, originally part of the collection of S. Sabas, which I consulted in July 2010, does not contain these prayers.

Appendix 2

Table of Prayers

A total of sixteen different prayers for *adelphopoiesis* appear in the *euchologia*, sometimes alone, often in combination. The sequence of the prayers in this table (A to P) is determined by the date when they first appear in the manuscripts, with A being the oldest, P being the youngest. As there is often more than one prayer in a manuscript, their sequence is indicated by numbers.

Manuscript total: 66 (57 of known content)	A *Ho poiêsas ton anthrôpon*	B *Ho panta pros sôtêrian*	C *Ho endoxazo-menos en boulê hagiôn*	D *Anthêron hêmin kai polypothêton hê tês agapês euôdia*	E *Ho panta pros to sympheron*	F *Ho ton choron tôn hagiôn sou apostolôn*	G *Ho einteila-menos hêmin agapan allêlous*
Earliest appearance	8th century	9th century	10th century	10th century	10th century	11th century	12th century
Frequency of occurrence	30	41	2	1	2	6	4
8th century							
1 Vatican, Barb. gr. 336	1						
9th century							
2 Sinai, gr. 957		1					
10th century							
3 Grottaferrata, Gamma beta VII	1		2	3			
4 Grottaferrata, Gamma beta IV	1	2					
5 Grottaferrata, Gamma beta X	1	2					
6 Sinai, gr. 958	2	1					
7 St. Petersburg, gr. 226	1				2		
11th century							
8 Paris, BN, Coislin 213		1				2	
9 Grottaferrata, Gamma beta II	1	2					
10 Sinai, gr. 959		1					
Euchologium Sinaiticum (Slavonic)	2	1					
11 Sinai, gr. 961		1					
12 Sinai, gr. 962		1					
12th century							
13 Vatican, gr. 1811	1						2
14 Sinai, gr. 973					1		
15 Vatican, Ottob. gr. 434		1					

H	I	J	K	L	M	N	O	P
Hê tachinê akoê, ta tachina splagchna	*Ho en hypsistois* (**variant:** *hypsêlois) katoikôn*	*Ho en tê kata sarka sou oikonomia*	*Ho dia tês aphatou sou oikonomias kataxiôsas adelphous kalesai tous hagious sou apostolous*	*Ho eipôn tois hagiois sou mathêtais kai apostolois: eirênên tên emên didômi hymin*	*Ho kataxiôsas dia tês sês epiphanias* (**variant:** *epiphoitôseôs) tou hagiou sou pneumatos*	*Ho enischysas tois hagiois sou mathêtais kai apostolois*	*Ho synathroisas tous hagious sou*	*Ho dia stomatos Dauid*
12th century	12th century	12th century	12th century	12th century	13th century	14th century	15th century	16th century
1	6	6	2	1	3	1	2	2
2								

(continued)

Manuscript total: 66 (57 of known content)	A *Ho poiêsas ton anthrôpon*	B *Ho panta pros sôtêrian*	C *Ho endoxazo-menos en boulê hagiôn*	D *Anthêron hêmin kai polypothêton hê tês agapês euôdia*	E *Ho panta pros to sympheron*	F *Ho ton choron tôn hagiôn sou apostolôn*	G *Ho einteila-menos hêmin agapan allêlous*
16	Bodleian, Auct. E.5.13		1					
17	Escurial, X.IV.13 (=408)	1						
18	Paris, BN, Coislin 214		1					
19	Paris, BN, gr. 330	1						
20	Paris, BN, gr. 392		1					
21	Vatican, Barb. gr. 329 (first prayer fragmentary, unidentified)	2						3
22	Vatican, Barb. gr. 345	2						3
23	Vatican, Barb. gr. 431	1						
24	Vatican, gr. 1552		2					
25	Vatican, gr. 1554	2						3
26	Vatican, gr. 1872		1					
27	Vatican, gr. 1875	1						
28	Sinai, gr. 1036	1						
	13th century							
29a	Patmos, 104							
29b	Patmos, 104 (bis)		2					
30	Athens, Ethnikê Bibliothêkê 662		1				2	
31	Athens, Ethnikê Bibliothêkê 2795		1					
32	Athos, Laura 189	3	2					
33	Grottaferrata, Gamma beta I		1				2	
34	Patmos 105	1						

H	I	J	K	L	M	N	O	P
Hê tachinê akoê, ta tachina splagchna	*Ho en hypsistois* (**variant:** *hypsêlois*) *katoikôn*	*Ho en tê kata sarka sou oikonomia*	*Ho dia tês aphatou sou oikonomias kataxiôsas adelphous kalesai tous hagious sou apostolous*	*Ho eipôn tois hagiois sou mathêtais kai apostolois: eirênên tên emên didômi hymin*	*Ho kataxiôsas dia tês sês epiphanias* (**variant:** *epiphoitôseôs*) *tou hagiou sou pneumatos*	*Ho enischysas tois hagiois sou mathêtais kai apostolois*	*Ho synathroisas tous hagious sou*	*Ho dia stomatos Dauid*
			2	3				
	1							
		1						
	1							
	2							
		1						
					1			

(continued)

	Manuscript total: 66 (57 of known content)	A *Ho poiêsas ton anthrôpon*	B *Ho panta pros sôtêrian*	C *Ho endoxazo-menos en boulê hagiôn*	D *Anthêron hêmin kai polypothêton hê tês agapês euôdia*	E *Ho panta pros to sympheron*	F *Ho ton choron tôn hagiôn sou apostolôn*	G *Ho einteila-menos hêmin hêmin agapan allêlous*
35	St. Petersburg, National Library, gr. 559		1				2	
36	Vatican, Barb. gr. 293		1					
37	Vatican, Barb. gr. 443	1						
38	Vatican, gr. 1840		1					
39	Grottaferrata, Gamma beta VI (prayer difficult to read)							
40	Sinai, gr. 960		1					
41	Sinai, gr. 966	1	2	4				
42	Sinai, gr. 971	1	2					
43	Sinai, gr. 982 (only the introduction to the prayer is present)							
	14th century							
44	Grottaferrata, Gamma beta III	2	3					
45	Athos, Laura, Beta 7							
46	Sinai, gr. 981		1					
47	Paris, BN, gr. 324	3	1				2	
48	Athens, Ethnikê Bibliothêkê 2724	3	1					
	15th century							
49	Athos, Kostamonites, 19 (20)		1					
50	Athos, Panteleemon, 364	1	4					
51	Athos, Pantokrator, 149							

H	I	J	K	L	M	N	O	P
Hê tachinê akoê, ta tachina splagchna	*Ho en hypsistois* (**variant:** *hypsêlois*) *katoikôn*	*Ho en tê kata sarka sou oikonomia*	*Ho dia tês aphatou sou oikonomias kataxiôsas adelphous kalesai tous hagious sou apostolous*	*Ho eipôn tois hagiois sou mathêtais kai apostolois: eirênên tên emên didômi hymin*	*Ho kataxiôsas dia tês sês epiphanias* (**variant:** *epiphoitôseôs*) *tou hagiou sou pneumatos*	*Ho enischysas tois hagiois sou mathêtais kai apostolois*	*Ho synathroisas tous hagious sou*	*Ho dia stomatos Dauid*
					2			
	5		3					
	3							
	1							
		2						
						2		
		3					2	

(continued)

	Manuscript total: 66 (57 of known content)	A *Ho poièsas ton anthrôpon*	B *Ho panta pros sôtêrian*	C *Ho endoxazomenos en boulê hagiôn*	D *Anthêron hêmin kai polypothêton hê tês agapês euôdia*	E *Ho panta pros to sympheron*	F *Ho ton choron tôn hagiôn sou apostolôn*	G *Ho einteilamenos hêmin agapan allêlous*
52	Athos, Xeropotamou, 51							
53	Jerusalem, Metochion tou Taphou 8 (182), now in Athens	1	4					
54	Patmos, 703							
55	Sinai, gr. 972		1					
56	Athos, Philotheou, 164							
	16th century							
57	Sinai, gr. 977	1 (variant)						
58	Athos, Laura, Omega 129							
59	Jerusalem, Metochion tou Taphou (now Athens), 615 (757)	2 (variant, cf. Sinai, gr. 977)	1				3	
60	Karditsa, Monastery of Korone, 8		1					
61	Athens, Ethnikê Bibliothêkê, 2064	2 (variant, cf. Sinai, gr. 977)	1					
62	Athos, Panteleêmon, 780							
63	Athos, Konstamonites, 60 (63)	2	1					
64	Athos, Kutlumousiou, 341							
65	Athos, Kutlumusiou, 358	2	1					
66	Sinai, gr. 989		2					

H	I	J	K	L	M	N	O	P
Hê tachinê akoê, ta tachina splagchna	*Ho en hypsistois* (**variant:** *hypsêlois*) *katoikôn*	*Ho en tê kata sarka sou oikonomia*	*Ho dia tês aphatou sou oikonomias kataxiôsas adelphous kalesai tous hagious sou apostolous*	*Ho eipôn tois hagiois sou mathêtais kai apostolois: eirênên tên emên didômi hymin*	*Ho kataxiôsas dia tês sês epiphanias* (**variant:** *epiphoitôseôs*) *tou hagiou sou pneumatos*	*Ho enischysas tois hagiois sou mathêtais kai apostolois*	*Ho synathroisas tous hagious sou*	*Ho dia stomatos Dauid*
		2					3	
								3
								3
		3		1				

Appendix 3

Prayers in Translation

Since this list of sixteen prayers is more complete that those given by Boswell, *Same-Sex Unions*, or Panagou, the numbers assigned to them here do not correspond to those in these earlier publications.

Prayer A: *Ho poiêsas ton anthrôpon*

First manuscript occurrence: late eighth century (Vatican, ms. Barb. gr. 336, no. 1)

Printed in Parenti and Velkovska, *L'eucologio Barberini gr. 336*, 199–200; Panagou, 337 (both based on this manuscript)

Frequency: 30.

Lord God, ruler of all, who has created man in your image and likeness and has given him eternal life, who has deemed it right that your holy and most famous apostles Peter, the head, and Andrew, and James and John the sons of Zebedee, and Philip and Bartholomew, become each other's brothers, not bound together by nature, but by faith and through the Holy Spirit, and who has deemed your holy martyrs Sergius and Bacchus, Cosmas and Damian, Cyrus and John worthy to become brothers:

Bless also your servants NN and NN, who are not bound by nature, but by faith. Grant them to love one another, and that their brotherhood remain without hatred [*amisêton*] and free from offense [*askandaliston*] all the days of their lives through the power of your Holy Spirit, the intercession of the All-Holy [Mother of God], our immaculate Lady the holy Theotokos and ever-virgin Mary, and of holy John the forerunner and baptizer, the holy and truly renowned apostles and all your holy martyrs.

For you are the unity and security and lord of peace, Christ our God, and to you we raise up glory and thanks.

Prayer B: *Ho panta pros sôtêrian*

First manuscript occurrence: ninth century (Sinai, ms. gr. 957, no. 2)
  Printed in Goar, 707, Panagou, 338 (both based on this manuscript)
  Frequency: 41.

Lord our God, who has granted everything for our salvation, and who has ordered us to love [*agapan*] one another and to forgive each other's trespasses. Even now, benevolent Lord, that these your servants who love one another with spiritual love [*pneumatikê agapê*] have come to your holy church to be blessed by you:
  Grant them faith without shame [*pistin akataischynton*], love without suspicion [*agapên anhypokriton*], and just as you granted your peace to your holy disciples, grant also to them everything that they ask for their salvation and grant them eternal life.
  For you are a merciful and benevolent God, and to you we raise up our praise, the Father, the Son and the Holy Spirit.

Prayer C: *Ho endoxazomenos en boulê hagiôn*

First manuscript occurrence: first half of the tenth century (Grottaferrata, ms. Gamma beta VII, no. 3)
  Printed in Passarelli, 131, Panagou, 338 (both based on this manuscript).
  Frequency: 2.

Lord our God, who is praised in the council of the saints, who is fearsome to all those around him:
  Bless these your servants, NN, give them the knowledge of your Holy Spirit, guide them in holy fear of you, give them gladness [*euphranon*], so that they may become spiritual brothers more than brothers according to the flesh.
  For it is you who blesses and sanctifies those who trust in you and to you we give glory.

Prayer D: *Anthêron hêmin kai polypothêton hê tês agapês euôdia*

First manuscript occurrence: first half of the tenth century (Grottaferrata, ms. Gamma beta VII, no. 3)
  Printed in Panagou, 339 (based on this manuscript).
  Frequency: 1.
  Context: monastic.

The scent of love [*agapê*] is like flowers to us and much desired. It is built on the foundation of our fathers, is guided by the voices of the prophets, and is sanctified by the proclamation of the apostles: love surpasses all the goods of this world. Our forefather Abraham perfected love under the oak of Mamre, and with love as a beginning "he believed in the Lord and he counted it to him for righteousness [Genesis 15:6]" and as an heir of love he received his firstborn son Isaac as a blessing, the pledge of faith, the censer of sacrifice, the announcer of the Savior, the inheritor of righteousness, the father of many peoples and the foundation of the church.

Lord God, give also to these your servants NN and NN the love and the peace of your holy disciples, which you gave to them saying "my peace I give unto you and my peace I leave with you [cf. John 14:27]." This love has brought the holy apostles together to the calm harbor of the church through brotherly love [*philadelphias*]. Love has instructed your holy martyrs to endure the toils of their struggles, so that they shall inherit the unfading wreath of eternal glory. Love has enabled the prophets to fulfill their angelic service, love has become the forerunner of the Savior enabling the service of all the saints, love has offered her children to God as a sacrifice, those who cherish brotherly love, and those who practice hospitality in God towards the poor, for which they are rewarded thousandfold by Christ.

Through love we glorify God, the Father of our Lord Jesus Christ, who has called us together from manifold places to come and see the treasure of love, which all the saints desire and, weaving an unfading wreath, offer to God as a worthy gift. Desiring this love Abel brought before God his first-born male lamb, desiring this love Enoch the scribe pleased God in righteousness, love made Abraham prepare a reception for the angels, love saved Lot from Sodom. Desiring such love Abraham brought his only son before God as a sacrifice, desiring such love the most wise Jacob inherited the blessing of Esau. Love saved Daniel from the mouth of the lion, love made Elijah to be taken up in Heaven in a fiery chariot, love saved Elisha on the mountain. Desiring such love the three holy children in the fiery furnace stripped and offered God a hymn of sweet scent.

We recognize you through love as the God of all, the servants recognize the Lord, the mortal ones the Immortal, those who last but a moment the Eternal, those on earth the one in Heaven. We do not order, but we beseech you, we plead with you and ask that you hear our plea.

For you, Lord, have said, "ask, and it shall be given you; seek, and ye shall find; knock, and it shall be opened unto you. For everyone that asketh receiveth; and he that seeketh findeth; and to him that knocketh it shall be opened [Matthew 7:7]."

As we, benevolent Lord, are mindful of your commandments in your awesome and glorious testament, and are knocking on earth, open to us in the

Heavens, give us a portion of faith and love with all your holy angels, grant us an angel like the one who guided Abraham, like the one who led Isaac, like the one who accompanied Jacob, like the one who woke up Lazarus, like the one who went into the house of Zacchaeus the chief tax collector and said to him "this day salvation has come to this house [Luke 19:9]." For where there is love, the enemy can do no harm, the demon has no strength, sin does not happen. For these are three: faith, hope, but the greatest of all is love [cf. 1 Corinthians 13:13].

The marvelous and much-desired scent of love brings forth on earth the grain of piety and in Heaven gathers the fullness of righteousness. "He has dispersed, he has given to the poor; his righteousness endureth forever [Psalm 111:9]." And because of love we beseech your benevolence "incline thine ear [cf. Psalm 97:3]" to our prayer. For you are the provider of all goodness and the savior of our souls, and to you we offer glory, the Father, the Son, and the Holy Spirit.

Prayer E: _Ho panta pros to sympheron_

First manuscript occurrence: tenth century (St. Petersburg, National Library, ms. gr. 226, no. 7).

Printed in Dmitrievskij, 122; Panagou, 346 (both based on Sinai, gr. 973, no. 14).

Frequency: 2.

Context: court, Constantinople.

Lord our God, who has granted everything for the benefit humankind, who has also instated spiritual brotherhood [_pneumatikên adelphotêta systêsamenos_] and given the desire for love [_agapês_], even now that these your servants want to enter into brotherhood and want to profess, before angels and people, spiritual love in everything, and who want to call each other brothers in the church and before witnesses, and who want to be sanctified through your words by the priest:

Lord our God, give them love without suspicion [_agapên anhypokriton_], faith without shame [_pistin akataischynton_], and the light of understanding, so that they may guard the declarations of spiritual brotherhood, forgive each other's trespasses, and not do evil in their hearts like Cain. But grant them, Lord, your love that you hold toward humankind, lighten their lamps which are filled with the oil of their works and your earthly benefits, and fill them also with your heavenly [benefits]. Prepare them for the ages without end and eternal life, and grant them peace and brotherly love [_philadelphian_]. For only you have the power to forgive sins, for you are merciful.

For you are the progenitor of love, Christ our God, and to you we give glory.

Prayer F: *Ho ton choron tôn hagiôn sou apostolôn*

First manuscript occurrence: 1027 (Paris, Bibliothèque Nationale, ms. Coislin 213, no. 8).

Printed in Dmitrievskij, 190 (based on St. Petersburg, National Library, ms. gr. 559, no. 35); Panagou, 342 (based on Paris, Bibliothèque Nationale, ms. Coislin 213, no. 8).

Frequency: 6.

Context: court, Constantinople.

Ruler and Lord, our God, who has gathered the choir of your holy disciples and apostles into one church, one herd, one brotherhood and has sent them out to the ends of the world to teach your commandments:

Even now, our God, as these your servants NN have come to stand in the face of your holy glory and to become spiritual brothers, preserve them in your name and sanctify them in your truth, so that, having conducted themselves according to your commandments, they may become heirs of your kingdom.[1]

Prayer G: *Ho einteilamenos hêmin agapan allêlous*

First manuscript occurrence: 1147 (Vatican, ms. gr. 1811, no. 13).

Printed in Goar, 707.

Frequency: 4.

Context: lay community, Southern Italy.

Lord our God, who has commanded us to love one another, and to forgive each other's transgressions, benevolent and most merciful Ruler:

Bless also these your servants who love one another with spiritual love and have come to this your church to be blessed by you. Grant them faith without shame [*pistin akataischynton*], love without suspicion [*agapên anhypokriton*], and just as you granted to your holy disciples and apostles your peace and your love, thus also grant to these your servants all their requests for salvation and eternal life.

For yours is the power and yours is the kingdom.

---

[1] Translation based on Dmitrievkskij, with minor alterations based on my transcription of Paris, Bibliothèque National, ms. Coislin 213.

Prayer H: *Hê tachinê akoê, ta tachina splagchna*

First manuscript occurrence: 1153 (Sinai, ms. gr. 973, no. 14).
   Printed in Panagou, 342 (based on this manuscript).
   Frequency: 1.
   Context: lay community.

Lord our God, who is quick to hear and quick to have mercy, hear us as we pray to you:
   Send your plentiful mercy on these your servants for spiritual brotherhood, so that they think alike and love each other, and send down on them your Holy Spirit, as you have done on your holy apostles and prophets, preserve them in good conduct and in the observance of your will for all the days of their life.
   For you are the sanctification and to you . . .

Prayer I: *Ho en hypsistois katoikôn*

First manuscript occurrence: twelfth century (Vatican, ms. Barb. gr. 345, no. 22).
   Printed in Panagou, 343–44 (based on Vatican, ms. gr. 1554, no. 25).
   Frequency: 6.[2]
   Context: lay community, Southern Italy.

Lord our God, who lives in the Highest and who has regard for the things that are humble, who has sent down your only-begotten Son, our Lord Jesus Christ, for the salvation of the human race, who has received Peter and Paul, Peter from Caesarea Philippi, Paul from Tiberias, and has brought them together and made them brothers:
   Make also these your brothers, NN and NN, like these two apostles. Preserve them without blame [*amemptôs*] all the days of their lives.
   So that your most precious and exalted holy name may be sanctified.[3]

Prayer J: *Ho en tê kata sarka sou oikonomia*

First manuscript occurrence: twelfth century or earlier (Escurial, ms. X.IV.13, no. 17)

---

  [2] Instead of *en hypsistois*, nos. 25, 26, 41, 42 read: *en hypsêlois*.
  [3] Translation based on Goar, but with corrections based on my transcription of Vatican, ms. Barb. gr. 329.

Printed in Dmitrievskij, 466–67 (based on Jerusalem, Metochion tou Taphou, ms. 182, no. 53); Panagou, 343 (based on Vatican, ms. gr. 1552, no. 24).
   Frequency: 6.

Lord our God, who in your dispensation according to the flesh has deemed James and John the sons of Zebedee worthy of being brothers and disciples and apostles.
   Even now, Ruler, preserve these your servants, NN, in peace and unity of mind [*homonoia*] all the days of their lives, enacting your commandments. Keep their lamp unextinguished, counting them among the five wise virgins, preserve them, have mercy on them for the sake of your name which is invoked by them. And grant them to find favor in your sight, for the things of the flesh are not like those of the spirit.
   For you are merciful and benevolent.

Prayer K: *Ho dia tês aphatou sou oikonomias kataxiôsas adelphous kalesai tous hagious sou apostolous*

First manuscript occurrence: twelfth century (Escurial, ms. X.IV.13, no. 17).
   Printed in Panagou, 347 (based on Sinai, ms. gr. 966, no. 41).
   Frequency: 2.
   Context: Southern Italy.

Lord our God, who in your indescribable dispensation has deemed the holy apostles and heirs to your kingdom worthy to be called brothers:
   Make these your servants NN and NN spiritual brothers and let there be between them no scandal from the machinations of the devil and his evil spirits, so that, as they grow in virtue, righteousness and pure love, through them and through us all your most holy name be praised, Father, Son and Holy Spirit . . .

Prayer L: *Ho eipôn tois hagiois sou mathêtais kai apostolois eirênen tên emên didômi hymin*

First manuscript occurrence: twelfth century (Escurial, ms. X.IV.13, no. 17).
   No printed version.
   Frequency: 1.
   Context: Southern Italy.

Prayer M: *Ho kataxiôsas dia tês epiphaneias tou hagiou sou pneumatos*

First manuscript occurrence: thirteenth century (Athos, Laura, ms. 189, no. 32).

Printed in Dmitrievskij, 179–80 (based on this manuscript); Panagou, 344 (based on Vatican, ms. Barb. gr. 293, no. 36).

Frequency: 3.[4]

Context: lay community, Southern Italy.

Ruler, Lord our God, who through the manifestation of your Holy Spirit has deemed worthy to unite [*synaphênai*] your holy apostles Peter and Paul from the ends of the earth, and has bound them [*syzeuxas*] through your Holy Spirit:

Even now, benevolent Emperor,[5] give to these your servants the grace that you gave between Peter and Paul, for by you every perfect and marvelous work is created for your saints.

For you are praised . . .

Prayer N: *Ho enischysas tois hagiois sou mathêtais kai apostolois*

First manuscript occurrence: fourteenth to fifteenth century (Athens, Ethnikê Bibliothêkê, ms. 2724, no. 48).

Printed in Panagou, 345 (based on this manuscript).

Frequency: 1.

Lord our God, who has strengthened your holy disciples and apostles to proclaim the good news of your dispensation to all peoples and who has through them gathered the whole world to your Word, who has drawn us all together into oneness and brotherhood, so that we give praise from one mouth and one heart to your most holy name.

Now also, Lord, give to these your servants NN and NN who love each other with spiritual love and who have come to this holy house, to be blessed by your goodness. Grant them the blessing of the spirit and strengthen them to serve and be subservient to one another in the fear of God so that, guarded by your generous grace and the love they desire, you grant them to enjoy the reward of your eternal goodness in your kingdom.

---

[4] Instead of *epiphanias*, no. 66 reads: *epiphoitêseôs*.

[5] I.e. ruler in Heaven.

Prayer O: *Ho synathroisas tous hagious sou*

First manuscript occurrence: fifteenth century (Athos, Panteleemon, ms. 364, no. 50).

Printed in Dmitrievskij, 467 (based on Jerusalem, Metochion tou Taphou, ms. 182, no. 53); Panagou, 345–46 (based on Athos, Panteleemon, ms. 364, no. 50).

Frequency: 2.

Lord our God, who has gathered your holy apostles in the clouds and has united them in the Holy Spirit:

Unite also the brothers here in holy love [*philêmati*], in peace, and in love without suspicion [*agapê anhypokritô*], so that they may fulfill your commandments.

Through the grace and implorations . . .

Prayer P: *Ho dia stomatos Dauid*

First manuscript occurrence: sixteenth century (Athos, Konstamonites, ms. 60, no. 63).

Printed (incompletely) in Dmitrievskij, 855 (from this manuscript).

Frequency: 2.

Context: monastic, Athos.

Lord who has spoken through the mouth of your servant David: Behold how good and delightful it is when brothers live together, and who has chosen and gathered together your holy disciples and apostles in unity and spiritual love . . . through the bond of love [*tô syndesmô tês agapês*].

{ BIBLIOGRAPHY }

Sources

Acta et diplomata graeca medii aevi
Ed.: F. Miklosich and J. Müller, *Acta et diplomata graeca medii aevi*, 6 vols. (Vienna, 1871–90).

Actes de Lavra
Ed.: G. Rouilland and P. Collomp, Archives de l'Athos, 1 (Paris, 1937).

Acts of Protaton
Ed.: D. Papachryssanthou, *Actes du Prôtaton*, Archives de l'Athos 7 (Paris, 1975).

Acts of the Council of Chalcedon
Ed.: E. Schwartz, *Concilium Universale Chalcedonense*, 6 vols., *Acta Conciliorum Oecumenicorum*, vol. 2 (Berlin and Leipzig, 1933–38).
Trans.: R. Price and M. Gaddis, *The Acts of the Council of Chalcedon (451)*, 3 vols. (Liverpool, 2005; repr. with minor corrections, 2010).

Canons of the Council of Chalcedon
Ed.: P. P. Joannou, *Discipline générale antique*, vol. 2: *Les canons des Pères Grecs* (Grottaferrata, 1962).
Trans.: J. Hefele, *A History of the Councils of the Church*, vol. 3 (Edinburgh, 1883).

Anna Komnena, *Alexias*
Ed.: D. R. Reinsch and A. Kambylis, *Annae Comnenae Alexias*, 2nd ed., CFHB 40 (Berlin and New York, 2001).
Trans.: E. A. Dawes, *The Alexiad of the Princess Anna Comnena being the History of the Reign of her Father, Alexius I, Emperor of the Romans, 1081–1118 A.D.* (London, 1928; repr. New York, 1978).

Anonymous Professor, *Letters*
Ed.: A. Markopoulos, *Anonymi Professoris Epistulae*, CFHB 37 (Berlin and New York, 2000).

John Apokaukos, *Letters*
Ed.: I. Delêmarê, *Hapanta Iôannou Apokaukou* (Naupaktos, 2000).

Apophthegmata Patrum (*Sayings of the Desert Fathers*). *Alphabetical Collection*
Ed.: PG 65, cols. 71–440.
Trans.: B. Ward, *The Sayings of the Desert Fathers: The Alphabetical Collection* (London, 1975; rev. ed. Kalamazoo, MI, 1984).

J. Wortley, *Give me a Word: The Alphabetical Sayings of the Desert Fathers* (New York, 2014).

Apophthegmata Patrum (Sayings of the Desert Fathers). Anonymous Collection
Ed.: F. Nau, "Histoires des solitaires égyptiens," *ROC* 12 (1907), 43–69 [nos. 1–37]; 171–89 [nos. 38–62]; 393–413 [nos. 63–132]; *ROC* 13 (1908), 47–66 [nos. 133–174]; 266–97 [nos.175–215]; *ROC* 14 (1909), 357–79 [nos. 216–297]; *ROC* 17 (1912), 204–11 [nos. 298–334]; 294–301 [nos. 335–358]; *ROC* 18 (1913), 137–46 [nos. 359–400].
Trans.: J. Wortley, *The "Anonymous" Sayings of the Desert Fathers: A Select Edition and Complete English Translation* (Cambridge, 2013).

Apophthegmata Patrum (Sayings of the Desert Fathers). Systematic Collection
Ed. and French trans.: J.-C. Guy, *Les Apophthegmes des Pères. Collection Systematique*, 3 vols., SC 387, 474, 498 (Paris, 1993–2005).
Trans.: J. Wortley, *The Book of the Elders. Sayings of the Desert Fathers: The Systematic Collection*, Cistercian Studies Series, 240 (Collegeville, MN, 2012).

Apophthegmata Patrum (Sayings of the Desert Fathers). Coptic
French trans.: L. Regnault, *Les sentences des pères du désert. Nouveau recueil: Apophthegmes inédits ou peu connus*, 2nd ed. (Solesmes, 1977).

Apophthegmata of Makarios the Egyptian
Ed.: PG 34, cols. 232–64.
Ed. and French trans.: E. Amélineau, *Histoire des Monastères de la Basse-Égypte, Vies des Saints Paul, Antoine, Macaire, Maxime et Domèce, Jean le Nain, etc.*, Annales du Musée Guimet 25 (Paris, 1894), 203–34.
Trans.: T. Vivian, *Saint Macarius the Spiritbearer: Coptic Texts Relating to Saint Macarius the Great*, Popular Patristics Series (Crestwood, NY, 2004).

Archive of Nepheros
Ed. and German trans.: B. Kramer, *Das Archiv des Nepheros und verwandte Texte*, Aegyptiaca Treverensia 4 (Mainz, 1987).

Athanasius of Alexandria, *Orations against the Arians (Orationes contra Arianos)*
Ed.: PG 26, cols. 12–468.
Trans.: P. Schaff, *Select Works and Letters*, Nicene and Post-Nicene Fathers, ser. 2, vol. 4 (New York, 1892; repr. Peabody, MA, 1995). http://www.newadvent.org/fathers/28161.htm.

Augustine, *Confessions*
Ed.: J. J. O'Donnell, *Augustine: Confessions*, 3 vols. (Oxford, 1992).
Trans.: R. S. Pine-Coffin, *The Confessions* (Harmondsworth, 1961).

Barsanuphius and John, *Letters*
Ed.: F. Neyt and P. de Angelis-Noah, *Correspondance*, 5 vols., SC 426, 427, 450, 451, 468 (Paris, 1997–2002).
Trans.: D. J. Chitty, *Varsanuphius and John, Questions and Answers*, PO 31/3 (Paris, 1966) [partial translation].
J. Chryssavgis, *Letters from the Desert: A Selection of Questions and Responses*, Popular Patristics Series (Crestwood, NY, 2003).

Basil of Caesarea, *Sermon at a Time of Famine and Drought (Homilia dicta tempore famis et siccitatis)*

Ed.: PG 31, cols. 304–28.

Basil of Caesarea, *Liturgia*
Ed.: PG 31, cols. 1629–56.

Basil of Caesarea, *In Praise of the Forty Martyrs* (*Oratio in laudem ss. quadraginta martyrum*)
Ed.: PG 31, cols. 507–26.

Basilika
Ed.: H. J. Scheltema, N. van der Wal, and D. Holwerda, *Basilicorum libri LX*, Text, 8 vols., Scholia, 9 vols. (Groningen, 1953–88).

Byzantine Monastic Foundation Documents
Ed.: J. Thomas and A. Constantinides Hero, *Byzantine Monastic Foundation Documents*,
Trans.: J. Thomas and A. Constantinides Hero, *Byzantine Monastic Foundation Documents*, 5 vols. (Washington, DC, 2000). http://www.doaks.org/resources/publications/doaks-online-publications/byzantine-monastic-foundation-documents.

Chronicle of the Morea
Ed.: J. Schmitt, *The Chronicle of Morea* (London, 1904; repr. Groningen, 1967).
Trans.: H. E. Lurier, *Crusaders as Conquerors: The Chronicle of Morea* (New York and London, 1964).

Codex Iustinianus (Justinianic Code)
Ed.: P. Krueger, rev. ed. (Berlin, 1912, repr. Hildesheim, 1989).
Trans.: F. H. Blume. http://www.uwyo.edu/lawlib/blume-justinian/

Codex Theodosianus (Theodosian Code)
Ed.: T. Mommsen and P. Meyer, *Theodosiani libri XVI* (Berlin, 1905). http://ancientrome.ru/ius/library/codex/theod/
Trans.: C. Pharr, *The Theodosian Code* (Nashville, 1944–46).

Constantine Harmenopoulos, *Epitome canonum*
Ed.: PG 150, cols. 45–168.

Constantine Harmenopoulos, *Hexabiblos*
Ed.: G. E. Heimbach, *Constantini Harmenopuli Manuale legum sive Hexabiblos* (Leipzig, 1851; repr. Aalen, 1969).

Constantine Prophyrogennetos, *Book of Ceremonies (De ceremoniis)*
Ed.: J. J. Reiske, *Constantini Porphyrogeniti imperatoris de cerimoniis aulae Byzantinae libri duo*, vol. 1 (Bonn, 1829).
Ed. and trans.: A. Moffat and M. Tall, *The Book of Ceremonies*, 2 vols., Byzantina Australiensia, 18 (Canberra, 2012).

Cyril of Scythopolis, *Life of Sabas*
Ed.: E. Schwartz, *Kyrillos von Skythopolis*, TU 49, no. 2 (Leipzig, 1939).
Trans.: R. M. Price, *Cyril of Scythopolis, Lives of the Monks in Palestine*, Cistercian Studies 114 (Kalamazoo, MI, 1991).

Demetrios Chomatenos, *Canonicae quaestiones (Canonical Questions)*

Ed.: J. B. Pitra, *Analecta sacra et classica spicilegio Solesmensi parata*, vol. 6, pt. 2 (Paris and Rome, 1891), col. 710.

Demetrios Chomatenos, *De gradibus (On the Degrees of Consanguinity)*
Ed.: J. B. Pitra, *Analecta sacra et classica spicilegio Solesmensi parata*, vol. 6, pt. 2 (Paris and Rome, 1891), cols. 719–28 (= PG 119, cols. 937B–945D).

Demetrios Chomatenos, *Ponêmata diaphora (Various Works)*
Ed.: G. Prinzing, *Ponêmata diaphora*, CFHB 38 (Berlin and New York, 2002).

Dionysios Solomos, *The Free Besieged (Hoi eleutheroi poliorkêmenoi)*
Ed. and trans.: P. Mackridge et al., eds., *The Free Besieged and Other Poems*, trans. P. Thompson et al. (Nottingham, 2000).

Ekloga
Ed.: L. Burgmann, *Ecloga. Das Gesetzbuch Leons III. und Konstantinos' V.*, Forschungen zur Byzantinischen Rechtsgeschichte 10 (Frankfurt, 1983).

Ekloga aucta
Ed.: D. Simon and S. Troianos, *Eklogadion und Ecloga private aucta*, Fontes minores 2, vol. 2 (Frankfurt, 1977).

Ephrem the Syrian, *Ad imitationem proverbiorum (Regarding the Imitation of Proverbs)*
Ed.: K. G. Phrantzolas, *Hosiou Ephraim tou Syrou erga*, vol. 1 (Thessalonike, 1988; repr. 1995).

Euchologia
Ed.: A. Dmitrievskij, *Opisanie liturgitseskich rukopisej*, vol. 2 (Kiev, 1901; repr. Hildesheim, 1965).

Euchologion
Ed.: Rome, 1873.

Euchologium Sinaiticum
Ed. and French trans.: J. Frček, *Euchologium Sinaiticum: Texte slave avec sources grecques et traduction française*, PO 24/5 (Paris, 1933), 605–802.
Ed.: R. Nahtigal, *Euchologium Sinaiticum* (Ljubljana, 1941–42).

Eustathios Romaios, *Peira*
Ed.: J. Zepos and P. Zepos, *Jus Graecoromanum*, vol. 4 (Athens, 1931; repr. Aalen, 1962).

Evagrius Scholasticus, *Church History (Historia ecclesiastica)*
Ed.: J. Bidez and L. Parmentier, *The Ecclesiastical History of Evagrius with the Scholia* (London, 1898; repr. Amsterdam, 1964).
Trans.: M. Whitby, *The Ecclesiastical History of Evagrius Scholasticus*, TTH 33 (Liverpool, 2000).

George Akropolites, *History*
Ed.: A. Heisenberg, *Georgii Acropolitae Opera*, 2 vols. (Leipzig, 1903); repr. with corrections by P. Wirth (Stuttgart, 1978).

George the Monk, *Chronicle*
Ed.: V. M. Istrin, *Chronika Georgija Amartola* (St. Petersburg, 1922).
Ed.: C. de Boor, *Georgii monachi chronicon*, 2 vols. (Leipzig, 1904; corr. repr. Stuttgart, 1978).

Ed.: I. Bekker, *Theophanes Continuatus, Ioannes Cameniata, Symeon Magister, Georgius Monachus*, CSHB (Bonn, 1838).

George Pachymeres, *History*
Ed. and French trans.: A. Failler and V. Laurent, *Georges Pachymérès, Relations historiques*, 5 vols. (Paris, 1984–2000).

Gregory of Nazianzus, *Oration 43: In Praise of Basil the Great*
Ed.: J. Bernardi, *Grégoire de Nazianze, Discours 42–43*, SC 405 (Paris, 1992).
Trans.: L. P. McCauley, *Funeral Orations by Saint Gregory Nazianzen and Saint Ambrose*, FOTC 22 (New York, 1953). http://www.newadvent.org/fathers/310243.htm.

Gregory of Nyssa, *Life of Makrina*
Ed.: P. Maraval, *Grégoire de Nysse: Vie de sainte Macrine*, SC 178 (Paris, 1971).
Trans.: V. Woods Callahan, *Saint Gregory of Nyssa, Ascetical Works*, FOTC 58 (Washington, DC, 1967).

Hesychius, *Lexikon*
Ed.: K. Latte, *Hesychii Alexandrini Lexicon (A–O)*, 2 vols. (Copenhagen, 1953–66).
Ed.: P. Λ. Hansen, *Hesychii Alexandrini Lexicon (Π–Ω)*, 2 vols. (Berlin and New York, 2005–09).

Hilarius of Arles, *Life of Honoratus*
Ed. and French trans.: M.-D. Valentin, *Vie de Saint Honorat*, SC 235 (Paris, 1977; repr. 2006).

History of the Monks in Egypt (*Historia Monachorum*)
Ed.: E. Schulz-Flügel, *Tyrannius Rufinus, Historia monachorum sive De vita sanctorum patrum*, Patristische Texte und Studien, 34 (Berlin and New York, 1990).
Ed. and French trans.: A.-J. Festugière, *Historia monachorum in Aegypto* (Brussels, 1971).
Trans.: N. Russell, *The Lives of the Desert Fathers: The Historia Monachorum in Aegypto* (London and Kalamazoo, MI, 1981).

Ignatius the Deacon, *Life of Patriarch Tarasius*
Ed.: S. Efthymiadis, *The Life of the Patriarch Tarasios by Ignatios the Deacon*, Birmingham Byzantine and Ottoman Monographs, 4 (Aldershot, 1998).

Jerome, *Letters*
Ed.: I. Hilberg, *Sancti Eusebii Hieronymi Epistulae*, CSEL 54–56 (Vienna, 1910–18).
Trans.: NPNF, ser. 2, vol. 6.

John Cassian, *Conferences*
Ed.: M. Petschenig, *Iohannis Cassiani opera*, vol. 2, CSEL 13 (Vienna, 1886).
Trans.: C. Luibheid, *John Cassian, Conferences* (New York, 1985). http://www.ccel.org/ccel/cassian/conferences.

John Cassian, *Institutes*
Ed.: M. Petschenig, *Iohannis Cassiani opera*, vol. 1, CSEL 17 (Vienna, 1888).
Trans.: NPNF, ser. 2, vol. 9. http://www.ccel.org/ccel/schaff/npnf211.iv.iii.html.

John Chrysostom, *Epitimia LXXIII*
Ed.: J. B. Pitra, *Spicilegium Solesmense*, vol. 4 (Paris, 1858 repr. Graz, 1963).

John Chrysostom, *To the People of Antioch* (*Ad populum Antiochenum*)
Ed.: PG 49, cols. 15–222.

John Chrysostom, *On the Letter to the Hebrews* (*In epistulam ad Hebraeos*)
Ed.: PG 63, cols. 9–236.

John of Damascus, *Barlaam and Joasaph*
Ed.: R. Volk, *Historia animae utilis de Barlaam et Ioasaph (spuria)*, Patristische Texte und
    Studien 60 (Berlin, 2006).

John of the Ladder (John Climacus), *The Ladder of Divine Ascent* (*Scala Paradisi*)
Ed.: PG 88, cols. 631–1164.
Trans.: C. Luibheid and N. Russell, *John Climacus, The Ladder of Divine Ascent*
    (New York, 1982).

John Moschus, *The Spiritual Meadow* (*Pratum Spirituale*)
Ed.: PG 87/3, cols. 2852–3112.
Trans.: J. Wortley, *The Spiritual Meadow* (Kalamazoo, MI, 1992).

John of Ephesus, *Lives of the Eastern Saints*
Ed. and trans.: E. W. Brooks, *Lives of the Eastern Saints*, PO 17, 18, 19 (Paris, 1923–26).

John the Little, *Life of Paisios*, included in Nikodemos Hagioreites, *New Eklogion*, and
    now part of *The Great Synaxaristes of the Orthodox Church*
Trans.: L. Papadopoulos and G. Lizardos (Jordanville, NY, 1998).

John Tzetzes, *Letters*
Ed.: P. L. Leone, *Ioannis Tzetzae epistulae* (Leipzig, 1972).

John VI Kantakouzenos, *History*
Ed.: L. Schopen, *Ioannis Cantacuzeni eximperatoris historiarum libri IV*, 3 vols., CSHB
    (Bonn, 1828–32).
Trans. German: J. Fatouros, T. Krischer, *Johannes Kantakuzenos, Geschichte* (Stuttgart,
    1982–2011).

Joseph Genesius, *Regum libri quattuor (Four Books about Kings)*
Ed.: A. Lesmüller-Werner and J. Thurn, *Iosephi Genesii regum libri quattuor*, CFHB 14
    (Berlin and New York, 1978).

Justinian, *Digest*
Ed.: T. Mommsen, rev. by P. Krüger (Berlin, 1912).
Trans.: S. P. Scott (Cincinnati, 1932). http://droitromain.upmf-grenoble.fr/Anglica/
    digest_Scott.htm.

Kekaumenos, *Strategikon*
Ed.: B. Wassiliewsky and V. Jernstedt, *Cecaumeni strategicon et incerti scriptoris de officiis
    regiis libellus* (St. Petersburg, 1896; repr. Amsterdam, 1965).
Ed. and Italian trans.: M. D. Spadaro, *Raccomandazioni e consigli di un galantuomo
    (Stratêgikon)* (Alessandria, 1998). http://www.ancientwisdoms.ac.uk/library/
    kekaumenos-consilia-et-narrationes/.

Kievan Caves Paterikon
Trans.: M. Heppell, *The Paterika of the Kievan Caves Monastery* (Cambridge, MA, 1989).

Leo the Grammarian, *Chronicle*
Ed.: I. Bekker, *Leonis Grammatici chronographia*, CSHB (Bonn, 1842).

Leo VI the Wise, *Novellae* (*Novels*)
Ed. and French trans.: A. Dain and P. Noailles, *Les novelles de Léon VI le Sage: Texte et traduction* (Paris, 1944).

Leontius of Neapolis, *Life of Symeon Salos*
Ed. and French trans.: A. J. Festugière and L. Rydén, *Léontios de Néapolis, Vie de Symeon le Fou, Vie de Jean de Chypre* (Paris, 1974).
Trans.: D. Krueger, *Symeon the Holy Fool. Leontius' Life and the Late Antique City* (Berkeley, 1996), 121–70.

Leontius of Neapolis, *Life of John the Almsgiver* (BHG 886b, 886c, 886d)
Ed. and French trans.: A. J. Festugière and L. Rydén, *Léontios de Néapolis, Vie de Symeon le Fou, Vie de Jean de Chypre* (Paris, 1974).
Trans. German: H. Gelzer, *Leontios' von Neapolis Leben des heiligen Iohannes des Barmherzigen, Erzbischofs von Alexandrien* (Freiburg and Leipzig, 1893).
Trans.: E. Dawes and N. H. Baynes, *Three Byzantine Saints* (Oxford, 1977) [first published in 1948, with different chapter divisions than the edition]. http://www.fordham.edu/halsall/basis/john-almsgiver.asp.

Leontius of Neapolis, *Life of John the Almsgiver* (BHG 887v)
Ed.: H. Delehaye, 'Une vie inédite de saint Jean l'Aumonier,' *AB* 45 (1927), 5–74.
Trans.: E. Dawes and N. H. Baynes, *Three Byzantine Saints* (Oxford, 1977) [first published in 1948, with different chapter divisions than the edition]. http://www.fordham.edu/halsall/basis/john-almsgiver.asp.

Leontius of Neapolis, *Life of John the Almsgiver* (BHG 887w)
Ed.: E. Lappa-Zizikas, "Un épitomé inédit de la Vie S. Jean l'Aumonier par Jean et Sophronios," *AB* 88 (1970), 265–78.

Liber confraternitatum Augiensis
Ed.: J. Autenrieth, D. Geuenich, and K. Schmid, *Das Verbrüderungsbuch der Abtei Reichenau*, MGH, Libri memoriales et necrologia, n.s. 1 (Hanover, 1979).

Life of Athanasius the Athonite (*Vita A and Vita B*)
Ed.: J. Noret, *Vitae duae antiquae sancti Athanasii Athonitae*, CCh, ser. gr. 9 (Turnhout, 1982).

Life of Basil (*Vita Basilii*), see Theophanes Continuatus

Life of Basil the Younger
Ed. and trans.: A.-M. Talbot et al., *The Life of Saint Basil the Younger* (Washington, DC, 2012).

Life of Cyril Phileotes by Nikolaos Kataskepenos
Ed.: E. Sargologos, *La vie de Saint Cyrille le Philéote moine Byzantin (†1110)*, Subsidia Hagiographica, 39 (Brussels, 1964).

Life of Euthymios, Patriarch of Constantinople
Ed. and French trans.: P. Karlin-Hayter, *Vita Euthymii patriarchae Constantinopolitani*, Bibliothèque de Byzantion, 3 (Brussels, 1970).

Life of George of Choziba by his disciple Antony
Ed.: C. Houze, "Sancti Georgii Chozebitae confessoris et monachi vita auctore Antonio eius discipulo," *AB* 7 (1888), 95–144.

Life of Niphon
Ed.: F. Halkin, "La vie de saint Niphon," *AB* 58 (1940), 12–27.

Life of John Kolobos
Ed. and French trans.: E. Amélineau, *Histoire des monastères de la Basse-Égypte: Vies des Saints Paul, Antoine, Macaire, Maxime et Domèce, Jean le Nain, etc.*, Annales du Musée Guimet, 25 (Paris, 1894), 316–410.

Life of the Jura Fathers
Ed. and French trans.: F. Martine, *Vie des pères du Jura*, SC 142 (Paris, 1968).
Trans.: T. Vivian et al., *The Life of the Jura Fathers*, Cistercian Studies Series, 178 (Kalamazoo, MI, 1999).

Life of Mary the Younger
Ed.: AASS Nov. IV (Brussels, 1925), cols. 692–705.
Trans.: A. Laiou, "Life of Mary the Younger," in *Holy Women of Byzantium*, ed. A.-M. Talbot, 239–89 (Washington, DC, 1996). http://www.doaks.org/resources/publications/doaks-online-publications/holy-women-of-byzantium/talbch8.pdf.

Life of Pachomius (Bohairic)
Ed.: L.-T. Lefort, *S. Pachomii vita bohairice scripta*, CSCO 89 (Louvain, 1925; repr. 1953).
Trans.: A. Veilleux, *Pachomian Koinonia*, vol. 1, Cistercian Studies Series, 45 (Kalamazoo, MI, 1980), 23–266.

Life of Pachomius (Greek)
Ed.: F. Halkin, *Sancti Pachomii vitae Graecae*, Subsidia hagiographica, 19 (Brussels, 1932), incl. *Vita Prima*.

Life of Paul of Qentos
Trans.: H. Arneson, E. Fiano, C. Luckritz Marquis, and K. R. Smith, *The History of the Great Deeds of Bishop Paul of Qentos and Priest John of Edessa*, Texts from Christian Late Antiquity, 29 (Piscataway, NJ, 2010).

Life of Philaretos the Merciful by Niketas of Amnia
Ed. and trans.: L. Rydén, *The Life of St. Philaretos the Merciful Written by His Grandson Niketas*, Studia Byzantina Upsaliensia, 8 (Uppsala, 2002).

Life of Severus of Antioch
Ed. and trans.: L. Ambjörn, *The Life of Severus by Zachariah of Mytilene*, Texts from Christian Late Antiquity, 9 (Piscataway, NJ, 2008).
Trans.: S. Brock and S. Fitzgerald, *Two Early Lives of Severos, Patriarch of Antioch*, TTH 59 (Liverpool, 2013).

Life of Stephanos and Nikon by Pseudo-Athanasius
Ed.: W. Imnaišwili, *Das Leben der Väter (Georgische Handschrift des 11. Jahrhunderts aus dem British Museum)* (Tbilisi, 1975).
German trans.: W. Imnaišwili, "Ps.-Athanasios, 'Vita' von Stephanos und Nikon," *JÖB* 26 (1977), 53–64.

Life of Thekla,
Ed. and French trans.: G. Dagron, *Vie et miracles de sainte Thècle*, Subsidia hagiographica 62 (Brussels, 1978).
Trans.: A.-M. Talbot and S. F. Johnson, *Miracle Tales from Byzantium*, DOML 12 (Cambridge, MA, 2012).

Life of Theodore of Sykeon
Ed. and French trans.: A.-J. Festugière, *Vie de Théodore de Sykéôn*, 2 vols., Subsidia hagiographica, 48 (Brussels, 1970).
Trans.: N. H. Baynes, *Three Byzantine Saints* (Oxford, 1977; first published in 1948). http://legacy.fordham.edu/Halsall/basis/theodore-sykeon.asp

Lives of Coptic Monks
Ed. and Italian trans.: T. Orlandi, *Vite di monaci copti* (Rome, 1984).

Manuel Malaxos, *Nomokanon*
Ed.: D. S. Gkines and N. I. Pantazopoulos, *Nomokanôn Manouêl notariou tou Malaxou* (Thessaloniki, 1985).

Marcellinus Comes, *Chronicle*
Ed.: T. Mommsen, *Marcellini V. C. comitis chronicon*, MGH, Auctores Antiquissimi 9 (Berlin, 1894), 60–108.
Trans.: B. Croke, *The Chronicle of Marcellinus*, Byzantina Australiensia, 7 (Sydney, 1995).

Martyrdom of Saint Theodore (Martyrium sancti Theodori Orientalis)
Ed.: I. Balestri and H. Hyvernat, *Martyrium S. Theodori, Orientalis nuncupati, fortis I. Christi martyris, et sociorum eius martyrum, quos dominus ad eumdem martyrii agonem invitavit, scilicet S. Leontii Arabis, ac beati Panygiridis e Persarum gente,* CSCO, Scriptores Coptici, 3, no. 1 (Paris, 1908), 30–46.

Matthaios Blastares, *Syntagma canonum*
Ed.: G. A. Rhalles and M. Potles, *Syntagma tôn theiôn kai hierôn kanonôn tôn te hagiôn kai paneuphêmôn apostolôn, kai tôn hierôn oikoumenikôn kai topikôn synodôn, kai tôn kata meros hagiôn paterôn*, vol. 6 (Athens, 1859).

Maurikios, *Strategikon*
Ed. and German trans.: G. Dennis and E. Gamillscheg, *Das Strategikon des Maurikios*, CFHB 17 (Vienna, 1981).
Trans.: G. Dennis, *Maurice's Strategikon: Handbook of Byzantine Military Strategy* (Philadelphia, 1984).

Michael Psellos, *Chronicle*
Ed.: É. Renauld, *Michel Psellos, Chronographie ou histoire d'un siècle de Byzance (976–1077)*, 2 vols. (Paris, 1926–28; repr. 1967).
Trans.: E. R. A. Sewter, *The Chronographia* (London, 1953).

Michael Psellos, *Letters*
Ed.: E. Kurtz and F. Drexl, *Michaelis Pselli scripta minora: Magnam partem huc inedita*, vol. 2: *Epistulae* (Milan, 1941).

Minucius Felix, *Octavius*
Ed.: PL 3, cols. 231–366.

Miracula Theclae (*Miracles of Thecla*)
Ed. and French trans.: G. Dagron, *Vie et miracles de saint Thècle*, Subsidia hagiographica 1978 (Brussels, 1978).
Trans.: S. F. Johnson, *Miracle Tales from Byzantium*, DOML 12 (Cambridge, 2012).

Nikephoros I, *Refutatio et eversio*
Ed.: J. Featherstone, *Nicephori Patriarchae Constantinopolitani refutatio et eversio definitionis synodalis anni 815*, CCh, ser. gr. 33 (Turnhout, 1997).

Niketas Choniates, *History*
Ed.: J. A. van Dieten, *Nicetae Choniatae historia*, CFHB 11, no. 1 (Berlin and New York, 1975).
Trans.: H. J. Magoulias, *O City of Byzantium. Annals of Niketas Choniates* (Detroit, 1984).

Niketas Stethatos, *Life of Symeon the New Theologian*
Ed.: I. Hausherr, *Vie de Syméon le Nouveau Théologien par Nicétas Stéthatos (949–1022)*, Orientalia Christiana 12 (Rome, 1928).
Trans.: R. P. H. Greenfield, *Niketas Stethatos, The Life of Saint Symeon the New Theologian*, DOML 20 (Cambridge, MA, 2013).

Nikos Kazantzakis, *Ho Kapetan Michalis*
Trans.: J. Griffin, *Freedom or Death, a Novel* (New York, 1956; repr. 1966; first published in Greek, 1950).

Oxyrhynchus Papyri
Ed.: B. P. Grenfell and A. S. Hunt, *The Oxyrhynchus Papyri*, vols. 1– (London, 1898–).

Palladius, *Lausiac History* (*Historia Lausiaca*)
Ed. and Italian trans.: G. J. M. Bartelink and M. Barchiesi, *Palladio. La storia Lausiaca* (Rome, 1974).
Trans.: R. T. Meyer, *The Lausiac History*, ACW 34 (London, 1965).

Paphnutius, *Narration about Saint Onuphrios* (*Narratio de sancto Onuphrio*)
Ed.: F. Halkin, *Hagiographica inedita decem*, CCh, ser. gr. 21 (Turnhout, 1989).
Trans.: T. Vivian, *Histories of the Monks of Upper Egypt and the Life of Onnophrius by Paphnutius*, Cistercian Studies Series 140 (Kalamazoo, MI, 1993; rev. ed. Piscataway, NJ, 2009).

Patria of Constantinople
Ed.: T. Preger, *Scriptores originum Constantinopolitanarum*, 2 vols. (Leipzig, 1901–07).

Paul Evergetinos, *Synagogê*
Ed.: V. Matthaios, *Evergetinos, êtoi Synagogê tôn theophthoggôn rhêmatôn kai didaskaliôn tôn theophorôn kai hagiôn paterôn* (Athens, 1957).

Paul of Monembasia, *Narrationes*
Ed.: J. Wortley, *Les récits édifiants de Paul, évêque de Monembasie et d'autres auteurs* (Paris, 1987).
Trans.: J. Wortley, *The Spiritually Beneficial Tales of Paul, Bishop of Monembasia and of Other Authors* (Kalamazoo, MI, 1996).

Peira

Ed.: J. Zepos and P. Zepos, *Jus Graecoromanum*, 8 vols. (Athens, 1931, repr. Aalen, 1962), vol. 4.

Pero Tafur, *Travels*

Ed.: M. J. de la Espada, *Andanças e viajes de Pero Tafur por diversas partes del mundo avidos, 1435–1439* (Madrid, 1874).

Trans.: M. Letts, *Travels and Adventures, 1435–1439* (New York and London, 1926).

Philo of Alexandria, *On the Contemplative Life* (*De vita contemplativa*)

Ed.: L. Cohn and S. Reiter, *Philonis Alexandrini opera quae supersunt* (Berlin, 1915; repr. 1962).

Photius, *Lexikon*

Ed.: C. Theodoridis, *Photii patriarchae lexicon (A–Δ)*, vol. 1 (Berlin, 1982).

Ed.: R. Porson, *Photiou tou patriarchou lexeôn synagôgê*, 2 vols. (Cambridge, 1822).

Plutarch, *On Having Many Friends* (*De amicorum multitudine*)

Ed. and trans.: F. C. Babbitt, *Plutarch's moralia*, vol. 2 (Cambridge, MA, 1928; repr. 1962).

Prochiron auctum

Ed.: J. Zepos and P. Zepos, *Jus Graecoromanum*, vol. 7 (Athens, 1931; repr. Aalen, 1962).

Pseudo-Codinus, *On the Buildings of Constantinople* (*De aedificiis Constantinopolitanis*)

Ed.: PG 157, cols. 515–612.

Pseudo-Zonaras, *Lexikon*

Ed.: J. A. H. Tittmann, *Iohannis Zonarae lexicon ex tribus codicibus manuscriptis*, 2 vols. (Leipzig, 1808; repr. Amsterdam, 1967).

Quintilian, *Institutio Oratoria*

Ed.: M. Winterbottom, *M. Fabi Quintiliani institutionis oratoriae libri duodecim*, 2 vols. (Oxford, 1970).

Trans.: H. Edgeworth, http://www.perseus.tufts.edu/hopper/text?doc=Perseusext: 2007.01.0060.

Rule of Abbot Isaiah (*Regula Isaiae abbatis*)

Ed.: PL 103, cols. 427–34.

Rhalles, Potles

G. A. Rhalles and M. Potles, *Syntagma tôn theiôn kai hierôn kanonôn tôn te hagiôn kai paneuphêmôn apostolôn, kai tôn hierôn oikoumenikôn kai topikôn synodôn, kai tôn kata meros hagiôn paterôn*, 6 vols. (Athens, 1859).

Socrates, *Church History* (*Historia ecclesiastica*)

Ed.: G. C. Hansen, *Sokrates, Kirchengeschichte*, GCS (Berlin, 1995).

Trans.: NPNF ser. 2, vol. 2. http://www.newadvent.org/fathers/2601.htm.

Sophronius of Jerusalem, *In Praise of Saints Cyrus and John*

Ed. and French trans.: P. Bringel, *Panégyrique des saints Cyr et Jean: Réédition d'après de nouveaux manuscrits*, PO 51/1, no. 226 (Turnhout, 2008). 16–72.

Sophronius of Jerusalem, *On the Holy Apostles Peter and Paul* (*In SS. Apost. Petrum et Paulum*)
Ed.: PG 87, cols. 3335–64.

Sozomenos, *Church History* (*Historia ecclesiastica*)
Ed.: J. Bidez, rev. C. Hansen, *Sozomenus, Kirchengeschichte*, GCS (Berlin, 1960, 2nd rev. ed., 1995).
Trans.: NPNF ser. 2, vol. 2. http://www.newadvent.org/fathers/2602.htm.

Suda
Ed.: A. Adler, *Suidae lexicon*, 4 vols. (Leipzig, 1928–35; reprint 1994–2001).

Sylvester Syropoulos, *Histories*
Ed. and French trans.: V. Laurent, *Les "Mémoires" du Grand Ecclésiarque de l'Église de Constantinople Sylvestre Syropoulos sur le Concile de Florence (1438–1439)* (Rome, 1971).

Symeon Magister (Logothetes), *Chronicle*
Ed.: I. Bekker, *Theophanes Continuatus, Ioannes Cameniata, Symeon Magister, Georgius Monachus*, CSHB (Bonn, 1838).

Symeon of Thessaloniki, *De sacris ordinationibus*
Ed.: PG 155, cols. 361–469.

Symeon the New Theologian, *Catecheses*
Ed. and French trans.: B. Krivochéine and J. Paramelle, *Catéchèses*, SC 96, 104, 113 (Paris, 1963–65).

Symeon the New Theologian, *Letters*
Ed. and trans.: H. J. M. Turner, *The Epistles of Symeon the New Theologian* (Oxford and New York, 2009).

Symeon the Stoudite, *Ascetical Discourse* (*Oratio ascetica*)
Ed. and French trans.: H. Alfeyev and L. Neyrand, *Syméon le Stoudite: Discours ascétique*, SC 460 (Paris, 2001).

Synodicon, West Syrian
Ed.: A. Vööbus, *The Synodicon in the West Syrian Tradition*, CSCO 367–68, 375–76, Scriptores syri 161–64 (Louvain, 1975–76).

Theodore the Stoudite, *Letters*
Ed.: G. Fatouros, *Theodori Studitae Epistulae*, 2 vols., CFHB 31 (Berlin and New York, 1992).

Theodore the Stoudite, *Iambi de variis argumentis*
Ed. and German trans.: P. Speck, *Theodoros Stoudites, Jamben auf verschiedene Gegenstände*, Supplementa Byzantina 1 (Berlin, 1968).

Theodore the Stoudite, *Monachorum poene quotidianae*
Ed.: PG 99, cols. 1748–1757.

Theodore the Stoudite, *Parva catechesis*
Ed.: E. Auvray, *Sancti patris nostri et confessoris Theodori Studitis praepositi Parva catechesis* (Paris, 1891).
French trans.: A.-M. Mohr, *Petites Catéchèses*, Les Pères dans la foi 52 (Paris, 1993).

Theodore the Stoudite, *Poenae monasteriales*
Ed.: PG 99, cols. 1733–1748.

Theodore the Stoudite, *Testament*
Ed.: PG 99, cols. 1813–24.
Trans.: T. Miller, in *Byzantine Monastic Foundation Documents*, vol. 1 (Washington, DC, 2000), 67–83. http://www.doaks.org/resources/publications/doaks-online-publications/byzantine-monastic-foundation-documents/typ009.pdf.

Theodoret of Cyrrhus, *History of the Monks of Syria* (*Historia religiosa*)
Ed.: P. Canivet and A. Leroy-Molinghen, *Théodoret de Cyr, L'histoire des moines de Syrie*, 2 vols., SC 234, 257 (Paris, 1977–79).
Trans.: R. M. Price, *A History of the Monks of Syria*, Cistercian Studies 88 (Kalamazoo, MI, 1985).

Theophanes Continuatus, *Chronicle*
Ed.: I. Bekker, *Theophanes Continuatus, Ioannes Cameniata, Symeon Magister, Georgius Monachus*, CFHB (Bonn, 1838), 3–481.

Theophanes Continuatus, *Life of Basil* (*Vita Basilii*)
Ed. and trans.: I. Ševčenko, *Chronographiae quae Theophanis Continuati nomine fertur Liber quo Vita Basilii imperatoris amplectitur*, CFHB 42 (Berlin, 2011).
Modern Greek trans.: C. Sidere, *Bios Basileiou: Hē biographia tu autokratora Basileiu I. tu Makedonos apo ton estemmeno engono tu* (Athens, 2010).

Theophylactos of Ohrid, *Letters*
Ed. and French trans.: P. Gautier, *Theophylacte d'Achrida*, CFHB 16, no. 2 (Thessaloniki, 1986).

Typikon of Athanasios the Athonite for the Lavra Monastery
Ed.: P. Meyer, *Die Haupturkunden der Athosklöster* (Leipzig, 1894, repr. Amsterdam, 1965), 102–22.
Trans.: G. Dennis, in *Byzantine Monastic Foundation Documents*, vol. 1 (Washington, DC, 2000), 245–70. http://www.doaks.org/resources/publications/doaks-online-publications/byzantine-monastic-foundation-documents/typ020.pdf.

Typikon of John for the Monastery of St. John the Forerunner of Phoberos
Ed.: A. I. Papadopoulos-Kerameus, *Noctes Petropolitanae* (St. Petersburg, 1913; repr. Leipzig, 1976).
Trans.: R. Jordan, in *Byzantine Monastic Foundation Documents*, vol. 3 (Washington, DC, 2000), 872–953. http://www.doaks.org/resources/publications/doaks-online-publications/byzantine-monastic-foundation-documents/typ041.pdf.

Typikon of John for the Monastery of St. John the Forerunner on Pantelleria
Ed.: I. Dujcev, "Il Tipico del monastero di S. Giovanni nell' isola di Pantelleria," *Bollettino della Badia Greca di Grottaferrata*, n.s. 25 (1971), 3–17.
Trans.: G. Fiaccadori, in *Byzantine Monastic Foundation Documents*, vol. 1 (Washington, DC, 2000), 59–66. http://www.doaks.org/resources/publications/doaks-online-publications/byzantine-monastic-foundation-documents/typ008.pdf.

Typikon of Nikon of the Black Mountain for the Monastery and Hospice of the Mother of God tou Roidiou

Ed.: V. Beneševič, *Taktikon Nikona Chernogortsa* (Petrograd, 1917).

    Trans.: R. Allison, in *Byzantine Monastic Foundation Documents*, vol. 1 (Washington, DC, 2000), 425–39. http://www.doaks.org/resources/publications/doaks-online-publications/byzantine-monastic-foundation-documents/typ028.pdf.

Typikon of Patriarch Athanasius I
T. S. Miller and J. Thomas, "The Monastic Rule of Patriarch Athanasios I: An Edition, Translation and Commentary," *OCP* 62 (1996), 353–71. http://www.doaks.org/resources/publications/doaks-online-publications/byzantine-monastic-foundation-documents/typ069.pdf.

Typikon of Sabbas the Serbian for the Kellion of St. Sabbas at Karyes on Mount Athos
Trans.: G. Dennis, in *Byzantine Monastic Foundation Documents*, vol. 4 (Washington, DC, 2000), 1331–37. http://www.doaks.org/resources/publications/doaks-online-publications/byzantine-monastic-foundation-documents/typ055.pdf.

Typikon of the Sebastokrator Isaac Komnenos for the Monastery of the Mother of God Kosmosoteira near Bera
Ed.: L. Petit, "Typikon du monastère de la Kosmosotira près d'Aenos (1152)," *Bulletin de l'Institut d'Archéologie Russe a Constantinople/Izvestiia Russago Archeologicheskago Instituta v Konstantinople* 13 (1908), 11–77.
Trans.: N. P. Ševčenko, in *Byzantine Monastic Foundation Documents*, vol. 2 (Washington, DC, 2000), 782–858. http://www.doaks.org/resources/publications/doaks-online-publications/byzantine-monastic-foundation-documents/typ039.pdf.

Typikon of Timothy for the Monastery of Theotokos Evergetis
Ed. and French trans.: P. Gautier, "Le typikon de la Théotokos Évergétis," *REB* 40 (1982), 5–101.
Trans.: R. Jordan, in *Byzantine Monastic Foundation Documents*, vol. 2 (Washington, DC, 2000), 454–506. http://www.doaks.org/resources/publications/doaks-online-publications/byzantine-monastic-foundation-documents/typ031.pdf.

Scholarly Literature

Aasgaard, R., "Brotherhood in Plutarch and Paul: Its Role and Character," in *Constructing Early Christian Families: Family as Social Reality and Metaphor*, ed. H. Moxnes, 166–82 (London and New York, 1997).

Ahrweiler, H., "Recherches sur la société byzantine au XIe siècle: Nouvelles hiérarchies et nouvelles solidarités," *Travaux et mémoires* 6 (1976), 99–104.

Althoff, G., *Verwandte, Freunde und Getreue: Zum politischen Stellenwert der Gruppenbindungen im Mittelalter* (Darmstadt, 1990).

Althoff, G., "Friendship and Political Order," in *Friendship in Medieval Europe*, ed. J. Haseldine, 91–105 (Stroud, 1999).

Alwis, A., *Celibate Marriages in Late Antique and Byzantine Hagiography: The Lives of Saints Julian and Basilissa, Andronikos and Athanasia, and Galaktion and Episteme* (London and New York, 2011).

Amantos, K., "Epitimion kata tês adelphopoiias," *EEBS* 4 (1927), 280–84.

Anagnostakes, E., "To epeisodio tês Daniêlidas: Plêrophrories kathêmerinou biou ê mythoplastika stoicheia?" in *Hê kathêmerinê zôê sto Byzantio: Praktika tou prôtou diethnous symposiou*, ed. C. Angelidi, 375–90 (Athens, 1989).

Angold, M., *The Byzantine Empire, 1025–1204: A Political History* (London and New York, 1984).

Aravecchia, N., "Hermitages and Spatial Analysis: Use of Space at Kellia," in *Shaping Community: The Art and Archaeology of Monasticism*, ed. S. McNally, 29–40 (Oxford, 2001).

Armstrong, P., ed., *Authority in Byzantium* (Farnham, 2013).

Arranz, M., *L'eucologio costantinopolitano agli inizi del secolo XI. Hagiasmatarion & Archieratikon (Rituale & Pontificale) con l'aggiunta del Leiturgikon (Messale)* (Rome, 1966).

Arranz, M., "La Liturgie des Présanctifiés de l'ancien Euchologe byzantin," *OCP* 47 (1981), 332–88.

Auzépy, M.-F., and G. Saint-Guillain, eds., *Oralité et lien social au Moyen Âge (Occident, Byzance, Islam): Parole donnée, foi jurée, serment*, Centre de recherche d'histoire et civilisation de Byzance, Monographies 29 (Paris, 2008).

Bács, T., "The So-Called 'Monastery of Cyriacus' at Thebes," *Egyptian Archaeology. The Bulletion of the Egypt Exploration Society* 17 (Autumn 2000), 34–36.

Baldanza, G., "Il rito del matrimonio nell'Eucologio Barberini 366: Analisi della sua visione teologica," *Ephemerides liturgicae* 93 (1979), 316–51.

Bamborschke, U., et al., *Die Erzählung über Petr Ordynskij: Ein Beitrag zur Erforschung altrussischer Texte* (Berlin, 1979).

Barton, S. C., "The Relativisation of Family Ties in the Jewish and Graeco-Roman Traditions," in *Constructing Early Christian Families: Family as Social Reality and Metaphor*, ed. H. Moxnes, 81–100 (London and New York, 1997).

Baun, J., *Tales from Another Byzantium: Celestial Journey and Local Community in the Medieval Greek Apocrypha* (Cambridge, 2007).

Bébén, A., "Frères et membres du corps du Christ: Les fraternités dans les *typika*," *Cahiers de civilisation médiévale* 44 (2001), 105–19.

Beck, H.-G., *Kirche und theologische Literatur im byzantinischen Reich* (Munich, 1959).

Beck, H.-G., "Byzantinisches Gefolgschaftswesen," *Bayerische Akademie der Wissenschaften, Philos.-hist. Kl., Sitzungsberichte* 1965, no. 5 (Munich, 1965).

Betz, H. D., ed., *Plutarch's Ethical Writings and Early Christian Literature* (Leiden, 1978).

Biedenkopf-Ziehner, A., *Koptische Ostraka*, vol. 1: *Ostraka aus dem Britischen Museum in London* (Wiesbaden, 2000).

Bitton-Ashkelony, B., "Penitence in Late Antique Monastic Literature," in *Transformations of the Inner Self in Ancient Religions*, ed. J. Assman and G. Stroumsa, 179–94 (Leiden, 1999).

Boero, D., "Symeon and the Making of a Stylite," PhD diss., University of Southern California, 2015.

Booth, P., "Saints and Soteriology in Sophronius Sophista's Miracles of Cyrus and John," in *The Church, the Afterlife and the Fate of the Soul*, ed. P. Clarke and T. Claydon, 52–63, Studies in Church History 45 (Oxford, 2009).

Børtnes, J., "Eros Transformed: Same-Sex Love and Divine Desire. Reflections on the Erotic Vocabulary in St. Gregory of Nazianzus's Speech on St. Basil the Great," in *Greek Biography and Panegyric in Late Antiquity*, ed. T. Hägg and P. Rousseau, 180–93 (Berkeley, CA, 2000).

Boswell, J., *Christianity, Social Tolerance and Homosexuality: Gay People in Western Europe from the Beginning of the Christian Era to the Fourteenth Century* (Chicago, 1980).

Boswell, J., *Rediscovering Gay History: Archetypes of Gay Love in Christian History* (London, Gay Christian Movement, 1982).

Boswell, J., "Revolutions, Universals and Sexual Categories," *Salmagundi* 58–59 (1982–83), 89–113.

Boswell, J., *Same-Sex Unions in Pre-Modern Europe* (New York, 1994); published in the UK as *The Marriage of Likeness: Same-Sex Unions in Pre-Modern Europe* (London, 1996).

Bowers, J. M., "Three Readings of *The Knight's Tale*: Sir John Clanvowe, Geoffrey Chaucer, and James I of Scotland," *Journal of Medieval and Early Modern Studies* 34 (2004), 279–307.

Bracewell, W., "Frontier Blood-Brotherhood and the Triplex Confinium," in *Constructing Border Societies on the Triplex Confinium*, ed. D. Roksandić and N. Stefaneć (Budapest, 2000), 29–45.

Bracewell, W., "Friends, Lovers, Rivals, Enemies: Blood-Brotherhood on an Early-Modern Balkan Frontier," *Caiete de antropolgie istorica* 2, nos. 1–3 (2003), 103–30.

Brakke, D., "Research and Publications in Egyptian Monasticism, 2000–2004," in *Huitième congrès international d'études coptes (Paris 2004): Bilans et perspectives, 2000–2004*, ed. A. Boud'hors and D. Vaillancourt, 111–26 (Paris, 2006).

Brakke, D., *Demons and the Making of the Monk: Spiritual Combat in Early Christianity* (Cambridge, MA, 2006).

Brandes, W., "Die 'Familie der Könige' im Mittelalter: Ein Diskussionsbeitrag zur Kritik eines vermeintlichen Erkenntnismodells," *Rechtsgeschichte / Legal History* 21 (2013), 262–84.

Brandes, W., "Taufe und soziale / politische Inklusion und Exklusion in Byzanz," *Rechtsgeschichte / Legal History* 21 (2013), 75–88.

Bray, A., "Friendship, the Family and Liturgy: A Rite for Blessing Friendship in Traditional Christianity," *Theology and Sexuality* 13 (2000), 15–33.

Bray, A., *The Friend* (Chicago and London, 2003).

Brock, S., "Regulations for an Association of Artisans from the Late Sasanian or Early Arab Period," in *Transformations of Late Antiquity: Essays for Peter Brown*, ed. P. Rousseau and M. Papoutsakis, 51–62 (Farnham and Burlington, VT, 2009).

Brown, E. A. R., "Ritual Brotherhood in Ancient and Medieval Europe: A Symposium. Introduction," *Traditio* 52 (1997), 261–83.

Brown, E. A. R., "Ritual Brotherhood in Western Medieval Europe," *Traditio* 52 (1997), 357–81.

Brown, W., *Unjust Seizure: Conflict, Interest, and Authority in Early Medieval Society* (Ithaca, NY, 2001).

Brubaker, L., and S. Tougher, eds., *Approaches to the Byzantine Family* (Farnham, 2013).

Burgmann, L., "Die Novellen der Kaiserin Eirene," in *Fontes Minores*, vol. 4, ed. D. Simon, 1–36 (Frankfurt, 1981).

Burgmann, L., and S. Troianos, "Appendix Eclogae," in *Fontes Minores*, vol. 3, ed. D. Simon, 24–125 (Frankfurt, 1979).

Burgtorf, J., "'Blood-Brothers' in the Thirteenth-Century Latin East: The Mamluk Sultan Baybars and the Templar Matthew Sauvage," in *From Holy War to Peaceful Cohabitation: Diversity of Crusading and the Military Orders*, ed. Z. Hunyadi and J. Laszlovszky (Budapest, forthcoming).

Cameron, A., "Cyprus at the Time of the Arab Conquests," *Cyprus Historical Review* 1 (1992), 27–49. Reprinted in A. Cameron, *Changing Cultures in Early Byzantium* (Aldershot, 1996).

Canart, P., *Codices Vaticani graeci: Codices 1745–1962* (Vatican City, 1970).

Carmichael, L., *Friendship: Interpreting Christian Love* (London and New York, 2004).

Castellan, G., *La vie quotidienne en Serbie au seuil de l'Indépendance, 1815–1839* (Paris, 1967).

Chabot, J.-B., "Le livre de la chasteté composé par Jésusdenah, évêque de Baçrah," *Mélanges d'archéologie et d'histoire de l'École française de Rome* 16 (1896), fasc. 3–4, 1–80, and 225–91.

Chadwick, H., "John Moschus and his Friend Sophronius the Sophist," *JThSt* n.s. 25 (1974), 41–74. Reprinted in H. Chadwick, *History and Thought of the Early Church* (London, 1982).

Chaplais, P., *Piers Gaveston: Edward II's Adoptive Brother* (Oxford, 1994).

Chapman, C. R., "'Oh that You Were Like a Brother to Me, One Who Had Nursed at My Mother's Breasts': Breast Milk as a Kinship-Forging Substance," *Journal of Hebrew Scriptures* 12 (2012), article 7.

Cheynet, J. C., *Pouvoirs et contestations à Byzance (963–1210)* (Paris, 1990).

Cheynet, J. C., "Aristocratie et héritage (XIe–XIIIe siècle)," in *La transmission du patrimoine: Byzance et l'aire méditéranée*, ed. J. Beaucamp and G. Dagron, 53–80 (Paris, 1998).

Cheynet, J. C., "Foi et conjuration à Byzance," in *Oralité et lien social au Moyen Âge (Occident, Byzance, Islam): Parole donnée, foi jurée, serment*, ed. M.-F. Auzépy and G. Saint-Guillain, 265–79, Centre de recherche d'histoire et civilisation de Byzance, Monographies 29 (Paris, 2008).

Chitty, D. J., *The Desert a City: An Introduction to the Study of Egyptian and Palestinian Monasticism under the Christian Empire* (London, 1966; repr. 1977).

Choat, M., "Philological and Historical Approaches to the Search for the 'Third Type' of Egyptian Monk," in *Coptic Studies on the Threshold of a New Millennium*, ed. M. Immerzeel and J. van der Vliet, vol. 2, 857–65 (Leuven, 2004).

Ciggaar, K. N., "Une description de Constantinople traduite par un pèlerin anglais," *REB* 34 (1976), 211–67.

Ciggaar, K. N., "Une description de Constantinople dans le Tarragonensis 55," *REB* 53 (1995), 117–40.

Clogg, R., *The Movement for Greek Independence, 1770–1821: A Collection of Documents* (London, 1976).

Constantinides, C. N., and R. Browning, eds., *Dated Greek Manuscripts from Cyprus to the Year 1570* (Washington, DC, 1993).

Cooper, K., *The Fall of the Roman Household* (Cambridge, 2007).

Coquin, R.-G., "Évolution de l'habitat et évolution de la vie érémitique aux Kellia," in *Le site monastique copte des Kellia: Sources historiques et explorations archéologiques. Actes du Colloque de Genève, 13 au 15 août* (Geneva, 1986), 261–72.

Coulie, B., and J. W. Nesbitt, "A Bilingual Rarity in the Dumbarton Oaks Collection of Lead Seals: A Greek/Armenian Bulla of the Later 10th/Early 11th Centuries," *DOP* 43 (1989), 121–23.

Crislip, A., *From Monastery to Hospital: Christian Monasticism and the Transformation of Health Care in Late Antiquity* (Ann Arbor, MI, 2005).

Crum, W. E., *Varia Coptica* (Aberdeen, 1939).

Dagron, G., *Constantinople imaginaire: Étude sur le recueil des "Patria"* (Paris, 1984).

Dagron, G., "'Ainsi rien n'échappera à la réglementation': État, église, corporations, confréries: À propos des inhumations à Constantinople (IVe–Xe siècle)," in *Hommes et richesses dans l'Empire byzantin*, ed. V. Kravari, J. Lefort, and C. Morrison, 155–82 (Paris, 1991).

Dagron, G., *Emperor and Priest: The Imperial Office in Byzantium* (Cambridge, 2003); first published in French as *Empereur et prêtre: Étude sur le "césaropapisme" byzantin* (Paris, 1996).

Dahlman, B., *Saint Daniel of Sketis: A Group of Hagiographic Texts* (Uppsala, 2007).

Darling Young, R., "Gay Marriage: Reimagining Church History," *First Things: The Journal of Religion, Culture and Public Life*, November 1994: http://www.firstthings. com/article/1994/11/gay-marriage-reimagining-church-history.

Davidson, J. N., *The Greeks and Greek Love: A Bold New Exploration of the Ancient World* (New York, 2007); published in the United Kingdom as *The Greeks and Greek Love: A Radical Reappraisal of Homosexuality in Ancient Greece* (London, 2007).

de Andrés, G., *Catálogo de los códices griegos de la Real Biblioteca de El Escorial*, vol. 2: *Códices 179–420* (Madrid, 1965).

de Gregorio, G., *Il copista greco Manuel Malaxos: Studio biografico e paleografico-codicologico* (Vatican City, 1991).

De Leo, P., "L'adoptio in fratrem in alcuni monasteri dell'Italia meridionale (sec. XII–XIII)," *Atti del 7° Congresso internazionale di studi sull'alto Medioevo: Norcia, Subiaco, Cassino, Montecassino, 29 settembre–5 ottobre, 1980* (Spoleto, 1982), 657–65.

Delehaye, H., "Une vie inédite de saint Jean l'Aumonier," *AB* 45 (1927), 5–74.

Delehaye, H., "Un groupe de récits 'utiles à l'âme,'" *Annuaire de l'Institut de philologie et d'histoire orientales* 2 (1934 = Mélanges Bidez), 255–66.

Delouis, O., "Église et serment à Byzance: Norme et pratique," in *Oralité et lien social au Moyen Âge (Occident, Byzance, Islam): Parole donnée, foi jurée, serment*, ed. M.-F. Auzépy and G. Saint-Guillain, 212–46, Centre de recherche d'histoire et civilisation de Byzance, Monographies 29 (Paris, 2008).

Demosthenous, A. A., *Friendship and Homosexuality in Byzantine 11th and 13th Centuries* (Thessaloniki, 2004) (in Greek).

Demosthenous, A., "The Power of Friendship in 11th and 12th Centuries [*sic*] Byzantium," in *Byzantium: Life and Fantasy*, 29–41 (Nicosia, 2008).

Dendrinos, C., "Co-operation and Friendship among Byzantine Scholars in the Circle of Emperor Manuel II Palaeologus (1391–1425) as Reflected in their Autograph Manuscripts," paper given at the conference "Unlocking the Potential of Texts: Perspectives on Medieval Greek," Centre for Research in the Arts, Social Sciences, and Humanities, University of Cambridge, July 18–19, 2006. http://www.mml.cam.ac.uk/ greek/grammarofmedievalgreek/unlocking/pdf/Dendrinos.pdf.

Deroche, V., *Études sur Léontios de Néapolis*, Acta Universitatis Upsaliensis, Studia Byzantina Upsaliensia 3 (Uppsala, 1995).

Devreesse, R., *Catalogue des manuscrits grecs*, vol. 2: *Le fonds Coislin* (Paris, 1945).

Dickey, E., "Literal and Extended Use of Kinship Terms in Documentary Papyri," *Mnemosyne* 67, no. 2 (2004), 131–76.

Diem, A., "Organisierte Keuschheit. Sexualprävention im Mönchtum der Spätantike und des frühen Mittelalters," *Invertito* 3 (2001), 8–37, http://www.invertito.de/en/annual/inv03_02en.html.

Diem, A., *Das monastische Experiment: Die Rolle der Keuschheit bei der Entstehung des westlichen Klosterwesens* (Münster, 2005)

Dmitrievskij, A., *Opisanie liturgitseskich rukopisej*, vol. 2 (Kiev, 1901; repr. Hildesheim, 1965).

Dobschütz, E., "Maria Romaia: Zwei unbekannte Texte," *BZ* 12 (1903), 173–214.

Dölger, F., "Chronologisches und Prosopographisches zur byzantinischen Geschichte des 13. Jahrhunderts," *BZ* 27 (1927), 291–320.

Dölger, F., "Die Familie der Könige im Mittelalter," *Historisches Jahrbuch* 60 (1940), 397–420. Reprinted in F. Dölger, *Byzanz und die europäische Staatenwelt* (Ettal, 1953).

Dölger, F., "Brüderlichkeit der Fürsten," *Reallexikon für Antike und Christentum*, vol. 2 (Stuttgart, 1954), cols. 642–46.

Dölger, F., "Johannes VI. Kantakuzenos as dynastischer Legitimist (1938)," in *Paraspora: 30 Aufsätze zur Geschichte, Kultur und Sprache des byzantinischen Reiches*, ed. F. Dölger, 194–207 (Ettal, 1961).

Dover, K., *Greek Homosexuality* (Cambridge, MA, 1978; repr. with a new postscript, 1989).

Drakopoulou, E., *Hellênes zôgraphoi meta tên halôsê (1450–1850)*, 3 vols. (Athens, 1987–2010).

Du Fresne, C., Sieur Du Cange, *Glossarium mediae et infimae latinitatis*, ed. L. Favré (Paris, 1883–87; repr. Graz 1954; first published 1681). http://ducange.enc.sorbonne.fr.

Duncan, J., *Coislin 213: Euchologe de la Grande Église* (Rome, 1983).

Durham, M. E., *Some Tribal Origins, Laws and Customs of the Balkans* (London, 1928).

Elm, S., *"Virgins" of God: The Making of Asceticism in Late Antiquity* (Oxford, 1994).

Eustratiades, S., *Katalogos tôn kodikôn tês megistês Lauras* (Paris, 1925).

Favre, L., ed., *Sur l'Histoire de Saint Louis: Des adoptions d'honneur en frère, et, par occasion, des frères d'armes* (Paris, 1887); http://sul-derivatives.stanford.edu/derivative?CSNID=00003340&mediaType=application/pdf.

Feron, A., and F. Battaglini, eds., *Codices manuscripti graeci Ottoboniani Bibliothecae Vaticanae* (Rome, 1903).

Ferrarini, E., "'Gemelli cultores': Coppie agiografiche nella letteratura latina del VI secolo," *Reti Medievali Rivista* 11, no. 1 (2010), 1–17.

Filipović, M. S., "Forms and Function of Ritual Kinship among South Slavs," in *VIe Congrès international des sciences anthropologiques et ethnologiques*, vol. 3, 77–80 (Paris, 1963).

Florensky, P., *The Pillar and Ground of the Truth: An Essay in Orthodox Theodicy in Twelve Letters*, trans. B. Jakim (Princeton, NJ, 1997).

Flusin, B., "Démons et sarrasins: L'auteur et le propos des Diègèmata stèrikta d'Anastase le Sinaite," *Travaux et mémoires* 11 (1991), 381–409.

Fögen, M. T., "Harmenopoulos, Constantine," *ODB*, 2: 902.

Foucault, M., *The History of Sexuality*, vol. 1: *An Introduction*; vol. 2: *The Use of Pleasure*; vol. 3: *The Care of the Self* (New York, 1978–84; first published in French, 1976–84).

Fourmy, M.-H., and M. Leroy, "La Vie de S. Philarète," *Byzantion* 4 (1934), 85–170.

Frangos, G. D., "The *Philike Etaireia*, 1814–1821: A Social and Historical Analysis," PhD diss., Columbia University, 1971.

Fraser, P. M., *Rhodian Funerary Monuments* (Oxford, 1977).

Fritze, W., "Die fränkische Schwurfreundschaft der Merovingerzeit," *Zeitschrift der Savigny-Stiftung für Rechtsgeschichte, Germanistische Abteilung* 71 (1954), 74–125.

Galatariotou, C., "Byzantine *ktetorika typika*: A Comparative Study," *REB* 45 (1987), 77–138.

Gardthausen, V., *Catalogus codicum graecorum Sinaiticorum* (Oxford, 1886).

Garitte, G., " 'Histoires édifiantes' géorgiennes," *Byzantion* 36 (1966), 396–423.

Gaspar, C., " 'The Spirit of Fornication, whom the Children of the Hellenes Used to Call Eros': Male Homoeroticism and the Rhetoric of Christianity in the Letters of Nilus of Ancyra," in *Chastity: A Study in Perception, Ideals, Opposition*, ed. N. van Deusen, 151–83 (Leiden and Boston, 2008).

Gastgeber, C., "Kaiserliche Schreiben des 9. Jahrhunderts in den Westen," in *Quellen zur byzantinischen Rechtspraxis*, ed. C. Gastgeber, 89–106, Österreichische Akademie der Wissenschaften, Philosophisch-historische Klasse, Denkschriften, vol. 413, 89–106 (Vienna, 2010).

Gautier, P., "Le chartophylax Nicéphore," *REB* 27 (1969), 159–95.

Gay, J., "Le patriarche Nicolas le Mystique et son rôle politique", in *Mélanges Diehl*, vol. 1, 91–100 (Paris, 1930).

Gelsi, D., "Punti sull'ufficio bizantino per la 'incoronazione' degli sposi," in *La celebrazione cristiana del matrimonio: Simboli e testi. Atti del II Congresso internazionale di Liturgia, Roma, 27–31 maggio 1985*, ed. G. Farnedi, 283–306 (Rome, 1986).

Georgopapadakis, A. M., "Hê adelphopoiia eis tên Manên," *Laographia* 13 (1951), 28–32.

Giannelli, C., *Codices Vaticani graeci: Codices 1485–1683* (Vatican City, 1950).

Giladi, A., *Infants, Parents and Wet Nurses: Medieval Islamic Views on Breastfeeding and Their Social Implications* (Leiden, 1999).

Giorda, M., *Il regno di Dio in terra: Le fondazioni monastiche egiziane tra V e VII secolo* (Rome, 2011).

Goar, J., *Euchologion, sive rituale Graecorum* (Venice, 1730; repr. Graz, 1960).

Godlewski, W., "Excavating the Ancient Monastery at Naqlun," in *Christianity and Monasticism in the Fayoum Oasis*, ed. G. Gabra, 155–71 (Cairo and New York, 2005).

Goehring, J., *Ascetics, Society and the Desert: Studies in Early Egyptian Monasticism* (Harrisburg, PA, 1999).

Goody, J., *The Development of the Family and Marriage in Europe* (Cambridge, 1983).

Graham, L., and J.-M. Kantor, *Naming Infinity: A True Story of Religious Mysticism and Mathematical Creativity* (Cambridge, MA, and London, 2009).

Grossmann, P., *Christliche Architektur in Ägypten*, Handbook of Oriental Studies, vol. 26 (Leiden, Boston, Cologne, 2002).

Grotowski, P. L., *Arms and Armour of the Warrior Saints: Tradition and Innovation in Byzantine Iconography (843–1261)* (Leiden and Boston, 2010).

Grumel, V., and J. Darrouzès, *Les regestes des actes du patriarcat du Constantinople*, vol. 1– (Paris, 1972–).

Guran, P., "Une théorie politique du serment au XIVe siècle: Manuel Moschopoulos," in *Oralité et lien social au Moyen Âge (Occident, Byzance, Islam): Parole donnée, foi jurée, serment*, ed. M.-F. Auzépy and G. Saint-Guillain, 161–85, Centre de recherche d'histoire et civilisation de Byzance, Monographies 29 (Paris, 2008).

Guy, J.-C., *Recherches sur la tradition grecque des Apopthegmata Patrum*, Subsidia hagiographica 36 (Brussels, 1962).

Hadot, I., "The Spiritual Guide," in *Classical Mediterranean Spirituality: Egyptian, Greek, Roman*, ed. A. H. Armstrong, 436–59 (London, 1986).

Haelst, J. van, "Une nouvelle reconstitution du papyrus liturgique de Dêr-Balizeh,' *Ephemerides Theologicae Lovanienses* 45 (1969), 444–55.

Haldon J. F., *Byzantium in the Seventh Century: The Transformation of a Culture* (Cambridge, 1990).

Haldon, J. F., ed., *The Social History of Byzantium* (Oxford, 2009).

Halkin, F., "Un diacre réconcilié avec son ami défunt (BHG 1322d)," *RSBN* n.s. 26 (1989), 197–202.

Halperin, D. M., *One Hundred Years of Homosexuality* (New York and London, 1990).

Halperin, D. M., *Saint Foucault: Towards a Gay Hagiography* (New York and Oxford, 1995).

Halsall, P., "Early Western Civilization under the Sign of Gender: Europe and the Mediterranean (4000 BCE–1400 CE)," in *The Blackwell Companion to Gender History*, ed. T. A. Meade and M. E. Wiesner-Hanks, 285–306 (Cambridge, 2005).

Harmless, W., "Remembering Poemen Remembering," *Church History: Studies in Christianity and Culture* 69 (2000), 483–518.

Harmless, W., *Desert Christians: An Introduction to the Literature of Early Monasticism* (Oxford and New York, 2004).

Hartmann, W., and K. Pennington, eds., *The History of Byzantine and Eastern Canon Law to 1500* (Washington, DC, 2012).

Hatlie, P., "Friendship and the Byzantine Iconoclast Age," in *Friendship and Friendship Networks in the Middle Ages*, ed. J. Haseldine, 137–52 (London, 1990).

Hatlie, P., "The City a Desert: Theodore of Stoudios on *porneia*," in *Desire and Denial in Byzantium: Papers from the Thirty-First Spring Symposium of Byzantine Studies, University of Sussex, Brighton, March 1997*, ed. L. James, 67–74 (Aldershot, 1999).

Hatlie, P., *The Monks and Monasteries of Constantinople, ca. 350–850* (Cambridge and New York, 2007).

Hausherr, I., *Spiritual Direction in the Early Christian East* (Kalamazoo, MI, 1990); first published in French as *La direction spirituelle en Orient autrefoi*, OCA 144 (Rome, 1955).

Heckmann, M.-L., "Das Doppelkönigtum Friedrichs des Schönen und Ludwigs des Bayern (1325–1327): Vertrag, Vollzug und Deutung im 14. Jahrhundert," *Mitteilungen des Österreichischen Instituts für Geschichtsforschung* 109 (2001), 53–81.

Hefele, C. J., *A History of the Councils of the Church*, 5 vols. (Edinburgh, 1879?–1896).

Herman, G., "Le parrainage, l'hospitalité et l'expansion du Christianisme," *Annales ESC* 52, no. 6 (1997), 1305–38.

Hevelone-Harper, J., *Disciples of the Desert: Monks, Laity and Spiritual Authority in Sixth-Century Gaza* (Baltimore, MD, 2005).

Holosnjaj, B., "Zajkovski Trebnik N. 960 der Nationalbibliothek 'Hl. Kirill und Methodij' in Sofia (Bulgarien)," PhD diss., Pontificio Istituto Orientale, Rome, 1995.

Hörandner, E., Review of Kretzenbacher, "Rituelle Wahlverbrüderung," *Byzantinische Zeitschrift* 67 (1974), 147–48.

Horden, P., "The Confraternities of Byzantium," in *Voluntary Religion*, ed. W. J. Shiels and D. Wood, 25–45, Studies in Church History 23 (Oxford, 1986).

Horn, J., "Tria sunt in Aegypto genera monachorum: Die ägyptischen Bezeichnungen für die 'dritte Art' des Mönchtums bei Hieronymus und Johannes Cassianus," in

Quaerentes scientiam: Festgabe für Wolfhart Westendorf zu seinem 70. Geburtstag, ed. H. Behlmer, 63–82 (Göttingen, 1994).

Hunger, H., "Das Testament des Patriarchen Matthaios I (1397–1410)," *BZ* 51 (1958), 288–309.

Hunger, H., "Christliches und Nichtchristliches im byzantinischen Eherecht," *Österreichisches Archiv für Kirchenrecht* 18 (1967), 305–25. Reprinted in H. Hunger, *Byzantinische Grundlagenforschung* (London, 1973).

Iorga, N., *Anciens documents de droit roumain* (Paris and Bucharest, 1930).

Ivanov, S. A., *Holy Fools in Byzantium and Beyond* (Oxford, 2006).

Jacob, A., "L'euchologe de Porphyre Uspenski. Cod. Leningr. gr. 226 (Xe siècle)," *Le Muséon* 78 (1965), 173–214.

Jacob, A., "Les euchologes du fonds Barberini grec de la Bibliothèque Vaticane," *Didaskalia* 4 (1974), 131–222.

Jacob, A., "Un euchologe du Saint-Sauveur 'in lingua Phari' de Messine: Le Bodleianus Auct. E.5.13," *Bulletin de l'institut historique belge de Rome* 50 (1980), 283–364.

Jacob, A., "Les sacrements de l'ancien euchologe constantinopolitain (1)," *OCP* 48 (1982), 284–335.

Jacob, A., "Une édition de l'Euchologe Barberini," *Archivio storico per la Calabria e la Lucania* 64 (1997), 5–31.

Jacob, A., "Une seconde édition 'revue' de l'Euchologe Barberini," *Archivio storico per la Calabria e la Lucana* 66 (1999), 175–81.

Jacob, A., "La prière pour les troupeaux de l'Euchologe Barberini: Quelques remarques sur le texte et son histoire," *OCP* 77 (2011), 1–16.

Jaeger, C. S., *Ennobling Love: In Search of a Lost Sensibility* (Philadelphia, PA, 1999).

Janin, R., *La géographie ecclésiastique de l'Empire byzantin*, vol. 1: *Le siège de Constantinople et le Patriarcat oecuménique*, part 3: *Les églises et les monastères* (Paris, 1953).

Joannou, P. P., *Discipline générale antique*, vol. 2: *Les canons des Pères Grecs* (Grottaferrata, 1962).

Jones, A. H. M., J. R. Martindale, and J. Morris, eds., *Prosopography of the Later Roman Empire*, 3 vols. (Cambridge, 1971–92).

Jullien, F., "Aux sources du monachisme oriental: Abraham de Kashkar et le développement de la légende de Mar Awgin," *Revue de l'histoire des réligions* 225, no. 1 (2008), 37–52.

Kalaitzidis, P. L., "To hyp' arithm. 662 cheirographo-euchologio tês Ethnikês Bibliothêkês tês Hellados," PhD diss., Pontificio Istituto Orientale, Rome, 2004.

Kalavrezou-Maxeiner, I., *Byzantine Icons in Steatite* (Vienna, 1985).

Karadžić, V. S., *Srpski rječnik*, 4th ed. (Belgrade, 1935; first published Vienna, 1818).

Karayannopoulos, J., and G. Weiss, eds., *Quellenkunde zur Geschichte von Byzanz*, 2 vols. (Wiesbaden, 1982).

Karlin-Hayter, P., "The Title or Office of Basileopator", *Byzantion* 38 (1968), 278–80.

Kazhdan, A. P., "Small Social Groupings (Microstructures) in Byzantine Society," *XVI Internationaler Byzantinistenkongress, Wien, 4.–9. Oktober 1981, Akten II/2 = JÖB* 32, no. 2 (1982), 3–11.

Kazhdan, A. P., "Basileopator", *ODB*, 1: 263–64.

Kazhdan, A. P., "Bryennios, Nikephoros", *ODB*, 1: 330–31.

Kazhdan, A. P., "The Constantinopolitan Synaxarium as a Source for the Social History of Byzantium," in *The Christian Near East, Its Institutions and Its Thought*, ed. R. F. Taft, 484–515, OCA 251 (Rome, 1996).

Kazhdan, A. P., and G. Constable, *People and Power in Byzantium: An Introduction to Modern Byzantine Studies* (Washington, DC, 1982; repr. 1991).

Kazhdan, A. P., and A. Wharton Epstein, *Change in Byzantine Culture in the Eleventh and Twelfth Centuries* (Berkeley, CA, 1985).

Keen, M., "Brotherhood in Arms," *History* 47 (1962), 1–17.

Keenan, J. G., "A Christian Letter from the Michigan Collection," *ZPE* 75 (1988), 267–71.

Kiousopoulou, A. *Ho thesmos tês oikogeneias stên Êpeiro kata ton 130 aiôna* (Athens, 1990).

Konidarês, I. M., and K. A. Manaphês, "Epiteuleutios boulêsis kai didaskalia tou oikoumenikou patriarchou Matthaiou A' (1397–1410)," *EEBS* 45 (1981–82), 462–515.

Konidarês, I. M., and K. A. Manaphês, *Nomikê theôrêsê tôn monastêriakôn typikôn* (Athens, 1984).

Kondyli, F., "Changes in the Structure of the Late Byzantine Family and Society," in *Approaches to the Byzantine Family*, ed. L. Brubaker and S. Tougher, 371–93 (Farnham 2013).

Konstan, D., *Friendship in the Classical World* (Cambridge and New York, 1997).

Konstan, D., "How to Praise a Friend," *in Greek Biography and Panegyric*, ed. T. Hägg and P. Rousseau, 160–79 (Berkeley, CA, 2000).

Köpstein, H., and F. Winkelmann, eds., *Studien zum 8. und 9. Jahrhundert in Byzanz*, Berliner Byzantinistische Arbeiten 51 (Berlin, 1983).

Koster, S. J., "Das Euchologion Sevastianov 474 (X. Jhdt.) der Staatsbibliothek in Moskau," PhD diss., Pontificio Istituto Orientale, Rome, 1996.

Koukoules, P., *Byzantinôn bios kai politismos*, 6 vols. (Athens, 1948–57).

Koumarianos, P., *Il codice 226 della Biblioteca di San Pietroburgo: L'eucologio bizantino di Porfyrio Uspensky* (London, ON, 1996).

Krause, M., "Die Testamente der Äbte des Phoibammon-Klosters in Theben," *Mitteilungen des Deutschen Archäologischen Instituts, Abteilung Kairo* 25 (1969), 57–67.

Krause, M., "Zwei Phoibammon-Klöster in Theben-West," *Mitteilungen des Deutschen Archäologischen Instituts, Abteilung Kairo* 37 (1981), 261–66.

Krause, M., "Die Beziehungen zwischen den beiden Phoibammon-Klöstern auf dem thebanischen Westufer," *BSAC* 27 (1985), 31–44.

Krause, M., "Das Mönchtum in Ägypten," in *Ägypten in spätantik-christlicher Zeit. Einführung in die koptische Kultur*, ed. M. Krause, 149–74 (Wiesbaden, 1988).

Krause, M., "Die koptischen Kaufurkunden von Klosterzellen des Apollo-Klosters von Bawit aus abbasidischer Zeit," in *Monastic Estates in Late Antique and Early Christian Egypt: Ostraca, Papyri, and Essays in Memory of Sarah Clackson (P. Clackson)*, ed. A. Boud'hors et al., 159–69, American Studies in Papyrology 46 (Cincinnati, OH, 2009).

Krausmüller, D., "Abbots and Monks in Eleventh-Century Studios: An Analysis of Rituals of Installation and Their Depictions in Illuminated Manuscripts," *REB* 65 (2007), 255–82.

Krausmüller, D., "Moral Rectitude vs. Ascetic Prowess: The Anonymous Treatise On Asceticism (Edition, Translation and Dating)," *BZ* 100 (2007), 101–24.

Krausmüller, D., "Byzantine Monastic Communities: Alternative Families?" in *Approaches to the Byzantine Family*, ed. L. Brubaker and S. Tougher, 345–58 (Farnham, 2013).

Krawiec, R., *Shenoute and the Women of the White Monastery: Egyptian Monasticism in Late Antiquity* (Oxford, 2002).

Kresten, O., "Datierungsprobleme isaurischer Eherechtsnovellen. I. Coll. I 26," in *Fontes Minores*, vol. 4, ed. D. Simon, 37–106 (Frankfurt, 1981).

Kretzenbacher, L., "Gegenwartsformen der Wahlverwandtschaft pobratimstvo bei den Serben und im übrigen Südosteuropa," in *Beiträge zu Kenntnis Südosteuropas und des Nahen Orients*, vol. 2, 167–82 (Munich 1967).

Kretzenbacher, L., "Rituelle Wahlverbrüderung in Südosteuropa: Erlebniswirklichkeit und Erzählmotiv," *Bayerische Akademie der Wissenschaften, Philosophisch-historische Klasse, Sitzungsberichte* 1971, no. 1 (Munich, 1971), 3–32.

Kretzenbacher, L., "Serbisch-orthodoxe 'Wahlverbrüderung' zwischen Gläubigenwunsch und Kirchenverbot von heute," *Südost-Forschungen* 38 (1979), 163–83.

Krueger, D., *Symeon the Holy Fool: Leontius' Life and the Late Antique City* (Berkeley, CA, 1996).

Krueger, D., "Between Monks: Tales of Monastic Companionship in Early Byzantium," *Journal of the History of Sexuality* 20, no. 1 (2011), 28–61.

Krumbacher, K., "Ein vulgärgriechischer Weiberspiegel," *Bayerische Akademie der Wissenschaften, Philosophisch-historische Klasse, Sitzungsberichte* 1905, no. 1 (Munich, 1905), 335–432.

Kuefler, M., ed., *The Boswell Thesis* (Chicago and London, 2006).

Kypriakides, S., "Adelphopoiia (kai adelphopoiesis)," in *Megalê Hellênikê Enkyklopaideia*, ed. P. Drandakes, vol. 1, 569–71 (Athens 1927; repr. 1963).

Laiou, A., *Marriage, amour et parenté à Byzance aux XIe–XIIIe siècles*, Travaux et mémoires; Monographies 7 (Paris, 1992).

Laiou, A., "Family Structure and the Transmission of Property," in *A Social History of Byzantium*, ed. J. Haldon, 51–75 (Chichester, 2009). Reprinted in A. Laiou, *Women, Family and Society in Byzantium*, ed. C. Morrison and R. Dorin (Farnham and Burlington, VT, 2011).

Laiou, A., *Women, Family and Society in Byzantium*, ed. C. Morrison and R. Dorin (Farnham and Burlington, VT, 2011).

Lampros, S. P., *Catalogue of the Greek Manuscripts on Mount Athos*, 2 vols. (Cambridge, 1895–1900; repr. Amsterdam, 1966).

Latjar, A., "Minima epigraphica: Aus dem christlichen Ägypten," *Journal of Juristic Papyrology* 26 (1996), 65–71.

Laurent, V., ed., *Les "mémoires" du Grand Ecclésiarque de l'Église de Constantinople Sylvestre Syropoulos sur le Concile de Florence (1438–1439)* (Rome, 1971).

Lauritzen, F., "Christopher of Mytilene's Parody of the Haughty Mauropus," *BZ* 100, no. 1 (2007), 125–32.

Lazarovich-Hrebelianovich, S. L. E., *The Servian People: Their Past Glory and Their Destiny* (New York, 1910).

Leclerq, H., "Confréries," *Dictionnaire d'archéologie et de liturgie chrétienne*, vol. 3, pt. 2 (Paris, 1914), cols. 2553–60.

Leclerq, J., "Saint Antoine dans la tradition monastique médiévale," in *Antonius Magnus Eremita*, ed. B. Steidle, 229–47, Studia Anselmiana 38 (Rome, 1956).

Lefebvre, M. G., *Recueil des inscriptions grecques-chrétiennes d'Égypte* (Cairo, 1907).

Legrand, E., *Bibliographie hellénique ou description raisonnée des ouvrages publiés en grec par des Grecs*, 4 vols. (Paris, 1885–1906; repr. Brussels, 1963).

Leroy, J., "La vie quotidienne du moine stoudite," *Irénikon* 27 (1954), 21–50.

Lilie, R.-J., "Der Kaiser in der Statistik: Subversive Gedanken zur angeblichen Allmacht der byzantinischen Kaiser," in *Hypermachos. Studien zur Byzantinistik, Armenologie und Georgistik: Festschrift für Werner Seibt zum 65. Geburtstag*, ed. C. Stavrakos, A.-K. Wassiliou, and M. K. Krikorian, 211–33 (Wiesbaden, 2008).

Lilie, R.-J., et al., eds., *Prosopographie der mittelbyzantinischen Zeit* (Berlin, 1988–2013).

Loraux, N., *The Divided City: On Memory and Forgetting in Ancient Athens* (New York, 2002; first published in French, 1997).

Ludwig, C., *Sonderformen byzantinischer Hagiographie und ihr literarisches Vorbild: Untersuchungen zu den Viten des Äsop, des Philaretos, des Symeon Salos und des Andreas Salos* (Frankfurt, 1997).

Ludwig, C., "Social Mobility in Byzantium? Family Ties in the Middle Byzantine Period," in *Approaches to the Byzantine Family*, ed. L. Brubaker and S. Tougher, 233–45 (Farnham, 2013).

MaCoull, L., "The Bawit Contracts: Texts and Translations (Plates 36–54)," *BASP Bulletin of the American Society of Papyrologists* 31 (1994), 141–58.

Macrides, R. J., "The Byzantine Godfather," *Byzantine and Modern Greek Studies* 11 (1987), 139–162. Reprinted in R. Macrides, *Kinship and Justice in Byzantium, 11th–15th Centuries* (Aldershot, 2000).

Macrides, R. J., "Kinship by Arrangement: The Case of Adoption," *DOP* 44 (1990), 109–18. Reprinted in R. Macrides, *Kinship and Justice in Byzantium, 11th–15th Centuries* (Aldershot, 2000).

Magdalino, P., "Church, Bath and Diakonia in Medieval Constantinople," in *Church and People in Byzantium*, ed. R. Morris, 165–88 (Birmingham, 1990).

Magdalino, P., "Innovations in Government," in *Alexios I Komnenos*, ed. M. Mullett and D. Smythe, 146–66, Belfast Byzantine Texts and Translations 4.1 (Belfast, 1996).

Magdalino, P., "Knowledge in Authority and Authorized History: The Intellectual Programme of Leo VI and Constantine VII," in *Authority in Byzantium*, ed. P. Armstrong, 187–209 (Farnham, 2013).

Maj, J. M., SJ, "Coislin 213: Eucologio della grande chiesa," PhD diss., Pontificio Istituto Orientale, Rome, 1995.

Mango, C., "A Byzantine Hagiographer at Work: Leontios of Neapolis," in *Byzanz und der Westen. Studien zur Kunst des europäischen Mittelalters*, ed. I. Hutter, 24–41, Sitzungsberichte der Österreichischen Akademie der Wissenschaften, Philosophisch-historische Klasse 432 (Vienna, 1984).

Markopoulos, A., "Oi metamorphôseis tês 'mythologias' tou Basileiou A'," in *Antecessor: Festschrift für Spyros N. Troianos zum 80. Geburtstag*, ed. V. A. Leontaritou, K. A. Bourdara, and E. S. Papagianni, 947–70 (Athens, 2013).

Maspero, J., and E. Drioton, *Fouilles exécutées à Baouît*, Mémoires de l'Institut français d'archéologie orientale du Caire 59 (Cairo, 1931–43).

Masterson, M., "Impossible Translation: Antony and Paul the Simple in the *Historia Monachorum*," in *The Boswell Thesis: Essays on "Christianity, Social Tolerance, and Homosexuality*," ed. M. Kuefler, 215–35 (Chicago and London, 2006).

McCormick, M., "Emperor and Court," in *Cambridge Ancient History*, vol. 14: *Late Antiquity: Empire and Successors, A.D. 425–600*, ed. A. Cameron, B. Ward-Perkins, M. Whitby, 135–63 (Cambridge, 2008).

McGeer, E., *Sowing the Dragon's Teeth: Byzantine Warfare in the Tenth Century* (Washington, DC, 1995).

McGing, B. C., "Melitian Monks at Labla," *Tyche* 5 (1970), 67–94.

McGuire, B. P., *Friendship and Community: The Monastic Experience, 350–1250* (Kalamazoo, MI, 1988; repr. Ithaca, NY, 2010).

Messis, C., "Des amitiés à l'institution d'un lien social: l"adelphopoiia' à Byzance," *Corrispondenza d'amorosi sensi: L'omoerotismo nella letteratura medievale*, ed. P. Odorico, N. Pasero, and M. P. Bachmann, 31–64 (Alessandria, 2008).

Meyer, P., *Die Haupturkunden der Athosklöster* (Leipzig, 1894; repr. Amsterdam, 1965).

Miller, T. S., and J. Thomas, "The Monastic Rule of Patriarch Athanasios I: An Edition, Translation and Commentary," *OCP* 62 (1996), 353–71.

Moraux, P., D. Harlfinger, D. Reinsch, and J. Wiesner, *Aristoteles Graecus: Die griechischen Manuskripte des Aristoteles*, Peripatoi 8 (Berlin, 1976).

Moravcsik, G., "Sagen und Legenden über Kaiser Basilieios I", *DOP* 15 (1951), 59–126.

Morris, R., "Spiritual Fathers and Temporal Patrons: Logic and Contradiction in Byzantine Monasticism in the Tenth Century," in *Le monachisme à Byzance et en Occident du VIIIe au Xe siècle*, ed. A. Dierkens, D. Missone, and J.-M. Sansterre, 273–88, *Revue Bénédictine* 103 (1993).

Morris, R., *Monks and Laymen in Byzantium, 843–1118* (Cambridge, 1995).

Mullett, M., "Byzantium: A Friendly Society?," *Past & Present* 118 (1988), 3–24.

Mullett, M., "Friendship in Byzantium: Genre, Topos and Network," in *Friendship in Medieval Europe*, ed. J. Haseldine, 166–84 (Stroud, 1999).

Nahtigal, R., *Euchologium Sinaiticum* (Ljubljana, 1941–42).

Nenci, G., "Materiali e contributi per lo studio degli otto decreti da Entella," *Scuola Normale Superiore, Annali Classe di Lettere e Filosofia* 12, no. 3 (1982), 771–1103.

Nesbitt, J., and J. Wiita, "A Confraternity of the Comnenian Era," *BZ* 68 (1975), 360–84.

Neville, L., *Authority in Byzantine Provincial Society, 950–1100* (Cambridge, 2004).

Nichanian, M., "Iconoclasme et prestation de serment à Byzance: du contrôle social à la nouvelle alliance," in *Oralité et lien social au Moyen Âge (Occident, Byzance, Islam): Parole donnée, foi jurée, serment*, ed. M.-F. Auzépy and G. Saint-Guillain, 81–101, Centre de recherche d'histoire et civilisation de Byzance, Monographies 29 (Paris, 2008).

Nikol'skii, K., *O sluzhbakh russkoi tserkvi byvshikh v prezhnikh pechatnykh bogolushevnykh knigakh* (St. Petersburg, 1885).

Odorico, P., "Le saint amour: Introduction au colloque," in *Corrispondenza d'amorosi sensi: L'omoerotismo nella letteratura medievale*, ed. P. Odorico and N. Pasero, (Alessandria, Italy, 2008).

Odorico, P., and N. Pasero, eds., *Corrispondenza d'amorosi sensi. L'omoerotismo nella letteratura medievale* (Alessandria, Italy, 2008).

Omont, H., *Inventaire sommaire des manuscrits grecs de la Bibliothèque Nationale* (Paris, 1898).

O'Rourke, S., *Warriors and Peasants: The Don Cossacks in Late Imperial Russia* (Basingstoke and New York, 2000).

Oschema, K., "Blood-Brothers: A Ritual of Friendship and the Construction of the Imagined Barbarian in the Middle Ages," *Journal of Medieval History* 32, no. 3 (2006), 275–301.

Panagou, C., *Hê adelphopoiêsê: Akolouthia tou evchologiou . . .* (Athens, 2010).

Papachryssanthou, D., "La vie monastique dans les campagnes byzantines du VIIIe au XIe siècle," *Byzantion* 43 (1973), 158–80.

Papadopoulos-Kerameus, A., *Hierosolymitikê Bibliothêkê êtoi katalogos tôn en tais Bibliothêkais tou agiôtatou apostolikou te kai katholikou orthodoxou patriarchikou thronou tôn Hierosolymôn kai pasês Palaistinês apokeimenôn ellênikôn cheirographôn*, 5 vols. (St. Petersburg, 1891–1915; repr. Brussels, 1963).

Papaioannou, S., "On the Stage of *Eros*: Two Rhetorical Exercises by Nikephoros Basilakes," in *Theatron: Rhetorische Kultur in Spätantike und Mittelalter*, ed. M. Grünbart, 57–66 (Berlin and New York, 2007).

Papaioannou, S., "Michael Psellos on Friendship and Love: Erotic Discourse in Eleventh-Century Constantinople," *Early Medieval Europe* 19, no. 1 (2011), 43–61.

Parenti, S., *L'eucologio manoscritto Gamma beta IV della Biblioteca di Grottaferrata* (Rome, 1994).

Parenti, S., *L'eucologio slavo del Sinai nella storia dell'eucologio bizantino*, Filologia Slava 2 (Rome, 1997).

Parenti, S., "Per la datazione dell'eucologio Gamma beta III di Grottaferrata," *Segno e Testo* 7 (2009), 239–43.

Parenti, S., "Towards a Regional History of the Byzantine Euchology of the Sacraments," *Ecclesia Orans* 27 (2010), 109–21.

Parenti, S., "Un eucologio poco noto del Salento El Escorial X.IV.13," *Studi sull'Oriente Cristiano* 15 (2011), 157–97.

Parenti, S., and E. Velkovska, *L'eucologio Barberini gr. 336* (Rome, 1995; rev. ed. Rome, 2000).

Parenti, S., and E. Velkovska, "A Thirteenth-Century Manuscript of the Constantinopolitan Euchology: Grottaferrata I, Alias of Cardinal Bessarion," *Bollettino della Badia Greca di Grottaferrata* 3, no. 4 (2007), 175–96.

Parkes, P., "Milk Kinship in Southeast Europe: Alternative Social Structures and Foster Relations in the Caucasus and the Balkans," *Social Anthropology* 12, no. 3 (2004), 341–58.

Passarelli, G., *L'eucologio cryptense Gamma beta VII (sec. X)*, Analekta Blatadon 36 (Thessaloniki, 1982).

Patlagean, E., "Christianisme et parentés rituelles: Le domaine de Byzance," *Annales ESC* 33 (1978), 625–36. English translation: "Christianization and Ritual Kinship in the Byzantine Area," in *Ritual, Religion and the Sacred: Selections from the Annales, Economies, Sociétés, Civilisations*, ed. R. Foster and O. Ranum, 81–94 (Baltimore, MD, 1982).

Patlagean, E., "Une représentation byzantine de la parenté et ses origines occidentales," *L'Homme* 6, no. 4 (1966), 59–83. Reprinted in E. Patlagean, *Structure sociale, famille, chrétienté à Byzance, IVe–XIe siècle* (London, 1981).

Patlagean, E., "Self and Others," in *A History of Private Life*, ed. P. Veyne, vol . 1, 551–643 (London, 1987).

Patrich, J., *Sabas, Leader of Palestinian Monasticism: A Comparative Study in Eastern Monasticism, Fourth to Seventh Centuries* (Washington, DC, 1995).

Pavković, N. F., "Pobratimstvo," in *The Lexicon of the Serbian Middle Ages*, ed. S. Ćirković and R. Mihaličić, 526–27 (Belgrade, 1999).

Pavlov, A., "Kanonicheskie otviety Nikiy, mitropolita Solunskago (XII vieka?)," *Vizantijskij Vremmenik* 2 (1895), 378–87.

Pétridès, S., "Spoudaei et Philopones," *Échos d'Orient* 7 (1904), 341–8.

Philemon, I., *Dokimion historikon peri tês Philikês Hetairias* (Nauplio, 1834; available on Google Books).

Pieler P., "Rechtsliteratur," in *Die hochsprachliche Literatur der Byzantiner,* ed. H. Hunger, vol. 2, 343–480 (Munich, 1978).

Pieler P., "Pediasimos, Johannes," in *Lexikon des Mittelalters,* vol. 6 (Munich, 1993), col. 1850.

Pitsakis, K., "Hê thesê tôn homophylophilôn stê Byzantinê koinônia," in *Hoi perithôria-koi sto Byzantio,* ed. C. Maltezou, 171–269 (Athens, 1993).

Pitsakis, K., "Parentés en dehors de la parenté: Formes de parenté d'origine extra-législative en droit byzantin et post-byzantin," in *Parenté et societé dans le monde grec de l'antiquité à l'âge moderne: Colloque international, Volos (Grèce), 19–21 juin 2003,* ed. A. Bresson et al., 297–385, Ausonius Éditions Études 12 (Paris and Bordeaux, 2006).

Politês, L., *Katalogos cheirographôn tês ethnikês bibliothêkês tês Hellados, ar. 1857–2500* (Athens, 1991).

Pontieri, E., *De rebus gestis Rogerii Calabriae et Siciliae comitis et Roberti Guiscardi Ducis fratris eius,* Raccolta dei Storici italiani, vol. 1 (Bologna, 1927). Translated by K. B. Wolf, *The Deeds of Count Roger of Calabria and Sicily and of his Younger Brother Guiscard by Robert Malaterra* (Ann Arbor, 2005).

Pott, T., "La 'Prière pour faire des frères' de l'Euchologe slave du Sinai (Xe siècle): Essai d'approche théologique," *Studia Monastica* 38, no. 2 (1996), 269–89.

Pratsch, T., *Theodoros Studies (759–826)—zwischen Dogma und Pragma: Der Abt des Studioslosters von Konstantinopel im Spannungsfeld von Patriarch, Kaiser und eige-nem Anspruch,* Berliner Byzantinistische Studien 4 (Frankfurt, 1998).

Preiser-Kapeller, J., "Eine 'Familie der Könige'? Anrede und Bezeichnung 'auslän-discher' Machthaber in den Urkunden des Patriarchatsregisters von Konstantinopel im 14. Jahrhundert," in *Das Patriarchatsregister von Konstantinopel: Eine zentrale Quelle zur Geschichte und Kirche im späten Byzanz,* ed. C. Gastgeber, E. Mitsiou, and J. Preiser-Kapeller, 257–90, Denkschriften der philosophisch-historischen Klasse 457, Veröffentlichungen zur Byzanzforschung 32 (Vienna, 2013).

Preisigke, F., *Wörterbuch der griechischen Papyrusurkunden* (Berlin, 1925).

Prinzing, G., "Spuren einer religiösen Bruderschaft in Epiros um 1225? Zur Deutung der Memorialtexte im Codex Cromwell 11," *BZ* 101, no. 2 (2008), 751–72.

Prinzing, G., "The Authority of the Church in Uneasy Times: The Example of Demetrios Chomatenos, Archbishop of Ohrid, in the State of Epiros 1216–1236," in *Authority in Byzantium,* ed. P. Armstrong, 137–50 (Farnham, 2013).

Puchner, W., "Griechisches zur 'Adoptio in fratrem,'" *Südost-Forschungen* 53 (1994), 187–224.

Rapp, C., "Ritual Brotherhood in Byzantium," *Traditio* 52 (1997), 285–326.

Rapp, C., "'For Next to God, You are My Salvation': Reflections on the Rise of the Holy Man in Late Antiquity," in *The Cult of Saints in Late Antiquity and the Early Middle Ages: Essays on the Contribution of Peter Brown,* ed. J. Howard-Johnston, and P. A. Hayward, 63–81 (Oxford, 1999).

Rapp, C., "All in the Family: John the Almsgiver, Nicetas and Heraclius," *Nea Rhome: Rivista di ricerche bizantinistiche* 1 (2004 = *Studi in onore di Vera von Falkenhausen*), 121–34.

Rapp, C., "Spiritual Guarantors at Penance, Baptism and Ordination in the Late Antique East," in *A New History of Penance,* ed. A. Firey, 121–48 (Leiden, 2008).

Rapp, C., "Safe-Conducts to Heaven: Holy Men, Mediation and the Role of Writing," in *Transformations of Late Antiquity: Essays for Peter Brown*, ed. P. Rousseau and E. Papoutsakis, 187–203 (Farnham and Burlington, VT, 2009).

Rapp, C., "Early Monasticism in Egypt: Between Hermits and Cenobites," in *Female "vita religiosa" between Late Antiquity and the High Middle Ages: Structures, Developments and Spatial Contexts*, ed. G. Melville and A. Müller, 21–42 (Zürich, 2011).

Rapp, C., "Christianity in Cyprus in the Fourth to Seventh Centuries: Chronological and Geographical Frameworks," in *Cyprus and the Balance of Empires: Art and Archaeology from Justinian I to the Coeur de Lion*, ed. C. A. Stewart, T. W. Davis, and A. Weyl Carr, 29–38 (Boston, 2014).

Ritzer, K., *Formen, Riten und religiöses Brauchtum der Eheschliessung in den christlichen Kirchen des ersten Jahrtausends*, Liturgiewissenschaftliche Quellen und Forschungen 38 (Münster, 1962).

Roberts, C. H., and B. Capelle, *An Early Euchologium: The Dêr-Balizeh Papyrus Enlarged and Re-Edited*, Bibliothèque du Muséon 23 (Louvain, 1949).

Rocchi, A., *Codices Cryptenses seu Abbatiae Cryptae Ferratae* (Tusculo, 1883).

Rochette, R., "Empereurs et serment sous les Paléologues," *Oralité et lien social au Moyen Âge (Occident, Byzance, Islam): Parole donnée, foi jurée, serment*, ed. M.-Γ. Auzépy and G. Saint-Guillain, 157–67, Centre de recherche d'histoire et civilisation de Byzance, Monographies 29 (Paris, 2008).

Rosenwein, B., *Emotional Communities in the Early Middle Ages* (Ithaca, NY, 2006).

Rousseau, P., "Blood-Relationships among Early Eastern Saints," *JThS* 23 (1972), 135–44.

Rousseau, P., *Pachomius: The Making of a Community in Fourth-Century Egypt* (Berkeley, CA, 1985).

Ruggieri, V., "The Cryptensis Euchology Gamma beta XI," *OCP* 52 (1986), 325–60.

Ruggieri, V., and G. C. Zaffanella, "La valle degli eremiti nel canyon del Koça Çay a Kizilbel in Licia," *OCP* 66 (2000), 69–88.

Runciman, S., "The Widow Danelis," in *Etudes dediées à la mémoire d'André Andréadès* (Athens, 1940), 425–31.

Rydén, L., *Bemerkungen zum Leben des heiligen Narren Symeon von Leontios von Neapolis* (Uppsala, 1970).

Rydén, L., "The Bride-Shows at the Byzantine Court: History or Fiction?" *Eranos* 83 (1985), 175–91.

Sakkelion, A. I., *Katalogos tôn cheirographôn tês ethnikês bibliothêkês tês Hellados* (Athens, 1892).

Safran, L., *The Medieval Salento: Art and Identity in Southern Italy* (Philadelphia, PA, 2014).

Sauneron, S., and R.-G. Coquin, *Les ermitages chrétiennes du désert d'Esna*, vol. 4: *Essai d'histoire* (Cairo, 1972).

Schiwietz, S., *Das morgenländische Mönchtum*, 3 vols. (Mainz and Vienna, 1904–38).

Schminck, A., "Der Traktat *Peri gamôn* des Johannes Pediasimos," in *Fontes Minores*, vol. 1, ed. D. Simon, 126–74 (Frankfurt, 1976).

Schminck, A., "Kritik am Tomos des Sisinnios," in *Fontes Minores*, vol. 2, ed. D. Simon, 215–54 (Frankfurt, 1977).

Schneider, G. A., "Der hl. Theodor von Studion, Sein Leben und Wirken: Ein Beitrag zur byzantinischen Mönchsgeschichte," PhD diss., Münster, 1900.

Schroeder, C. T., *Monastic Bodies: Discipline and Salvation in Shenoute of Atripe* (Philadelphia, PA, 2007).

Scott, J. M., *Adoption as Sons of God: An Exegetical Investigation into the Background of Hyiothesia in the Pauline Corpus* (Tübingen, 1992).

Seidl, E., *Der Eid im römisch-ägyptischen Provinzialrecht* (Munich, 1935).

Selb, W., *Orientalisches Kirchenrecht*, vol. 2: *Die Geschichte des Kirchenrechts der Westsyrer (von den Anfängen bis zur Mongolenzeit)*, Österreichische Akademie der Wissenschaften, Philosophisch-historische Klasse, Sitzungsberichte 543 (Vienna, 1989).

Ševčenko, I., "Re-reading Constantine Porphyrogenitus", in *Byzantine Diplomacy: Papers from the Twenty-Fourth Spring Symposium of Byzantine Studies, Cambridge, March 1990*, ed. J. Shepard and S. Franklin, 167–95 (Aldershot, 1992).

Shaw, B., "Ritual Brotherhood in Roman and Post-Roman Societies," *Traditio* 52 (1997), 327–55.

Shepard, J., "'Father' or 'Scorpion'? Style and Substance in Alexios' Diplomacy," in *Alexios I Komnenos*, ed. M. Mullett and D. Smythe, 68–132, Belfast Byzantine Texts and Translations 4.1 (Belfast, 1996).

Sidéris, G., "L'*adelphopoièsis* aux VIIe–Xe siècles à Byzance: Une forme de fraternité jurée," in *Oralité et lien social au Moyen Âge (Occident, Byzance, Islam): Parole donnée, foi jurée, serment*, ed. M.-F. Auzépy and G. Saint-Guillain, 281–92, Centre de recherche d'histoire et civilisation de Byzance, Monographies 29 (Paris, 2008).

Simon, D., "Zur Ehegesetzgebung der Isaurier," in *Fontes Minores*, vol. 1, ed. D. Simon, 16–43 (Frankfurt, 1976).

Simon, D., "Byzantinische Hausgemeinschaftsverträge," in *Beiträge zur europäischen Rechtsgeschichte und zum geltenden Zivilrecht: Festgabe für Johannes Sontis*, ed. F. Baur, K. Larenz, and F. Wieacker, 91–128 (Munich, 1977).

Smythe, D., "In Denial: Same-Sex Desire in Byzantium," in *Desire and Denial in Byzantium: Papers from the Thirty-First Spring Symposium of Byzantine Studies, University of Sussex, Brighton, March 1997*, ed. L. James, 139–48 (Aldershot, 1999).

Sniveley, C., "Invisible in the Community? The Evidence for Early Womens' Monasticism in the Balkan Peninsula," in *Shaping Community: The Art and Archaeology of Monasticism*, ed. S. McNally, 57–68, BAR International Series 941 (Oxford, 2001).

Stahl, P. H., "La consanguinité fictive: Quelques exemples balkaniques," *Quaderni fiorentini per la storia del pensiero giuridico moderno* 14 (1985), 122–47.

Stassi, G., "L'eucologio Gamma beta 1 'Bessarione' di Grottaferrata," PhD diss., Pontificio Istituto Orientale, Rome, 1982.

Stevenson, K., *Nuptial Blessing: A Study of Christian Marriage Rites* (New York, 1983).

Strittmatter, A., "The 'Barberinum S. Marci' of Jacques Goar," *Ephemerides liturgicae* 47 (1933), 329–67.

Svoronos, N., "Le serment de fidelité à l'empereur byzantin et sa signification constitutionelle," *REB* 9 (1951), 106–42. Reprinted in N. Svoronos, *Études sur l'organisation intérieure, la societé et l'économie de l'Empire byzantin* (London, 1973).

Taft, R. F., *Beyond East and West: Problems in Liturgical Understanding* (Washington, DC, 1984).

Taft, R. F., *The Byzantine Rite: A Short History* (Collegeville, MN, 1992).

Thiermeyer, A.-A., "Das Euchologion Ottoboni gr. 434 (12. Jahrhundert)," PhD diss., Pontificio Istituto Orientale, Rome, 1992.

Till, W., *Koptische Heiligen- und Martyrerlegenden*, 2 vols., OCA 102, 108 (Rome, 1935–36).

Till, W., *Die koptischen Rechtsurkunden aus Theben*, Österreichische Akademie der Wissenschaften, Philosophisch-historische Klasse, Sitzungsberichte 244/3, no. 77 (Vienna, 1964).

Tinnefeld, F., "'Freundschaft' in den Briefen des Michael Psellos. Theorie und Wirklichkeit," *JÖB* 22 (1973), 151–68.

Tougher, S., *The Reign of Leo VI (886–912): Politics and People* (Leiden, 1997).

Tougher, S., "Michael III and Basil the Macedonian: Just Good Friends?" in *Desire and Denial in Byzantium: Papers from the 31st Spring Symposium of Byzantine Studies, University of Sussex, March 1997*, ed. L. James, 149–58 (Aldershot, 1999).

Tougher, S., "Imperial Families: The Case of the Macedonians (867–1025)," in *Approaches to the Byzantine Family*, ed. L. Brubaker and S. Tougher, 303–26 (Farnham 2013).

Treadgold, W., "The Bride-Shows of the Byzantine Emperors," *Byzantion* 49 (1979), 395–413.

Troianos, S., "Kirchliche und weltliche Rechtsquellen zur Homosexualität in Byzanz," *JÖB* 39 (1989), 29–48.

Troianos, S., *Hoi pêges tou Byzantiou dikaiou*, 3rd ed. (Athens and Komotini, 2011).

Troianos, S., "Byzantine Canon Law from the Twelfth to the Fifteenth Centuries," in *The History of Byzantine and Eastern Canon Law to 1500*, ed. W. Hartmann and K. Pennington, 170–214 (Washington, DC, 2012).

Tsamakda, V., *The Illustrated Chronicle of Ioannes Skylitzes in Madrid* (Leiden, 2002).

Tsantsanoglu, E., "Hoi adelphopoitoi [*sic*]: Hena metakinoumeno Solômiko thema," in *Aphieroma ston Kathêegete Lino Polite* (Thessaloniki, 1979), 145–51.

Tulchin, A. A., "Same-Sex Couples Creating Households in Old Regime France: The Uses of the *Affrèrement*," *Journal of Modern History* 79 (2007), 613–47.

Ubl, K., *Inzestverbot und Gesetzgebung: Die Konstruktion eines Verbrechens (300–1100)*, Millennium Studies 20 (Berlin and New York, 2008).

Usener, H., *Der heilige Tychon* (Leipzig and Berlin, 1907).

von Boeselager, P., with F. and J. Fehrenbach, *Valkyrie: The Plot to Kill Hitler* (London, 2009). Originally published in French as *Nous voulions tuer Hitler: Le dernier survivant du complot du 20 juillet 1944* (Paris, 2008).

von Staden, H., "'In a Pure and Holy Way': Personal and Professional Conduct in the Hippocratic Oath," *Journal for the History of Medicine and Allied Sciences* 51 (1996), 406–08.

Vuolanto, V., "Family and Asceticism: Continuity Strategies in the Late Roman World," PhD diss., Tampere, 2008.

Watts, E. J., "Student Travel to Intellectual Centers: What Was the Attraction?" in *Travel, Communication and Geography in Late Antiquity*, ed. L. Ellis and F. Kidner, 13–23 (Aldershot, 2004).

Watts, E. J., *City and School in Late Antique Athens and Alexandria* (Berkeley, CA, 2006).

Watts, E. J., *Riot in Alexandria: Tradition and Group Dynamics in Late Antique Pagan and Christian Communities* (Berkeley, CA, 2010).

White, C., *Christian Friendship in the Fourth Century* (Cambridge, 1992).

White, M., *Military Saints in Byzantium and Rus, 900–1200* (Cambridge, 2013).

Winkelmann, F., *Quellenstudien zur herrschenden Klasse von Byzanz im 8. und 9. Jahrhundert* (Berlin, 1987).

Wipszycka, E., "Apports d'archéologie à l'histoire du monachisme égyptien," in *The Spirituality of Ancient Monasticism: Acts of the International Colloquium, Cracow-Tyniec, 16–19 November 1994*, ed. M. Starowieyski, 63–78 (Cracow, 1995).

Wipszycka, E., "Les confréries dans la vie religieuse de l'Égypte chrétienne," in *Proceedings of the Twelfth International Congress of Papyrology, Ann Arbor, 13–17 August 1968*, ed. D. H. Samuel, 511–25 (Toronto, 1970). Reprinted in E. Wipszycka, *Études sur le christianisme dans l'Égypte de l'antiquité tardive*, Studia Ephemeridis Augustinianum 52 (Rome, 1996).

Wipszycka, E., "Recherches sur le monachisme égyptien, 1997–2000," in *Coptic Studies on the Threshold of a New Millennium: Proceedings of the Seventh International Congress of Coptic Studies, Leiden, 27 August–2 September 2000*, ed. M. Immerzeel and J. van der Vliet, 831–55 (Leuven, 2004).

Wipszycka, E., "Les formes institutionelles et les formes d'activité économique du monachisme égyptien," in *Les formes institutionelles et les formes d'activité économique du monachisme égyptien*, ed. A. Camplani and G. Filoramo, 109–54 (Leuven, 2007).

Wipszycka, E., *Moines et communautés monastiques en Égypte (IVème au VIIIème siècle)* (Warsaw, 2009).

Zachariä von Lingenthal, K. E., *Geschichte des griechisch-römischen Rechts*, 3rd ed. (Berlin, 1892; repr. Aalen, 1955).

Zaninović, O. A., "Dva Latinska spomenika o sklapanju pobratimstva u Dalmaciji," *Zbornik za narodni zivot i obicaje Juznih Slavena* 45 (1971), 713–24.

Zhishman, J., *Das Eherecht der orientalischen Kirche* (Vienna, 1864).

{ INDEX }